MW00611604

METROPOLITAN HILARION ALFEYEV

ORTHODOX CHRISTIANITY

Volume V:
Sacraments and
Other Rites

Translated from the Russian by Nathan Williams

ST VLADIMIR'S SEMINARY PRESS
YONKERS, NEW YORK 10707
2019

*The publication of this book was made possible by a generous contribution
from Archbishop Melchisedek (Pleska)*

*In remembrance of his sister Sandra, his parents and grandparents:
Alexander and Eugenia Pleska; Peter and Olga Pleska; Alexey and Charitina Stachuk.*

Library of Congress Cataloging-in-Publication Data

Ilarion, Hieromonk.
  [Pravoslavie. English]
  Orthodox Christianity / Metropolitan Hilarion Alfeyev.
    p. cm.
  Includes bibliographical references.
  ISBN 978–0–88141–878–1
    1. Russkaia pravoslavnaia tserkov'—History.   2. Orthodox Eastern Church—Russia
(Federation)—History.   3. Russkaia pravoslavnaia tserkov'—Doctrines.   4. Orthodox
Eastern Church—Russia (Federation)—Doctrines.   5. Russkaia pravoslavnaia tserkov'.
6. Orthodox Eastern Church—Russia (Federation).   I. Title.
  BX485.I4313 2011
  281.9'47—dc22

                                                                2011002385

Pravoslavie, Tom II.
originally published by Sretensky Monastery, 2008

Copyright © 2019 by Hilarion Alfeyev

ST VLADIMIR'S SEMINARY PRESS
575 Scarsdale Rd, Yonkers, NY 10707
1-800-204-2665
www.svspress.com

978-0-88141-643-5 paper
978-0-88141-644-2 ebook

All Rights Reserved

PRINTED IN THE UNITED STATES OF AMERICA

Table of Contents

Preface

THIS IS THE FIFTH VOLUME of a detailed and systematic exposition of the history, canonical structure, doctrine, moral and social teaching, liturgical services, and spiritual life of the Orthodox Church.

The basic idea of this work is to present Orthodox Christianity as an integrated theological and liturgical system—a world view. In this system all elements are interconnected: theology is based on liturgical experience, and the basic characteristics of church art—including icons, singing, and architecture—are shaped by theology and the liturgy. Theology and the services, in their turn, influence the ascetic practice and the personal piety of each Christian. They shape the moral and social teaching of the Church as well as its relation to other Christian confessions, non-Christian religions, and the secular world.

Orthodoxy is traditional and even conservative (we use this term in a positive sense, to emphasize Orthodoxy's reverence for church tradition). The contemporary life of the Orthodox Church is based on its historical experience. Orthodoxy is historic in its very essence: it is deeply rooted in history, which is why it is impossible to understand the uniqueness of the Orthodox Church—its dogmatic teaching and canonical structure, its liturgical system and social doctrine—outside of a historical context. Thus, the reference to history—to the sources—is one of the organizing principles of this book.

This series covers a wide range of themes relating to the history and contemporary life of the Orthodox Church. It contains many quotations from works of the church fathers, liturgical and historical sources, and works of contemporary theologians. Nevertheless, we do not claim to give an exhaustive account of the subjects discussed: this work is not an encyclopedia, a dictionary, or a reference work. It is rather an attempt to understand Orthodoxy in all its diversity, in its historical and contemporary existence—an understanding through the prism of the author's personal perception.

A special feature of these books is that they strive to provide a sufficiently detailed wealth of material. It is addressed to readers who are already acquainted with the basics of Orthodoxy and who desire to deepen their knowledge and, above all, to systematize it.

The first volume focused on the history and canonical structure of the Orthodox Church, and the second volume on the fundamental teachings of the Church, grounded in Scripture and Tradition. The third volume delved into the unique aspects of Orthodox art as expressed in its architecture, icons, and liturgical music.

The fourth volume explored the liturgical life of the Orthodox Church—the history, structure, and meaning of the daily, weekly, yearly, and festal services—in all its variety and richness.

This fifth and final volume is dedicated to the mysteries (or sacraments) of the Orthodox Church: baptism, chrismation, the Eucharist, repentance (confession), holy orders (ordination), unction, and marriage. This list of seven sacraments, however, is not absolute. The services of monastic tonsure, burial (funeral), the blessing of water, and the consecration of a church building were also regarded as mysteries by some of the fathers of the Church, and they certainly have a sacramental character or dimension. Finally, this volume also explains the remaining non-sacramental church services or rites that fall outside the daily, weekly, and annual liturgical cycle, such as molebens and akathists, and various blessings for people, objects, and occasions.

PART FIVE

Sacraments and Rituals

I

Sacraments in the Orthodox Understanding

THE CONCEPT OF A SACRAMENT has a long history in the Eastern Orthodox Church. In modern Orthodox linguistic usage, *sacrament* is the term for a sacred rite in which the grace of the Holy Spirit is bestowed upon a believer.

In the so-called symbolic books of the Orthodox Church, and in Greek and Russian textbooks on dogmatic theology from the eighteenth and nineteenth centuries, the teaching on the sacraments was presented in the terms of Latin scholastic theology. It was asserted that there were seven sacraments in the Church, neither more or less: baptism, chrismation, communion, penance, holy orders, matrimony, and unction.[1] The reason for there being seven sacraments "is concealed in the will of the Institutor of the sacraments, the Lord Jesus." Furthermore, there are seven because they "supply all the needs of a person's Christian life and the needs of the Church itself."[2]

To perform any sacrament three things are required, writes the author of one seventeenth-century textbook: (1) "a visible thing presented to be sanctified, which we call matter or substance"; (2) "certain words by which we invoke the Holy Spirit to sanctify the things presented: this we call the form"; and (3) "a clergyman or person lawfully appointed by a bishop for this ministry."[3]

This conceptualization has been the cause of many strained interpretations. Firstly, the sevenfold number of sacraments artificially emphasized seven church rites, while passing over numerous others of no less importance and categorizing them as "rituals." Why, for example, is matrimony a sacrament, while the monastic tonsure is a rite? To this the textbooks could provide no clear answer.

Secondly, it was necessary to prove the divine origin of each sacrament, something that could not always be done convincingly. In particular, while it was clear that baptism and the Eucharist were divinely instituted, in the case of certain other sacraments—such as chrismation or unction—this was not clear at all. And so

[1]Archim. Makary, *Dogmaticheskoe bogoslovie* [Dogmatic Theology], vol. 2 (Moscow: 1786), 314, 512.
[2]Ibid., 512–513.
[3]Ibid., 179.

*Hieromartyr Dionysius the
Areopagite. Fresco. Church of
the Great Martyr George. Staro
Nagoričane, Macedonia. 14th c.*

the divine origin of the sacrament of chrismation was demonstrated by citing the promise of the Holy Spirit that Jesus gave to his disciples (cf. Jn 7.37–39).[4] The sacrament of unction was declared to have existed in the apostolic era (cf. Jas 5.14–15), and since the apostles preached nothing of themselves, but taught only what Jesus had commanded them, it followed that this sacrament was of divine origin.[5] Regarding the sacrament of matrimony it was said that Christ established it either while present at the marriage in Cana of Galilee (cf. Jn 2.1–11), or when he said to the Pharisees, "What therefore God hath joined together, let not man put asunder" (Mt 19.6); or at some other point unknown to us.[6]

Thirdly, it was not easy to define the "matter" for three of the seven sacraments. Obviously, in the Eucharist the matter is bread and wine; in baptism, water; in chrismation, chrism; and in unction, oil. But what matter is present in the sacraments of matrimony, holy orders, and penance?

Finally, the necessity of defining the verbal formula by which the sacrament is performed for each sacrament led to particular words, deemed the "consecratory words," being artificially emphasized in the sacramental service orders. In the sacrament of penance the consecratory formula came to be the prayer of absolution (which is absent in the Greek order of the sacrament, and which appeared in the Russian practice no earlier than the seventeenth century). In the sacrament of matrimony the most important words came to be the following: "The servant of God *N.* is crowned unto the handmaiden of God *N.*; the handmaiden of God *N.* is crowned unto the servant of God *N.*," and the brief prayer "O Lord our God, crown them with glory and honor."

The foregoing teaching on the seven sacraments was borrowed from medieval Latin theology, and has no counterpart in the works of the Eastern fathers of the Church from the first millennium. In the West it was formulated by the twelfth

---

[4]Makary (Bulgakov), *Dogmaticheskoe bogoslovie* [Dogmatic Theology], vol. 2, 346.
[5]Ibid., 465.
[6]Ibid., 479.

century and was made dogma at the Council of Lyons in 1274 and the Council of Florence in 1439 (it should be noted that at both councils unions were established between the Orthodox and the Latins). On March 3, 1547, the Council of Trent (by Catholic reckoning the Nineteenth Ecumenical Council) decreed that whoever held that the sacraments were not established by our Lord Jesus Christ, or that they were greater or fewer than seven in number, was to be excommunicated from the Church.[7]

In the Orthodox East the first attempt at systematization (and schematization) of the church sacraments was a treatise by Dionysius the Areopagite titled *The Ecclesiastical Hierarchy*. In this work the two threefold hierarchies of the clerical ranks correspond to the two threefold hierarchies of the sacraments: (1) illumination (baptism, including chrismation); (2) synaxis ("assembly," i.e., the Eucharist); (3) the consecration of chrism; (4) the ordination of clergy; (5) monastic initiation (the tonsure); and (6) sacred rites for the departed (the funeral). The venerable Theodore the Studite lists the sacraments in this same order, citing "the all-wise Dionysius."[8]

The teaching of seven sacraments first appears in the Orthodox East in the third quarter of the thirteenth century, and is in fact an attempt at adapting Orthodox teaching to that of the Catholics. In 1267 the emperor Michael Palaiologos sent Pope Clement IV of Rome a "Confession of Faith," the objective of which was a union with the Latins: this "Confession" included the teaching of the seven sacraments, along with other Catholic dogmas, particularly concerning purgatory and the filioque.

In this same period the seven sacraments were mentioned in a letter by the Byzantine monk Job (†1270): "Seven are the mysteries of the Holy Church of God: (1. firstly, baptism, (2) secondly, chrism, (3) thirdly, communion, (4) fourthly, priesthood, (5) fifthly, honorable marriage, (6) sixthly, monastic habit, and (7) seventhly, anointing, i.e., penance."[9] Thus, the monastic tonsure was numbered with the seven sacraments, while unction was combined with penance into a single sacrament.

In the fourteenth century Gregory Palamas and Nicholas Cabasilas mention the sacraments in their writings, but neither gives a list of seven sacraments. Only in the fifteenth century does a list of this sort appear, written by Symeon of Thessalonica, who mentions the following sacraments: baptism, chrismation, the

---

[7]Council of Trent, first canon regarding the sacraments. Cf. *Khristianskoe verouchenie* [Christian Doctrine], 375.

[8]Theodore the Studite, *Letters* 2.165 (PG 99:1524AB).

[9]Translation in Christiaan Kappes, "A New Narrative for the Reception of Seven Sacraments into Orthodoxy," *Nova et Vetera*, 15.2 (2017): 465–501, at 472.

Eucharist, penance, holy orders, matrimony, and unction. However, in the section on penance he includes a complete description of the monastic tonsure.[10]

Only in the seventeenth century did the teaching of seven sacraments become generally accepted in the Orthodox East, finding its way first into the "symbolic books," then into seminary textbooks on theology. And only in the late nineteenth and twentieth centuries, along with a resurging interest in the works of the church fathers, did Orthodox theology begin to free itself from the artificial and schematic concept of the sacraments characteristic of the medieval Latin Church. "Scholastic theology"[11] gave way to a theological school that tended toward a patristic synthesis, and the teaching of the sacraments was rethought in order to redirect it back into patristic channels. Contributing to this rethinking were theologians of the "Parisian school," such as Archimandrite Cyprian (Kern), Protopresbyter Alexander Schmemann, and Protopresbyter John Meyendorff.

As the latter notes, "Byzantine theology ignores the Western distinction between 'sacraments' and 'sacramentals,' and never formally committed itself to any strict limitation of the number of sacraments." The very term *sacrament,* or *mystery* (μυστήριον/*mystērion*),[12] is used by the holy fathers not so much to signify a sacred rite as to refer to the "mystery of salvation" in the broader sense.[13] In a similar vein, Gregory of Nyssa speaks of the "mystery which Christians cherish,"[14] meaning the whole body of Christian tradition. In John Chrysostom's instructions to catechumens the term *mystery* is variously used to refer to baptism and the Eucharist as a single entity, to refer to one of these two sacraments, and to refer to all the divine services of the baptismal cycle.[15]

---

[10]Cf. Symeon of Thessalonica, *On the Sacraments,* 265–275, from the section "On Repentance" (PG 155:489A–504B).

[11]The term scholastic theology was used by the hieromartyr Hilarion (Troitsky) in his historical article "*Bogoslovie I svoboda Tserkvi: o zadachakh osvoboditel'noi voiny v oblasti russkogo bogosloviya*" [Theology and Freedom of the Church: On the Goals of the War of Liberation in the Sphere of Russian Theology], in his *Collected Works,* vol. 2, 259. Later the term was widely used by theologians of the Russian immigration to designate a theological school strongly influenced by Latin scholasticism.

[12]Throughout this section it should be born in mind that the terms *sacrament* and *mystery* are the same word in Russian and Greek (*tainstvo* and *mystērion,* respectively). Hence, whereas in English *sacrament* is always a church service through which God's grace is bestowed, in Russian and Greek the word can also simply mean "mystery."—*Trans.*

[13]John Meyendorff, *Byzantine Theology,* 2nd ed., rev. (New York: Fordham University Press, 1983), 191.

[14]Gregory of Nyssa, *Against Eunomius* 11.5 (*NPNF*² 5:236–239).

[15]Irina Prolygina, "*Katekhizatsiya i chin kreshcheniya v Antiokhii*" [Catechesis and the Rite of Baptism in Antioch], in *Svyatitel' Ioann Zlatoust. Oglasitel'nye gomilii* [St John Chrysostom. Catechetical Homilies], D.E. Afinogenov, literary advisor, Irina Prolygina, trans. (Tver: Germenevtika, 2006), 56.

Events from Christ's life and from church feasts were also called sacraments.[16] *Feast* and *sacrament* could be perceived as synonyms: every feast was mystical and mysterious in nature, and every sacrament, particularly baptism, was perceived as a feast. To this Gregory the Theologian refers in one of his sermons: "Again my Jesus, and again a mystery, a mystery not deceitful or disorderly, nor belonging to the disorder and drunkenness of the [pagan] Greeks . . . will—but a mystery exalted and divine and bringing the radiance from above."[17] Here the "mystery," or sacrament, is the feast of Theophany, the topic of the sermon.

If we speak of the sacraments as sacred rites, the sacraments as we have seen included the monastic tonsure and the order for the burial of the departed. Other sacred rites, categorized today as rituals, such as the great blessing of water on the feast of Theophany, are also sacramental in nature. The prayers of this rite have vivid "eucharistic" overtones: the priest asks God to send down the Holy Spirit upon the water, after which it is changed into the "great agiasma"—something sacred that is reverently consumed, with which the faithful are anointed and sprinkled. The order for the consecration of a church is also sacramental in nature.

The majority of church sacraments are genetically linked to the Eucharist, from which as a rule they were not separated during the Byzantine period. The orders of baptism and chrismation concluded with the Eucharist; ordinations to all the holy orders took place (as they still do) during the Eucharist; the sacrament of matrimony likewise grew out of a blessing that the bishop would bestow upon the bride and groom during the Eucharist. Not a single one of these sacraments was perceived as a "private" service, a "service of need," that could be served in isolation from the eucharistic community.

Subsequently, certain sacraments (such as matrimony) were separated from the Eucharist, but they retained traces of their connection with it. The concept of the sacrament as a "conciliar" action was also retained, even if performed outside the Eucharist and outside the church building, as in the case of the sacrament of unction, which may be served in the home. In the latter instance, represented by the seven priests by whom, according to the Typicon, this sacrament is to be performed, the Church itself comes into the home of the sick person who is unable to come to church.

All the sacraments are performed within the Church; they are inseparable from the Church. The Latin teaching that a sacrament is valid *ex opera operato* ("by

[16]Cf. G.W.H. Lampe, *A Patristic Greek Lexicon* (Oxford: Oxford University Press, 1991), 891–893.

[17]Gregory of Nazianzus, *Orations* 39.1. *Festal Orations: St Gregory of Nazianzus*, Popular Patristics Series 36, Nonna Verna Harrison, trans. (Crestwood, NY: St Vladimir's Seminary Press, 2008), 79

virtue of the action having been performed") is foreign to Orthodox consciousness. According to this teaching, the validity of the seven sacraments is ensured by their proper performance, with the sacraments viewed as instruments of grace over which the Church has no power, which act on their own, independent of the Church.[18] For Orthodox theology, posing the matter in such terms is unacceptable, since for it the concept of a sacrament outside the Church, apart from the Church, or contrary to the will of the Church does not exist.

The significance of each sacrament may be expressed by the term *transformation* (μετάληψις/*metalēpsis*), used with respect to the holy gifts at the Eucharist. In the liturgy of Basil the Great, this term, which literally means "change," refers to what happens to the bread and the wine when they become the body and blood of Christ. The form of bread and wine remains, but the reality changes: the bread and the wine cease to be such, and they become the body and blood of Christ. Through communing a person undergoes an analogous change: his physical qualities do not change, but he receives God into himself and, by uniting with him, is spiritually transfigured. A person undergoes a similar change in the sacrament of baptism: he descends into the font an old man, but emerges a man new and reborn.

The sacraments give a person a glimpse of otherworldly reality and facilitate his spiritual rebirth. Of this Nicholas Cabasilas writes, "Through these sacred Mysteries as through windows the Sun of Righteousness enters this dark world. He puts to death the life which accords with this world, but raises up that which is above the world."[19] A believer is made able to be united with Christ "by being initiated into the Mysteries, being washed and anointed and partaking of the holy table. When we do these things, Christ comes to us and dwells in us, He is united to us and grows into one with us. He stifles sin in us and infuses into us His own life and merit and makes us to share in His victory."[20] The sacraments reveal to a person the path to deification:

> That which belongs to the Head[21] becomes ours as well. Now, then, we depart from this water without sin. Because of the chrism we partake of His graces, and because of the banquet we live with the same life He does. In the world to come we shall be gods with God, fellow-heirs with Him of the same riches,

---

[18]Cf. Benedetto Testa, *Tainstva v Katolicheskoi Tserkvi* [Sacraments in the Catholic Church] (Moscow: Khristianskaya Rossiya, 2000), 69–75. [Translated from Italian.—*Trans.*]

[19]Nicholas Cabasilas, *The Life in Christ* 1.6, Carmino J. DeCatanzaro, trans. (Crestwood, NY: St Vladimir's Seminary Press, 1974), 50.

[20]Ibid., 1.11, 60.

[21]To Christ.

reigning with Him in the same kingdom—that is, unless we of our own free will blind ourselves in this life and rend asunder the royal garment. This alone we contribute to this life—that we submit to His gifts, retain His graces, and do not reject the crown which God by many toils and labours has prepared for us. This is the life in Christ which the Mysteries confer.[22]

In uniting a person with God, at the same time the sacraments of the Church help the person to achieve his own "humanness," his potential for freedom, his vocation of life in the Holy Spirit:

A sacrament is not an imaginary abstraction. It is an experience where man is not involved alone, but where he acts in communion with God. In a sacrament, humanity participates in the higher reality of the Spirit, without, however, ceasing to be fully humanity. Actually, as we have said above, it becomes more authentically human and fulfills its original destiny. A sacrament is a "passage" to true life; it is man's salvation. It is an open door into true, unadulterated humanity. A sacrament, therefore, is not magic. The Holy Spirit does not suppress human freedom but, rather, liberates man from the limitations of sinfulness. In the new life, the impossible becomes truly possible, if only man freely accepts what God gives.[23]

Hierarchal succession in the imparting of the sacraments of the Church may be traced from the apostolic era to our own time. The same sacraments imparted by the apostles are imparted today by the bishops and priests, as Symeon the New Theologian emphasizes:

Since these sacraments are administered today not by the holy apostles, nor by their holy successors, our forefathers who have passed away, but by men who exist now and are alive and living amongst us, it is very clear that these provide us now with what those who then were in the world imparted to believers, and that these are also their equals. How so? As those baptized in water and the divine Spirit, so too do these now; those imparted the body and blood of Christ, and these impart the same to us, and there was no extra allotted to those recipients then, nor for us, to whom the sacrament is imparted now, is there anything lacking; those taught faith in Christ and in the Father, Son, and Holy

---

[22]Cabasilas, *The Life in Christ* I.II, 63.

[23]John Meyendorff, *Marriage: An Orthodox Perspective,* 3rd ed. (Crestwood, NY: St. Vladimir's Seminary Press, 2000), 20.

Spirit, the indivisible Trinity, three Persons equal in honour, while our fathers teach us the same.[24]

As has already been said, modern linguistic usage differentiates between sacraments and rituals. The latter include sacred rites that resemble sacraments in every aspect, yet which are not numbered among the seven sacraments. The division between sacraments and rituals is just as arbitrary as emphasizing seven sacraments out of all the sacred rites of the Church. Certain modern theologians call rituals "lesser mysteries," thereby emphasizing their sacramental, mystical nature.[25] The number of church rituals in existence is past counting. Some rituals existed in ancient times but have fallen into disuse, while others are being established even as we speak.

In this section we will not attempt to examine all the sacraments and rituals in the arsenal of the Church. We will discuss the most significant of these: (1) baptism, chrismation, and consecration of chrism; (2) the Eucharist; (3) penance (confession); (4) ordination to holy orders (the ranks of bishop, priest, and deacon), as well as elevation to minor orders (the ranks of reader and subdeacon); (5) unction (anointing of the sick); (6) matrimony; (7) the monastic tonsure; (8) burial (the funeral); (9) the consecration of a church; (10) the blessing of water; and (11) molebens (services of supplication) for various occasions.

The service orders for most sacraments and rituals may be found in a book called the Book of Needs—in Slavonic, the *Trebnik* (from the Slavonic word *treba*, meaning a service performed for a particular need). There is no universal version of the Book of Needs, and the book's contents vary depending on the time and place of publication. The complete version of the Book of Needs is called the Great Book of Needs and consists of two parts. The first part contains the service orders for baptism, chrismation, matrimony, unction, penance, burial, the blessing of water, and the monastic tonsure. The second part contains the service orders for the blessings of buildings, objects, and foodstuffs, molebens for various circumstances, and several liturgical service orders of more recent origin, such as the rite of the washing of the feet on Great Thursday. The Small Book of Needs is an abbreviated version of the Great Book of Needs and is the version most widely used.[26]

[24]Symeon the New Theologian, *The Epistles of St Symeon the New Theologian*, H.J.M. Turner, trans., Henry Chadwick, ed. (New York: Oxford University Press, 2009), 121–123.

[25]Cf., for example, John Anthony McGuckin, *The Orthodox Church* (West Sussex: Wiley-Blackwell, 2011), 277.

[26]Both of these works are published in English by St Tikhon's Monastery Press (*The Great Book of Needs* in five volumes, and *A Small Book of Needs* in one volume). —*Ed.*

2

Baptism and Chrismation

B APTISM IS THE SACRAMENT that grants entry into the Church to one who has come to believe in Christ. Without receiving baptism it is impossible to be an Orthodox Christian. In the modern practice of the Orthodox Church the sacrament of chrismation is also incorporated into the order of the sacrament of baptism. It is therefore logical that we examine the sacraments of baptism and chrismation in the same chapter.

FORMULATION OF THE SERVICE ORDER

Historically, before Christian baptism there was the baptism of John, described in the Gospel (cf. Mt 3.1–12, Mk 1.4–8, Lk 3.3–17). Outwardly this baptism resembled the ritual ablutions commonly practiced among the Jews. In content, however, it was "the baptism of repentance for the remission of sins" (Lk 3.3). It was preparatory in nature, for John said to those who came to him, "I indeed baptize you with water; but one mightier than I cometh . . . he shall baptize you with the Holy Spirit and with fire" (Lk 3.16, Mt 3.11, Mk 1.8). Jesus himself was also baptized by John (cf. Mt 3.13–17, Mk 1.9–11, Lk 3.21–22).

Apostle Philip baptizing the eunuch. Fresco. Dečani, Kosovo. 14th c.

As far as may be judged from the Gospel, after John baptized him Jesus also began to baptize. At any rate, in one passage the Gospel of John directly states that Jesus was dwelling with his disciples in the land of Judea and baptizing at the same time that John "was baptizing in Aenon near to Salim" (Jn 3.22–23). In the same Gospel, however, another passage clarifies that "Jesus himself baptized not, but his disciples" (Jn 4.2). Whatever the case may be, this original baptism most probably resembled the baptism of John in

Apostle Philip instructing the eunuch. Fresco. Dečani, Kosovo. 14th c.

both form and content.[1] The Gospel is silent regarding whether Christ's subsequent preaching included baptizing those who believed. Likewise we know nothing of whether Jesus baptized his disciples.[2]

At his ascension into heaven after his resurrection, Jesus commanded his disciples, "Go ye therefore and teach all nations, baptizing them in the name of the Father, and of the Son, and of the Holy Spirit" (Mt 28.19). "He that believeth and is baptized shall be saved; but he that believeth not shall be damned" (Mk 16.16). At the express command of their teacher the disciples began to preach and to receive believers into the community through baptism. It was baptism—immersion in water—that became the act that signified entry into the Church, and it was baptism that opened the path to participation in the Eucharist, to full participation in the life of the Church.

Even in apostolic times baptism was preceded by catechesis. During the apostles' lifetime this was usually brief, lasting no more than a few hours or a few days. In the book of Acts there is an account of a eunuch of great authority under the

---

[1]Cf. Tertullian, *On Baptism* 11 (*ANF* 3:674): "It was with the selfsame 'baptism of John' that His disciples used to baptize, as ministers, with which John before had baptized as forerunner. Let none think it was with some other, because no other exists, except that of Christ subsequently; which at that time, of course, could not be given by His disciples, inasmuch as the glory of the Lord had not yet been fully attained, nor the efficacy of the font established through the passion and the resurrection; because neither can our death see dissolution except by the Lord's passion, nor our life be restored without His resurrection" (cf. Rom 6.4–5).

[2]In *On Baptism* 12 (*ANF* 3:674–675) Tertullian gives no clear answer as to whether the apostles were baptized. However, in the words that Christ spoke to Peter—"He that is washed needeth not save to wash his feet, but is clean every whit" (Jn 13.10)—Tertullian sees an intimation that the apostles had been baptized.

queen of the Ethiopians, who was riding in a chariot and reading the book of the prophet Isaiah—namely, the passage describing the Messiah (cf. Is 53.7–8). Approaching the chariot, the apostle Philip asked, "Understandest thou what thou readest?" The eunuch responded with a question of his own: "How can I, except some man should guide me?" And he asked Philip to join him in the chariot. Then Philip "opened his mouth and began at the same Scripture, and preached unto him Jesus." As this was happening they came to some water, and the eunuch said, "See, here is water; what doth hinder me to be baptized?" Philip replied, "If thou believest with all thine heart, thou mayest." The eunuch said, "I believe that Jesus Christ is the Son of God." And they entered the water, and Philip baptized the eunuch, after which the Holy Spirit descended upon him, and Philip disappeared (Acts 8.27–39).

In this instance the catechesis consisted of Philip's discourse on Jesus, based on the prophecies of Holy Scripture. In other instances described in Acts, baptism was likewise preceded by preaching, whether private or public. In Caesarea, in the home of Cornelius the centurion, Peter preached concerning Jesus, and while he was yet speaking the Holy Spirit descended upon all those present. Then Peter said, "Can any man forbid water, that these should not be baptized, which have received the Holy Spirit as well as we?" And immediately he commanded them all to be baptized in the name of Jesus Christ (Acts 10.25–48). In Philippi the apostle Paul conversed with a group of women gathered in a house of prayer, one of whom believed and was baptized together with her household (cf. Acts 16.13–15).

Apostle Paul and Ananias. Fresco. Dečani, Kosovo. 14th c.

In the account of Paul's conversion (cf. Acts 9.3–19) no catechetical discourse is mentioned. This does not mean, however, that none took place: the apostle Ananias who came to him, after being commanded by God to baptize Paul, must have conversed with Paul before baptizing him. Furthermore, after baptism Paul spent several days in company with Jesus' disciples in Damascus, which probably indicates that his catechesis continued even after he had received baptism. It is worth noting that catechesis in the apostolic era did not necessarily end at baptism: not infrequently the apostles would remain in the home of the newly baptized in order to strengthen him in the faith by discourse (cf. Acts 10.48, 16.15).

Catechesis is also mentioned in the *Didache*—the first Christian manuscript in which the order of baptism is mentioned:

> Now with regard to baptism: baptize thus. When you have said all these things beforehand,[3] baptize in the name of the Father and of the Son and of the Holy Spirit in living water. If you have no living water baptize in another water, in warm, if you are unable (to do so) in cold. If you have neither pour out water onto the head three times in the name of the Father and of the Son and of the Holy Spirit. Now before baptism the one who baptizes should fast in advance, and the one being baptized, and others if they are able. You order the one being baptized to fast one or two days before.[4]

This description confirms that, as the second century dawned, baptism was preceded by catechesis (as shown by the words "when you have said all these things beforehand"). From the *Didache* we also learn that in baptism, in accordance with Christ's commandment, a trinitarian formula was used. Baptism took place in living, or flowing, water (in rivers and lakes); at the same time baptism by affusion (pouring) was also permitted. The manuscript mentions fasting before baptism—a tradition that has since been lost.

We find a significantly more detailed description of baptism in the *Apostolic Tradition*. This treatise testifies to the fact that in the third century catechesis took place over a lengthy period of time, with the catechumens not only attending catechetical talks, but also obliged to demonstrate their compliance with Christian moral standards:

> When those who are to receive baptism are chosen their lives should be examined; whether they lived uprightly as catechumens, whether they honored the widows, whether they visited the sick, whether they were thorough in performing good works; and if those who brought them bear witness that they have acted thus, so they should hear the Gospel.[5]

Thus, each catechumen is sponsored by some member of the community, whose duty it is to affirm the moral compliance of the candidate. The expression "then let

---

[3]That is, the fundamentals of Christian doctrine.

[4]*Didache*, 7.1–4, in *On the Two Ways*, Popular Patristics Series 41, Alistair Stewart(-Sykes), ed. (Yonkers, NY: St Vladimir's Seminary Press, 2011), 42.

[5]Hippolytus, *On the Apostolic Tradition* 20.1–2. In *On the Apostolic Tradition*, 2nd ed., Popular Patristics Series 54, Alistair C. Steward, trans. (Yonkers, NY: St Vladimir's Seminary Press, 2015), 127.

them hear the Gospel" indicates that those preparing for baptism are allowed to be present at the liturgy of the catechumens, at which the Gospel is read.

Throughout the period of preparation for baptism, hands are laid upon each of the catechumens, and on the eve of the baptism, which takes place on a Saturday, the bishop performs the rite of the "exorcism" of evil spirits:

> From the time they are set apart a hand is laid on them daily whilst they are exorcized. When the day draws near the bishop should exorcize each of them so that he may be sure that they are pure. If there is any uncertainty he should be put to shame, and set to one side because he has not heard the word in faith. Indeed, an alien being should not remain in him. Those who have been set apart for baptism should be instructed to bathe themselves on the fifth day of the week. . . . Those who are to be baptized should fast on the day of preparation and the Sabbath.[6] On the Sabbath those who are to be baptized are gathered at the will of the bishop. They shall be instructed to pray and to bend the knee. And when he lays his hand on them he shall exorcize them saying: "May every alien spirit flee away from them and not return." And when he has finished exorcizing them he should blow on their faces; and when he has sealed their forehead, their ears and their noses he should make them stand up. They should spend the entire night in vigil, hearing readings and receiving instruction.[7]

The rite of exorcism, as we see, has a twofold significance: on the one hand it drives away every alien spirit from the person being baptized, and on the other it helps to determine which of the candidates for baptism are pure and which are "not good or pure" (a clear reference to demonic possession). As in the *Didache*, fasting before baptism is mentioned. The catechumens must spend the night before their baptism in prayer, without leaving the church. Early in the morning, "when the cock crows," the bishop prays over the water. The water "should be flowing, or at least running." If, however, there is "continuous and sudden necessity use any water you can find."[8] This later instruction echoes what we encountered in the *Didache*: baptism in flowing water is the standard, but where necessary any water may be used.

---

[6]The Russian translation specifies only the eve of Saturday: "Let those preparing for baptism fast on the eve of the Sabbath."—*Trans.*

[7]Hippolytus, *Apostolic Tradition* 20.3–9 (PPS 54:127–128).

[8]Hippolytus, *Apostolic Tradition* 21.1–2 (PPS 54:133).

The description that follows contains numerous valuable details, which testify as to how the sacrament of baptism was performed in the early Christian Church:

> And they should take off their clothes. You are to baptize the little ones first. All those who are able to speak for themselves should speak. With regard to those who cannot speak for themselves, their parents, or somebody who belongs to their family, should speak. Then baptize the grown men and finally the women, after they have let down their hair and laid down the gold and silver ornaments which they have on them. Nobody should take any alien object down into the water. When they are to receive the oil of exorcism the bishop shall give thanks over the oil in a vessel. And he shall exorcize another. A deacon shall take the oil of exorcism and stand beside the presbyter, and another the same with the oil of thanksgiving. He should stand to the right, and the presbyter who exorcizes at the left. And he takes them one by one asking them about their faith. He says "I renounce you, Satan, and all your service and all your works and all your filth." And when he has made this profession he is anointed with the exorcized oil, praying that he be cleansed from every alien spirit. Then he is handed over to the bishop or the presbyter who is to baptize him, and stands naked in the water.[9]

From this description it follows that baptisms were performed en masse, and that not only adults but also children took part, including infants who could not yet talk. The parents and relatives of the candidates would be present. The bishop would preside over the rite of baptism, but presbyters and deacons also took part. The clergy performed the baptism in special vestments; conversely, the candidates took off their finery and approached the water naked. The baptism (immersion) itself was performed by the bishop or presbyter, but it was a deacon who entered the water together with the candidate. The baptism was performed by three immersions:

> And a deacon likewise goes down with him into the water. When the one being baptized goes down into the waters the one who baptizes, placing a hand on him, should say thus: "Do you believe in God the Father Almighty?" And he who is being baptized should reply: "I believe." Let him baptize him once immediately, having his hand placed upon his head. And after this he should

[9]Hippolytus, *Apostolic Tradition* 21.3–11 (PPS 54:133–134).

say: "Do you believe in Christ Jesus, the son of God, who was born of the Holy Spirit and Mary the virgin and was crucified under Pontius Pilate and was dead and buried and rose on the third day alive from the dead and ascended in the heavens and sits at the right hand of the Father and will come to judge the living and the dead?" And when he has said, "I believe," he is baptized again. And again he should say: "Do you believe in the Holy Spirit and the holy church and the resurrection of the flesh?" And he who is being baptized should say: "I believe." And so he should be baptized a third time. And afterwards, when he has come up, he is anointed by the presbyter with that sanctified oil, saying: "I anoint you with holy oil in the name of Jesus Christ." And afterwards, each drying himself, they shall dress themselves, and afterwards let them go into the church.[10]

In concluding the sacrament the bishop lays his hand upon the head of the newly baptized, then anoints him with the "oil of thanksgiving":

And the bishop, laying his hand on them invokes, saying: "Lord God, you have made these worthy to deserve the remission of sins through the washing of regeneration: grant that they may be filled with the Holy Spirit, sending your grace upon them so they may serve you in accordance with your will; for to you be glory, to the Father and the Son with the Holy Spirit in the holy church both now and to the ages of the ages. Amen." After this, pouring the sanctified oil from his hand and putting it on his head he shall say: "I anoint you with holy oil in God the Father Almighty and Christ Jesus and the Holy Spirit." And signing him on the forehead he shall give him the kiss and say: "The Lord be with you." And he who has been signed shall say: "And with your spirit." And thus he shall do to each. And thenceforth they shall pray with all the people; they shall not pray with the people until they have performed all these things.[11]

It should be noted that Hippolytus mentions two types of oil—the oil of exorcism and the oil of thanksgiving. The presbyters anoint with the former, the bishop with the latter. Before the anointing with the oil of thanksgiving the bishop reads a prayer, asking that the Holy Spirit be sent down upon the newly baptized. In the fourth century the "oil of thanksgiving" would come to be called chrism; subsequently in the Orthodox East the rite of chrismation would be set apart as

[10]Hippolytus, *Apostolic Tradition* 21.11–20 (PPS 54:134).
[11]Hippolytus, *Apostolic Tradition* 21.21–25 (PPS 54:134–135).

a separate sacrament, performed together with baptism (in the West chrismation would be performed separately from baptism).

Tertullian also speaks of anointing after baptism, pointing out the direct link between Christian anointing, the Old Testament anointing to the priesthood, and the ministry of Christ, the Lord's Anointed:

> When we have issued from the font, we are thoroughly anointed with a blessed unction—(a practice derived) from the old discipline, wherein on entering the priesthood, *men* were wont to be anointed with oil from a horn, ever since Aaron was anointed by Moses. Whence Aaron is called "Christ," from the "chrism," which is "the unction"; which, when made spiritual, furnished an appropriate name to the Lord, because He was "anointed" with the Spirit by God the Father; as *written* in the Acts: "For truly they were gathered together in this city against Thy Holy Son whom Thou hast anointed" [cf. Acts 4.27]. Thus, too, in *our* case, the unction runs carnally (*i.e.* on the body), but profits spiritually; in the same way as the *act* of baptism itself too is carnal, in that we are plunged in water, *but* the *effect* spiritual, in that we are freed from sins.[12]

Hippolytus' description does not contain the baptismal formula "In the name of the Father, and of the Son, and of the Holy Spirit." It is apparently understood, however, inasmuch as the three immersions of which Hippolytus speaks are not performed silently, but while speaking this formula. This is confirmed by a contemporary of Hippolytus, the martyr Justin the Philosopher, in his description of the order of baptism:

> So that we should not remain children of necessity and ignorance, but [become sons] of free choice and knowledge, and obtain remission of the sins we have already committed, there is named at the water, over him who has chosen to be born again and has repented of his sinful acts, the name of God the Father and Master of all. Those who lead to the washing the one who is to be washed call on [God by] this term only. For no one may give a proper name to the ineffable God. . . . This washing is called illumination, since those who learn these things are illumined within. The illuminand is also washed in the name of Jesus Christ, who was crucified under Pontius Pilate, and in the name of the Holy Spirit, who through the prophets foretold everything about Jesus.[13]

---

[12]Tertullian, *On Baptism* 7 (ANF 3:672).

[13]Justin the Philosopher, *The First Apology of Justin, the Martyr* 61. In *The Library of Christian Classics*, *vol. 1: Early Christian Fathers*, Cyril C. Richardson, trans. (Philadelphia, PA: The Westminster Press, 1953), 282–283.

Baptism is also called an "initiation" in the *Apostolic Constitutions*, in which the chapter "On the Formation of the Character of Believers, Thanksgiving, and Christian Initiation" contains the following directions:

> Now concerning baptism, O bishop, or presbyter, we have already given direc-
> tion, and we now say, that you shall so baptize as the Lord commanded us,
> saying: *Go, and teach all nations, baptizing them in the name of the Father, and
> of the Son, and of the Holy Spirit* . . . of the Father who sent, of Christ who
> came, of the Comforter who testified. But you shall beforehand anoint the
> person with the holy oil, and afterward baptize him with the water, and in the
> conclusion shall seal him with the ointment; that the anointing with oil may
> be the participation of the Holy Spirit, and the water the symbol of the death
> of Christ, and the ointment the seal of the covenants. But if there be neither oil
> nor ointment, water is sufficient both for the anointing, and for the seal, and
> for the confession of him that is dead, or indeed is dying together *with Christ.*
> But before baptism, let him that is to be baptized fast.[14]

This text equates the participation or communion of the Holy Spirit with the oil before immersion into the water, and not with the chrism after immersion. As is apparent from the context, the words regarding the sufficiency of water alone pertain to the baptism of someone who is at the point of death. This is the sole instance in which the ancient Church recognized the validity of baptism performed by a layman.

According to the *Apostolic Constitutions*, baptism was to be preceded by a lengthy catechesis, in the course of which a candidate for baptism had to be "instructed . . . in the knowledge of the unbegotten God, in the understanding of his only begotten Son, in the assured acknowledgment of the Holy Spirit." The catechesis had to include a complete course in the history of the Old Testament: "Let him be instructed why the world was made, and why man was appointed to be a citizen therein; let him also know his own nature, of what sort it is; let him be taught how God punished the wicked with water and fire . . . and how God still took care of and did not reject mankind, but called them from their error and vanity to the acknowledgment of the truth at various seasons." When the course of catechesis is completed, the bishop or the priest lays his hand on the catechumen and prays that God might save him and cleanse him of every impurity of flesh and spirit, that he might be vouchsafed the "laver of regeneration." After this the catechumen is given

---

[14]*Apostolic Constitutions* 7.22 (*ANF* 7:469).

a course in New Testament history—instruction "in the doctrines concerning our Lord's incarnation, and in those concerning his passion, and resurrection from the dead, and assumption."[15] Thus, the catechetical course is divided into two parts, the Old Testament and the New Testament, and in between these two parts the bishop prays while laying hands upon the catechumen.

Upon completion of both parts of the catechetical course the candidate for baptism must say aloud, "I renounce Satan, and his works, and his pomps, and his worships, and his angels, and his inventions, and all things that are under him."[16] Then the candidate unites himself to Christ, reading a brief creed that begins with the words, "And I associate myself to Christ, and believe, and am baptized into one unbegotten Being, the only true God Almighty, the Father of Christ, the Creator and Maker of all things, from whom are all things; and into the Lord Jesus Christ, his only begotten Son, the First-born of the whole creation."[17] In its content this creed resembles the Nicene-Constantinopolitan Creed with which we are familiar.

After reading this creed the candidate "comes in order to the anointing with oil." The oil "is blessed by the high priest for the remission of sins, and the first preparation for baptism." After this follows the blessing of the water: the priest reads a prayer similar in content to the eucharistic anaphora, giving thanks for the whole history of the economy of man's salvation. The blessing of the water is performed by pronouncing the words, "Look down from heaven, and sanctify this water, and give it grace and power, that so he that is to be baptized, according to the command of Thy Christ, may be crucified with Him, and may die with Him, and may be buried with Him, and may rise with Him to the adoption which is in Him, that he may be dead to sin and live to righteousness."[18]

After the blessing of the water the priest immerses the candidate in the water in the name of the Father, the Son, and the Holy Spirit, then anoints him with chrism. The priest concludes the sacrament of baptism by reading the prayer "Our Father," followed by another prayer in which he asks God to bestow "a body undefiled, a heart pure, a mind watchful, an unerring knowledge"[19] upon the newly baptized.

---

[15]Ibid., 7.39 (*ANF* 7:476).
[16]That is, all the evil spirits that are subject to him.
[17]*Apostolic Constitutions* 7.41 (*ANF* 7:476).
[18]*Apostolic Constitutions* 7.43 (*ANF* 7:477).
[19]Ibid., 7.45 (*ANF* 7:477).

A very similar order of catechesis and baptism is described in the *Catechetical Lectures* of Cyril of Jerusalem, which reflect the baptismal practice of fourth-century Jerusalem. The *Catechetical Lectures* as a body are no less than a series of talks addressed to catechumens on the subject of the Christian faith. These talks are based on the Jerusalem Creed, which is textually quite close to the Nicene Creed and is in fact a point-by-point explanation thereof. The cycle of talks is divided into two parts: the first part (catechetical lectures) is given before baptism, and the second (lectures on the sacraments) is given immediately after baptism. The second part of the cycle expounds the teaching on the sacraments of baptism and the Eucharist. The cycle is divided in this way because it was considered improper to reveal the meaning of these sacraments to catechumens, since it is impossible to understand their meaning without the aid of the Holy Spirit, which is bestowed in baptism.[20] Catechumens could hear the Gospel, study Christian dogma using the Creed, and be present at the "liturgy of the word," but they were not permitted to participate in the liturgy of the faithful and to have the sacraments of baptism and the Eucharist explained to them.

The usual season for catechesis was Great Lent (the period of fasting preceding Pascha), and the catechesis itself—lectures focused on individual aspects of the Christian faith—could last several months. Chrysostom speaks of thirty days of catechesis;[21] the complete catechetical lectures of Cyril of Jerusalem include nineteen lectures, which also probably took about a month to deliver. The lectures on the mysteries were given after the sacrament of baptism, during the week after Pascha (Bright Week).

The service order for the sacrament of baptism is set forth by Cyril in his first and second lectures on the mysteries. This sacrament began in the narthex of the church, where the catechumens, facing west, would renounce Satan. The formula for the renunciation was the words, "I renounce you, Satan, and all your works, and all thy pomp, and all your worship."[22] After this the candidates would turn toward the east and pronounce this confession of faith: "I believe in the Father and in the Son and in the Holy Spirit and in one baptism of repentance."[23] The

---

[20]Cf. Athanasius of Alexandria, *Defense Against the Arians* 11 (*NPNF²* 4:106): "We ought not then to parade the holy mysteries before the uninitiated, lest the heathen in their ignorance deride them, and the Catechumens being over-curious be offended."

[21]John Chrysostom, *Instructions to Catechumens* 1.4 (*NPNF¹* 9:162).

[22]Cf. Cyril of Jerusalem, *On the Mysteries* 1.4–8. In Cyril of Jerusalem, *Lectures on the Christian Sacraments: The Procatechesis and the Five Mystagogical Catecheses Ascribed to St Cyril of Jerusalem*, Popular Patristics Series 57, Maxwell E. Johnson, trans. (Yonkers, NY: St Vladimir's Seminary Press, 2017), 87–91.

[23]Ibid., 1.9 (PPS 57:93).

candidates were then led into the church, and they would undress completely.[24] Then followed the anointing "from the top of the hairs of your head to the lower parts of your body."[25] Then the candidates were led to the baptismal font: they were asked whether they believed in the Father, the Son, and the Holy Spirit, and this confession of faith was followed by a triple immersion.[26]

The third lecture on the mysteries expounds the order of chrismation. This was performed immediately after the triple immersion: Cyril calls it "the sacramental representation [τὸ ἀντίτυπον] of the Holy Spirit."[27] Chrism is blessed with a prayer invoking the Holy Spirit.[28] The brow, ears, nostrils, and breast are anointed with chrism.[29]

We find a detailed description of the service order for the sacrament of illumination (baptism) in a tract by Dionysius the Areopagite titled *The Ecclesiastical Hierarchy*. This work first describes the process of registering a catechumen. According to the Areopagite, the person wishing to be baptized first approaches one of the Christians and asks to be brought to the hierarch (the bishop). The latter first offers up a prayer of thanksgiving, then gathers "a full religious assembly into the sacred place, for co-operation, and common rejoicing over the man's salvation, and for thanksgiving for the Divine Goodness." Then "a certain hymn, found in the Oracles"[30] is chanted, after which the hierarch kisses the holy table, goes out to the newcomer, and asks for what purpose he has come. When, as instructed by his sponsor, he denounces godlessness and asks to be baptized, then the hierarch "testifies to him, that his approach ought to be entire, as to God Who is All Perfect, and without blemish." Finally, "when he has expounded to him fully the godly course of life, and has demanded of him, if he would thus live—after his promise he places his right hand upon his head, and when he has sealed him, commands the priests to register the man and his sponsor."[31]

Then follows a description of the rituals of renouncing Satan and uniting oneself to Christ, followed by the anointing with oil, the blessing of the water, and baptism:

[24]Ibid., 2.2 (PPS 57:97–99).
[25]Ibid., 2.3 (PPS 57:99).
[26]Ibid., 2.4 (PPS 57:99–101).
[27]Ibid., 3.1 (PPS 57:105).
[28]Ibid., 3.3 (PPS 57:107)
[29]Ibid., 3.4 (PPS 57:107–109).
[30]That is, the word of God.—*Trans.*
[31]Dionysius the Areopagite, *The Ecclesiastical Hierarchy* 2.2. In *The Celestial and Ecclesiastical Hierarchy of Dionysius the Areopagite*, John Parker, trans. (London: Skeffington & Son, 1894), 55.

[The bishop] unlooses his sandals, and removes his clothing by means of the Deacons. Then when he has placed him facing the west, and whilst he beats with his hands with aversion towards the same quarter, he thrice commands him to breathe scorn upon Satan, and further, to profess the words of the renunciation. When he has witnessed his threefold renunciation, he turns him to the east, after he has confessed this three times, and has looked up to heaven, and extended his hands in this direction, he commands him to be subject to Christ. . . . When the man has done this, he witnesses again for him his threefold confession, and again, when he has thrice confessed, after prayer, he gives thanks and lays his hand upon him. When the Deacons have entirely unclothed him, the Priests bring the holy oil of the chrism.[32] Then he begins the chrism, through the threefold sealing, and assigns the man to the Priests for the anointing of his whole body, while he himself advances to the mother of filial adoption,[33] and dedicates the water within it by the sacred invocations, and consecrates it by three cruciform effusions of the holy myrrh. And when he has invoked three times, as in the injection of the myrrh, the holy melody of the inspiration of the Divinely rapt Prophets, he orders the man to be brought forward. When one of the Priests, from the register, has announced the name of himself and his surety, he is conducted by the Priests over the water to the hand of the Hierarch, being led by the hand to him. Then the Hierarch, standing above, when the Priests have again called aloud, near the Hierarch, within the water, the name of the initiated, the Hierarch dips him three times, invoking the threefold Subsistence of the Divine Blessedness.[34]

From this description it follows that the rite of the making of the catechumen was performed by the bishop: he would question the candidate, turning him first toward the west, then toward the east. The bishop would bless the water and begin the anointing with oil, which the priests would then complete. The candidate would be led to the baptismal font by the presbyters, while the baptism itself was performed by the bishop, "standing above" (that is, not going down into the font together with the candidate). From this description it follows that the whole church community would be present for baptisms.

---

[32]Here, according to the author in the paragraph that follows, by "chrism" St Dionysius is actually referring to blessed oil, not to chrism in the modern liturgical sense.—*Trans.*

[33]The baptismal font or baptistery.

[34]Dionysius the Areopagite, *The Ecclesiastical Hierarchy* 2.2. In *The Celestial and Ecclesiastical Hierarchy*, John Parker, trans., 55–56.

Regarding the role of deacons at the sacrament of baptism, the author of the *Corpus Areopagiticum* says:

> For which reason, during the service of Regeneration, the Leitourgoi[35] strip him who draws nigh of his old clothing, and even take off his sandals, and make him stand towards the west for renunciation. And again, they lead him back to the east . . . commanding those who approach to entirely cast away the coverings of their former life; and, showing the darkness of their former conduct, and teaching those who have said farewell to the darkness, to transfer their allegiance to the Light.[36]

Whereas in the apostolic age baptism was simple in form (entailing a descent into water and the laying on of hands by the apostles), by the third century it had become a solemn religious rite in which the entire church community participated. In the third and fourth centuries there was a custom of performing the sacrament of baptism on great feast days. Tertullian names Pascha and Pentecost as the days most suitable for receiving baptism.[37] Basil the Great likewise speaks of baptism on Pascha: "What time is more closely connected with baptism than Easter day, since the day itself is a memorial of the resurrection, and baptism is the powerful means for our resurrection? On resurrection day, then, let us receive the grace by which we rise again."[38] Gregory the Theologian mentions Theophany, Pascha, and Pentecost as customary days for baptism, but holds that one need not necessarily wait for one of these feasts in order to be baptized.[39]

The custom of serving baptisms exclusively on great feasts was not universal. Hippolytus of Rome, as we have seen above, spoke of baptism on Saturdays. Tertullian emphasizes that "every day is the Lord's; every hour, every time, is apt for baptism: if there is a difference in the solemnity, there is no distinction in the grace."[40] Tertullian is echoed by Gregory the Theologian: "Every moment is right for your washing."[41]

---

[35] That is, the deacons.—*Trans.*

[36] Dionysius the Areopagite, *The Ecclesiastical Hierarchy* 5.1. In *The Celestial and Ecclesiastical Hierarchy*, John Parker, trans., 80–81.

[37] Tertullian, *On Baptism* 19 (*ANF* 3:678).

[38] Basil the Great, *Sermon 13.* In *A Treatise on Baptism,* Francis Patrick Kenrick, trans. (Philadelphia, PA: King and Baird, 1843), 226.

[39] Gregory the Theologian, *Orations* 40.24 (PPS 36.118).

[40] Tertullian, *On Baptism* 19 (*ANF* 3.678).

[41] Gregory the Theologian, *Orations* 40.13 (PPS 36:109).

In the sacrament of baptism, Tertullian notes, a person is immersed in water with "simplicity, without pomp, without any considerable novelty of preparation, finally, without expense."[42] These words indicate that in addition to group baptisms on great feast days, less formal "private" baptisms were also permitted, performed apparently by arrangement at a time convenient for the candidates. Likewise important is his mention of the fact that baptism was performed "without expense": although the ancient Church encouraged voluntary donations, no payment was levied for performing the sacraments.

In the period that followed, baptism gradually dissociated from communal worship and transformed into one of the "private" services of need, performed in the presence of an intimate group at a time apart from the divine services. The order of the making of a catechumen also gradually shrunk, eventually being reduced to a single, fairly brief service order, performed as a rule immediately before baptism. The abbreviation and virtual disappearance of lengthy catechetical courses before baptism was due primarily to the practice of infant baptism, which became universally widespread in the fourth to eighth centuries. In Christian society of both East and West, adult baptisms became an extraordinary event, while infant baptism became the accepted standard.

Despite this change in the external form of baptism, its essence has remained unchanged since apostolic times. All the primary formative elements of the sacrament have also survived: the making of the catechumen, the renunciation of Satan, the confession of faith in Christ, the anointing with oil, the immersion in (or affusion with) water, and the blessing of the bishop (now bestowed in the form of a separate sacrament—chrismation). Many prayers and formulae used in the sacrament of baptism in the Orthodox Church have remained unchanged since the third century. Furthermore, the modern service order of the sacrament of baptism retains the form of the adult baptism in its entirety, preserved from the days when adult baptism was the most prevalent form.

PATRISTIC TEACHING ON BAPTISM

The fathers of the Church—both Eastern and Western—have given considerable attention to the sacrament of baptism. The first serious theological tract on the subject was Tertullian's composition *On Baptism*. In the fourth century individual

---

[42]Tertullian, *On Baptism* 2 (*ANF* 3:669).

Noah and his family in the ark. Mosaic. Cathedral of Monreale. Sicily. 12th c.

tracts or lectures were devoted to the sacrament of baptism by the holy hierarchs Cyril of Jerusalem, Basil the Great, Gregory the Theologian, Gregory of Nyssa, and John Chrysostom. Chapters devoted to baptism are found in the tracts *On the Mysteries* by Ambrose of Milan and *On the Catechizing of the Uninstructed* by Blessed Augustine, in Dionysius the Areopagite's composition *The Celestial Hierarchy*, in the *Mystagogy* of Maximus the Confessor, in the *Exposition of the Faith* of John of Damascus, and in numerous other compositions. Several basic themes permeate all these works of the holy fathers.

First and foremost, Christian authors speak of the significance of water as a religious symbol. Water "is one of those things which, before all the furnishing of the world, were quiescent with God in a yet unshapen state."[43] In the words of Scripture, "In the beginning God created the heaven and the earth. And the earth was without form, and void; and darkness was upon the face of the deep. And the Spirit of God moved upon the face of the waters" (Gen 1.1–2). These words, says Tertullian, indicate the purity of water as an element that was more pleasing to God than the other elements then in existence: "For the darkness was total thus far, shapeless, without the ornament of stars; and the abyss gloomy; and the earth unfurnished; and the heaven unwrought: water alone—always a perfect, gladsome, simple material substance, pure in itself—supplied a worthy vehicle to God."[44]

[43]Tertullian, *On Baptism* 3 (*ANF* 3:670).
[44]Ibid.

Water is an element of life: it is water that "was the first to produce that which had life, that it might be no wonder in baptism if waters know how to give life."[45] Through the presence of the Holy Spirit "the nature of the waters, sanctified by the Holy One, itself conceived withal the power of sanctifying."[46] Water acquires this power anew each time the Holy Spirit is invoked upon it:

> All waters, therefore, in virtue of the pristine privilege of their origin, do, after invocation of God, attain the sacramental power of sanctification; for the Spirit immediately supervenes from the heavens, and rests over the waters, sanctifying them from Himself; and being thus sanctified, they imbibe at the same time the power of sanctifying.[47]

In the Old Testament water was viewed not only as an element of life, but as an instrument of death, as evinced by the biblical account of the flood. Since apostolic times this account has been seen as one of the prefigurations of baptism (cf. 1 Pet 3.20–21). According to Gregory the Theologian, "This is the grace and power of baptism, not a flood inundating the world as of old, but the purification of each from sin and their complete cleansing from the heaps and defilements introduced by evil."[48]

Another Old Testament prefiguration of baptism was Moses' crossing of the Red Sea: "Israel was baptized in Moses in the cloud, and in the sea, presenting therein types for thy instruction, and sensibly exhibiting the truth which was to be shown in the latter days."[49] But the story of the flood is also perceived as a prefiguration of Pascha: with good reason it is read on the eve of Pascha as one of the fifteen Old Testament readings. The dual meaning of the flood's symbolism in Christian tradition is largely due to the fact that the paschal celebration was also a day of baptism.

The baptism of John likewise prefigured Christian baptism. The difference between these two baptisms is in keeping with the difference between a symbol and

Crossing of the Red Sea. Paris Psalter. Byzantium, early 10th c.

---

[45]Ibid.
[46]Ibid., 4 (*ANF* 4:670).
[47]Ibid. (*ANF* 4:671).
[48]Gregory Nazianzen, *Oration on Holy Baptism* 40.7 (PPS 36:103–104).
[49]Basil the Great, *Exhortation to Baptism*. In *A Treatise on Baptism*, Francis Patrick Kenrick, trans., 228–229.

*John the Baptist baptizing
the people. Book miniature.
Athos. 11th c.*

the reality, between a prefiguration and its materialization. In the words of Basil the Great, "John preached a baptism of penance, and all Judea went forth to him: the Lord proclaims a baptism whereby we are adopted as children. . . . That baptism was introductory: this is perfective: that separated from sin: this unites with God."[50]

Baptism is an agreement, or a covenant, between man and God. In the words of Gregory the Theologian, "the power of baptism is to be understood as a covenant with God for a second life and a purer lifestyle."[51] John Chrysostom describes baptism using an example that was familiar to any Byzantine: an agreement for the purchase of a slave. When we purchase slaves, says Chrysostom, we ask the persons who are being sold whether they wish to leave their former masters and enter into our service, and only after obtaining their consent do we make payment. In the same way Christ asks us whether we wish to renounce the authority of the devil, and "does [not] compel those who are unwilling, to serve him." The payment to the devil for our liberation from slavery is that great price (cf. 1 Cor 7.23) that he paid with his blood. After this "he does not require of us witnesses, or registration, but is content with the single word, if thou sayest it from thy heart. 'I renounce thee, Satan, and thy pomp,' has included all."[52]

Baptism is only valid when it is performed in the name of the Holy Trinity. Confession of the Trinity is an essential attribute of baptism, its theological nucleus. Gregory the Theologian says, "Guard . . . the confession of Father and Son and Holy Spirit. I entrust this to you today. With this I will both submerge you [in the water] and raise you up. This I give you as a companion and protector for all your life, the one divinity and power."[53] In the words of John of Damascus, we "are baptized into the Holy Trinity because those things which are baptized have need of the Holy Trinity for their maintenance and continuance, and the three subsistences cannot be otherwise than present, the one with the other. For the Holy Trinity is indivisible."[54]

[50]Ibid., 226.
[51]Gregory Nazianzen, *Oration on Holy Baptism* 40.8 (PPS 36:104).
[52]John Chrysostom, *Instructions to Catechumens* 2.5 (*NPNF*[1] 9:170).
[53]Gregory Nazianzen, *Oration on Holy Baptism* 40.41 (PPS 36:136).
[54]John of Damascus, *Concerning Faith and Baptism* 4.9 (*NPNF*[2] 9:78b).

A prefiguration of the Trinitarian baptism was the three days that Christ spent in the bowels of the earth after his death on the cross. Addressing the newly baptized, Cyril of Jerusalem says:

> You professed this saving confession and you descended three times into the water and ascended again, thereby also re-enacting through symbol the three-day burial of Christ. For just as our Savior spent "three days and three nights in the heart of the earth" (Mt 12.40), so also you in your first ascent imitated the first day of Christ in the earth and in your descent the night. . . . And in this same time you died and were reborn, and that saving water became both grave and mother for you. . . . And one time brought about both of these, and your birth was brought together with your death.[55]

At the same time, as John of Damascus emphasizes, Christ's death occurred not three times, but once, and so one also need be baptized but once.[56] From this it follows that rebaptism is inadmissible: those who are baptized a second time "crucify the Christ afresh." On the other hand, those who are not baptized in the name of the Holy Trinity must be baptized anew, since their baptism is invalid.[57]

As the apostle Paul teaches, baptism into the death of Christ unites a person with Christ through the "likeness of his resurrection": by dying unto sin, a person is resurrected unto "newness of life" (Rom 6.2–11). This imagery is developed by various fathers of the Church, among them Basil the Great and Gregory the Theologian:

> Let us then die, that we may live. Let us mortify the carnal feeling, which cannot be subject to the law of God, that a strong spiritual affection may arise in us, through which we may enjoy life and peace [cf. Rom 8.6–7]. Let us be buried together with Christ, who died for us, that we may arise again with Him, who proffers new life to us.[58]

So let us be buried with Christ through baptism, that we may also rise with him. Let us descend with him, that we may also be exalted with him. Let us ascend with him, that we may also be glorified with him.[59]

---

[55]Cyril of Jerusalem, *On the Mysteries* 2.4 (PPS 57:99–101).
[56]John of Damascus, *An Exact Exposition of the Orthodox Faith* 4.9 (*NPNF*² 9:77b).
[57]Ibid. (*NPNF*² 9:77b–78b).
[58]Basil the Great, *Exhortation to Baptism.* In *A Treatise on Baptism*, Francis Patrick Kenrick, 225.
[59]Gregory Nazianzen, *Oration on Holy Baptism* 40.9 (PPS 36:105).

The various names for baptism attest to its diverse effects upon a person's soul:

> We call it gift, grace, baptism, illumination, anointing, robe of incorruption, bath of rebirth, seal. . . . It is a gift because no offering is given for it beforehand; and grace, as given even to debtors; and baptism, as burying sin in the water; and anointing, as priestly and royal, since they were the ones anointed; and illumination, as most radiant; and robe, as entirely covering shame; and bath, as washing clean, and seal, as a safeguard and a sign of authority.[60]

In the words of Gregory the Theologian, "The word of Scripture recognizes three births for us: one from the body, one from baptism, and one from resurrection." Birth through baptism wholly frees a man from sin: it "releases from passions, cutting away all the veil that has surrounded us since birth and leading us back toward the life on high."[61]

Continuing the subject of a second birth, John Chrysostom avows that baptism not only frees from all sin, but also makes holy those who receive it:

> We promise to show you that they who approach the laver become clean from all fornication: but the word has shown more, that they have become not only clean, but both holy and just. . . . as a spark falling into the wide sea would straightway be quenched, or would become invisible, being overwhelmed by the multitude of the waters, so also all human wickedness, when it falls into the pool of the divine fountain, is more swiftly and easily overwhelmed, and made invisible, than that spark. . . . [The laver] does not simply take away our sins, nor simply cleanse us from our faults, but so as if we were born again. For it creates and fashions us anew not forming us again out of earth, but creating us out of another element, namely, of the nature of water. For it does not simply wipe the vessel clean, but entirely remoulds it again. . . . As therefore any one who takes and recasts a golden statue which has been tarnished by time, smoke, dust, rust, restores it to us thoroughly cleansed and glistening: so too this nature of ours, rusted with the rust of sin, and having gathered much smoke from our faults, and having lost its beauty, which He had from the beginning bestowed upon it from himself, God has taken and cast anew, and throwing it into the waters as into a mould, and instead of fire sending forth the grace of the Spirit,

---

[60]Gregory Nazianzen, *Oration on Holy Baptism* 40.4 (PPS 36:101); cf. John Chrysostom, *Instructions to Catechumens* 1.3 (*NPNF*¹ 9:161).

[61]Ibid., 40.2 (PPS 36:99).

then brings us forth with much brightness, renewed, and made afresh, to rival the beams of the sun, having crushed the old man, and having fashioned a new man, more brilliant than the former.[62]

While baptism frees a man from sin, by the same token it lays upon him the obligation not to return to his former sins. In the words of Gregory the Theologian, baptism must be followed by a change in one's way of life, for the purpose of eliminating the "old man" and of complete spiritual renewal: "Let us purify every limb and organ, brothers and sisters, let us sanctify every sense. Let there be nothing imperfect in us, nothing of the first birth; let us leave nothing unillumined."[63] John Chrysostom says:

> For the laver is able to remit former sins, but there is no little fear, and no ordinary danger lest we return to them, and our remedy become a wound. For by how much greater the grace is, by so much is the punishment more for those who sin after these things. [If] thou hast a habit of doing of things unlawful . . . away with the habit, in order that thou mayest not return to it, after baptism. The laver causes the sins to disappear. Correct thy habits, so that when the colors are applied, and the royal likeness is brought out, thou mayest no more wipe them out in the future; and add damage and scars to the beauty which has been given thee by God.[64]

These words establish a link between the sacrament of baptism and the moral character of the one who has received it. If baptism is not accompanied by a virtuous life, it may prove of no use to a person. Cyril of Jerusalem puts it laconically: "For although the water may receive you, the Spirit will not."[65] In another place Cyril says, "If thou play the hypocrite, though men baptize thee now, the Holy Spirit will not baptize thee."[66] Gregory of Nyssa speaks in a similar vein:

> Now if the washing is applied to the body, and the soul has not expunged the stains of the passions, but life after initiation should be on a par with uninitiated life, though it may be daring to say, I will say it and not be deterred, that

---

[62]John Chrysostom, *Instructions to Catechumens* 1.3 (*NPNF*[1] 9:161–162).
[63]Gregory Nazianzen, *Oration on Holy Baptism* 40.38 (PPS 36:133).
[64]John Chrysostom, *Instructions to Catechumens* 2.2–3 (*NPNF*[1] 9:167).
[65]Cyril of Jerusalem, *Procatechesis* 4 (PPS 57:69).
[66]Cyril of Jerusalem, *Catechetical Lectures* 17.36 (*NPNF*[2] 7:132).

in these cases the water is [mere] water, since the gift of the Holy Spirit is
nowhere manifest in what takes place.[67]

The fathers of the Church devote attention to various external aspects of the
sacrament of baptism. In the words of Gregory the Theologian, it does not matter
whether the baptism is performed by a bishop, a metropolitan, or a priest.[68] The
grace of the sacrament is not dependent on the date, or the place, or the merits of
the baptizer: every priest is suitable for the sacrament, if he has not been excommunicated from the Church. In general, all distinctions—between the virtuous
and the morally imperfect, between rich and poor, slave and freeman—vanish
before the baptismal font:

> Do not judge your judges, you who need healing. Do not judge the rank of
> those who purify you, and do not make distinctions regarding those who give
> you birth. One may be greater or another more lowly, but all are more exalted
> than you. . . . Let it be thus to you in regard to every baptizer. One may excel
> in his way of life, but the power of baptism is equal. And let every initiator
> be alike to you who has been formed by the same faith. Do not disdain to be
> baptized with a poor person if you are rich, with one lowly born if you are
> noble, with one up to now a slave if you are a master. You are not yet humbling
> yourself as much as Christ, into whom you are baptized today, who for your
> sake even accepted "the form of a slave." From the day you are transformed,
> all the old imprints have withdrawn; Christ has placed himself upon all as a
> single form.[69]

The works of the church fathers devoted to baptism are filled with exhortations
not to delay baptism until old age or the hour of death. These exhortations were
necessitated by the belief, widespread in the fourth century, that since baptism
bestows purification of sins it is best to receive it just before death. Some would
receive baptism only on their deathbed (a classic example being the emperor Constantine). Addressing those who put off baptism, Basil the Great inquires:

> Who has marked out for thee the limit of life? who has defined for thee the
> length of old age? who is the surety on which thou reliest for what is to befall

---

[67]Gregory of Nyssa, *Catechetical Discourse* 40.3. In St Gregory of Nyssa, *Catechetical Discourse: An
Ancient Catechist's Handbook*, Popular Patristics Series 59, Ignatius Green, trans. (Yonkers, NY: St Vladimir's
Seminary Press, forthcoming).

[68]Gregory Nazianzen, *Oration on Holy Baptism* 40.26 (PPS 36:121).

[69]Gregory Nazianzen, *Oration on Holy Baptism* 40.26–27 (PPS 36:121–122).

thee? Dost thou not see infants snatched away, and others in the age of man-
hood carried off? Life has no fixed boundary. Why dost thou await that baptism
should be for thee as a gift brought by a fever? Wilt thou wait until thou shalt
not be able to utter the saving words, and scarcely to hear them distinctly, thy
malady having its seat in thy head? Thou wilt not be able to raise thy hands to
heaven, or to stand on thy feet, or to bend thy knee in adoration, or to receive
suitable instruction, or to confess accurately, or to enter into covenant with
God, or to renounce the enemy; probably not even to follow the sacred minister
in the mystic rites; so that the by-standers may doubt whether thou perceivest
the grace, or art unconscious of what is done, and if even thou receivest the
grace, with consciousness, thou hast but the talent, without the increase.[70]

Echoing Basil, Gregory the Theologian insists that a person must hasten to
baptism while he is still of sound mind, while he is not yet mortally ill, while his
tongue can yet pronounce the words of the mystic rites. Why wait for the last few
minutes before death, why turn the feast of baptism into a ritual ablution before
burial? All times are fitting for baptism, for death is always close at hand.[71] The devil
suggests to a person, "Give the present to me, the future to God; your youth to me,
your old age to God." But there is great danger of accident and sudden death:

War has liquidated you, or an earthquake overwhelmed you, or the sea engulfed
you, or a wild beast seized you, or a disease killed you, or a crumb going down
the wrong way . . . or drinking was excessive, or a wind knocked you down, or
a horse ran away with its rider, or a drug was prepared in a plot against you . . .
or a judge was inhuman, or an executioner inexorable.[72]

John Chrysostom gives a vivid description of a deathbed baptism, praising
those who do not wait for the hour of death to receive baptism:

Wherefore, I count you blessed already before those sacred nuptials, and I do
not only count you blessed, but I praise your prudence in that you have not
come to your illumination . . . at your last breath. . . . For they indeed receive
it on their bed, but you in the bosom of the Church, which is the common
mother of us all; they indeed with lamentation and weeping, but you rejoicing, and exceeding glad: they sighing, you giving thanks; they indeed lethargic

---

[70]Basil the Great, *Exhortation to Baptism*. In *A Treatise on Baptism*, 235–236.
[71]Gregory Nazianzen, *Oration on Holy Baptism* 40.11–13 (PPS 36:107–109).
[72]Ibid., 40.14 (PPS 36:109–110).

with much fever, you filled with much spiritual pleasure; wherefore in your case all things are in harmony with the gift, but in theirs all are adverse to it. For there is wailing and much lamentation on the part of the initiated, and children stand around crying, wife tearing her cheeks, and dejected friends and tearful servants; the whole aspect of the house resembles some wintry and gloomy day. And if thou shalt open the heart of him who is lying there, thou wilt find it more downcast than are these. . . . Then in the midst of its tumult and confusion, the Priest enters, more formidable than the fever itself, and more distressing than death to the relatives of the sick man. For the entrance of the Presbyter is thought to be a greater reason for despair than the voice of the physician despairing of his life, and that which suggests eternal life seems to be a symbol of death.[73]

In the fourth century there was a widespread custom of not receiving baptism until one reached the age of thirty or until completion of one's secular education. Supporters of this practice cited the example of Christ, who was baptized at thirty years of age. In response to this opinion Gregory the Theologian (who was himself baptized at the age of thirty) says that "his conduct has been handed down to the extent of being a model for ours while avoiding a complete likeness."[74] Christ himself had power both his birth and his death, but a man is at risk of dying before being born unto a new life.

What age is most suitable for baptism? Different eras and different regions have given different answers to this question. Tertullian held that "according to the circumstances and disposition, and even age, of each individual, the delay of baptism is preferable; principally, however, in the case of little children." Tertullian gave a rather unusual explanation of Christ's words regarding children—"Suffer little children to come unto me, and forbid them not: for of such is the kingdom of God" (Lk 18.16):

Let them "come," then, while they are growing up; let them "come" while they are learning, while they are learning whither to come; let them become Christians when they have become able to know Christ. Why does the innocent period of life hasten to the "remission of sins"? For no less cause must the unwedded also be deferred—in whom the ground of temptation is prepared, alike in such as never were wedded by means of their maturity, and in the

[73]John Chrysostom, *Instructions to Catechumens* 1.1 (*NPNF*[1] 9:160).
[74]Gregory Nazianzen, *Oration on Holy Baptism* 40.30 (PPS 36:125).

widowed by means of their freedom—until they either marry, or else be more fully strengthened for continence. If any understand the weighty import of baptism, they will fear its reception more than its delay: sound faith is secure of salvation.[75]

Basil the Great held that youth is a perfectly suitable season for baptism: "Art thou young? secure thy youth against vice, by the restraint which baptism imposes. Has the vigor of life passed away? Do not neglect the necessary provision for thy journey: do not lose thy protection: do not consider the eleventh hour, as if it were the first; since it even behoves him who is beginning life, to have death before his eyes."[76]

Christ with the children

Is infant baptism permissible? From Tertullian's perspective, no. In the fourth century, however, the view began to prevail that one need not necessarily wait for the age of reason to be baptized. Gregory the Theologian writes, "Do you have a small child? Let evil not seize this time, let him be sanctified from babyhood, let him be consecrated by the Spirit from when his nails grow."[77] Gregory does not actually object to the idea that baptism must be received with awareness, but for him the danger of sudden death remains an irrefutable argument in favor of infant baptism. He holds that the age of three years, by which time the child is able to consciously comprehend what is taking place, is optimal for receiving baptism. In response to the question of whether to baptize infants, who experience neither harm nor grace, he writes:

> Absolutely, if indeed there is some immediate danger. For it is better to be sanctified without perceiving it than to depart unsealed and uninitiated. . . . But as for the rest I give my recommendation to wait for the third year, or a little more or a little less, when they can also hear something of the mystery and respond, so even if they do not understand completely, at any rate they are imprinted. And then sanctify them in both soul and body by the great mystery of initiation. For indeed the situation is as follows. They begin to be responsible for their lives at the time when their reason is matured and they learn the

[75]Tertullian, *On Baptism* 18 (*ANF* 3:678).
[76]Basil the Great, *Exhortation to Baptism*. In *A Treatise on Baptism*, Francis Patrick Kenrick, 233.
[77]Gregory Nazianzen, *Oration on Holy Baptism* 40.17 (PPS 36:112).

mystery. . . . And it is more useful in every respect to be fortified by the bath because the sudden assaults of danger that befall us are beyond help.[78]

Although in the fourth century the optimal age for receiving baptism was still being disputed, with various perspectives being voiced in this regard, subsequently the practice of infant baptism became predominant throughout the Christian world. The broad proliferation of this practice led to a change in the function of the sponsors. Whereas in the time of Justin Martyr [c. AD 100–165] the sponsors' primary function was to bring the person desiring to be baptized to the church and to vouch for his good behavior over the course of his catechesis, later the sponsors came to be entrusted with the religious education of infants baptized before the age of reason. The sponsors would respond to the priest's questions during the sacrament of baptism on behalf of the candidate, if the latter were not yet able to speak and rationally comprehend his surroundings.

Infant baptism and the role of the sponsors are discussed by the author of the *Corpus Areopagiticum,* in the *The Ecclesiastical Hierarchy.* The Areopagite disputes with those who find it "a fit subject for reasonable laughter, upon the supposition that the Hierarchs teach Divine things to those not able to hear, and vainly transmit the sacred traditions to those who do not understand. And this is still more laughable—that others, on their behalf, repeat the abjurations and the sacred compacts." Refuting the opinion of the opponents of infant baptism, the author of the *Corpus Areopagiticum* writes:

> Infants being brought up according to a Divine institution will attain a religious disposition, exempt from all error, and inexperienced in an unholy life. When our Divine leaders came to this conclusion, it was determined to admit infants upon the following conditions, viz.: that the parents of the child to be presented should transfer him to some one of the instructed, who is a faithful teacher of children in Divine things, so that the child should lead the rest of his life under his instruction, as under a godfather, and security for his religious safe-keeping.[79]

By participating in the sacrament of baptism it is as if the sponsor were saying, "I promise that when this infant reaches the age of reason, and is in a condition to understand holy things, I will exhort him to wholly renounce all that is of the enemy and to confess and fulfill the divine vows." As the Areopagite concludes,

---

[78]Gregory Nazianzen, *Oration on Holy Baptism* 40.28 (PPS 36:123–124).
[79]Dionysius the Areopagite, *The Ecclesiastical Hierarchy* 7.3.11, 96.

"There is nothing absurd, then, in my judgment, if the child is brought up in a religious training, in his having a guide and religious surety, who implants in him a disposition for Divine things, and keeps him inexperienced in things contrary."[80]

A recurring theme in patristic literature was the assertion that salvation without baptism is impossible. This assertion was based on the words of Christ (cf. Mk 16.16). At the same time, no definitive answer was given concerning the fate of those who died unbaptized through no fault of their own, such as infants or those who did not receive baptism "through ignorance." According to Gregory the Theologian, such persons "will neither be glorified nor punished by the just judge,84 since they did not receive the seal yet were not wicked, but suffered rather than did the damage."[81] This does not, however, extend to those who deliberately defer baptism and die unbaptized due to their own negligence.

In patristic tradition the term *baptism* was applied not only to the sacrament of baptism performed by priests in the church. In the era of persecutions (the second and third centuries) some of those who believed in Christ received a martyric death before they could be baptized. Concerning these people the Church believed that their baptism by blood stood in lieu of sacramental baptism:

> If a catechumen should be arrested for the sake of the name of the Lord he should be constant in respect of his witness. For if violence is brought against him and he is killed before receiving remission of his sins, he has received baptism in his own blood and is justified.[82]

> We have indeed, likewise, a second font, (itself withal *one with the former,*) of blood, to wit; concerning which the Lord said, "I have to be baptized with a baptism," when He had been baptized already [cf. Lk. 12.50]. For He had come "by means of water and blood" [1 Jn. 5.6], just as John has written; that He might be baptized by the water, glorified by the blood; to make us, in like manner, called by water, chosen by blood. These two baptisms He sent out from the wound in His pierced side, in order that they who believed in His blood might be bathed with the water; they who had been bathed in the water might

---

[80]Ibid., 97.

[81]Gregory Nazianzen, *Oration on Holy Baptism* 40.23 (PPS 36:117). The fate of unbaptized infants has been previously discussed in vol. 2, pp. 350, 352, and 503. [St Gregory of Nyssa also wrote a treatise on the subject: *On Infants' Early Deaths* (NPNF² 5:372–381). —*Ed.*]

[82]Hippolytus, *Apostolic Tradition* 19.2 (PPS 54:126).

likewise drink the blood. This is the baptism which both stands in lieu of the
fontal bathing when that has not been received, and restores it when lost.[83]

In Christian sources of the period that followed (the fourth to eighth centuries)
the term *baptism* began to take on other meanings as well. In particular the labor of
repentance and the sacrament of confession came to be called a "baptism of tears."
John of Damascus lists eight senses in which the term *baptism* is used in Eastern
Christian literature:

> The first baptism was that of the flood for the eradication of sin. The second was
> through the sea and the cloud: for the cloud is the symbol of the Spirit and the
> sea of the water. The third baptism was that of the Law: for every impure person
> washed himself with water, and even washed his garments, and so entered into
> the camp. The fourth was that of John. . . . The fifth was the baptism of our
> Lord, whereby He Himself was baptized. . . . But we, too, are baptized in the
> perfect baptism of our Lord, the baptism by water and the Spirit. . . . The sixth
> is that by repentance and tears, which baptism is truly grievous. The seventh is
> baptism by blood and martyrdom, which baptism Christ Himself underwent
> in our behalf, He Who was too august and blessed to be defiled with any later
> stains. The eighth is the last, which is not saving, but which destroys evil: for
> evil and sin no longer have sway: yet it punishes without end.[84]

Pre-Baptismal Rituals

The Naming

In the contemporary Book of Needs of the Orthodox Church the sacrament of
baptism is preceded by several rituals, which as a rule are performed separately
from baptism: the prayers on the first day, the naming on the eighth day, and the
prayers on the fortieth day. All these rituals were not originally a part of the sacrament of baptism and are not included in it. They appeared when infant baptism
became the norm.

On the first day after the birth of a child the priest reads three prayers over the
mother. In these prayers he asks God to heal the child's mother and to raise her
up from her bed of sickness, to preserve her "from every oppression of the devil,"

---

[83]Tertullian, *On Baptism* 16 (*ANF* 3.677).
[84]John of Damascus, *An Exact Exposition of the Orthodox Faith* 4.9 (*NPNF*[2] 9.78b–79b).

and to cleanse her of impurity; and he asks that the child be preserved "from every cruelty and storm of adversity, and from evil spirits, whether of the day or of the night."

On the eighth day, according to custom, the naming of the child takes place, at which the priest reads this prayer:

> O Lord our God, we entreat thee and supplicate thee: let the light of thy countenance be signed upon this thy servant *N.* and let the Cross of thine Only-begotten Son be signed in his heart and understanding. . . . And grant, O Lord, that thy holy Name may remain unrejected by him, and that, in due time, he may be joined to thy holy Church and be perfected by the dread Mysteries of thy Christ.

In our time a name is no more than an identifier, needed in order to distinguish one person from another. Every person has a name, but the original meaning of that name is not generally connected to that person's personality. Frequently people do not even know what their name means. In naming a child the parents usually choose from a very limited pool of names that are more or less common in their culture, and they pay more attention to euphony than to meaning. Secular specialists in anthroponymy recommend that the meaning of the name be disregarded entirely when choosing a name for a child.[85]

In ancient times it was another matter. Names were treated not merely as an identifier or a sobriquet, but as a mystic symbol that served as a key to the fundamental characteristics of its bearer and was directly linked to him. In the Old Testament a person was viewed on the principle of "as his name is, so is he" (1 Sam. 25.25). In the Bible a name is practically equated with the personality of its bearer: a glorious name means that its bearer is glorious, a dishonorable name means that its bearer has lost his dignity, and the destruction of a name means that its bearer has perished.[86] The name was ascribed an almost magical significance: whoever possessed a person's name possessed the person of its bearer.[87] Hence the important role of name changes in the Bible, which signified a loss of independence

---

[85]Cf. for example A.V. Suslova and A.V. Superanskaya, *O russkikh imenakh* [On Russian Names] (Leningrad: Lenizdat, 1985), 189–190: "To correlate name meanings when choosing a name for a child is an idle and fruitless undertaking. . . . Knowing the meaning of this or that name in the source language is of interest only in that it allows us to trace the historical path of a name from nation to nation. . . . In our time however this is of no practical value in selecting a name."

[86]Cf. Neofit (Osipov), *"Mysli ob Imeni"* [Thoughts on the Name], *Nachala* 1–4 (1998): 51–58.

[87]Louis Bouillé, *O Biblii i Evangelii* [On the Bible and the Gospel] (Brussels: Zhizn' s Bogom, 1998), 23; H.O. Thomson, "Yahweh," in *Anchor Bible Dictionary* 6 (New Haven, CT: Yale University Press, 1992), 1012.

and subjection to the changer of the name (cf. 2 Kg 23.34, 24.17). At the same time, a change of name could betoken a more intimate relationship with the name changer. For example, Moses changed the name of Oshea the son of Nun to Joshua before sending him into the land of Canaan in command of a company of spies (cf. Num 13.17). With this name the son of Nun not only subjected himself to Moses, but also became his most intimate assistant, and later his successor.

When God himself changes a person's name, this is a sign that the person has lost his independence and become a slave of God, while at the same time entering into a new, more intimate relationship with God. God changes the names of his chosen ones—those whom he has taken into his confidence, whom he has entrusted with some mission, with whom he has entered into a covenant. After God covenanted with Abram that he would become the father of many nations, Abram became Abraham (cf. Gen 17.1–5), and his wife Sarai became Sarah (cf. Gen 17.15). Jacob received the name Israel ("Contender with God," or, in another interpretation, "Godseer") after he wrestled with God and God blessed him (cf. Gen 32.27–28).

If receiving a name from God means to subject oneself to God, to embark on the saving path that leads to heaven, then "to make a name for oneself" (cf. Gen 11.4) means, conversely, to oppose God: this expression indicates the sinful aspiration of men to abandon subjection to God, to reach heaven without God's help.

In view of this theology of the name it becomes clear why in Orthodox tradition the naming is a pre-baptismal church ritual. Receiving a name from the priest is the first step a Christian takes on the path of obedience to God and the Church. In practice the name is given by the parents, and the priest simply repeats it on the eighth day after the child is born. However, with the parents' consent the priest may change the name they had chosen, especially if it is not a Christian name.

In the Russian Orthodox Church there is a custom of naming those being baptized in honor of saints. This has been the custom in Russia ever since it adopted Christianity, and it was borrowed from Byzantium. The princes of Russia, descendants of the Vikings, received the names of Greek saints at baptism: Olga was named Elena (Helen); Vladimir, Vasily (Basil); Boris and Gleb, Roman and David. As a result, a significant number of traditional names of Slavic origin fell into disuse and Russians began giving their children predominantly Greek names. Only a few Slavic names belonging to Russian saints (who were themselves baptized with other names) are included among the names given at baptism in the Russian Church.

In the Greek Church the custom of naming people after saints was not always strictly followed, and in modern Greece there are Christians with names such as Panayiotis and Christos.[88] In the Serbian Church various names of Slavic origin but not connected with saints are common (Radoslav, Radomir, Milka): a person's heavenly patron is considered to be not the saint whose name he bears, but the saint whom his family chooses to be their patron. Thus, a single saint is considered the

Ancient baptistery.
Shivta, Israel.

heavenly patron of the whole family; his feast day is called a *slava*, and the family celebrates it with particular festivity.

The fortieth day after the birth of a child marks the end of the postpartum purification of the mother. The Christian Church inherited the concept of postpartum impurity from the Old Testament (cf. Lev 12.1–5, Lk 2.22). In the Bible the concept of birth is inseparably linked with the concept of sin: "For behold, I was conceived in iniquities, and in sins did my mother bear me" (Ps 50.7). This by no means implies that the act of conception and giving birth is sinful, as some suppose. The Bible has no underlying antisexual message: on the contrary, in the Old Testament conception and giving birth had a sacred significance, and the highest manifestation of God's blessings was the bestowal of "seed," or progeny. The words of the psalm concerning conception in iniquity and sin refer to the hereditary transmission of sinfulness, that is, the transmission of Adam's sin from one generation to the next (cf. Rom 5.12–19). Through his parents each person inherits not only all the good accumulated by previous generations, but also the propensity to sin and liability for it. For this reason, in addition to the birth "of the flesh" one also has need of the birth "of water and of the Spirit" (Jn 3.5–6), this being the sacrament of baptism.

---

[88]Both these names are connected with Christianity but are not saints' names. The name Panayiotis is a title of the Most Holy Theotokos, meaning "All Holy," but in masculine form [and the common woman's name Despoina is likewise a title of the Theotokos, meaning "Lady"—*Ed.*]. The name Christos (Χρῆστος/Chrēstos) means "good, kind" (it is a homophone, but not identical to the name of Christ, as the spelling differs). [Greeks also take the names of feast days, e.g., the women's names Υραραντē/Υπαπαντή (Meeting of the Lord), Eisōdia/Εἰσώδια (Entrance of the Lord), Evangelia/Εὐαγγελία (Annunciation).—*Ed.*]

The Making of the Catechumen

The baptism of an infant traditionally takes place around the fortieth day after his birth. There is no firmly set time for the baptism, however; it may take place either before or after the fortieth day. An adult may be baptized at any age.

The first part of the sacrament of baptism is called the making of the catechumen. It comprises the final stage of what the term *catechesis* was understood to mean in the ancient Church—the process of preparation for baptism. In our time the rite of the making of the catechumen immediately precedes baptism, though it may also be performed separately, since it has retained the format of a complete service order.

The rite begins in the Book of Needs with these words: "The priest looses the garment of the person who desires Illumination, and removes it, and puts it off from him; and places him with his face towards the east, clothed in one garment only, unshod, and with head uncovered, and with his arms hanging by his sides." These words describe the ancient custom whereby the catechumen would approach for the sacrament clothed only in a long shirt covering his naked body (this was removed before his immersion in the water). This custom is mentioned by John Chrysostom: "Our fathers . . . settled that . . . after the instruction from us, removing your shoes and raiment, unclad and unshod, with but one garment on, they conduct you to hear the words of the exorcisers."[89] In modern times special baptismal robes are used for infant baptisms; in some churches long white robes are also sold for adult baptisms.

The candidate for baptism stands facing east; the priest lays his hand upon his head and reads this prayer:

> In thy Name, O Lord of truth, and in the Name of thine Only-begotten Son, and of thy Holy Spirit, I lay my hand upon thy servant, *N.*, who has been found worthy to flee unto thy holy Name, and to take refuge under the shelter of thy wings. Remove far from him his former delusion, and fill him with the faith, hope, and love which are in thee; that he may know that thou art the only true God, with thine Only-begotten Son, our Lord Jesus Christ, and thy Holy Spirit. Enable him to walk in all thy commandments, and to fulfill those things which are well-pleasing unto thee. . . . Inscribe him in thy Book of Life, and unite him to the flock of thine inheritance. And may thy holy Name be glorified in him, together with that of thy beloved Son, our Lord Jesus Christ,

---

[89]John Chrysostom, *Instructions to Catechumens* 1.2 (*NPNF*[1] 9:160).

and of thy life-creating Spirit. Let thine eyes ever regard him with mercy, and let thine ears attend unto the voice of his supplication. Make him to rejoice in the works of his hands, and in all his generation; that he may render praises unto thee, may sing, worship and glorify thy great and exalted Name always, all the days of his life.

It should be noted that the prayer begins with the words "In thy Name"; that the priest refers to the candidate as one who has been vouchsafed to flee to the holy name of God; and that he prays that the candidate glorify the "great and exalted" name of God. In the prayers that follow in the order of the sacrament of baptism, the name of God is mentioned numerous times. The baptismal formula itself, as commanded by Christ, consists of pronouncing the name of the Father, the Son, and the Holy Spirit. The early Christian Church, as we have noted elsewhere,[90] ascribed tremendous importance to the name of God. In discussing the name of God, John Chrysostom exclaims, "By it we perform the sacred mysteries."[91] According to Chrysostom, the name of God possesses particular power in the sacrament of baptism:

> Nothing is equal to this Name, marvelous is it everywhere. . . . He that hath uttered it is straightway filled with fragrance. . . . Such great things doth this Name work. If thou hast said, "In the Name of Father, and Son, and Holy Spirit," with faith, thou hast accomplished everything. See, what great things thou hast done! Thou hast created a man, and wrought all the rest (that cometh) of Baptism! . . . We have been regenerated by this Name. This if we have, we beam forth.[92]

Chrysostom speaks of two "spiritual charms": the first is the name of God; the second, the might of the cross.[93] Chrysostom's words should not, however, be understood to mean that the name of God or the sign of the cross possesses magical powers. In the sacrament of baptism in particular both the name of God and the sign of the cross play an important role, but they do not work magically, apart from the other prayers and sacred actions comprising the service order.

In the ancient Church a person would begin his path to baptism by coming to the bishop and declaring his desire to become a Christian. The bishop would then

---

[90]Cf. vol. I, from 376 on.
[91]John Chrysostom, *Explanation of Psalm 110.*
[92]John Chrysostom, *Homilies on Colossians* 9 (*NPNF*[1] 13:303).
[93]John Chrysostom, *Homilies on Romans* 8 (*NPNF*[1] 11:392).

register him as a catechumen. It is this ritual, of which Hippolytus of Rome spoke as early as the third century, that is referred to in the prayer "In thy Name." How this ritual was performed in fourth-century Jerusalem is related by Egeria:

> And when the priest has written down the names of all, after the next day of Quadragesima, that is, on the day when the eight weeks begin,[94] the chair is set for the bishop in the midst of the great church, that is, at the martyrium, and the priests sit in chairs on either side of him, while all the clergy stand. Then one by one the competents are brought up, coming, if they are males (*viri*) with their fathers, and if females (*feminae*), with their mothers.[95] Then the bishop asks the sponsors of every one who has entered concerning each individual, saying: "Does this person lead a good life, is he obedient to his parents, is he not given to wine, nor deceitful?" making also inquiry about the several vices which are more serious in man. And if he has proved him in the presence of witnesses to be blameless in all these matters concerning which he has made inquiry, he writes down his name with his own hand. But if he is accused in any matter, he orders him to go out, saying: "Let him amend, and when he has amended then let him come to the font (*lavacrum*)." And as he makes inquiry concerning the men, so also does he concerning the women. But if any be a stranger, he comes not so easily to Baptism, unless he has testimonials from those who know him.[96]

Above we cited a description of the ritual of registering a catechumen, found Dionysius the Areopagite's tract *The Ecclesiastical Hierarchy*. As we recall, the ritual ended with the bishop laying his hand upon the one come to be baptized. This gesture had profound symbolic meaning in the era when the Church was persecuted: it testified that from the moment that person entered the Church he was under its protection and prayerful patronage. His registration as a catechumen also had a symbolic meaning: it signified that henceforth that person, though not yet a full member, was not a stranger to the Church. In addition it indicated that when a person comes to Christ his name is written into "the book of life" (cf. Phil 4.3; Rev 3.5, 13.8, 17.8, 20.12–15, 21.27).

---

[94]In Jerusalem Great Lent lasted for eight weeks, since on Saturdays and Sundays the fast was suspended (eight weeks, excluding Saturdays and Sundays, is exactly forty days).

[95]This refers to the sponsors—the godfathers and godmothers.

[96]Etheria, *The Pilgrimage of Etheria* 7.1, M.L. McLure and C.L. Feltoe, trans. (London: Society for Promoting Christian Knowledge, 1919), 90–91.

After the prayer "In thy Name" is read, the exorcism and renunciation of the devil begin (a ritual so ancient as to be described in detail by Hippolytus of Rome). The first two exorcisms are unique in that they are addressed not to God, but to the devil.[97] These exorcisms are exactly that—exorcisms, casting the devil out of the person:

> The Lord lays thee under ban, O Devil: He who came into the world, and made his abode among men, that he might overthrow thy tyranny and deliver men, who also upon the tree did triumph over the adverse powers . . . who also by death annihilated death, and overthrew him who exercized the dominion of death, that is thee, the devil. I adjure thee by God, who hath revealed the Tree of Life, and arrayed in ranks the cherubim and the flaming sword which turns all ways to guard it: Be thou under ban. . . . Fear, be gone and depart from this creature, and return not again, neither hide yourself in him, neither seek to meet him, nor to influence him, either by night or by day, either in the morning or at noonday: but depart hence to thine own Tartarus, until the great Day of Judgment which is ordained. . . . Be gone, and depart from this sealed, newly-enlisted warrior of Christ our God . . .

This exorcism is of very ancient origin (it is found in the late eighth-century *Barberini Euchologion*). The second exorcism is similar in content.

The two exorcisms are followed by two prayers addressed to God. In the first of these the priest asks God to cast out impure spirits from the candidate, to drive away from him all activity of the devil, to crush Satan beneath his feet, and to grant him victory over Satan and the other impure spirits. In the second prayer the priest asks God to open the inner eyes of the candidate, to enlighten him with the light of the Gospel, and to assign him a guardian angel to deliver him from all activity of the devil. In the course of the prayer the priest breathes thrice upon the mouth, brow, and breast of the candidate (this breathing is mentioned as early as the *Apostolic Tradition*),[98] saying:

> Expel from him every evil and unclean spirit which hides and makes its lair in his heart. (Thrice.) The spirit of deceit, the spirit of evil, the spirit of idolatry and of every covetousness; the spirit of falsehood and of every uncleanness which operates through the prompting of the Devil. And make him a reason-endowed

---

[97]It is unlikely that saying, "Let us pray to the Lord" before these exorcisms is appropriate, despite its being prescribed in the Book of Needs.

[98]Hippolytus, *Apostolic Tradition* 20.8, 128.

sheep in the holy flock of thy Christ, an honorable member of thy Church, a consecrated vessel, a child of the light and an heir of thy kingdom, that having lived in accordance with thy commandments, and preserved inviolate the seal, and kept his garment undefiled, he may receive the blessedness of the saints in thy kingdom.

Two exorcisms and two prayers comprise the rite of exorcism—the casting out of the demons. Exorcism is one of the ancient church institutions that has been preserved in the Orthodox Church. In the third century there was a special rank of exorcist, whose duty it was to cast out demons from catechumens and the possessed. The rank of exorcist was below the rank of deacon, but above the ranks of reader and gatekeeper. In some churches exorcists were ordained by the bishop. In other churches exorcists were not ordained, since their ministry was perceived as charismatic rather than hierarchal.[99] In the third century either a layman or a presbyter could be an exorcist. Later, however, the authority to cast demons out of catechumens became the exclusive domain of the presbyters, and the rank of lay exorcists ceased to exist.[100]

To the modern man the rite of exorcism may appear frightening and repellent. Some laymen view it as a vestige of the Dark Ages, while some priests either entirely omit or significantly abbreviate it when serving the sacrament of baptism. And yet the exorcism is an integral part of the rite of the making of the catechumen. This failure to understand its significance is due to the fact that some Christians have only a loose knowledge of the Orthodox teaching on the devil and demons: they think the devil a mythological figure and refuse to believe in his existence.

The experience of the Church, however, shows that demonic reality exists in the lives of men. Furthermore, demons do "hide and make their lair in the heart" of a man, as it is said in the prayer at the making of the catechumen. This expression may be understood as a reference to the vices and sinful inclinations that, as Christ said, come out of the heart of a man: "Out of the heart proceed evil thoughts, murders, adulteries, fornications, thefts, false witness, blasphemies" (Mt 15.19). As the Christian ascetic writers saw it, each of the vices has its own demon (John of the

---

[99]For more information on exorcists see *Istoriya katakhizatsii v Drevnei Tserkvi* [History of Catechesis in the Ancient Church], Pavel Gavrilyuk (Moscow: Svyato-Filaretovskiy pravoslavno-khristianskiy institut, 2001), 156–159, 187–188.

[100]In the modern practice of the Orthodox Church, in addition to being part of the pre-baptismal rite of the making of the catechumen, exorcism is practiced by some priests as a separate rite. In the vernacular it is called *otchitka* or *otchityvanie*—a "reading out" of the evil spirit. In many cases this is done without the blessing of the ecclesiastical authorities and can be detrimental to a person's spiritual and mental wellbeing.

Ladder speaks of the demons of sensuality, sorrow, love of money, cowardice, despondency, and vainglory).[101]

It is characteristic of modern man to become desensitized to manifestations of the demonic world and, at the same time, to the vices through which the demonic world materializes in the world of men. A distorted understanding of the devil's role in a person's life, an inability to see the demonic presence behind every sin and vice, leads to a permissive attitude toward vice, indifference toward evil, and an inability to recognize evil in oneself. Paradoxically, another consequence of the same is an inclination to superstition, to which modern man is no less susceptible—indeed perhaps far more so—than ancient man. The idea that the devil is

Orthodox baptistery in Ravenna. Interior view. Mid-5th c.

a mythical being, the product of medieval imagination, together with the wide proliferation of horoscopes and magic, the industrious activities of psychics and sorcerers, the interest of the general public in demonic themes in art—such is the reality of life in our modern, "civilized" society.

The Christian Church opposes superstitions specifically because it believes that the devil is real. According to the teaching of the Church, demonic reality requires active opposition on the part of a Christian. Concerning this the apostle Paul writes that "we wrestle not against flesh and blood, but against principalities, against powers, against the rulers of the darkness of this world, against spiritual wickedness in high places" (Eph 6.12). A Christian is "a good soldier of Jesus Christ" (2 Tim 2.3, 1 Tim 1.18), and he must be clothed in the armor of light (cf. Rom 13.12). One must be clothed in the whole armor of God in order "to stand against the wiles of the devil" (Eph 6.11). In accordance with this teaching, the order of the making of the catechumen calls the person who has approached for baptism a "newly-enlisted warrior of Christ our God." In embarking on the path of Christian life, a person becomes a warrior of Christ and throws down the gauntlet to the devil.

In the order of baptism this is represented by a wide range of words and symbolic actions. Immediately after the prayers that the devil be cast out, the priest turns the candidate to face west, turning to face the same direction himself. This action is of profound significance. In the ancient Church the east was perceived as a symbol of God, and the west as a symbol of the devil. For this reason churches

---

[101]Cf. vol. 1, 498–500.

were built with their altars toward the east, and people offered up prayers facing east, while the exorcism of the devil was pronounced facing west. Addressing catechumens, Cyril of Jerusalem says, "For the West is the place where darkness appears, and that one [Satan] is darkness and possesses his power in darkness. Therefore, symbolically keeping your eyes toward the West, you renounced that dark and gloomy prince."[102]

Having turned the candidate toward the west, the priest asks him thrice, "Dost thou renounce Satan, and all his works, and all his angels, and all his service, and all his pride?" (We find this formula in the writings of Hippolytus of Rome in the third century, and of Cyril of Jerusalem and John Chrysostom in the fourth century.) The candidate thrice responds, "I do renounce him." Then the question is asked thrice, "Hast thou renounced Satan?" followed by the response, "I have renounced him." After this the priest says, "Breathe and spit upon him," at which the candidate must breathe and spit (symbolically) toward the west.

For some modern individuals this ancient ritual evokes a smile or bewilderment. Yet there is no better expression of the essential Christian attitude toward the devil. The power of the devil is illusory: where God is at work the devil is powerless, and he is incapable of harming a person unless the person himself gives him opportunity to do so. The devil gains entry to the human heart through sins and vices, as well as through various forms of magic, sorcery, and witchcraft. If a person is a stranger to these things, if he does not commit mortal sins, he need not fear the devil. On the contrary, living according to Christ's commandments gives him strength and confidence in his fight against evil—against Satan and all his works, his helpers, his service, and his pride.

The renunciation of Satan is an indispensable condition of embarking on the path of Christian life. A person cannot become a Christian without renouncing voluntary adherence to vice, evil, and sin. This refers not to involuntary sins, which every Christian may commit and for which he offers repentance in confession. This refers to conscious opposition to the will of God, to a sinful and wicked way of life that is incompatible with Christianity, to a worldview grounded in anti-Christian values. Against this worldview one must declare war when embarking on the path of Christian life:

> To renounce Satan thus is not to reject a mythological being in whose existence one does not even believe. It is to reject an entire "worldview" made up of pride

---

[102]Cyril of Jerusalem, *On the Mysteries* 1.4 (PPS 57:87–89).

Baptism of Prince Vladimir. V.M. Vasnetsov. Fresco.

and self-affirmation, of that pride which has truly taken human life from God and made it into darkness, death, and hell. And one can be sure that Satan will not forget this renunciation, this rejection, this challenge. "Breathe and spit upon him!" A war is declared! A fight begins whose real issue is either eternal life or eternal damnation. For this is what Christianity is about![103]

As soon as the renunciation of the devil has taken place, the catechumen turns to the east, and the priest asks him thrice, "Dost thou unite thyself unto Christ?" He replies, "I do." The dialogue then continues: "Hast thou united thyself unto Christ?" "I have." "And dost thou believe in him?" "I believe in him as King and God." The Nicene-Constantinopolitan Creed is read. After a threefold repetition of this dialogue the priest calls upon the candidate to bow down before God, and the candidate makes the sign of the cross and a prostration with the words, "I bow down before the Father, the Son, and the Holy Spirit, the Trinity one in essence and indivisible." The priest then says, "Blessed is God, who desires that all men should be saved and come to a knowledge of the truth, now and ever and unto the ages of ages." And a prayer is read that concludes the rite of the making of the catechumen (similar in content to the initial prayer of the rite):

O Master, Lord our God, call thy servant, *N.*, to thy holy Illumination, and grant unto him that great grace of thy holy Baptism. Put off from him the old

[103]Alexander Schmemann, *Of Water and the Spirit* (Crestwood, NY: St Vladimir's Seminary Press, 1974), 30.

man, and renew him unto life everlasting; and fill him with the power of thy
Holy Spirit, in the unity of thy Christ: that he may be no more a child of the
body, but a child of thy kingdom.

The Creed is one of the most ancient elements of the sacrament of baptism. In
the early Church there were various creeds; each local church had its own creed.
Originally these creeds were brief; over time, as heresies spread and the battle
against them intensified, the content of these creeds expanded. Moreover, gradually the local creeds underwent a process of synchronization and unification, which
reached completion in the Christian East in the late fifth century. By this time the
Nicene-Constantinopolitan Creed had taken hold as the common creed for the
whole Church.

Uniting oneself to Christ is also an integral part of the sacrament of baptism,
both in the practice of the ancient Church and in our own time, and it immediately follows the renunciation of the devil. Once again, this action had a profound
meaning: it signified no less than an oath of allegiance to Christ. Whereas the
renunciation of Satan was a termination of the agreement with the devil, uniting
oneself to Christ was the signing of an agreement with God. If all biblical history
may be viewed as a series of covenants made between God and men, "in baptism
a person became a participant in the history of salvation and a member of the
covenant, writing his name into the history of salvation."[104]

The idea of a covenant is developed in the instructions from the *Barberini
Euchologion,* which dates back to the late eighth century. This euchologion contains a detailed description of the ritual of renouncing Satan and uniting oneself
to Christ. This ritual took place on Great Friday in the presence of the archbishop.
Upon entering the church at about midday he would say to the catechumens,
"Peace be unto all," and instruct them to remove their clothing (their outerwear)
and shoes. Then he would address them with these words:

> This is the end of our instruction: the occasion of your redemption. Today you
> are here to publish before Christ the contract of faith: for our pen and ink we
> use our understanding, our tongue and our behavior. Watch therefore how you
> write your confession. . . . Each of you shall look at the devil and hate him,
> and thus you shall blow upon him. Each of you must enter into his conscience,
> search his heart, and see what he has done. If after you have blown upon the
> devil there is still anything evil in you, spit it out. . . . The devil stands now

---

[104]Gavrilyuk, *Istoriya katakhizatsii,* 206.

to the west, gnashing his teeth, tearing his hair, wringing his hands, biting his lips, crazed, bewailing his loneliness, disbelieving your escape to freedom. For this cause Christ sets you opposite the devil, that having renounced him and having blown upon him you may take up the warfare against him. The devil stands to the west because it is from there that darkness comes: renounce him, blow upon him, and then turn to the east and join yourselves unto Christ. . . . All that is happening is most awful and horrifying. All the powers of the heavens are there, all angels and archangels. Unseen, the Cherubim and Seraphim record your voices: at this moment they look down from heaven to receive your vows and carry them to the Master. Take care therefore how you renounce the enemy and accept the Creator.[105]

Then follows the ritual of renouncing Satan and uniting oneself to Christ in the very form in which it has been preserved in modern editions of the Book of Needs of the Orthodox Church. At the conclusion of this ritual, after the catechumens have bowed down before God, the bishop says:

Behold, you have renounced the devil and adhered to Christ. The contract is fully written. The Master preserves it in heaven. Study the articles of your agreement: remember, it is brought forth at the day of judgment. . . . Watch then, and secure yourselves: you have renounced the devil, hate him to the end: you have united yourselves to Christ, praise him to your last breath, sojourn with this orthodox confession to God the Master. Be not *shipwrecked concerning the faith* [1 Tim. 1.19].[106]

The Blessing of the Water in the Sacrament of Baptism

The order of the sacrament of baptism in the modern Book of Needs is preceded by the following remark: "The priest enters the sanctuary and putts on white vestments, and his gauntlets. And when he has lighted all the tapers . . . he takes the censer, and goes to the Font, and censes round about it; and having given the censer to be held, he makes a reverence." While the priest may perform the making of the catechumen in a ryassa (or exorasson) and epitrachelion, before the baptism begins he vests in a white robe, as a reminder of the paschal character of the sacrament.

---

[105] *Barberini Euchologion* fol. 260ff. In *Documents of the Baptismal Liturgy* by Edward Charles Whitaker, revised and expanded by Maxwell E. Johnson, 3rd ed. (Collegeville, MN: Liturgical Press, 2003), 110.

[106] Ibid., 111–112.

The rite of baptism begins with the exclamation, "Blessed is the Kingdom of the Father, and of the Son, and of the Holy Spirit, now and ever and unto the ages of ages." Of all the sacraments of the Church, only the Eucharist, baptism, and matrimony begin with this exclamation. This is due to the fact that the latter two sacraments were formerly included in eucharistic worship, and only in later years separated from it into independent service orders.

As at the liturgy, at baptism the initial exclamation is followed by the great litany. To it are added petitions for the water: that it be sanctified by the power, effectual operation, and descent of the Holy Spirit; that upon it there be sent down the grace of redemption and the blessing of Jordan; that there descend upon it the purifying operation of the super-substantial Trinity; that it receive the power to avert the snares of all enemies, both visible and invisible. A petition is added for all those present (the priest and the members of the church community), that through the inspiration of the Holy Spirit they might be enlightened by the illumination of their understanding and piety. Special petitions are offered for the candidate: that he be made worthy of the incorruptible kingdom of God; for his salvation; that he prove to be a child of the light and an heir of eternal good things; that he be a partaker of the death and resurrection of Christ; that he preserve his baptismal garment and the pledge of the Spirit undefiled and blameless unto the dread day of judgment.

While this litany is being chanted the priest prays for himself (this prayer is similar in content to the prayer "No one who is bound"[107] from the divine liturgy):

> O compassionate and merciful God, who triest the heart and the reins . . . thou who knowest all things concerning me, regard me not with loathing, neither turn thy face from me; but consider not my iniquities at this present hour. . . . And wash away the vileness of my body, and the pollution of my soul. And sanctify me wholly by thine all-perfect, invisible might, and by thy spiritual right hand, lest, while I proclaim liberty unto others, and administer this rite with perfect faith in thine unutterable love toward mankind, I myself may become the base slave of sin.

The content of the prayer shows that in the sacrament of baptism the priest must not be merely an instrument in the Lord's hands, a passive receptor and conductor of grace that is outside of and foreign to him. The sacrament of baptism can have a purifying effect on him also, and the descent of the Holy Spirit can be

[107]The prayer of the cherubic hymn.—*Trans.*

a source of sanctification and enlightenment of the mind and piety both for him and for the whole church community. In this prayer a connection is established between the priest, the candidate, the church community, and the sacrament that is taking place. In the words of Protopresbyter Alexander Schmemann, "The prayer of the priest 'for himself' reminds us . . . of our total dependence on one another for spiritual growth and fulfillment. It reveals Baptism not to be 'an end in itself' but the beginning of a process in which the whole community, but especially the pastor, is to have a decisive part."[108]

Next the priest exclaims thrice, "Great art thou, O Lord, and wondrous are thy works, and there is no word which sufficeth to hymn thy wonders." A prayer then follows that resembles the eucharistic anaphora in structure: it includes thanksgiving to God, a recollection of the history of mankind from the creation of the world, a recollection of the economy of the Savior's coming into the world, and, finally, a petition for the sending down of the Holy Spirit. But while the prayer of the anaphora primarily emphasizes the mystical supper and the transformation of the bread and wine into the body and blood of Christ, the prayer of the blessing of the water recalls Jesus' baptism in the Jordan:

> For thou, of thine own good will, hast brought into being all things which before were not, and by thy might thou dost uphold creation, and by thy providence thou dost order the world. When thou hadst joined together the universe out of four elements, thou didst crown the circle of the year with four seasons. Before thee tremble all the powers endowed with intelligence. The sun sings unto thee. The moon glorifies thee. The stars meet together before thy presence. The light obeys thee. The deeps tremble before thee. The water-springs are subject unto thee. Thou hast spread out the heavens like a curtain. Thou hast established the earth upon the waters. Thou hast set around the sea barriers of sand. Thou hast shed abroad the air for breathing. The angelic powers serve thee. The choirs of the archangels fall down in adoration before thee. The many-eyed cherubim and the six-winged seraphim, as they stand round about and fly, veil their faces in awe before thine ineffable glory. For thou, who art God inexpressible, existing uncreated before the ages, and ineffable, didst descend upon earth, and didst take on the semblance of a servant, and wast made in the likeness of man. . . . We confess thy grace. We proclaim thy mercy. We conceal not thy gracious acts. Thou hast delivered the generation of our

[108]Schmemann, *Of Water and the Spirit*, 52.

mortal nature. By thy birth thou didst sanctify a virgin's womb. All creation
magnifieth thee, who hast revealed thyself. For thou, O our God, hast revealed
thyself upon earth, and hast dwelt among men. Thou didst hallow the streams
of Jordan, sending down upon them from heaven thy Holy Spirit, and didst
crush the heads of the dragons who lurked there.

In the eucharistic anaphora the divine incarnation is viewed as an event pertaining primarily to the salvation of man, but in the prayer of the blessing of the
water the divine incarnation is woven into the cosmological context: it is spoken
of as an event that concerns the whole universe. In descending into the waters of
the Jordan, by his presence the incarnate God sanctified the whole nature of water,
and together with it all the elements, all creation, all of cosmic space.[109]

In the Christian understanding, the fate of the universe is inseparably linked to
the fate of man. In the words of the apostle Paul, because of the fall creation "was
made subject to vanity" and along with man it "groaneth and travaileth in pain
together until now"; likewise together with man, and not apart from him, it awaits
deliverance "from the bondage of corruption" (Rom 8.19–22). The ultimate fate of
creation is tied to the fate of man, and the transfiguration of creation is impossible
without the salvation of man. In the sacrament of baptism, through the descent of
the Holy Spirit upon the water, the lost connection between man and the world
of nature is restored.

Holy water is needed so that men can be baptized in it, and through the descent
of the Holy Spirit upon it the water itself acquires healing and wonderworking
properties:

> Wherefore, O King who lovest mankind, come thou now and sanctify this
> water, by the indwelling of thy Holy Spirit. (*Thrice.*) And grant unto it the grace
> of redemption, the blessing of Jordan. Make it the fountain of incorruption,
> the gift of sanctification, the remission of sins, the remedy of infirmities, the
> final destruction of demons, unassailable by hostile powers, filled with angelic
> might. Let those who would ensnare thy creature flee far from it. For we have
> called upon thy Name, O Lord, and it is wonderful, and glorious, and awesome
> unto adversaries.

Then, immersing his hand in the water and signing the water thrice with the
sign of the cross, the priest says thrice, "Let all adverse powers be crushed beneath

---

[109]Cf. Bishop Athanasius (Yevtich), *Christ: The Alpha and Omega* (Sebastian Press, 2007), 101.

*Patriarch Nicholas the Mystic baptizing the son of Leo VI, Constantine Porphyrogenitus.
Book miniature. 11th c.*

the sign of the image of thy cross." After this he continues: "We pray thee, O God, that every aerial and obscure phantom may withdraw itself from us; and that no demon of darkness may conceal himself in this water; and that no evil spirit which instilleth darkening of intentions and rebelliousness of thought may descend into it with him who is about to be baptized." Once again the priest is praying not only for the water and for the candidate, but for all those present—that all demonic illusions and apparitions will depart from them.

The words of the prayer concerning "aerial phantoms" should not be construed as a relic of archaic mythology. This prayer reflects the Christian understanding that matter is never neutral with regard to good and evil: matter is not merely some dead or passive substance. God created matter good, but if it is not used as a means of communion with God it becomes a vessel and a habitation of the powers of darkness.[110] In this world evil is often accomplished by means of material objects and elements, which may be used as instruments of crime. Water, for example, can be used to drown a person; fire, for arson; metal, to inflict bodily harm or to commit murder. In all such cases responsibility for the evil is borne not by the material object or element, but by the person who has succumbed to the influence of demonic forces or of his own sinful inclinations. The task of a Christian is to free matter from the oppression of the forces of evil, to use it for good, to restore it to God in an act of gratitude.

[110]Schmemann, *On Water and the Spirit*, 57.

Continuing the prayer, the priest asks God that the blessed water might become a source of spiritual change and transfiguration for the candidate for baptism:

> Do thou, O Master of all, show this water to be the water of redemption, the water of sanctification, the purification of flesh and spirit, the loosing of bonds, the remission of sins, the illumination of the soul, the laver of regeneration, the renewal of the Spirit, the gift of adoption to sonship, the garment of incorruption, the fountain of life. . . . Thou hast bestowed upon us from on high a new birth through water and the Spirit. Wherefore, O Lord, manifest thyself in this water, and grant that he who is baptized therein may be transformed; that he may put away from him the old man, which is corrupt through the lusts of the flesh, and that he may be clothed upon with the new man, and renewed after the image of him who created him: that being buried, after the pattern of thy death, in baptism, he may, in like manner, be a partaker of thy Resurrection.

In this prayer two "eucharistic" terms are used: *to show* and *to be transformed*. The term *to show* is used in the liturgy of Basil the Great along with two other terms (*to bless* and *to sanctify*) to indicate the action performed upon the bread and the wine by God the Father, aided by the Holy Spirit. The verb *to change* (meaning "to transform") is used in the same sense in the liturgy of John Chrysostom. In both cases this refers to a qualitative change in material objects, the bread and the wine: their transformation into the body and blood of Christ. The prayer at the blessing of the water, however, asks not only that the water be qualitatively changed, transformed from ordinary water into sanctified water, but also that this change take place in the candidate himself—that he, like the holy gifts at the Eucharist, might undergo a qualitative change, putting off the old man and being clad in the new.

The Anointing with Oil, Immersion in Water, and Clothing in a White Robe

The similarity between what happens to the holy water in the sacrament of baptism and what happens to the person being baptized is further underscored by the fact that both the water and the person are anointed with oil. The prayer at the blessing of oil resembles the prayer at the blessing of the water: in it the priest asks that the oil be unto the person an anointing of incorruption, a shield of righteousness, a renewal of soul and body, the driving away of every action of the devil. Then the priest dips a brush into the oil and immerses it cruciformly in the water to the singing of "Alleluia." After this he anoints the brow, breast, back (between the shoulders), ears, hands, and feet of the candidate, with these words: "The servant of God *N.* is anointed with the oil of gladness; in the name of the Father, and of the Son, and of the Holy Spirit, unto the healing of soul and body, unto the hearing of the faith. Thy hands have made me and fashioned me. That he may walk in the way of thy commandments."[111]

Before immersion in the font the candidate is anointed with the "oil of gladness," a rite recorded as early as the third century. (The significance of oil as a religious symbol will be discussed in the section devoted to the sacrament of unction.)

The word *baptism* (from the Greek βάπτισμα/*baptisma*) literally means "immersion," and the church Typicon prescribes baptism by full immersion. As we have seen, in the ancient Church baptism in living water, by full immersion, was considered the standard; at the same time baptism by affusion was also permitted when necessary.[112] Hence those priests are wrong who hold that baptism by affusion is always invalid (such priests are occasionally encountered in Orthodox circles). At the same time it should be recognized that in our time, as in antiquity, baptism by full immersion must be considered the norm. Infants can be baptized by immersion in a font; adults, in a specially built baptistery (a baptismal pool, which some Orthodox churches have) or in a natural body of water (a river or lake).

It is immersion in water, and not affusion or aspersion (sprinkling), that conveys the full symbolism of the sacrament of baptism as the death of the old man and the resurrection of the new. In ancient churches baptisteries typically had steps on the east and west sides: the candidate would enter the font from the west side, then exit toward the east. At this time he would be facing east.[113] This too had profound significance, as it indicated that after baptism a person must not return to his former sinful life. Passing through the baptistery from west to east symbolized a passage from darkness to light, from death to life.

---

[111]The Book of Needs calls for the priest to dip two fingers in the oil and anoint the candidate with them. In practice this anointing is performed using a special brush. The established practice is to anoint the brow, eyes, ears, mouth, breast, hands (back and palm), and top of the feet (for an adult) or top and bottom (for an infant baptism). [This describes the Russian practice. In Greek practice, when an infant is baptized the godparents bring a bottle of olive oil, and in addition to the specific anointings listed above, they lather the child's entire body with oil themselves, using their hands.—*Ed.*]

[112]See references to the *Didache* and the *Apostolic Tradition* above.

[113]The modern Book of Needs contains this instruction: "Holding the child upright and facing toward the east, the priest immerses the child in the baptismal water."

The baptism takes place with these words: "The servant of God *N.* is baptized, in the name of the Father. Amen. And of the Son. Amen. And of the Holy Spirit. Amen." In ancient times the threefold "amen" was spoken by the whole community; today the priest says it alone. In the Latin ritual, when baptizing the priest pronounces a somewhat different formula: "I baptize you in the name of the Father, and of the Son, and of the Holy Spirit." The reason that the rituals of East and West differ on this point is that in the East the action of God in the sacraments was emphasized: it is not the priest who baptizes, but God himself by the agency of the priest, as affirmed by the use of the third person passive ("is baptized"). Here, however, the difference is one of terminology, as the Western tradition also teaches that the sacrament is accomplished by God himself. As Ambrose of Milan says, "Damasus cleansed not, Peter cleansed not, Ambrose cleansed not, Gregory cleansed not; for ours is the ministry, but the sacraments are Thine. For it is not in man's power to confer what is divine, but it is, O Lord, Thy gift."[114]

The church Typicon prescribes for the candidate to enter the baptistery completely naked. In practice this injunction is observed only for infant baptisms. When adults are baptized it is not observed, and with good reason. In the perception of modern man the concept of nakedness is linked with the concept of debauchery: exposing oneself in public (for baptismal nakedness was exactly that, in an era when baptisms were performed publically) is perceived as indecent behavior.

In the Bible and the early Christian Church, nakedness was understood differently. The Bible says that God created man naked, and in this primordial nakedness there was nothing indecent or sinful. Nakedness became shameful after the fall into sin. In the sacrament of baptism the original meaning of nakedness is restored, and so in the context of baptism—and in that context alone—it symbolizes purity and sinlessness. Addressing those who have just been baptized, Cyril of Jerusalem said, "were naked in the sight of everyone and you were not ashamed."[115] This directly alludes to the words of Genesis concerning Adam and Eve, who "were naked, and were not ashamed" (cf. Gen 2.25). In addition, nakedness in the sacrament of baptism had christological connotations: "Having stripped, you were naked, imitating also by this the nakedness of Christ on the cross."[116]

The post-baptismal ritual of being clothed in a white robe also has christological significance. This is linked to the words of the apostle Paul: "For as many

---

[114]Ambrose of Milan, *On the Holy Spirit* 1.18 (*NPNF²* 10:96).
[115]Cyril of Jerusalem, *On the Mysteries* 2.2 (PPS 57:99).
[116]Ibid. (PPS 57:97).

of you as have been baptized into Christ have put on Christ" (Gal 3.27). Disrobing before baptism signified putting off the old man, while being robed after baptism indicates that those baptized have put on Christ, becoming children of God by faith and heirs according to the promise (cf. Gal 3.26, 29). The robe's white color symbolizes the spiritual purity and angelic state of a person who has emerged from the baptismal font—a person whose every sin has been forgiven. When robing the newly baptized the priest says, "The servant of God *N.* is clothed in the robe of righteousness, in the name of the Father, and of the Son, and of the Holy Spirit. Amen." The choir sings, "Grant unto me the robe of light, O most merciful Christ our God, who dost clothe thyself with light as with a garment."

Baptism of Blessed Augustine. Fragment of relief on the tomb of St Augustine. Pavia, Italy. 1362.

Traditionally, after the white robe the baptismal cross is placed on the newly baptized. The Book of Needs is silent regarding this custom, but the tradition of wearing a cross around one's neck is certainly of ancient Christian origin, as confirmed by the numerous baptismal crosses that have survived from the early Christian and Byzantine eras. There were two kinds of crosses—those with an image of Christ crucified and those without. These were not seen as being fundamentally different: every cross was considered a symbol of Christ's presence, possessing miraculous power. Nor was there any special rite for blessing the cross, since it was not presumed that the cross, being itself a source of sanctification, required any additional sanctification.

The tradition of wearing a cross around one's neck is universal and long established in the Orthodox Church. It did not disappear even during the persecution of the Church in the Soviet Union. Though few believers wore the baptismal cross on a chain (this being fairly noticeable), many concealed it in a pocket or sewed it beneath a shirt collar.

CHRISMATION

The meaning and significance of the church sacraments are most fully revealed in their service orders: the prayers and rituals comprising a sacrament are the best key to understanding it. In this regard the sacrament of chrismation is an exception. This is the shortest of all the sacraments of the church: it lasts about a minute, and consists of the declaration of a short formula and the anointing of the newly baptized with holy chrism—a special compound of fragrant oils. The formula of chrismation consists of nine words: "The seal of the gift of the Holy Spirit." The brow, eyes, nostrils, ears, mouth, breast, hands, and feet are anointed.[117] After this a prayer is read that gives no further explanation of the meaning of the sacrament just performed:

> Blessed art thou, O Lord God Almighty . . . who hast given unto us, unworthy though we be, blessed purification through hallowed water, and divine sanctification through life-creating chrismation; who now, also, hast been graciously pleased to regenerate thy servant that has newly received illumination, by water and the Spirit, and dost grant unto him remission of sins, whether voluntary or involuntary. Do thou, the same Master, compassionate King of kings, grant also unto him the seal of thy holy, and almighty, and adorable Spirit, and participation in the holy body and precious blood of thy Christ.

Thematically this prayer pertains to baptism and communion as much as to chrismation (as we recall, in the ancient Church baptism and chrismation were immediately followed by communion).

The very terseness of the service order for this sacrament may possibly explain the substantial difference in its interpretation in the Orthodox East and the Latin West. In the East chrismation was never liturgically established as a separate sacrament, but rather was always included as part of the sacrament of baptism. In the West, conversely, chrismation (confirmation) was segregated into a separate liturgical service order, which is not performed at infant baptisms, but is administered to children between seven and twelve years of age. Since persons who have not been chrismated may not receive the sacrament of the Eucharist, in the Western Church infants are not communed at all. In the Catholic Church first communion became

---

[117]Cyril of Jerusalem mentions the anointing of the brow, eyes, ears, and nostrils (*On the Mysteries* 3.4). The canons say to anoint the brow, eyes, ears, nostrils, and mouth (seventh canon of the Second Ecumenical Council and ninety-fifth canon of the Sixth Ecumenical Council).

a separate ritual.[118] As for those Christian communities that separated from the Roman Church in the age of Reformation (Lutherans, Calvinists, etc.), these do not consider chrismation to be a separate sacrament, and it is included as part of the rite of baptism.

Orthodox academic theology of the nineteenth century viewed the sacrament of chrismation primarily in a polemical context. Disputing the Catholic understanding of the sacrament, Orthodox theologians insisted on the liturgical link between chrismation and baptism, while in disputes with the Protestants they demonstrated that chrismation is an independent sacrament. As frequently occurred in such cases, they borrowed Protestant arguments to oppose the Catholics, while employing Catholic arguments in disputing with the Protestants.

In the Latin ritual only the bishop may administer the sacrament of chrismation. In the Orthodox Church a priest may administer the sacrament, but the chrism used in the sacrament is blessed by the bishop (the patriarch). This emphasizes the link between the believer and the primate of the local church to which he belongs. Through chrismation, even if performed by a priest and not the bishop, the bishop's blessing is bestowed upon the believer.

According to one theory on the origin of chrismation, the sacrament was established to replace the laying on of hands by the bishop after baptism. According to this theory, in the early Christian Church the sacrament of baptism was performed by the bishop, who would lay his hands upon the newly baptized after his immersion in the font: through this laying on of hands (χειροτονία/*cheirotonia*) the gift of the Holy Spirit was bestowed upon the newly baptized. Later, however, when the bishop ceased performing the sacrament of baptism personally and delegated this authority to the presbyters, the hierarchal blessing was replaced by chrismation.

The artificiality of this theory is demonstrated by the fact that surviving descriptions of the sacrament of baptism from the era of the early Church include both the laying on of hands by the bishop and chrismation, which the bishop performed. The *Apostolic Tradition* of Hippolytus of Rome, as we have seen, states that immediately after baptism the bishop lays his hand upon those newly baptized, saying a prayer that the Holy Spirit be sent down upon them. After this he pours chrism (oil) into his hand, again lays his hand upon the head of the newly baptized person, and anoints his brow.[119] Thus, the laying on of hands by the bishop is by no means

---

[118]In 1910 Pope Pius X lowered the age for first communion to the age of reason (usually around seven). In practice Roman Catholic children usually begin receiving communion before confirmation (chrismation).—*Ed.*

[119]Hippolytus, *Apostolic Tradition* 21.23 (PPS 54:135).

replaced by chrismation: both actions are performed, signifying the descent of the Holy Spirit upon the newly baptized.

Indeed, during the apostles' lifetime the descent of the Holy Spirit was associated with the laying on of hands, which was viewed as a supplement to baptism. The book of Acts contains an account of a group of Samaritans who had been baptized in the name of Jesus, but as yet the Holy Spirit had descended upon none of them. The apostles Peter and John were sent to them, and when they arrived, the apostles prayed for them and "laid they their hands on them," after which "they received the Holy Spirit" (Acts 8.14–17). This account affirms that baptism was not seen as sufficient for the bestowal of the Holy Spirit. For this an additional sacred rite was needed: prayer and the laying on of hands by the apostles. The account makes no mention of anointing with chrism.

On the other hand, anointing is mentioned on numerous occasions in the apostolic epistles. Addressing Christians, the apostle John says, "Ye have an anointing [χρῖσμα/chrisma] from the Holy One. . . . The anointing [χρῖσμα/chrisma] which ye have received of him abideth in you" (1 Jn 2.20, 27). The apostle Paul writes to the Corinthians, "He which stablisheth us with you in Christ, and hath anointed us, is God; who hath also sealed us, and given the earnest of the Spirit in our hearts" (2 Cor 1.21–22). Here the anointing may be understood figuratively—as the blessing of God, the inner action of the Spirit of God. It should, however, by no means be ruled out that the action of the Holy Spirit was outwardly expressed through anointing with chrism. It is thus that the latter fathers of the Church understood Paul's words.[120] The formula "The seal of the gift of the Holy Spirit" is also based on the words of the apostle Paul.

The Christian Church inherited the ritual of anointing from the Old Testament Church. Anointing with chrism was an important element of the ancient Hebrew religious tradition. Certain cult elements were anointed with chrism, such as the altar, which consequently became "an altar most holy" (cf. Ex 29.36–37, 30.26–29). Priests were anointed with chrism (cf. Ex 30.30–31, Lev 8.12). The term *anointing* was used with regard to the prophets (cf. Ex 61.1).[121] Particular significance was accorded the anointing to kingship: it was performed by a prophet (cf. 1 Sam 10.1, 16.13; 2 Kg 9.6) or a priest (cf. 1 Kg 1.39, 2 Kg 11.12). This royal anointing

---

[120]Cyril of Jerusalem, *On the Mysteries* 3.6; Dionysius the Areopagite, *The Ecclesiastical Hierarchy* 7.4; John Chrysostom, *Homilies on Second Corinthians* 3.4.

[121]The anointing in Is 61 may be understood figuratively. Elijah was commanded to anoint Elisha (cf. 1 Kg 19.16); however, when the time comes to pass on to him his prophetic mission, Elijah cast his mantle upon him and imparted his spirit to him (cf. 1 Kg 19.19, 2 Kg 2.9–15).

became a prefiguration of the anointing of Christ, and in the Christian tradition the "anointed one" (χριστός/*christos*) of the psalms (e.g. Ps 2.2) was understood to mean the Messiah (which in Hebrew means "anointed one").

An allusion to anointing may be discerned in the words of John the Theologian in Revelation concerning Christ: "Unto him that loved us, and washed us from our sins in his own blood, and hath made us kings and priests unto God and his Father; to him be glory and dominion for ever and ever. Amen" (Rev 1.5–6). As John the Theologian perceives it, blood and water are at once symbols of redemption and of baptism (cf. 1 Jn 5.6: "This is he that came by water and blood, even Jesus Christ; not by water only, but by water and blood"). If the words "and washed us from our sins in his own blood" are taken to mean baptism as well as redemption, it is perfectly logical to see the words concerning kings and priests as an allusion to anointing with chrism.

Whatever the case may be, manuscripts as early as the second century speak of anointing with chrism (oil) as an important religious rite. Theophilus of Antioch writes, "That which is anointed [χριστός/*christos*] is sweet and serviceable [χρήστος/ *chrēstos*]. . . . Wherefore we are called Christians on this account, because we are anointed with the oil of God."[122] Clement of Alexandria distinguishes between "rational baptism" and the "blessed seal."[123] In the third century Cyprian of Carthage spoke of baptism and anointing as two different sacraments.[124]

In the fourth century an explanation of the sacrament of chrismation was provided by Cyril of Jerusalem, who devoted a separate lecture to this sacrament. Echoing Theophilus of Antioch, he links the sacrament of chrismation with the name of Christ: "Having become worthy of this holy chrismation you are called "Christians," confirming the truth of the name by your new birth. For before you had become worthy of baptism and this grace of the Holy Spirit, you were not yet worthy of this proper title, but were advancing on the way toward becoming Christians."[125]

According to the hierarch of Jerusalem, anointing is "the spiritual protection of your body and for the salvation of your soul."[126] It is performed as an image of the descent of the Holy Spirit upon Christ:

---

[122]Theophilus of Antioch, *Theophilus to Autolycus* 1.12 (*ANF* 2:92).
[123]Clement of Alexandria, *The Stromata* 2.3 (*ANF* 2:349).
[124]Cyprian of Carthage, *Epistles* 72 (*ANF* 5:379 –386).
[125]Cyril of Jerusalem, *On the Mysteries* 3.5 (PPS 57:109).
[126]Ibid., 3.7 (PPS 57:111).

You became christs when you received the sacramental representation [τὸ
ἀντίτυπον/*to antitypon*] of the Holy Spirit, and all things happened to you in
images, since you are the images of Christ. When that one had washed in the
Jordan, and after he gave to the waters the fragrance of his divinity, he ascended
from the waters and the Holy Spirit came upon him in substantial form, like
resting upon like. In the same way to you also, when you ascended from the
pool of the sacred waters, you received the anointing, the sacramental representation of Christ's anointing. And this is the Holy Spirit.[127]

As Cyril goes on to explain, having foreordained from before the ages that his
Son would be the Savior of the world, God the Father anointed him with the Holy
Spirit (cf. Acts 10.38). In Christ an anointing similar to this is bestowed upon the
faithful:

And just as Christ was truly crucified and buried and raised up, and you, by
means of baptism, were made worthy to be crucified, buried, and raised up in
likeness, so also is it with the chrismation. For that one was anointed by the
spiritual oil of gladness, that is, the Holy Spirit. . . . But you were anointed with
myron, becoming sharers and companions of Christ.[128]

Holy chrism is used to anoint a person's sensory organs. In the anthropological
view of the ancient Church, the soul manifests itself through the sensory organs,
and so the various sensory organs must be sanctified in order to sanctify the various
faculties of the soul. In the words of St Cyril, "symbolizing this you were anointed
on your forehead and your other senses. And your body was anointed with visible *myron* but your soul was sanctified by the Holy and invisible Spirit."[129] The
hierarch of Jerusalem explains:

And first you were anointed on your forehead . . . so that "with an unveiled face
you might reflect the glory of the Lord" (2 Cor 3.18). Next, upon your ears, so
that you might receive ears for the hearing of the divine mysteries. . . . Next,
upon the nostrils, that having sensed the divine *myron*. . . . After these upon
the breast that "having put on the breastplate of righteousness, you might stand
against the tricks of the devil" (Eph 6.14, 11).[130]

[127]Ibid., 3.1 (PPS 57:105).
[128]Cyril of Jerusalem, *On the Mysteries* 3.2 (PPS 57:107).
[129]Ibid., 3.3 (PPS 57:107).
[130]Ibid., 3.4 (PPS 57:107–109).

The hierarch compares the chrism imparted in the anointing to the gifts of the Eucharist, over which a prayer of thanksgiving is offered:

> Stop supposing that this visible *myron* is ordinary oil. For just as the bread of the Eucharist, after the invocation of the Holy Spirit is no longer ordinary bread, but the body of Christ, so also this holy m*yron* is no longer . . . common . . . but it is the gift of Christ and the Holy Spirit being accomplished by the coming of his divinity.[131]

Thus, chrism is not merely a compound of fragrant oils: through the descent of the Holy Spirit, by the gift of Christ, it becomes a receptacle of the Holy Spirit—a place, instrument, and medium of his presence. A transformation or change takes place, in which the fragrant compound becomes holy chrism, through which the gift of the Holy Spirit is imparted to the faithful.

The Baptismal Procession, Epistle, and Gospel

The baptismal procession takes place around the font immediately after the neophyte is robed in white and chrismated: the priest, holding a cross, and the newly baptized with his sponsor walk around the font three times while the words of the apostle Paul are sung: "As many as have been baptized into Christ have put on Christ" (cf. Gal 3.27), with the addition of the word "Alleluia." This solemn procession serves as a reminder of the connection between baptism and Pascha.

As has already been noted, in the ancient Church baptism was performed in baptisteries, and at the end of the sacrament the newly baptized would solemnly process into the church to participate in the Eucharist. Today two processions serve as reminders of this: the baptismal procession around the font and the paschal procession around the church on the night of holy Pascha. The early Christian Church experienced baptism "as the paschal sacrament" and Pascha "as baptismal celebration."[132] After baptism was separated from the celebration of Pascha, and instead of a single paschal/baptismal procession there were now two processions, their meaning changed somewhat, but the conceptual link between them was not completely lost. Today at the paschal procession the clergy and laity exit the church, witnessing to Christ's resurrection before the world outside the Church. In this way the paschal procession emphasizes the missionary task of the Church. But the

---

[131]Ibid., 3.3 (PPS 57:107).
[132]Schmemann, *Of Water and the Spirit*, 113.

mission of the Church, like that of the apostles, is to teach all nations and to baptize them "in the name of the Father and of the Son and of the Holy Spirit" (Mt 28.19). The sacrament of baptism is the goal and the completion of this mission.

In receiving baptism a person becomes a missionary, since the task that was entrusted to the apostles is now entrusted to him as well. Each Christian must be an apostle, a missionary, a preacher, showing forth by his life the truth of the resurrection of Christ. The procession around the font serves as a reminder of the missionary calling of every person who receives holy baptism.

At the same time, the baptismal procession is a reminder that in this world the Church is a sojourner: it is still on the path to the kingdom of God. And each Christian participates in this sojourn, traversing the path of Christian life under the guidance of the Church. Baptism is the beginning of this path, and the kingdom of God is its end.

The link between baptism and Pascha, between baptism and the resurrection of Christ, is emphasized in the epistle reading that follows the baptismal procession:

> As many of us as were baptized into Jesus Christ were baptized into his death. Therefore we are buried with him by baptism into death: that as Christ was raised up from the dead by the glory of the Father, even so we also should walk in newness of life. For if we have been planted together in the likeness of his death, we shall be also in the likeness of his resurrection: knowing this, that our old man is crucified with him, that the body of sin might be destroyed, that henceforth we should not serve sin. For he that is dead is freed from sin. Now if we be dead with Christ, we believe that we shall also live with him: knowing that Christ being raised from the dead dieth no more; death hath no more dominion over him. For in that he died, he died unto sin once: but in that he liveth, he liveth unto God. Likewise reckon also yourselves to be dead indeed unto sin, but alive unto God through Jesus Christ our Lord.

This reading from the Apostolos (the Book of Epistles) summarizes the sacrament of baptism, as it were, while simultaneously expounding its profound significance. These words of the apostle Paul bring to life the full symbolism of immersion in the waters of the baptismal font as a likeness of the Lord's death. Through baptism, the life, death, and the resurrection of Christ become part of the spiritual experience of each Christian. At the same time the apostle emphasizes the moral meaning of baptism as a death to sin and a resurrection unto "newness of life." In the words of John Chrysostom, "If then thou hast died in baptism, remain dead, for any one that dies can sin no more; but if thou sinnest, thou marrest God's gift."[133]

The epistle reading is followed by a reading from the Gospel, recounting Christ's commandment to his disciples to baptize in the name of the Father and of the Son and of the Holy Spirit (cf. Mt 28.16–20). This reading restores an evangelic perspective to the sacrament, testifying to its divine institution and simultaneously reminding the faithful that Christ is continually present in the Church: "Lo, I am with you . . . even unto the end of the world" (Mt 28:20).

Conclusion of the Sacrament. Rituals of the Eighth Day

The reading of the Gospel concludes the symbolism of the sacrament of baptism. It actually goes beyond the bounds of the original rite of baptism as such, since it was read at the paschal liturgy (to this day at liturgy on Great Saturday the same epistle and Gospel readings are read as at the sacrament of baptism). The initiation of the new members of the Church did not end with baptism and the services on the night of Pascha. Throughout the paschal week they would come to the church to hear the lectures on the mysteries. On the eighth day—that is, on the Sunday following Pascha—they would come once again, and the rituals of the eighth day would be performed for them. In modern practice these rituals are often performed immediately after baptism and are even included in the baptismal rite (despite the Book of Needs' prescription that they be performed specifically on the eighth day).

The first of these rituals is the washing of the holy chrism from the body of the newly baptized. This begins with two prayers, in which the priest asks God to help the newly baptized person to preserve "the shield of his faith" and the garment of incorruption. Laying his hand upon the head of the one who has been baptized, the priest addresses God with these words: "Lay thine almighty hand upon him and preserve him by the power of thy goodness. Maintain unassailed the earnest of the Spirit, and make him worthy of life everlasting." After this a special sponge is used to wash away the traces of chrism from the body of the baptized person, with the words: "Thou art justified. Thou art illumined. Thou art sanctified. Thou art washed: in the name of our Lord, Jesus Christ, and by the spirit of our God. Thou art baptized. Thou art illumined. Thou hast been chrismated. Thou art sanctified. Thou art washed: in the name of the Father, and of the Son, and of the Holy Spirit."

---

[133]John Chrysostom, *Homilies on Romans* 11 (*NPNF*[1] 11:409).

This ritual is not merely the utilitarian removal of the traces of chrism from the body of the baptized person. The symbolic meaning of this ritual is that it signifies the end of the long baptismal path, which as we remember included a lengthy catechesis and an examination of one's morality, a renunciation of Satan and a unification with Christ, immersion in the baptismal font and anointing with chrism, participation in the paschal services and communion of the holy mysteries of Christ, and daily attendance at the lectures on the mysteries throughout the week of Pascha. Now the Christian has been given all he requires to set out on his own path toward the kingdom of heaven. Now he is clothed in the whole armor of God, thoroughly equipped for battle with the forces of evil, both external and internal. Now he has received all he requires to go out into the world and bear witness to the miracle of spiritual resurrection that has taken place in him.

After the chrism has been washed, the white robe is removed from the newly baptized, and he dresses in his usual clothing. This, however, is not a symbol that the holiday is over and mundane life has resumed. Rather, it is a symbol of embarking on a military campaign: "When the real fight begins the bright and colorful uniform is of no use and is replaced with battle fatigues. . . . The white garment is removed and the Holy Chrism is washed off, for they were given to be not signs but reality itself, to be transformed into life."[134]

The moment of baptism marks the beginning of the Christian's fight for his own soul and for the souls of those around him. In this fight he will need the protection and aid of the Church. The Church for its part will be able to help its member only if he lives in obedience to its institutions and laws.

In this lies the meaning of the last of the eighth-day rites: the tonsure. Since ancient times the tonsure has been a symbol of obedience: with good reason a person is tonsured upon entering monasticism and at elevation to the rank of reader—the first rank of the clergy. The prayers after baptism remind us of the need for obedience to the Church, its hierarchy, and its institutions. At the same time it speaks of the incorruptible crown that is prepared for those who conquer in the spiritual battle—a crown that not only the newly baptized, but also the priest and all the members of the church community hope to receive. For this reason in the prayer once again the first person plural is used:

> He who hath clothed himself in thee, O Christ our God, boweth also his head with us, unto thee. Keep him ever a warrior invincible in every attack of those who assail him and us; and make us all victors, even unto the end, through thy crown incorruptible.

[134]Schmemann, *Of Water and the Spirit,* 126–127.

3

The Eucharist (Communion)

W E HAVE ALREADY SPOKEN in detail concerning the service order for the sacrament of the Eucharist in the section devoted to the daily cycle of services.[1] In this section we will discuss the spiritual and theological significance of the sacrament of the Eucharist, as well as various practical aspects of individual preparation for this sacrament.

We understand the sacrament of the Eucharist to mean not only the actual act of communing of the holy mysteries of Christ, but the entire service order of the liturgy. Unlike the majority of the sacraments of the Church, which in current practice have been relegated to the category of private services, the sacrament of communion retains its communal, conciliar character. Communion is inseparable from the liturgy. Even in those exceptional circumstances when communion takes place outside the liturgy (such as when a priest communes one who is sick or dying in his home), it is seen as a continuation of the liturgy that was served in the church. Communion at the liturgy of the presanctified gifts, at which the bread and wine do not change into the body and blood of Christ, is thought of as a continuation of the preceding full Eucharist at which this transformation did take place.

The Eucharist is the heart of the life of the Christian Church, its axis and its anchor. The Eucharist is more ancient than the holy scriptures of the New Testament and all the dogmatic and canonical institutions of the Church. The Church grew up out of the Eucharist and has the Eucharist as its foundation. The sacrament of the Eucharist is not only the backbone of the life of the entire body of the Church, but is also the core of the spiritual life of a Christian.

Christ performed the first Eucharist using bread and wine. Bread and wine are among the most ancient and most universal symbols. In the Old Testament bread was a symbol of food, of plenty, and hence a symbol of life; wine was first and foremost a symbol of joy: "Wine maketh glad the heart of man . . . and bread strengtheneth man's heart" (Ps 103:15). Bread is a gift from God: an abundance of

[1]See vol. 4, pp. 101ff.

Melchizedek offering a sacrifice. Mosaic. Basilica of Sant'Apollinare in Classe. Ravenna. 6th c.

bread signifies God's blessing as a reward for righteousness (cf. Ps 36.25, 131.15) and industry (cf. Prov 12.11). A shortage of bread (cf. Jer 5.17, Ez 4.16, Lam 1.11), or of bread and wine (cf. Lam 2.12), is a punishment from God for sins. God endows the prophet Elisha with the miraculous gift of multiplying bread (cf. 2 Kg 4.42–44), a gift that Christ also possesses (cf. Mt 14.15–21). The Savior commands his disciples to pray for their daily bread (cf. Mt 6.11), and at the same time reminds them that the Heavenly Father knows all the needs of man (cf. Mt 6.25–32). Unlike John the Baptist (cf. Lk 1.15, Mt 11.18), Christ does drink wine (cf. cf. Mt 11.19, Lk 7.34), and at the wedding in Cana of Galilee he changes water into wine (cf. Jn 2.1–10).

Bread and wine have been known as elements of worship since the Old Testament. Melchizedek, king of Salem, who was "a priest of the most high God," came forth to meet Abraham with bread and wine (cf. Gen 14.18): in the Christian tradition Melchizedek is perceived as a prefiguration of Christ, and the bread and wine as a prefiguration of the Eucharist. The "showbread" was kept in the temple in Jerusalem upon a golden table (cf. 1 Kg 7.48); beside these loaves stood a vessel of wine (cf. Num 4.7). The "wave loaves" were part of the sacrificial ritual: they were offered in sacrifice to God along with the lambs (cf. Lev 23.17–18). Wine was also used as one of the sacrificial elements (cf. Ex 29.40; Lev 23.13; Num 15.5, 10, 28.7, 14; Hos 9.4).

In the Church from the very beginning bread and wine have been the primary elements of eucharistic worship. For the Eucharist pure grape wine must be used, to which water is added.[2] In the practice of the Russian Orthodox Church only red wine—as a rule, sweet (dessert) wine—is used for the Eucharist. Certain other local Orthodox churches also employ blush and white wines. In the Catholic Church white wine is sometimes used for the Eucharist. The use of red wine is usually explained by its outward resemblance to human blood, but this resemblance is not required either by patristic tradition or by canonical precepts. A more substantial factor than the color of the wine is its quality: the wine must be unmingled. For this reason it is impermissible to use wines containing grain alcohol, sugar, and flavorings for the Eucharist.

---

[2]See Justin the Martyr, *Apologies* 1.65; cf. seventh canon of the Seventh Council of Carthage.

Certain early Christian sects (the Ebionites, Encratites, Marcionites, Manichaeans, Aquarians, and others) performed the Eucharist using bread and water; the Church, however, absolutely rejected this practice.[3] The church canons prohibit performing the Eucharist using berry or fruit juices,[4] although in certain exceptional circumstances deviations from this rule have been permitted.[5]

PATRISTIC TEACHING ON THE EUCHARIST

The eucharistic theology of the eastern fathers of the Church is grounded in the Gospel account of the Last Supper (cf. Mt 26.26–29, Mk 14.22–25, Lk 22.19–20), Christ's discourse on the bread of life (cf. Jn 6.32–65), and the teaching of the apostle Paul on the Eucharist. These New Testament texts became the foundation for the patristic understanding of the Eucharist, its meaning and content, the means for performing it, and its significance for the spiritual life.

The subject of the Eucharist was already discussed by the apostolic fathers of the second century. The hieromartyr Ignatius the God-bearer wrote to the Ephesians, "Seek, therefore, to come together more closely to give thanks to God [εἰς εὐχαριστίαν θεοῦ][6] and to glorify him."[7] In his epistle to the Philadelphians he emphasized the unity of the Eucharist as the pledge of the unity of the Church with the bishop at its head: "Therefore be eager to celebrate one Eucharist. For there is one flesh of our Lord Jesus Christ and one cup of unity in his blood, one altar, just as there is one bishop together with the presbytery and the

Hieromartyr Ignatius the God-bearer. Fresco. Staro Nagorichino, Macedonia. 14th c.

[3]Irenaeus of Lyons, *Against Heresies* 5.1.3; John Chrysostom, *Explanation of Matthew* 82.2.

[4]*Apostolic Canons* 3.

[5]In particular, Metropolitan Macarius of Moscow (†1542–1563) permitted the liturgy to be served using cherry liqueur. The Local Council of the Russian Orthodox Church of 1917–1918 likewise permitted substituting juices for wine in exceptional circumstances, thereby permitting the new martyrs and confessors to serve the Eucharist in prisons and concentration camps (cf. "Vino" [Wine], Constantine Neklyudov and Alexander Tkachenko, in *Pravoslavnaya entsiklopediya* [The Orthodox Encyclopedia], vol. 8, 519–520 [Moscow: Tserkovno-nauchnyy tsentr "Pravoslavnaya entsiklopediya," 2004]).

[6]That is, for the Eucharist, which comes from the Greek word meaning "thanksgiving."—*Trans.*

[7]Ignatius the God-bearer, *Letter to the Ephesians* 13.1. In *Ignatius of Antioch: The Letters*, Popular Patristics Series 49, Alistair Stewart, trans. (Yonkers, NY: St Vladimir's Seminary Press, 2013), 37.

deacons."[8] In his epistle to the Smyrnaeans Ignatius speaks of heretics who "abstain from the Eucharist and prayer, since they do not confess that the Eucharist is the flesh of our Savior Jesus Christ who suffered on account of our sins, and whom the Father raised in his goodness."[9] Ignatius likewise emphasizes that the only true Eucharist is that which is performed by a bishop or by one whom he has appointed for this.[10]

For Ignatius the God-bearer the bread of the Eucharist is a source of inspiration to martyric labors. On the way to his execution, as he prepared to be thrown to the lions, Ignatius wrote:

> I have no pleasure in corruptible food nor in the pleasures of this life; I desire the bread of God which is the flesh of Jesus Christ, of the seed of David, and I desire his blood for my drink, which is incorruptible love.[11]

The sacrament of the Eucharist is mentioned repeatedly in the works of another second-century hieromartyr—Irenaeus of Lyons. Speaking of Christ's institution of the Eucharist, Irenaeus writes:

> Again, giving directions to His disciples to offer to God the first-fruits of His own, created things—not as if He stood in need of them, but that they might be themselves neither unfruitful nor ungrateful—He took that created thing, bread, and gave thanks, and said, "This is My body." And the cup likewise, which is part of that creation to which we belong, He confessed to be His blood, and taught the new oblation of the new covenant; which the Church receiving from the apostles, offers to God throughout all the world, to Him who gives us as the means of subsistence the first-fruits of His own gifts in the New Testament.[12]

Refuting the Gnostic concept that the flesh cannot participate in salvation, Irenaeus speaks of communion of the flesh of Christ as the pledge of the general resurrection:

> When, therefore, the mingled cup and the manufactured bread receives the Word of God, and the Eucharist of the blood and the body of Christ is made,

[8]Ignatius the God-bearer, *Letter to the Philadelphians* 4 (PPS 49:81).
[9]Ignatius the God-bearer, *Letter to the Smyrnaeans* 7.1 (PPS 49:93).
[10]*Smyrnaeans* 8.1 (ibid.).
[11]Ignatius the God-bearer, *Letter to the Romans* 7.3 (PPS 49:73).
[12]Irenaeus of Lyons, *Against Heresies* 4.17.5 (*ANF* 1:484).

from which things the substance of our flesh is increased and supported, how can they[13] affirm that the flesh is incapable of receiving the gift of God, which is life eternal, which [flesh] is nourished from the body and blood of the Lord, and is a member of Him? . . . [The flesh] is nourished by the cup which is His blood, and receives increase from the bread which is His body. And just as a cutting from the vine planted in the ground fructifies in its season, or as a corn of wheat falling into the earth and becoming decomposed, rises with manifold increase by the Spirit of God, who contains all things, and then, through the wisdom of God, serves for the use of men, and having received the Word of God, becomes the Eucharist, which is the body and blood of Christ; so also our bodies, being nourished by it, and deposited in the earth, and suffering decomposition there, shall rise at their appointed time, the Word of God granting them resurrection to the glory of God, even the Father.[14]

Among the writers of the third century, the subject of the Eucharist received particular attention from Origen in the East, and from Tertullian and Cyprian of Carthage in the West. In his *Epistle to Caecilius, on the Sacrament of the Cup of the Lord,* Cyprian speaks of the Eucharist as "the tradition of the Lord," performed as Christ originally performed it. Cyprian insists that water and wine, and not water only, must be used in the Eucharist.[15] The subject of the Eucharist is also touched on in his book *On the Lord's Prayer* in connection with the words, "Give us this day our daily bread."[16]

Beginning in the fourth century the Eucharist becomes a central focus for many fathers of the Church in the Greek East. An important contribution to the development of eucharistic theology was made by the holy hierarchs John Chrysostom and Cyril of Alexandria, as well as the venerable John of Damascus, Symeon the New Theologian, and Nicholas Cabasilas. It seems important, therefore, to examine the teaching of these fathers on the Eucharist.

In the sermons, lectures, and explanations of John Chrysostom we find a comprehensive teaching on the Eucharist, remarkable for its consistency and clarity. Chrysostom's frequent return to the theme of the Eucharist is primarily due to the fact that he was obliged to comment on the "eucharistic texts" of the Gospel and the apostolic epistles. Furthermore, the liturgical context of the majority of his

[13]The heretics.

[14]Irenaeus of Lyons, *Against Heresies* 5.2.3 (*ANF* 1:528).

[15]Cyprian of Carthage, *Epistles* 62.2–14: *Cæcilius, on the Sacrament of the Cup of the Lord* (ANF 5:359–362).

[16]See footnote on pages 372–373.

The Crucifixion. Fresco.
Church of St Nicholas in
Prilep, Macedonia. 13th c.

lectures, which were given in the church following the divine services, made the Eucharist a pertinent topic for his listeners.

Chrysostom always insists particularly on the reality of Christ's presence in the eucharistic bread and wine, and the reality of the believer's union with Christ through communion. The hierarch emphasizes that the body of Christ in the Eucharist is no different from that body that lay in the manger, hung upon the cross, and ascended in glory to the throne of the Heavenly Father:

This Body, even lying in a manger, Magi reverenced. . . . But thou beholdest Him not in the manger but on the altar, not a woman holding Him in her arms, but the priest standing by, and the Spirit with exceeding bounty hovering over the gifts set before us. Thou dost not see merely this Body itself as they did, but thou knowest also Its power, and the whole economy, and art ignorant of none of the holy things which are brought to pass by It, having been exactly initiated into all.[17]

When thou seest It set before thee, say thou to thyself, "Because of this Body am I no longer earth and ashes, no longer a prisoner, but free: because of this I hope for heaven, and to receive the good things therein, immortal life, the portion of angels, converse with Christ; this Body, nailed and scourged, was more than death could stand against; this Body the very sun saw sacrificed, and turned aside his beams; for this both the veil was rent in that moment, and rocks were burst asunder, and all the earth was shaken. This is even that Body, the blood-stained, the pierced, and that out of which gushed the saving fountains, the one of blood, the other of water, for all the world."[18]

But why adds he also, "which we break" [1 Cor 10.16]? For although in the Eucharist one may see this done, yet on the cross not so, but the very contrary. For, "A bone of Him," saith one, "shall not be broken" [Jn 19.36]. But that which He suffered not on the cross, this He suffers in the oblation for thy sake, and submits to be broken, that he may fill all men.[19]

---

[17]John Chrysostom, *Homilies on First Corinthians* 24.8 (*NPNF*¹ 12:143).
[18]John Chrysostom, *Homilies on First Corinthians* 24.7 (*NPNF*¹ 12:142).
[19]Ibid., 24.4 (*NPNF*¹ 12:140).

As many of us as partake of that Body and taste of that Blood, are partaking of that which is in no wise different from that Body, nor separate. Consider that we taste of that Body that sitteth above, that is adored by Angels, that is next to the Power that is incorruptible. . . . How many ways to salvation are open to us! He hath made us His own body, He hath imparted to us His own body.[20]

The blood of the Eucharist, according to Chrysostom, is the selfsame blood that Christ shed for the salvation of the world:

What [the apostle Paul] says is this: "This which is in the cup is that which flowed from His side, and of that do we partake." But he called it a cup of blessing, because holding it in our hands, we so exalt Him in our hymn, wondering, astonished at His unspeakable gift, blessing Him, among other things, for the pouring out of this self-same draught that we might not abide in error: and not only for the pouring it out, but also for the imparting thereof to us all.[21]

Lest the disciples be scandalized at the Last Supper, Christ himself first drank his own blood, Chrysostom points out.[22] For the believer Christ's blood possesses curative and life-creating properties:

This blood causeth the image of our King to be fresh within us, produceth beauty unspeakable, permitteth not the nobleness of our souls to waste away, watering it continually, and nourishing it. . . . This blood, if rightly taken, driveth away devils, and keepeth them afar off from us, while it calleth to us Angels and the Lord of Angels. For wherever they see the Lord's blood, devils flee, and Angels run together. This blood poured forth [upon the cross] washed clean all the world. . . . This blood is the salvation of our souls, by this the soul is washed, by this is beautiful, by this is inflamed, this causeth our understanding to be more bright than fire, and our soul more beaming than gold; this blood was poured forth, and made heaven accessible.[23]

By opening the gates of the kingdom of heaven to the believer, communion of the body and blood of Christ becomes a source of sanctification and salvation for the believer here and now, on earth:

---

[20]John Chrysostom, *Homilies on Ephesians* 3 (*NPNF*¹ 13:63).
[21]John Chrysostom, *Homilies on First Corinthians* 24.3 (*NPNF*¹ 12:139).
[22]John Chrysostom, *Homilies on the Gospel of Saint Matthew* 82.1 (*NPNF*¹ 10:492).
[23]John Chrysostom, *Homilies on the Gospel of St John* 46.3 (*NPNF*¹ 14:166).

For this Table is the sinews of our soul, the bond of our mind, the foundation of our confidence, our hope, our salvation, our light, our life. When with this sacrifice we depart into the outer world, with much confidence we shall tread the sacred threshold, fenced round on every side as with a kind of golden armor. And why speak I of the world to come? Since here this mystery makes earth become to thee a heaven.[24]

Chrysostom warns against communing unworthily, by which he means communing negligently, irreverently, "with insolence":

Those also shall then meet Him descending from heaven, who now worthily have this privilege, even as they who do so unworthily, shall suffer the extremest torments. . . . For if one would not inconsiderately receive a king (why say I a king? nay were it but a royal robe, one would not inconsiderately touch it with unclean hands) . . . what shall we say of the Body of Him Who is God over all, spotless, pure, associate with the Divine Nature, the Body whereby we are, and live; whereby the gates of hell were broken down and the sanctuaries of heaven opened? how shall we receive this with so great insolence?[25]

What does Chrysostom mean by communing "worthily"? This is communing with spiritual trembling and ardent love, with belief in the actual presence of Christ in the holy gifts, and with an awareness of the greatness of these holy things:

Do not see it as bread, neither think that it is wine. . . . While you approach, do not think that you partake of the Divine Body from a man; rather, believe that you partake of the Divine Body from the very Seraphim with the fiery spoon that Isaiah saw; and when we partake of the Saving Blood, let us believe that our lips touch the very Divine and Immaculate Side.[26]

How many now say, I would wish to see His form, the mark, His clothes, His shoes. Lo! thou seest Him, Thou touchest Him, thou eatest Him.

And thou indeed desirest to see His clothes, but He giveth Himself to thee not to see only, but also to touch and eat and receive within thee. Let then no one approach it with indifference, no one faint-hearted, but all with burning hearts, all fervent, all aroused.[27]

[24]John Chrysostom, *Homilies on First Corinthians* 24.8 (*NPNF*¹ 12:143).

[25]Ibid., 24.7 (*NPNF*¹ 12:142).

[26]John Chrysostom, *On Repentance and Almsgiving*, Gus George Christo, trans. In *The Fathers of the Church* (Washington, DC: The Catholic University of America Press, 1998), 96:127–128.

[27]John Chrysostom, *Homilies on the Gospel of Saint Matthew* 82.4 (*NPNF*¹ 10:495).

With particular force and an almost shocking naturalism Chrysostom speaks of the unification of the believer with Christ in the sacrament of the Eucharist. In communion Christ imparts unto us his whole self, in order that we might become his brothers and his friends; he gives us his body, so that we, by sinking our teeth into it, might satisfy all our desires:

> On this account He hath mixed up Himself with us; He hath kneaded up His body with ours, that we might be a certain One Thing, like a body joined to a head. For this belongs to them who love strongly. . . . Wherefore this also Christ hath done, to lead us to a closer friendship, and to show His love for us; He hath given to those who desire Him not only to see Him, but even to touch, and eat Him, and fix their teeth in His flesh, and to embrace Him, and satisfy all their love. Let us then return from that table like lions breathing fire, having become terrible to the devil; thinking on our Head, and on the love which He hath shown for us. Parents often entrust their offspring to others to feed; "but I," saith He, "do not so, I feed you with Mine own flesh. . . . I have willed to become your Brother, for your sake I shared in flesh and blood, and in turn I give out to you the flesh and the blood by which I became your kinsman."[28]

Developing the idea of the believer's union with Christ, Chrysostom turns to the apostle Paul's teaching concerning the Church as the body of Christ, and the faithful as the members of this body:

> We communicate not only by participating and partaking, but also by being united. For as that body is united to Christ, so also are we united to him by this bread. . . . Further, because [Paul] said, "a communion of the Body" [1 Cor 10.16], and that which communicates is another thing from that whereof it communicates; even this which seemeth to be but a small difference, he took away. For having said, "a communion of the Body," he sought again to express something nearer. Wherefore also he added, "For we, who are many, are one bread, one body" [1 Cor 10.17]. "For why speak I of communion?" saith he, "we are that self-same body." For what is the bread? The Body of Christ. And what do they become who partake of it? The Body of Christ: not many bodies, but one body. For as the bread consisting of many grains is made one, so that the grains no where appear; they exist indeed, but their difference is not seen

[28]John Chrysostom, *Homilies on the Gospel of Saint John* 46.3 (*NPNF*[1] 14:166).

by reason of their conjunction; so are we conjoined both with each other and with Christ.[29]

While Chrysostom developed the teaching of the Eucharist in an exegetical and liturgical context, for Cyril of Alexandria the definitive context was christological—namely, the context of his dispute with Nestorius concerning the two natures of Christ. He demonstrated that dividing the one Christ into "two sons," two entities, turns communion into "anthropophagy." In communing we partake not of the divinity, but of the deified flesh of Christ. Moreover, Christ comes to dwell in us with both his natures—the divine and the human:

> And Who was it who said, *He that eateth My Flesh and drinketh My Blood, abideth in Me and I in him* [Jn 6.56]? If then it be a man by himself and the Word of God have not rather been made as we, the deed were cannibalism and wholly unprofitable the participation (for I hear Christ Himself say, *The flesh profiteth nothing, it is the Spirit that quickeneth* [Jn 6.63], for as far as pertains to its own nature, the flesh is corruptible, and will in no wise quicken others, sick itself of the decay that is its own): but if thou say that it is the Own Body of the Word Himself . . . which do we eat, the Godhead or the flesh? . . . But we eat, not consuming the Godhead (away with the folly) but the Very Flesh of the Word Which has been made Life-giving. . . . And as the Body of the Word Himself is Life-giving, He having made it His own by a true union passing understanding and language; so we too who partake of His holy Flesh and Blood, are quickened in all respects and wholly, the Word dwelling in us Divinely through the Holy Spirit, humanly again through His Holy Flesh and Precious Blood.[30]

The means by which the bread and wine are changed into the body and blood of Christ is unknown to us, yet nevertheless we believe in the reality of that change. In imparting to us his flesh and blood in the form of bread and wine, Christ is "comingled" with our bodies and enlivens us:

> He said explicitly, "This is My Body" and, "This is My Blood" (Mt 26.26–28), so that you would not think that which is revealed to be an image, but that by a certain ineffable (action) of Almighty God the things offered are truly changed into the Body and Blood of Christ, and in communing thereof we

---

[29]John Chrysostom, *Homilies on First Corinthians* 24.4 (*NPNF*[1] 12:140).
[30]Cyril of Alexandria, *Against Nestorius* 4.5 (*LFC* 47:142–145).

receive the life-creating and sanctifying power of Christ. For it was necessary that, through the Holy Spirit and in a God-befitting manner, He might after a fashion become mingled with our bodies through His holy Flesh and precious Blood, which things we received as a life-creating blessing as though in bread and wine, that we might not be petrified upon seeing the Flesh and Blood present on the holy tables in the churches. For God, commensurate with our weakness, sends the power of life into the things there present and changes them unto the action of His life.[31]

The venerable John of Damascus devotes a separate chapter of the *Exposition of the Orthodox Faith* to a comprehensive analysis of the Orthodox teaching on the Eucharist. Echoing the other Eastern fathers, the Damascene asserts that God chose bread and wine for the Eucharist out of condescension to human weakness. To these material substances, however, he united his divine nature, that through them we might be joined to the Divinity. After their transformation the bread and wine of the Eucharist are not a symbol or an image of Christ's body and blood, but the true body and true blood of Christ:

> Bread and wine are employed: for God knoweth man's infirmity: for in general man turns away discontentedly from what is not well-worn by custom: and so with His usual indulgence He performs His supernatural works through familiar objects . . . since it is man's custom to eat [bread] and to drink water and wine, He connected His divinity with these and made them His body and blood in order that we may rise to what is supernatural through what is familiar and natural. The body which is born of the holy Virgin is in truth body united with divinity, not that the body which was received up into the heavens descends, but that the bread itself and the wine are changed into God's body and blood. . . . The bread and the wine are not merely figures of the body and blood of Christ (God forbid!) but the deified body of the Lord itself: for the Lord has said, "This is My body," not, this is a figure of My body: and "My blood," not, a figure of My blood.[32]

In the words of the Damascene, the body and blood of Christ "are making for the support of our soul and body, without being consumed or suffering corruption, not making for the draught . . . but for our being and preservation, a

---

[31]Cyril of Alexandria, *Explanation of the Gospel of Matthew* (PG 72:452CD). [Translated by the present translator.] See also his *Explanation of the Gospel of Luke* (PG 72:912AB).

[32]John of Damascus. *Exposition of the Orthodox Faith* 4.13 (*NPNF*[2] 9:83b).

Adoration of the sacrifice. Fresco.
Studenica Monastery. 14th c.

protection against all kinds of injury, a purging from all uncleanness." Communion has a purifying effect on a person: if the body and blood of Christ find "base gold" within someone, they purify him with the fire of judgment. This is the sense in which the Damascene understands the words of the apostle Paul about communing unworthily, due to which many become infirm and sick and even die (cf. 1 Cor 11.29–30). Through sicknesses and every kind of adversity the holy mysteries purify a person, that he might not be condemned in the age to come.[33]

Through communing "we are united to the body of Christ and to His Spirit and become the body of Christ," says the Damascene. By virtue of communion "we partake of the divinity of Jesus"; "we have communion with Christ and share in His flesh and His divinity." At the same time we enter into communion and are united to each other, "for since we partake of one bread, we all become one body of Christ and one blood, and members one of another, being of one body with Christ [cf. Eph 3.6]."[34]

Particularly noteworthy is the teaching of the venerable Symeon the New Theologian on the Eucharist. This late Byzantine spiritual writer was interested not so much in the objective reality of the transformation of the bread and wine into the body and blood of Christ (the reality of this transformation he never doubts) as in how communion affects the faithful. First and foremost Symeon underscores the spiritual union of the believer with Christ that results from communing of the holy mysteries:

Spiritually joined and cleaving to Him, we shall each one be with Him one Spirit and likewise one body, by virtue of our bodily eating His flesh and drinking His blood.[35]

Just as Eve was taken from the flesh and bones of Adam and the two were one flesh, so also Christ gives Himself to us to the extent of communion of His flesh

---

[33]John of Damascus, *Exposition of the Orthodox Faith* 4.13 (*NPNF*² 9:84b).

[34]John of Damascus, *Exposition of the Orthodox Faith* 4.13 (*NPNF*² 9:84b).

[35]St Symeon the New Theologian, *The Ethical Discourses* 2.7. In St Symeon the New Theologian, *On the Mystical Life: The Ethical Discourses*, vol. 1, Popular Patristics Series 14, Alexander Golitzin, trans. (Crestwood, NY: St Vladimir's Seminary Press, 1995), 112.

and bones. . . . From the same flesh and bones He gives us to eat, and through this communion makes us, too, one with Him.[36]

The Son of God cries out plainly that our union with Him through communion is such as the unity and life which He has with the Father. Thus, just as He is united by nature to His own Father and God, so are we united by grace to Him, and live in Him, by eating His flesh and drinking His blood.[37]

Echoing John Chrysostom and Cyril of Alexandria, Symeon says that through communion those who believe in Christ become his "kinfolk"[38] and "of one body."[39] In the words of the venerable one, Christ "has become our kinsman in the flesh, and has rendered us co-participants in His divinity, and so has made us all His kinsmen. Above all, the divinity imparted to us through this communion cannot be broken down into parts, is indivisible, and thus all of us who partake of it in the truth must necessarily and inseparably be one body with Christ in the one Spirit."[40] Hence, "when we receive the Spirit of our Master and God, we become participants of His divinity and essence, and when we eat of His all-pure flesh—I mean holy communion—we become truly His kin, of one body with Him."[41]

In its proper place we touched on Symeon's teaching on man's deification through the incarnation of the Son of God.[42] Through conscious communion of the holy mysteries of Christ this deification becomes a reality for the Christian. In the words of Symeon, in communion Christ imparts to us the selfsame flesh that he took from the Most Pure Virgin. In partaking of it "each one of us receives within himself the entirety of God made flesh, our Lord Jesus Christ, Son of God and son of the immaculate Virgin Mary, the very One Who sits at the right hand of God the Father." When we receive the body of Christ within ourselves, "He is no longer among us as an infant, and so known only according to the flesh. Rather, He is present in the body bodilessly, mingled with our essence and nature, and deifying us who share His body, who are become flesh of His flesh and bone of His bone."[43]

---

[36]Ibid., 1 (PPS 14:46).
[37]Ibid., 3 (PPS 14:133).
[38]Ibid., 2.7 (PPS 14:112).
[39]Cf. ibid., 1.10 (PPS 14:58).
[40]Ibid., 1.6 (PPS 14:44).
[41]Ibid., 1.3 (PPS 14:34).
[42]See vol. 2, pp. 381ff.
[43]Symeon, *Ethical Discourses* 1.10 (PPS 14:57).

Symeon speaks from his own spiritual experience regarding deification as a result of repentance and communion:

> Having been purified by repentance, and by rivers of tears, and having partaken of the deified body as God himself, I myself become God by this ineffable union. See the mystery! Therefore the soul and the body . . . are one in two essences. Therefore body and soul are one and two partaking of Christ and drinking his blood, united to both essences, and likewise to both natures of my God; they become God by participation.[44]

Frequently the venerable Symeon describes the Eucharist using the imagery of light and fire. This eucharistic symbolism is traditional in the Orthodox Church, being reflected both in the writings of the holy fathers and in liturgical texts. Symeon Metaphrastes, an older contemporary of Symeon the New Theologian, in his prayers before communion develops the theme of a fire that does not consume sinners, but purifies sin.[45] In the canon before holy communion we read, "May Thy most precious Body and Blood, my Savior, be to me as fire and light, consuming the fuel of my sin and burning the thorns of my passions, fully enlightening me to worship Thy Divinity."[46]

Using traditional symbolism, Symeon develops his teaching on the Eucharist in his characteristic mystical manner:

> Let [Him] . . . Who is Himself the bread which comes down from heaven and gives life to the world . . . be your unceasing and inexhaustible food and drink. And, as for wine, let it not be this visible wine, but that which appears as wine yet is perceived by the intellect as the blood of God, as light inexpressible, ineffable sweetness, everlasting joy.[47]

> [By means of holy communion] You make me a light, I who was darkened. . . . You shine around me with a ray of immortality, and I am both stupefied and burning within, yearning to fall down and worship You Yourself.[48]

---

[44]Symeon the New Theologian, *Hymns* 30.467–484. In *Divine Eros: Hymns of St Symeon the New Theologian*, Popular Patristics Series 40, Daniel K. Griggs, trans. (Crestwood, NY: St Vladimir's Seminary Press, 2010), 244.

[45]Symeon Metaphrastes, *Prayers* 3.

[46]*Canon in Preparation for Holy Communion*. From *Orthodox Daily Prayers*, 2nd ed. (South Canaan, PA: St. Tikhon's Seminary Press, 2008), 108.

[47]Symeon the New Theologian, *Ethical Discourses* 14 (PPS 14:179).

[48]Symeon the New Theologian, *Hymns* 20.27–31 (PPS 40:134).

The light is Christ Jesus, the Savior and King of all. The bread of His most pure Flesh is light; the cup of His precious Blood is light.[49]

A distinctive characteristic of Symeon's teaching on communion is his insistence that communion must be with "perception and knowledge" (μετὰ θεωρίας και γνώσεως/ *meta theōrias kai gnōseōs*).[50] In communing a person must contemplate God with the eyes of his soul and sense his living presence in the consecrated gifts:

> If you partake of such things with perception and knowledge, you do so worthily. If not thus, however, you certainly eat and drink unworthily. If it is with a pure contemplation that you have partaken of what you took, behold! You are become worthy of this table. If you have not become worthy, you will not be joined, you will in no way be united with God. Let those who partake unworthily of the divine mysteries not imagine then that they are simply joined by them and united to the invisible God.[51]

There is nothing unusual in the idea of communing with knowledge as such; it may be traced back to the teaching of the apostle Paul on the necessity of discerning the Lord's body (cf. 1 Cor 11.28–29), that is, of approaching consciously for communion. What is unusual in the teaching of Symeon is that the criterion of worthiness is called "pure contemplation," which is no less than the mystical experience of a vision of God. Symeon in fact acknowledges only that communion which is accompanied by this experience. In his opinion, those who partake without mystical contemplation feed only their bodies, and by no means their souls.[52] "How can you think," Symeon asks, "that you have partaken of eternal life if you do not sense that you have begun to live the heavenly life, and that you have received within you the all-illumining bread that burns with fire? The light shines for you, but you are blind; the flame warms you, but you are cold. "While you are thus receiving [the holy mysteries] . . . you remain without receiving, without eating, without having anything at all within yourself."[53] Developing this idea, Symeon makes the following radical statement:

---

[49]Symeon the New Theologian, *Traités théologiques et éthiques* [Theological Discourses] vol. 1, 3, J. Darrouzès, ed. (SC 122, 1966), 150–152. [Translated by the present translator.]

[50]Symeon the New Theologian, *Ethical Discourses* 10 (PPS 14:164).

[51]Symeon the New Theologian, *Ethical Discourses* 14 (PPS 14:179).

[52]Ibid. (PPS 14:180).

[53]Ibid. (PPS 14:181).

If those . . . who eat His flesh and drink His blood have eternal life, according to His own word, but we in eating these perceive nothing more happening in us than the material food, nor receive in knowledge another kind of life, we then partake of mere bread alone and not also of God.[54]

Such statements are fairly rare in patristic literature. For comparison, however, we may cite the words of Gregory of Nyssa quoted above, in which he states that if a person receives the sacrament of baptism, but in later life demonstrates no change for the better, for him "water is [mere] water," because in it "the gift of the Holy Spirit is nowhere manifest."[55] Thus, in the opinion of both writers—Gregory of Nyssa and Symeon the New Theologian—the reception of a sacrament, be it the Eucharist or baptism, presumes that the Holy Spirit must be manifested in the recipient of the sacrament. If the sacrament is not followed by the manifestation of the Holy Spirit, it was all for nothing: the water remained mere water, and the bread mere bread. Like Gregory of Nyssa, Symeon is referring to the state of the person participating in the sacrament: the bread remains mere bread for one who receives it unworthily.

One other particularity of Symeon's eucharistic piety is his statement that communion must unfailingly be accompanied by tears. Symeon borrowed this idea from his spiritual father, St Symeon the Studite, who wrote, "Never communicate without tears."[56] In one of his catechetical homilies Symeon the New Theologian describes how once, when he read these words of his spiritual father to a group of monks and laymen, his hearers scoffed in response, "Well then, we shall never again communicate, but we shall all go without communion."[57] Astounded by this reaction, Symeon elaborates on his teaching that whoever desires to attain true compunction and tears acquires them through fulfilling the commandments of God: "Do you wish, then, never to communicate without tears? Practice what you daily sing and read, and then you will be able continually to achieve this."[58] In other words, if in his life a person adheres to what he hears in church at the services, he will always be able to approach for communion with heartfelt tears.

---

[54]Symeon the New Theologian, *Ethical Discourses* vol. 1, 10, 166.

[55]Gregory of Nyssa, *Catechetical Discourse* 40.3 (PPS 59, forthcoming).

[56]Symeon the New Theologian, *Catechetical Discourses* 4.11–12. In *The Discourses*, trans. by C. J. De Catanzaro (Mahwah, NJ: Paulist Press, 1980), 70.

[57]Ibid., 4.13–18.

[58]Ibid., 4.517–519.

The reaction of Symeon's listeners seems perfectly natural, if we recall that in the ascetic tradition tears during prayer are viewed as a gift from God.[59] "Few have the gift of tears," we read in a composition attributed to Athanasius of Alexandria.[60] Symeon himself calls tears a "divine gift."[61] At the same time, however, he states that the inclination to weeping and tender feeling is dependent not on innate qualities, but on a person's own volition. Tears are a gift from God, sent to those who by their deeds have shown a favorable disposition. If we are unable to weep it is our own fault.[62] Whoever communes without tears must accuse himself, for if he had wished to shed them he could have kept all the commandments of God and received the gift of weeping and tender feeling. Where other authors treated this as the ideal, Symeon considers it the norm.

Though it is radical, Symeon's teaching on the Eucharist had an indisputable influence on the formulation of eucharistic piety in the Orthodox Church. In particular, many of Symeon's ideas are reflected in the order of preparation for holy communion. One of the prayers in the order of preparation, which begins with the words, "From sullied lips, from an abominable heart," bears the name of Symeon the New Theologian and is compiled on the basis of one of his hymns.[63]

The theme of man's deification through the Eucharist, to which the venerable Symeon ascribes such importance, was continued in the works of the late Byzantine author Nicholas Cabasilas. He notes the change or transformation that comes over the believer through communion:

> Christ infuses Himself into us and mingles Himself with us. He changes and transforms us into Himself, as a small drop of water is changed by being poured into an immense sea of ointment.[64]

> When [Christ] has led the initiate to the table and has given him His Body to eat He entirely changes him, and transforms him into His own state. The clay

---

[59]Cf. Basil the Great, *The Short Rules* 16.

[60]Athanasius of Alexandria, *On Virginity* 17. Regarding the attribution of this composition see Clavis II, 46.

[61]Symeon the New Theologian, *Catechetical Discourses* 4.558.

[62]Abp Basil Krivocheine, *In the Light of Christ: St Symeon the New Theologian—Life, Spirituality, Doctrine*, Anthony P. Gythiel, trans. (Crestwood, NY: St Vladimir's Seminary Press, 1987), 38–39, 69, and 142–48.

[63]Cf. Valentin Asmus, "Gimny prepodobnogo Simeona Novogo Bogoslova v bogosluzhebnikh knigakh Russkoi Tserkvi" [The Hymns of the Venerable Symeon the New Theologian in the Liturgical Books of the Russian Church], lecture at the international conference in honor of the 1000-year anniversary of the Baptism of Russia, 2004.

[64]Nicholas Cabasilas, *The Life in Christ* 4.6. In Nicholas Cabasilas, *The Life in Christ*, Carmino J. Decatanzaro, trans. (Crestwood, NY: St Vladimir's Seminary Press, 1998), 122.

is no longer clay when it has received the royal likeness but is already the Body
of the King. It is impossible to conceive of anything more blessed than this. It
is therefore the final Mystery as well, since it is not possible to go beyond it or
to add anything to it.[65]

The soul and the body and all their faculties forthwith become spiritual, for our
souls, our bodies and blood, are united with His. What is the result? The more
excellent things overcome the inferior, things divine prevail over the human,
and that takes place which Paul says concerning the resurrection, "what is mortal is swallowed up by life" (2 Cor 5.4). . . . O how great are the Mysteries! What
a thing it is for Christ's mind to be mingled with ours, our will to be blended
with His, our body with His Body and our blood with His Blood![66]

So also man lives because of food, but not in the same way in this sacred rite.
Since natural food is not itself living it does not of itself infuse life into us, but
by aiding the life which is in the body it appears to those who eat to be the
cause of life. But the Bread of Life is Himself living, and through Him those to
whom He imparts Himself truly live. While natural food is changed into him
who feeds on it, and fish and bread and any other kind of food become human
blood, here it is entirely opposite. The Bread of Life Himself changes him who
feeds on Him and transforms and assimilates him into Himself.[67]

In summarizing what has been said regarding how the eastern fathers of the
Church understood the sacrament of the Eucharist, we can single out several key
statements:

(1) In communion the true body and blood of Christ, and not mere bread and
    wine, are imparted to the believer.

(2) In communion the believer receives the exact same body that was born
    of the Virgin Mary, suffered on the cross, died, rose again, and ascended
    to the Father, and the exact same blood that was shed for the salvation of
    the world.

(3) Communion unites a person unto Christ, making him a kinsman of Christ
    and of one body with him.

(4) Communion unites the faithful to one another.

[65]Ibid., 4.1, 113–114.
[66]Nicholas Cabasilas, *The Life in Christ* 4.3, 116.
[67]Ibid., 4.8, 125–126.

(5) One must commune with fear, reverence, and tender feeling.

(6) Through communion the believer becomes a god by grace.

(7) Worthy communion is the pledge of salvation and eternal life.

How Often Should One Commune?

In modern Orthodoxy there is no universal opinion regarding how often one ought to commune. The practice of one local Orthodox church in this regard may differ substantially from that of the next, and even within a single local church various practices may exist in different regions, dioceses, and parishes. At times even in a single parish two different priests may teach differently regarding how often one ought to approach for the sacrament of the Eucharist.

This state of affairs is the result of many centuries of evolution of the liturgical rite and of eucharistic piety—evolution that Protopresbyter Alexander Schmemann called a "metamorphosis in the perception—not only on the part of the people of the Church but also on the part of the episcopate, the clergy and, finally, the theologians—of the very essence of the Eucharist."[68] This metamorphosis lay in that the Eucharist first went from being a meal of fellowship to being a ceremonious public worship service, and later the idea of the Eucharist as an event in which the whole community participated gave way to the concept of communion as a private religious act. To this day the Eucharist remains a public worship service in form, but communion has become the private affair of each Orthodox Christian: being present at the Eucharist has ceased to entail invariably communing.

The order of the liturgy of the faithful does not in fact allow for worshippers to be present without communing. Over many centuries, however, the established practice has become exactly that: for many communion has become a rare event, requiring special preparation. For many believers the rhythms of communing and of going to church are not in sync: some come to liturgy on Sundays and feasts, but commune only once or a few times a year.

If we look to our roots we see that in the early Christian Church the Eucharist and communion were connected with the "Lord's day"—the first day of the week (cf. Acts 20:7, 1 Cor 16.2), which was devoted to the remembrance of Christ's resurrection. It was on this day that all members of the community would gather for the

---

[68]Alexander Schmemann, *The Eucharist: Sacrament of the Kingdom* (Crestwood, NY: St Vladimir's Seminary Press, 2003), 230–231.

Eucharist and commune of the body and blood of Christ in remembrance of his death and resurrection. The Lord's day, or Sunday (the "day of the sun"), remained the standard time for performing the Eucharist in the second century as well, as witnessed by Justin the Philosopher: "And on the day called Sunday, all who live in cities or in the country gather together to one place. . . . And there is a distribution to each, and a participation of that over which thanks have been given."[69]

By the third and fourth centuries, however, the number of days when the Eucharist was performed had increased: to the Lord's day were added Saturday, feast days, and days when the martyrs were commemorated. Basil the Great testifies regarding the days on which the Eucharist was performed in Caesarea in Cappadocia: "I, indeed, communicate four times a week, on the Lord's day, on Wednesday, on Friday, and on the Sabbath, and on the other days if there is a commemoration of any Saint."[70] Thus, in the fourth century in Caesarea the Eucharist was performed a minimum of four times per week.

The increase in the number of days on which the Eucharist was performed did not lead to more frequent communion. On the contrary, whereas in the early Christian community every member participated in the weekly Eucharist, now parishioners began attending services on those days they themselves thought best. Although present for the Eucharist, by no means did they always commune of the holy mysteries. This custom of approaching for communion with extreme rarity was confirmed by John Chrysostom in the late fourth century: "Many partake of this sacrifice once in the whole year, others twice; others many times." Chrysostom notes that not only laity, but also some "who are settled in the desert"—that is, hermits—"partake once in the year, and often indeed at intervals of two years."[71]

At the same time, Rufinus testifies that certain fourth-century monastic communities had the custom of communing daily: he describes the monastery of Abba Appolonius in the Egyptian desert, where all the monks received communion each day at about the ninth hour (that is, at three o'clock in the afternoon).[72] Daily communion, however, never became the universal norm in the monasteries of the Orthodox East.

In patristic literature we encounter various recommendations regarding frequency of communion. Sometimes these recommendations are of a very general nature. For example, in the second century Ignatius the God-bearer said, "Seek,

[69]Justin Martyr, *First Apology* 67 (*ANF* 1:186).
[70]Basil the Great, *Letters* 93, "To the Patrician Caesaria, concerning Communion" (*NPNF*[2] 8:179).
[71]John Chrysostom, *Homilies on Hebrews* 17.7 (*NPNF*[1] 14:449).
[72]Rufinus, *History of the Monks of Egypt* 7.13.4.

therefore, to come together more closely to give thanks to God [μετὰ θεωρίας καὶ γνώσεως/*meta theōrias kai gnōseōs/eis eucharistian Theou*] and to glorify him."[73] ("To gather to celebrate the Eucharist" means to commune, since in St Ignatius' time all those present for the Eucharist would commune.) In the fourth century Cyril of Jerusalem exhorted his flock, "Do not break yourselves away from communion."[74]

In other cases the recommendations are more specific. The venerable Nilus (fourth century) says, "Abstain from all that is corruptible and *every day* commune of the divine Supper, for by this means the body of Christ becomes our own." The holy hierarch Basil the Great writes, "It is good and beneficial to communicate *every day*, and to partake of the holy body and blood of Christ."[75] Both Cyprian of Carthage[76] and Blessed Augustine[77] mention daily communion.

In patristic literature the question of frequency of communion often dovetails with the subject of the worthiness and unworthiness of the communicants. By the fourth century the idea had arisen that, due to his unworthiness, a Christian should not approach the holy mysteries frequently. This idea was notably opposed by St Cyril of Jerusalem: "Do not, on account of the defilement of your sins, deprive yourselves of these holy and spiritual mysteries."[78]

Some would devote the forty days of Great Lent to preparing for communion, and then would commune on Pascha, and thereafter would refrain from communion for the entire year. Referring to this custom, John Chrysostom asks: "Which shall we approve? those [who receive] once [in the year]? those who [receive] many times? those who [receive] few times?" And he replies:

> Neither those [who receive] once, nor those [who receive] often, nor those [who receive] seldom, but those [who come] with a pure conscience, from a pure heart, with an irreproachable life. Let such draw near continually; but those who are not such, not even once. Why, you will ask? Because they receive to themselves judgment, yea and condemnation, and punishment, and vengeance. . . . Dost thou feast at a spiritual table, a royal table, and again pollute thy mouth

---

[73]Ignatius the God-bearer, *Ephesians* 13.1 (PPS 49:37).

[74]Cyril of Jerusalem, *On the Mysteries* 5.23 (PPS 57:135).

[75]Basil the Great, *Letters* 93, "To the Patrician Caesaria, concerning Communion" (*NPNF*² 8:179).

[76]Cyprian of Carthage, *On the Lord's Prayer* 18. In *On the Lord's Prayer: Tertullian, Cyprian, & Origen*, Popular Patristics Series 29, Alistair Stewart-Sykes, trans. (Crestwood, NY: St Vladimir's Seminary Press, 2004), 79.

[77]Augustine, *Explanation of John* 16.15.35.

[78]Cyril of Jerusalem, *On the Mysteries* 5:23 (PPS 57:135–137).

with mire? Dost thou anoint thyself with sweet ointment, and again fill thyself with ill savors? Tell me, I beseech thee, when after a year thou partakest of the Communion, dost thou think that the Forty Days are sufficient for thee for the purifying of the sins of all that time? And again, when a week has passed, dost thou give thyself up to the former things? . . . Thou assignest forty days for the health of the soul, or perhaps not even forty, and dost thou expect to propitiate God? Tell me, art thou in sport? These things I say, not as forbidding you the one and annual coming, but as wishing you to draw near continually.[79]

Thus, it is not the time spent in preparation for communion that makes a person worthy, but the life that he leads. The person who is unworthy to commune is not he who communes frequently, but he whose life is incompatible with the greatness and holiness of the body and blood of Christ.

Chrysostom emphasizes that one should not commune only during the fasts or on great feasts, but at every liturgy:

I observe many partaking of Christ's Body lightly and just as it happens, and rather from custom and form, than consideration and understanding. When, saith a man, the holy season of Lent sets in, whatever a man may be, he partakes of the mysteries, or, when the day of the Lord's Epiphany comes. And yet it is not the Epiphany, nor is it Lent, that makes a fit time for approaching, but it is sincerity and purity of soul. With this, approach at all times; without it, never. . . . Observe the vast inconsistency of the thing. At the other times ye come not, no, not though often ye are clean; but at Easter, however flagrant an act ye may have committed, ye come. Oh! the force of custom and of prejudice! In vain is the daily Sacrifice, in vain do we stand before the Altar; there is no one to partake.[80]

With great force of conviction Chrysostom says that if a person is unworthy to commune he is unworthy to be present in the church, and must leave together with the catechumens. If he is worthy to be present in the church, however, then he may also commune at the liturgy:

Art thou not worthy of the Sacrifice, nor of the participation? If so, then neither art thou of the prayer. Thou hearest the herald, standing, and saying, "As many as are in penitence, all depart." As many as do not partake, are in penitence. If

[79]John Chrysostom, *Homilies on Hebrews* 17.7 (*NPNF*[1] 14:449).
[80]John Chrysostom, *Homilies on Ephesians* 3 (*NPNF*[1] 13:63–64).

thou art one of those that are in penitence, thou oughtest not to partake; for he that partakes not, is one of those that are in penitence. . . . But no, thou art not of that number, thou art of the number of those who are qualified to partake, and yet art indifferent about it, and regardest the matter as nothing. Look, I entreat: a royal table is set before you, Angels minister at that table, the King Himself is there, and dost thou stand gaping? Are thy garments defiled, and yet dost thou make no account of it?—or are they clean? Then fall down and partake. . . . For every one, that partaketh not of the mysteries, is standing here in shameless effrontery. . . . Suppose any one were invited to a feast, and were to wash his hands, and sit down, and be all ready at the table, and after all refuse to partake; is he not insulting the man who invited him? were it not better for such an one never to have come at all? Now it is just in the same way that thou hast come here. Thou hast sung the Hymn with the rest: thou hast declared thyself to be of the number of them that are Worthy, by not departing with them that are unworthy. Why stay, and yet not partake of the table? I am unworthy, thou wilt say. Then art thou also unworthy of that communion thou hast had in prayers. For it is not by means of the offerings only, but also by means of those canticles that the Spirit descendeth all around. . . . [God] hath invited us to heaven, to the table of the great and wonderful King, and do we shrink and hesitate, instead of hastening and running to it? And what then is our hope of salvation?[81]

At the same time Chrysostom underscores the importance of carefully preparing to participate in the sacrament of communion:

In the past, and especially at the time when Christ entrusted to us these sacred mysteries, many a man approached the sacrificial banquet without thought or preparation. Since the Fathers realized that it was harmful for a person to approach the mysteries in this heedless fashion, they came together and marked out forty days for people to fast, pray, and gather together to hear the word of God. Their purpose was that we might all scrupulously purify ourselves during this time by our prayers, almsgiving, fasting, vigils, tears, confessions, and all the other pious practices, so that we might approach the mysteries with our consciences made as clean as we could make them.[82]

---

[81] John Chrysostom, *Homilies on Ephesians* 3 (*NPNF*[1] 13:64–65).

[82] John Chrysostom, *Discourses Against Judaizing Christians* 3.5. In *The Fathers of the Church* (Washington, DC: Catholic University of America Press, 1979), 68:60–61.

Avoiding communion is also mentioned in the canons of the Orthodox Church. The second canon of the Council of Antioch states, "All who enter the church of God and hear the Holy Scriptures, but do not communicate with the people in prayers, or who turn away, by reason of some disorder, from the holy partaking of the Eucharist, are to be cast out of the Church, until, after they shall have made confession, and having brought forth the fruits of penance, and made earnest entreaty, they shall have obtained forgiveness."[83] This is likewise reflected in the ninth apostolic canon.[84]

An awareness of one's sinfulness should not be an obstacle to communion, but should rather arouse in a Christian the desire to approach for communion more frequently for the healing of soul and body. St John Cassian the Roman spoke of this in the sixth century:

> We ought not to suspend ourselves from the Lord's Communion because we confess ourselves sinners, but should more and more eagerly hasten to it for the healing of our soul, and purifying of our spirit, and seek the rather a remedy for our wounds with humility of mind and faith, as considering ourselves unworthy to receive so great grace. Otherwise we cannot worthily receive the Communion even once a year, as some do, who . . . so regard the dignity and holiness and value of the heavenly sacraments, as to think that none but saints and spotless persons should venture to receive them, and not rather that they would make us saints and pure by taking them. And these thereby fall into greater presumption and arrogance than what they seem to themselves to avoid, because at the time when they do receive them, they consider that they are worthy to receive them. But it is much better to receive them every Sunday for the healing of our infirmities, with that humility of heart, whereby we believe and confess that we can never touch those holy mysteries worthily, than to . . . believe that at the year's end we are worthy to receive them.[85]

In the ninth century Theodore the Studite practiced daily communion and advised other monks to commune frequently.[86] One of his disciplinary rules prescribes a penance for monks who "avoid the day of the liturgy";[87] another prescribes

[83] *The Seven Ecumenical Councils: Antioch in Encaeniis* 2 (*NPNF²* 14:108–109).
[84] *The Canons of the Holy and Altogether August Apostles* 9 (*NPNF²* 14:594).
[85] John Cassian, *Conferences* 21 (*NPNF²* 11:531).
[86] Theodore the Studite, *Letters* 555 (*Epistulae S.* 849).
[87] Theodore the Studite, *Prohibitions* 2:31 (PG 99:1753A).

punishment for those who voluntarily avoid communing.[88] In once place Theodore reproaches those who do not commune for more than forty days without good reason.[89] Lamenting over the negligence of monks regarding communion, Theodore says, "If on Sunday people do still approach for the mysteries, when the assembly is held on another day no one draws near. Formerly even in the monastery those who desired were permitted to commune each day; but today this is encountered very rarely, or else it is not encountered at all in any place."[90] From Theodore's writings it is clear that he encouraged frequent communion, and that at one time—a time that he himself could remember—the custom of daily communion (for those who desired it) was widespread; nevertheless, in his time there were already many monks who received the holy mysteries only very rarely.

We find an analogous situation in the eleventh century, in the example of St Symeon the New Theologian and the monks in the monasteries of his day. Symeon himself communed daily and considered it possible "to commune of the dread mysteries *every day* with tears," whereas his opponents held this to be impossible.[91] In Symeon's opinion, one who keeps the commandments of God and leads his life in repentance "is very worthy not only on feasts, but *every day* . . . to abide in the communion of these divine mysteries. . . . In so doing and being thus disposed, he is illumined in soul *every day*, receiving help from the communion of the holy (mysteries), and soon is raised to perfect purification and sanctity."[92]

While insisting that daily communion is indeed possible, Symeon by no means considered it obligatory for every monk. Addressing one new monastic, he writes concerning with what feelings he ought to be present at the liturgy: "Stand with trembling, as one who beholds the Son of God, who is slain for you. And if you are worthy and have received permission to do so, approach with fear and joy to partake of the ineffable mysteries."[93] Thus, the condition he sets for communing is that the communicant be worthy and have permission from his spiritual father to commune. Consequently, if a monk has not prepared and has not received permission, he may be at the liturgy without communing.

We see that over the course of many centuries, both in monasteries and in the world, various practices existed regarding frequency of communion. A universal

---

[88]Theodore the Studite, *Prohibitions* 1:10 (PG 99:1733A).

[89]Ibid., 2:6 (PG 99:1749B).

[90]Theodore the Studite, *Lesser Catechism* 107.

[91]Symeon the New Theologian, *Catéchèses* [Catechetical Discourses] vol. 1, 4, B. Krivochéine and J. Paramelle, ed. (SC 96, 1963), 35–38. [Translated by the present translator.]

[92]Ibid., 612–622.

[93]Ibid., vol. 3, 26 (SC 113, 1965), 114–120.

*Sts Macarius of Corinth
and Nicodemus of the Holy
Mountain. Modern fresco.
Simonopetra Monastery. Athos.*

standard apparently existed only in the early Christian era, when all the faithful gathered for the Eucharist and communed every Sunday. By the fourth century we see considerable disparity, which continued for many centuries: in some eras it was customary to commune more frequently, in others less. Furthermore, how communion was practiced varied from one region to the next. By the seventeenth and eighteenth centuries throughout the Orthodox East, including the Greek-speaking world, the Balkans, and Russia, the practice of infrequent communion for the laity had become firmly established.[94]

But the voices of the advocates of frequent communion did not fall silent. In the late eighteenth century, activists of the Kollyvades movement—Sts Macarius of Corinth and Nicodemus of the Holy Mountain—compiled the book *Concerning Frequent Communion of the Divine Mysteries,* first published in 1783 in Venice. This book, written as though by a single author, presents a compilation of testimonials from various sources confirming the necessity and lawfulness of frequent communion.

First and foremost the author cites the order of the divine liturgy, pointing to all the priestly exclamations that invite those present to commune of the holy mysteries. He then asks:

> So, based on all of these sacred rituals of the Divine Liturgy, I ask you, my brothers, to tell me in the fear of God and in the good conscience of your soul, is it not obvious that Christians who attend the Liturgy are required to commune frequently? Are they not obligated to do this in order to show that it is a communion, a gathering, and a supper, and so that they may not be shown to be transgressors of those very things which they believe and confess during the

---

[94]It should be noted that, in the opinion of Mikhail Skaballanovich (cf. Skaballanovich, *Tolkovy Tipikon* [The Typicon with Commentary], 151), the discontinuance of general communion at every liturgy had the following effect upon the liturgical order: it exalted vespers and matins to a position close to that of the liturgy, and helped to prevent these services from being neglected (as occurred, for example, in the Roman Catholic Church). Reversing this process causes evening worship to gradually be displaced from parish usage (as essentially is already occurring in the Greek Church).

Liturgy? If, however, they do not receive Communion as they have confessed during the Liturgy, I fear, I truly fear, that they might be found to be transgressors. But also, regarding the priest's call to them to come forward, and the other sacred words, acts, and rituals which take place during the divine Liturgy—I no longer know if they are even in their correct places. For every single person withdraws, so that not even a single Christian is found to approach the Holy Mysteries, to obey such an invitation from the priest—or, to state it better, from God. But rather, the priest, having done nothing, turns back with the Holy Things, without anyone having accepted his invitation to come forward and receive Communion.[95]

In the words of the book's author, "This is the order: for the Holy Bread to be divided at every Divine Liturgy, and for the faithful (that is, the faithful who do not have an impediment) to partake of it."[96] Through frequent communion "the intellect is illumined, the mind is made to shine, and all of the powers of the soul are purified."[97] Frequent communion and being united with Christ become for a person the pledge of resurrection in eternal life:

> [Brother,] if you frequently approach the Mysteries and partake worthily of that immortal and glorified body and blood of our Lord Jesus Christ, and become one body and one blood with the all-holy body and blood of Christ, the life-giving power and energy; then, at the resurrection of the righteous, your own body will be brought to life and resurrected incorruptible.[98]

Conversely, without frequent communion "we cannot be freed from the passions and ascend to the heights of dispassion."[99] One who postpones communion grows heedless, does not keep his mind from harmful thoughts, falls into carelessness, and the warmth of divine grace grows cold in him. The person becomes thoughtless and negligent and loses the fear of God, continence in his feelings, and caution in his actions, allowing himself "total license with regard to food, words, and improper sights and sounds, and to become like a horse without a bridle, falling over every precipice of sin."[100]

---

[95]St Nikodemos the Hagiorite, *Concerning Frequent Communion of the Immaculate Mysteries of Christ* 2.1.3, trans. George Dokos (Thessalonica, Greece: Uncut Mountain Press, 2006), 92.

[96]Nikodemos the Hagiorite, *Concerning Frequent Communion* 2.1.3.97.

[97]Ibid., 2.2.110.

[98]Ibid., 2.2.121–122.

[99]Ibid., 2.2.110.

[100]Ibid., 2.3.123.

As for prohibitions against frequent communion, the authors of the book call it "wicked," a "bad habit," and a "very evil custom." This had become so deeply entrenched "that we not only do not receive Communion, but also, when we see others frequently receiving divine Communion, reproach them and judge them as if they were impious and scorners of the divine Mysteries, when actually we should be imitating them."[101]

By way of preparation for communion the book lists prayer, confession, and doing penance.[102] At the same time it recommends living in constant preparedness to receive communion, so that at the ringing of the bell one might break free from ordinary affairs, come to the church, and commune of the holy mysteries:

> Do you see the ineffable gift? He not only died for us, but He also gives himself to us as food. What could show more love than this? What is more salvific to the soul? Moreover, no one fails to partake every day of the food and drink of the common table. And, if it happens that someone does not eat, he becomes greatly dismayed. And we are not speaking here about ordinary bread, but about the Bread of life; not about an ordinary cup, but about the Cup of immortality. And do we consider Communion an indifferent matter, entirely unnecessary? How is this thought not irrational and foolish? If this is how it has been up until now, my children, I ask that we henceforth take heed to ourselves, and, knowing the power of the Gift, let us purify ourselves as much as possible and partake of the sanctified Things. And if it happens that we are occupied with a handicraft, as soon as we hear the sounding-board calling us to church, let us put our work aside and go partake of the Gift with great desire.[103]

Answering the question of whether it is beneficial to commune three times a year, Macarius and Nicodemus reply, "This too is good and beneficial. But for someone to receive Communion more frequently is much better." They go on to explain, repeating the argumentation of John Chrysostom:

> The more one approaches light, the more he is illumined; the more he approaches fire, the more he is warmed; and the more he draws near to holiness, the more is he made holy. Wherefore, the more frequently someone approaches God through Communion, the more is he illumined, warmed, and made holy. My brother, if you are worthy to receive Communion two or three times a year, you

---

[101]Ibid., *Epilogue* 193.
[102]Ibid., 2.3.129.
[103]Nikodemos the Hagiorite, *Concerning Frequent Communion* 2.2.108.

are also worthy, just as the divine Chrysostom says, to receive more frequently, performing the same preparation. What prohibits us from communing? Our negligence and our sloth. Being conquered by these, we do not prepare ourselves according to our abilities.[104]

If it is not possible to commune daily, the book's authors maintain, then one should at least commune on Saturdays, Sundays, and feasts:

Since infrequent Communion brings us so many great and inexpressible evils, while frequent Communion grants us such lofty, great, heavenly, and supranatural good things, in both the present and future life, why do we delay so much to receive it? Why should we not prepare ourselves properly to commune in the divine Mysteries, if not daily, then every Saturday or Sunday and at every Feast?[105]

Sts Macarius and Nicodemus emphatically opposed the custom, widespread in their time, of not communing on Pascha (a custom that endures in many parts of the Orthodox world to this day):

As many as fast for Pascha, but do not commune, do not celebrate Pascha. . . . And as many as are not prepared to receive the body and blood of our Lord cannot truly celebrate Sundays or the other Feasts of the year, because they do not possess the cause and occasion for the Feast, which is the most-sweet Jesus Christ, and they do not possess the spiritual joy that divine Communion brings.[106]

Conversely, those who commune frequently celebrate Pascha and the resurrection of the soul each day throughout the year:

Do you desire to rejoice every day? Do you wish to celebrate brilliant Pascha whenever you like and to exult with unspeakable joy during this sorrowful life? Run frequently to the Mysteries and partake of them with the proper preparation and you will enjoy such things. For the true Pascha and the true festival of the soul is Christ, Who is sacrificed in the Mysteries.[107]

---

[104]Ibid., 3.13.185.
[105]Ibid., 2.3.127.
[106]Nikodemos the Hagiorite, *Concerning Frequent Communion* 2.2.116–117.
[107]Ibid., 2.2.115–116.

The authors of *Concerning Frequent Communion* repeat almost verbatim the teaching of Symeon the New Theologian concerning life as a continual feast of communion with God. In Symeon's opinion, communion transforms our whole life into a Pascha, a transition from earthly existence to the heavenly: "If, then, you celebrate the feast and so partake as well of the divine mysteries, all your life will be to you one single feast. And not a feast, but the beginning of a feast and a single Pascha, the passage and emigration from what is seen to what is sensed by the intellect."[108]

Ancient Rus' apparently followed the Byzantine standard of frequent communion. Over the centuries, however, as in Greece, communion in Russia became an increasingly rare occurrence, and the rule of preparation for communion relentlessly grew more stringent. In Russia in the eighteenth and nineteenth centuries communion became an annual duty: the most pious laypeople and children communed five times a year—during the fasts and on their namedays. This practice was officially documented by the *The Longer Catechism of the Holy, Catholic, Eastern Church, in The Doctrine of the Russian Church* compiled by Metropolitan Philaret of Moscow: "Our Mother the Church calls on all, who would live religiously, to confess before their spiritual Father, and communicate in the Body and Blood of Christ, four times yearly, or even every month, but requires all, without exception, to receive it at the least once in the year."[109] Thus, communing once a year was presented as a universal standard, while communing four times a year or even every month was deemed a mark of particular piety.

Furthermore, annual communion and confession was required by ecclesiastical and state laws. In particular, a law dated February 8, 1716, mandated that "men of every rank make confession without fail every year." Those who failed to make confession were subject to fines, which were to be levied by the governors. A directive dated February 17, 1718, mandated that priests report those who failed to confess to the civil authorities, so that fines could be levied upon them based on the reports: one ruble from commoners and tradesmen, two rubles for a second offence, three rubles for a third. Country folk were fined ten *dengas* for the first offence, a *grivna* for a second offence, and five *altyn* for a third.[110] A directive dated November 19, 1721, assigned "as many officers and

---

[108]Symeon the New Theologian, *Ethical Discourses* vol. 1, 14, 181.

[109]Metropolitan Philaret of Moscow, *The Longer Catechism of the Holy, Catholic, Eastern Church*, in *The Doctrine of the Russian Church*, Richard W. Blackmore, trans. (Aberdeen: A. Brown and Co., 1845), 93.

[110]In the eighteenth century a ruble was equal to one hundred *denga* coins. One *altyn* equaled three such coins, and one *grivna* equaled twenty.—*Trans.*

soldiers as necessary"[111] to collect the fines. These curious mandates—directives of this sort were issued throughout the entire eighteenth century—were inspired not so much by concern for the piety of the populace as by the desire to identify clandestine schismatics and sectarians among them. Confessing and communing annually was viewed as proof of loyalty. In the nineteenth century "fines for non-confession" were abolished, but annual confession and communion remained the norm, as synodal and consistorial mandates regularly reminded.

Even in nineteenth-century Russia, however, there were not a few church figures who advocated more frequent communion. One of these was the holy hierarch Ignatius Brianchaninov, who advised people to commune frequently. Commenting on the words of Basil the Great—"Who doubts that to share frequently in life, is the same thing as to have manifold life?"[112]—St Ignatius says, "What does frequent communion mean, if not renewal in oneself of the properties of the God-man, if not renewal of oneself through these properties? Renewal, continually sustained and nourished, is assimilated. Through it and by it the decrepitude acquired through the fall is destroyed; eternal death is vanquished and slain by the eternal life abiding in Christ, which is poured forth from Christ; the life that is Christ comes to dwell in a man." In the words of the saint, "Communion of the holy mysteries is established as a daily occurrence. Daily participation in the life of Christ must daily enliven the Christian through spiritual life."[113]

Another eminent ecclesiastical figure who spoke out in favor of frequent communion was St Theophan the Recluse. Responding to the question of one lady, who complained that she met with no support for her desire to commune frequently, Theophan wrote, citing Basil the Great:

> People give you much grief regarding frequent communion. Do not be troubled. They will look closer, and then they will stop. Everyone ought to do as you do, but such is not our established tradition. In the East Christians commune frequently, not only during the great fasts but outside them also. Originally in the Church of Christ everyone communed at every liturgy. In the time of Saint Basil the Great a certain young lady asked him whether one might commune frequently and how often. He replied that one not only might, but must, and

---

[111]A.N. Almazov, *Tainaya ispoved' v Pravoslavnoy Vostochnoi Tserkvi* [Secret Confession in the Orthodox Eastern Church], vol. 2 (Odessa, 1894; reprinted by Palomnik: Moscow, 1995), 371–379.

[112]Basil the Great, *Letters* 93, "To the Patrician Caesaria, concerning Communion" (*NPNF*[2] 8:179).

[113]St Ignatius Brianchaninov, *Sochineniya svyatitelya Ignatiya Bryanchaninova*, tom IV, *asketicheskaya propoved'* [The Writings of the Holy Hierarch Ignatius Brianchaninov, vol. 4, Ascetic Preaching] (Moscow: Pravilo Very, 1993), 180.

regarding how often he said: "We commune four times a week—on Wednesday, Friday, Saturday, and Sunday." "We" naturally means all Caesareans, for the question at hand concerned not the clergy, but the laity. Having said this to his inquirer, he did not give her a definite number of times to commune, but only set her an example, leaving her free to do as she was able, while nevertheless leaving in force the counsel that one should commune frequently.[114]

Like Nicodemus of the Holy Mountain a century before him, St Theophan noted that the very words of the divine liturgy invite all those present to participate in the sacrament:

> Observe: what does the liturgy itself require? At every liturgy the clergyman invites, "With the fear of God and with faith draw nigh." Consequently, one may approach for communion at every liturgy, to say nothing of communing frequently. Some around us say even that it is a sin to commune frequently, while others claim that one must not commune before six weeks have passed. Perhaps besides these there are other incorrect ideas in this regard. Pay no attention to these comments, and commune as often as you have the need, doubting nothing. Strive only to prepare in every way to approach as you ought with fear and trembling, with faith, with compunction and feelings of penitence. And to those who plague you by commenting on this, answer thus: "After all, I do not come to holy communion illicitly; each time I have the permission of my spiritual father." And let this be sufficient.[115]

The call to frequent communion of the holy mysteries of Christ is found in many of St Theophan's letters to various persons and in his works addressed to the public at large. As the saint sees it, "Frequent communion of the holy mysteries of Christ (one might add 'as frequent as possible') vividly and effectively unites the Lord's new member unto him through his most pure body and blood, sanctifying him, establishing peace within him, and making him unassailable to the powers of darkness."[116] In his pastoral practice, however, St Theophan also took the individual spiritual constitution of each person into account. To one woman regarding frequency of communion he writes, "Regarding *frequently*, you should not increase

---

[114]Theophan the Recluse, *Pis'ma o raznykh predmetakh* [Letters on Various Subjects] (Moscow: Pravilo Very, 2008), 491–492.
[115]Ibid., 492.
[116]Theophan the Recluse, *Put' ko spaseniyu* [The Path to Salvation], 25.

frequency, since this frequency takes away no small part of the reverence for this greatest of affairs . . . I mean preparation and communion."[117]

At the turn of the twentieth century the practice of frequent and even daily communion was revived by St John of Kronstadt. In St Andrew Cathedral in Kronstadt, of which he was the rector, he served liturgy on a daily basis, and as a rule all those present at the liturgy would commune. In his theological diary John of Kronstadt called into question the widespread practice of communing rarely and insisted that one should commune with all possible frequency—each day, if possible:

> There are people who only come once a year to receive the holy mysteries, out of obligation and necessity. This . . . is not good, since they are fulfilling what is now their Christian duty under duress and out of necessity, as it were. . . . But if the Lord is the true bread, we must desire this bread not only once a year, but if possible every month, every week, even *every day*. Why so? Because this is daily bread for us, for our soul, and since we need our daily bread every day, we also have need of heavenly food—of the body and blood of Christ—*every day*. For this reason in the Lord's prayer we pray, "Give us this day our daily bread."[118]

THE RULE OF PREPARATION FOR COMMUNION

The Church has always recognized that communion of this great sacrament—the body and blood of Christ—requires that a person be inwardly prepared. The apostle Paul warned Christians:

> Wherefore whosoever shall eat this bread, and drink this cup of the Lord, unworthily, shall be guilty of the body and blood of the Lord. But let a man examine himself, and so let him eat of that bread, and drink of that cup. For he that eateth and drinketh unworthily, eateth and drinketh damnation to himself, not discerning the Lord's body. For this cause many are weak and sickly among you, and many sleep (1 Cor 11.27–30).

[117]Theophan the Recluse, *Sobranie Pisem* [Collected Letters] 500, 3rd ed. (Moscow: Pravilo Very, 2000), 177.

[118]John of Kronstadt, *Mysli o pokayanii i prichashchenii* [Thoughts on Penance and Communion] (Moscow: Palomnik, 1997), 60. Emphasis ours.

St Theophan the Recluse states that the words "examine himself" here refer to proper preparation. "In what does this lie? In cleansing the conscience. Offer repentance for your sins and firmly resolve to sin no more, but instead of sins to practice every virtue, and you will be properly prepared for communion."[119] Over time, as communion became a rare event in the life of the Christian, the practice of special outward preparation arose—in Russian, *govenye*—consisting of fasting and reading the appointed prayer rule.

The Typicon—the order of services employed in the Orthodox Church—contains the following injunction regarding communion: "When a person wishes to commune of the holy mysteries of Christ, it behooves him to observe the whole week, from Monday on abiding completely in fasting, prayer, and perfect sobriety—and then with fear and great reverence he shall receive the most pure mysteries."[120] In other words, before communing one must fast for a full week.

The 1651 edition of the Liturgical Psalter, at the beginning of "The Order of Preparation for Holy Communion," contains still more stringent instructions entitled, "From the Rules of the Holy Apostles of the Second Council."[121] These prescribe not only fasting for a week before communing, but abstaining from oil and wine[122] throughout the entire period of preparation, eating only one meal per day:

> When you wish to commune on Saturday or Sunday, spend the whole week before communing in strict fasting, without oil or drink. If it is necessary to commune sooner, due to illness or for some other reason, abstain for at least three days from oil and drink, eating only once at the ninth hour, and then commune. This however we say for the sake of necessity, since it is absurd; one must prepare for communion of the body and blood of Christ for seven days, with fear and trembling, through abstinence, fasting, vigil, prayer, and tears. Beginning the evening before one must guard oneself against every evil thought, and spend the night with all attention in numerous prostrations.[123]

It is clear that the instructions of the Typicon and the Liturgical Psalter quoted above (this Psalter is used to this day by the Old Believers) could not have origi-

---

[119]St Theophan the Recluse, *Pervoe poslanie k Korinfyanam* [First Epistle to the Corinthians], 425.

[120]*Typikon* (Leningrad: 1992), 32.39.

[121]This may refer to the Apostolic Canons, or to the canons of the Second Ecumenical Council; these injunctions, however, are not found in either document.

[122]In the text cited, "drink" (*pitie*) may actually be referring to wine, not to water.—*Trans.*

[123]Translated from the Slavonic text of *Psaltir' Sledovannaya* [The Liturgical Psalter] (Leningrad), 543.

nated in the era when believers communed regularly. Injunctions of this kind began appearing when communion became a rare event and began to be treated as a special, exceptional event in the life of a Christian, requiring several days of preparation.

To this same era belongs the formulation of the "Order of Preparation for Holy Communion"—a compilation of prayers that the believer must read the morning of the day of communion, before the liturgy. This order is not part of the daily cycle of divine services and is not mentioned in the Typicon. It is comprised of prayers ascribed to various authors, including Basil the Great, John Chrysostom, John of Damascus, Symeon Metaphrastes, and Symeon the New Theologian. These prayers, which are extraordinarily rich in their theological content, are not of a liturgical nature, but they are filled with allusions to liturgical texts. Their overall tone is one of penitence and tender feeling: they are designed to incline the believer to a eucharistic disposition, to help him to become permeated with reverence before the sacrament of the Eucharist.

In the mid-seventeenth century an order was used in Russia that differed significantly from the one in use today, both in content and in length.[124] It was comprised of eighteen prayers and a canon beginning with the words, "Behold, O soul, Christ who is slain." This order is used to this day in Old Believer communities. In the synodal era it was significantly abbreviated, with the result that only eleven of the eighteen prayers remain (ten in some editions), and the lengthier prayers have been abbreviated. The canon was replaced with a different one, beginning with the words, "May Thy holy Body be for me the bread of eternal life." Even in this abbreviated form, however, reading this order requires at least half an hour.

In the modern practice of the Russian Orthodox Church, reading "The Order of Preparation for Holy Communion" is considered obligatory for every Christian preparing to receive the holy mysteries. In addition to this, there is a fairly widespread injunction to read three canons before communion—the canons of repentance, to the Theotokos, and to the guardian angel, as well as the "Akathist to Sweetest Jesus," if desired.[125]

---

[124]Cf. *Psaltir' Sledovannaya* [The Liturgical Psalter] (Leningrad), 336 (reverse)–337 (reverse). See also Valentin Asmus, "Gimny Simeona Novogo Bogoslova v bogosluzhebnikh knigakh Russkoi Tserkvi" [The Hymns of Symeon the New Theologian in the Liturgical Books of the Russian Church], *Bogoslovskiy Vestnik* 4 (2004): 209–219, at 215–216.

[125]The injunction to read the three canons before communion is not only conveyed by word of mouth, but is also printed in many contemporary prayer books, thereby giving this injunction near-canonical status. The question of preparation for communion is a subject of much dispute and requires serious discussion on a Church-wide level.

The communion of Judas.
Book miniature.
Stuttgart Psalter, 9th c.

Regarding fasting before communion the instructions of various spiritual fathers can differ widely from one to the next. The strictest spiritual fathers require that believers have fasted a whole week, while others who are more "moderate" require that they have fasted three days (given that Wednesday is a fast day, a three-day fast in preparation for Sunday becomes a four-day fast). In both cases, however, Saturday is rendered a day of fasting. Fasting on Saturday has never been the tradition of the Orthodox Church. Furthermore, this was one of the accusations that Byzantium and Russia leveled against the Catholics over the course of several centuries, citing the sixty-fourth canon of the apostles: "If any of the clergy be found fasting on the Lord's day, or on the Sabbath, excepting the one only,[126] let him be deposed. If a layman, let him be excommunicated."[127] (The fifty-fifth canon of the Sixth Ecumenical Council clarifies that this canon must be observed in Rome as well.) Today fasting on Saturday has been abolished in the Catholic Church, yet in the Orthodox Church certain spiritual fathers turn Saturday into a day of fasting for those of their parishioners who are preparing to commune.

It is characteristic that the injunction to observe a fast of seven or three days before communing does not extend to the clergy. The usual explanation given for this is that the clergy commune frequently, and hence they are unable to fast continually. But this situation, in which a stricter ascetic rule is imposed on the laity than on the clergy (including monastics), seems inadmissible and in contradiction to the spirit of the liturgy, at which all—bishops, priests, and laymen—worship before God, standing before him in equal worthiness or, more appropriately, equal unworthiness. Additionally, in this situation Christ's words regarding the Pharisees may rightly be applied to the clergy: "They bind heavy burdens and grievous to be borne, and lay them on men's shoulders; but they themselves will not move them with one of their fingers" (Mt 23.4).

In our time the austere rules of preparation for communion, and the requirement of several days of fasting and of reading lengthy prayer rules, can sometimes

---

[126]The Russian translation clarifies by rendering this passage as "excepting Great Saturday only."
—*Trans.*

[127] *The Canons of the Holy and Altogether August Apostles* 66 (*NPNF²* 14:598).

repulse and frighten the faithful away from communion. Hence, certain parishes, particularly St Nicholas Church in Kuznetsk Sloboda, according to its rector, Archpriest Vladimir Vorobyev, practice a "mitigated" method of preparing for communion: "For those who live a profoundly Christian life, pray to God, attend services regularly, and observe the weekly and yearly fasts, in order to commune on Sunday they must fast on Wednesday and Friday, not eat meat on Saturday, and read 'The Order of Preparation for Holy Communion.'" Reading the three canons is not required.[128]

This method, we presume, could be introduced in other churches as well. It is even difficult to term this method "mitigated," since it presumes following all the instructions of the church Typicon, including observing all the fasts, whether one day or many. At any rate, it does not impose additional fasts upon believers beyond those prescribed by the Typicon. Most importantly, it is designed so that believers might commune frequently of the holy mysteries, and so that communion does not become an extraordinary event, requiring particular ascetic preparatory labors.

It should be noted that in the Greek Church fasting before communion is not obligatory, though it is practiced by the more pious believers. The Greeks also do not require confession before each communion. This custom, like many other church institutions, the Russians originally borrowed from the Greeks, but today it remains only in the Russian Church.

The link between confessing one's sins and communion is recorded in numerous sources, and the custom of confessing one's sins before communion dates back to the earliest days of Christianity. It existed already in the second century, as testified by the "Teaching of the Twelve Apostles" (the *Didache*): "In accordance with the ‹commandment› of the Lord,[129] gather together to break bread and give thanks, first confessing your failings, so that your sacrifice may be pure."[130] This, however, refers not to confession as a separate sacrament, but to general confession of sins in the context of eucharistic prayer. This kind of confession (*confessio*) is present in the Tridentine Mass, where the priest addresses it to God, the saints, and all those present in the church.[131] In the liturgies that remain in use in the Orthodox Church there is no special prayer of confession of sins; nevertheless, repentance of sins is one

---

[128]Vladimir Vorobyev, "Podgotovka ko svyatomu prichashcheniyu" [Preparation for Holy Communion]. Report given at the round table "Preparation for Holy Communion: Historic Practice and Modern Approaches to the Issue," held on December 27, 2006, at St Daniel Monastery in Moscow.

[129]In the Russian this passage is rendered, "On the Lord's day."—*Trans.*

[130]*Didache* 14.1 (PPS 41:42; emphasis added).

[131]During this prayer, beating his breast thrice, the priest says, "*Mea culpa, mea culpa, mea maxima culpa*" (Lat. "Through my fault, through my fault, through my most grievous fault").

The communion of the apostles. Fresco. St George Church.
Staro Nagorichino, Macedonia. 4th c.

of the themes that runs through many prayers of the liturgy. Additionally, before the beginning of the liturgy (at the end of the entrance prayers), as well as before communion, the chief celebrant asks forgiveness of the concelebrating clergy.

Confession of sins before communion is mentioned in a number of late Byzantine sources—for example, by Macarius of Corinth and Nicodemus of the Holy Mountain: "It is enough to make a contrite confession, fulfill a sound rule, and prepare properly, and immediately one can receive Communion and become one body and one blood with Christ."[132] In contrast to the *Didache,* this is referring to sacramental confession. The words quoted, however, should not necessarily be understood as requiring confession before *every* communion as an indispensible condition. Rather, this is stating that a person who desires to commune frequently must regularly make confession.

When confession is interpreted as an obligatory condition for communion, this can cause a variety of difficulties for believers. In certain parishes confessions take place throughout the liturgy in a separate wing of the church. As a result, those wishing to commune spend a large part of the time waiting in line instead of listening attentively to the words of the service; listening to the service is the privilege of those who are not communing. In other parishes, due to overwhelming numbers of the faithful (in certain Orthodox churches several thousand people commune on

[132]Nikodemos the Hagiorite, *Concerning Frequent Communion,* 2.3.129.

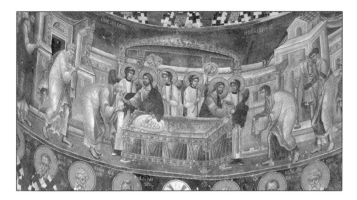

major feasts), confession takes place hurriedly or is replaced by so-called "general confession." Here confession becomes a formality, required solely in order that a person might approach to receive the sacrament of the Eucharist.

At the same time it is obvious that universally abolishing confession before communion could upset and offend the sensitivities of the faithful, and in the long term it could lead to a gradual loss of the sense of need for it and the erosion of ecclesiastical self-identity, as notably occurred in the Roman Catholic Church after the Second Vatican Council. Any steps in this area must be carefully gauged and thought through so as not to fracture the age-old traditions formulated by Russian ecclesiastical piety.

Obviously, under present-day conditions it would be an extremely complex matter to formulate universal rules of preparation for communion. Parishes vary so greatly in size from one to the next, and parishioners vary so greatly in their level of churchedness and the degree to which they follow the church canons, that formulating a unified common standard is hardly possible. Every pastor must have discernment and an individual approach that takes into account the particularities of the given region, his parish, and each particular parishioner.

Nevertheless, several guiding principles may be formulated by way of guidelines for pastors:

(1) Frequent communion must be encouraged—on all Sundays and feast days, if possible.

(2) Rules of preparation for communion must not be stricter for the laity than for the clergy. However, they must naturally be stricter for those who commune rarely than for those who commune frequently.

(3) Regular confession must be encouraged, but confession should not be absolutely required from *every* believer before *every* communion. With the consent of their spiritual father, an individual rhythm of confession and communion may be established for persons who regularly confess and commune, who observe the church canons and the fasts established by the Church.

We believe that following these principles as guidelines (given all the possible local and individual variations thereof) would help to revitalize the atmosphere in many parishes, and to restore the sacrament of the Eucharist to the central place which it must occupy in the life of the church community and of each individual believer.

4

Repentance (Confession)[1]

I N THE CHRISTIAN TRADITION the concept of repentance has a very broad
significance: it is not exhausted by the concept of acknowledging one's sinful
act and feeling remorse for it. Repentance is an entire spiritual system, one that
includes daily self-analysis, regret for sins committed and sinful thoughts, constant
labor to improve spiritually, and striving continually to do good.

REPENTANCE AND CONFESSION OF SINS
IN THE OLD AND NEW TESTAMENTS

Since Old Testament times repentance has been linked to the liturgical cult. One
of the most important institutions of the Old Testament cult was "the great day of
atonement" (Yom Kippur), when special liturgical rites were held with the object
of purification from sin. On this day sacrifices of purification were offered for sin.
The most important attribute of the Day of Atonement was the "scapegoat," which
was not burnt upon a fire, but was driven into the wilderness, bearing with it all
the sins of Israel:

> And Aaron shall lay both his hands upon the head of the live goat, and confess
> over him all the iniquities of the children of Israel, and all their transgressions
> in all their sins, putting them upon the head of the goat, and shall send him
> away by the hand of a fit man into the wilderness: and the goat shall bear upon
> him all their iniquities unto a land not inhabited. (Lev 16.21–22)

In addition to this symbolic act there were numerous injunctions regarding
individual acts of repentance after committing sinful acts. Here is one of them:

---

[1]In Russian this sacrament is called *pokayanie*—repentance. In English various terms are used, including
confession, penance and reconciliation, and simply *penance.—Trans.*

When a man or woman shall commit any sin that men commit, to do a trespass against the Lord, and that person be guilty; then they shall confess their sin which they have done: and he shall recompense his trespass with the principal thereof, and add unto it the fifth part thereof, and give it unto him against whom he hath trespassed. But if the man have no kinsman to recompense the trespass unto, let the trespass be recompensed unto the Lord, even to the priest; beside the ram of the atonement, whereby an atonement shall be made for him. (Num 5.6–8)

Here the act of repentance comprises three elements: confession of the sin, that is, recognizing and admitting it; correction of the sin by doing the good deed that is its opposite; and the participation of the priest, who cleanses the sinner by means of a sacrifice.

One function of the priest and the primary mission of the prophet in the Old Testament was to call people to repentance. When David sinned by taking the wife of another and killing her husband, the prophet Nathan was sent to him, and he brought David to repentance by means of a parable (cf. 2 Sam 11–12). In both the Judaic and the Christian traditions David has become a symbol of repentance, and Psalm 50, which he authored, is perceived as the most powerful penitential prayer ever written by man. In the Orthodox Church it is customary to read Psalm 50 several times a day, both during communal worship and during prayer at home.

The books of the prophets are filled with calls to repentance, both individual and collective. The book of the prophet Isaiah begins with a moving speech in which God says that sacrifices and whole-burnt offerings that are not accompanied by a change in one's way of life are of no use to him. A pleasing sacrifice to God is a change of life, good deeds: if a person deliberately converts to what is good, then God cleanses that person of sin (cf. Is 1.11–18).

Thus, conversion is a synonym for repentance. The Greek word μετάνοια/*metanoia*, which translates as "repentance," literally means "a change of mind," "a change of one's way of thinking"—in the grand scheme, a change of lifestyle, conversion from evil to good. The call to repentance with which John the Baptist began his preaching was a call to a change of lifestyle, to spiritual conversion, to moral rebirth. Expounding on the meaning of his own words, "Bring forth therefore fruits worthy of repentance" (Lk 3.8), John the Baptist said, "He that hath two coats, let him impart to him that hath none; and he that hath meat, let him do likewise." To the publicans John commanded that they demand nothing beyond what was due, and to the soldiers that they abuse no one, not make false accusations, and be content with their own wages (Lk 3.10–14). The call to repentance was a call to renunciation of sinful acts and to a virtuous life.

Confession of sins is the starting point on the path of repentance as a conversion from sin to virtue. Without confession of sins, spiritual purification and rebirth are impossible. The baptism of John, which was a baptism of repentance and purification, was accompanied by confession of sins (cf. Mt 3.6). After Christ's resurrection, when the Church began to spread and to receive new believers into her bosom, their entry into the Church was accompanied by confession of sins: "Many that believed came, and confessed, and showed their deeds" (Acts 19.18).

St John the Forerunner. Icon. Yaroslavl. 16th c.

Thus, since the earliest history of the Christian Church baptism has been linked with confession of sins. In the epistle of the apostle John the Theologian we read, "If we confess [ὁμολογῶμεν/*homologomen*] our sins, he is faithful and just to forgive us our sins, and to cleanse us from all unrighteousness" (1 Jn 1.9). The apostle James says, "Confess your faults one to another" (Jas 5.16). This refers not merely to private conversation, in the course of which one Christian might admit to another having done some deed. In all likelihood this refers to an act of a liturgical nature, which would take place during an assembly of the community. "One to another" means "in the church," at the assembly. This is confirmed by the words from "The Teaching of the Twelve Apostles" (the *Didache*): "You shall confess your transgressions in the assembly."[2] In another passage of the *Didache* confession of sins is directly associated with the Eucharist, as has been said above.[3]

Aside from confession of sins, the act of repentance entailed their remission. In the Old Testament cult the remission of sins took place through the priest and the prophet; in the New Testament Church it began to take place through the apostles. In Caesarea Philippi Jesus said to Peter, "And I will give unto thee the keys of the kingdom of heaven, and whatsoever thou shalt bind on earth shall be bound in heaven, and whatsoever thou shalt loose on earth shall be loosed in heaven" (Mt 16.19). Some time later, while in Capernaum, Jesus said to all the apostles, "Verily

[2]*Didache* 4.14, in *On the Two Ways* 38.
[3]Cf. p. 113.

Apostle Peter. Icon. 16th c.

I say unto you, whatsoever ye shall bind on earth shall be bound in heaven, and whatsoever ye shall loose on earth shall be loosed in heaven" (Mt 18.18). The power "to bind and to loose" is much broader in nature than remission of sins: essentially this refers to the authority to govern the church community. Nevertheless, remission of sins is one of the undeniable components of that authority.

After his resurrection Jesus Christ spoke explicitly concerning remission of sins: "When he had said this, he breathed on them, and saith unto them, 'Receive ye the Holy Spirit: whose soever sins ye remit, they are remitted unto them; and whose soever sins ye retain, they are retained'" (Jn 20.22–23). The words of the evangelist show that remission of sins is accomplished through the apostles with the cooperation of the Holy Spirit. More precisely, the Holy Spirit remits sins through the agency of the apostles. Concerning this Cyril of Alexandria writes, "They who have once been endued with the Spirit of Him Who is God and Lord should have power also to remit or retain the sins of whomsoever they would, the Holy Spirit That dwelt in them remitting or retaining them according to His Will, though the deed were done through human instrumentality."[4]

REPENTANCE IN THE ANCIENT CHURCH

In the Church of the post-apostolic period the power "to bind and to loose" was assimilated by the heirs of the apostles—the bishops. Ignatius the God-bearer wrote in the second century, "The Lord forgives all who repent if they repent in the unity of God and the council of the bishop. I have faith in the grace of Jesus Christ, who will release you from all your chains."[5] In the third century Firmilian, bishop of Caesarea, wrote to Cyprian of Carthage, "The power of remitting sins was given to the apostles, and to the churches which they, sent by Christ, established, and to the bishops who succeeded to them by vicarious ordination."[6] Cyprian himself says

[4]Holy Hierarch Cyril of Alexandria, *Commentary on the Gospel According to Saint John* vol. 2, Thomas Randell, trans. In *A Library of Fathers of the Holy Catholic Church* (London: Walter Smith [late Mozley], 1885), 48:680.

[5]Ignatius the God-bearer, *Letter to the Philadelphians* 8.1 (PPS 49:83).

[6]Firmilian of Caesarea, *Epistles of Cyprian* 74 (*ANF* 5:394).

likewise: "In smaller sins sinners may do penance for a set time, and according to the rules of discipline come to public confession, and by imposition of the hand of the bishop and clergy receive the right of communion."[7] In the *Apostolic Constitutions* the ministry of the bishop is linked to the remission of sins, which is described in terms of a court of law:

Prophet Ezekiel.
Book miniature. 9th c.

> Sit in the Church when thou speakest, as having authority to judge offenders. . . . Do thou therefore, O bishop, judge with authority like God, yet receive the penitent; for God is a God of mercy. Rebuke those that sin, admonish those that are not converted, exhort those that stand to persevere in their goodness, receive the penitent; for the Lord God has promised with an oath to afford remission to the penitent for what things they have done amiss. For He says by Ezekiel: "Speak unto them: 'As I live,' saith the Lord, 'I would not the death of a sinner, but that the wicked turn from his evil way, and live. Turn ye therefore from your evil ways; for why will ye die, O house of Israel?'" [Ezek 33.11] Here the word affords hope to sinners, that if they will repent they shall have hope of salvation, lest otherwise out of despair they yield themselves up to their transgressions; but that, having hope of salvation, they may be converted, and may address to God with tears, on account of their sins, and may repent from their hearts, and so appease His displeasure towards them; so shall they receive a pardon from Him, as from a merciful Father.[8]

The procedure of restoring one who has sinned (apparently gravely) to the Church is described as follows. First the bishop drives him from the church, and outside the church the deacons interrogate him, after which they return to the bishop and intercede for the one who has sinned. The bishop commands him to enter and inquires concerning the sin committed. After this he assigns him a fast lasting two, three, five, or seven weeks.[9] Remission of sins takes place through the laying on of hands by the bishop: "When with tears the offender begs readmission,

---

[7]Cyprian of Carthage, *Epistles of Cyprian* 9 (*ANF* 5:290).
[8]*Apostolic Constitutions* 3.11–12 (*ANF* 7:399–400).
[9]*Apostolic Constitutions* 2.16 (*ANF* 7:402).

receive him, and let the whole Church pray for him; and when by imposition of thy hand thou hast admitted him, give him leave to abide afterwards in the flock."[10]

Along with bishops, priests also are invested with the power "to bind and to loose." Testimonies of this abound in the Christian literature of both East and West, beginning in the third century. They are found, among other places, in the writings of Origen, Cyprian of Carthage, Basil the Great, John Chrysostom, Ambrose of Milan, Blessed Augustine, and Cyril of Alexandria:

> For, if we have done this and revealed our sins not only to God but also to those who can heal our wounds and our sins, our sins will be blotted out by him who says, "I shall blot out your transgressions like a cloud, and like a mist your sins [Is 44.22]."[11]

> Moreover, how much are they . . . greater in faith . . . who, although bound by no crime of sacrifice to idols or of certificate,[12] yet, since they have even thought of such things, with grief and simplicity confess this very thing to God's priests, and make the conscientious avowal . . . and seek out the salutary medicine even for slight and moderate wounds. . . . I entreat you . . . that each one should confess his own sin, while he who has sinned is still in this world, while his confession may be received, while the satisfaction and remission made by the priests are pleasing to the Lord.[13]

> Ought one who wishes to confess his sins confess them to all and sundry, or only to certain ones? . . . It seems necessary that sins be confessed to those entrusted with the stewardship of the Mysteries of God (cf. 1 Cor 4:1). For thus also those who repented of old are found to have confessed their sins before the saints. For it is written in the gospel that they confessed their sins to John the Baptist (cf. Mt 3.6; Mk 1.5) and in the Acts of the Apostles, to the apostles, by whom they were also baptized (cf. Acts 2.37).[14]

---

[10]Ibid., 2.18 (*ANF* 7:403–404).

[11]Origen, *Homilies on Luke* 17.8 (PG 13:1846A). In *Origen: Homilies on Luke*, The Fathers of the Church, vol. 94, Joseph T. Lienhard, S.J., trans. (Washington, DC: The Catholic University of America Press, 1996), 74.

[12]"Certificate" (Lat. *libelli*) here means a certificate of having sacrificed to the gods, which was issued by state agencies during the persecution under the emperor Decius. Christians who obtained these certificates, even if they had not actually sacrificed to the gods, were considered apostates.

[13]Cyprian of Carthage, *On the Lapsed* 28–29 (*ANF* 5:445).

[14]Basil the Great, *The Rule of St Basil the Great*, Anna M. Silvas, trans. (Collegeville, MN: Liturgical Press, 2013), 326.

For earth's inhabitants, having their life in this world, have been entrusted with the stewardship of heavenly things, and have received an authority which God has not given to angels or archangels. Not to them was it said, "What things soever ye shall bind on earth shall be bound also in heaven; and what things soever ye shall loose, shall be loosed." Those who are lords on earth have indeed the power to bind, but only men's bodies. But this binding touches the very soul and reaches through heaven. What priests do on earth, God ratifies above. The Master confirms the decisions of his slaves.[15]

"The Father hath given all judgment to the Son" [Jn 5.22]. But I see that the Son has placed it all in their [the priests'] hands. . . . The priests of the Jews had authority to cure leprosy of the body, or rather, not to cure it, but only to certify the cure. But our priests have received authority not over leprosy of the body but over uncleanness of the soul, and not just to certify its cure, but actually to cure it.[16]

Have you sinned? Enter into the church and wipe away your sin.[17]

There are people who think it sufficient for their salvation to confess their sins to God alone. . . . But do you rather invite the priest and confess to him your secrets. . . . Otherwise how will the command of God come to pass, given both under the law and under grace: "Go shew yourselves unto the priests" (Lk 17.14, cf. Lev 14.2)? Therefore, in place of God employ the presbyter as an intermediary of your wounds and reveal to him your ways, and he will give you the pledge of reconciliation.[18]

Who can forgive sins, but God alone? For God also forgives through those to whom he has given the power of forgiveness.[19]

They who have the Spirit of God . . . remit and retain sins, by rebuking erring children of the Church, and granting pardon to those who repent.[20]

[15]John Chrysostom, *Six Books on the Priesthood* 3.4. In John Chrysostom, *On the Priesthood*, Popular Patristics Series 1, Graham Neville, trans. (Crestwood, NJ: St Vladimir's Seminary Press, 1977), 71–72.

[16]John Chrysostom, *Six Books on the Priesthood* 3.5 (PPS 1:72).

[17]John Chrysostom, *Homilies on Repentance* 2. In *The Fathers of the Church*, trans. by Gus George Christo (Washington, DC: The Catholic University of America Press, 1998), 96:39.

[18]Augustine, *On Visiting the Infirm* 2.4 (PL 40:1154–1155). [Translated by the present translator.]

[19]Ambrose of Milan, *Exposition of the Gospel of Luke* 5.12–13. In *Ancient Christian Commentary on Scripture*, vol. 3, Arthur A. Just Jr., ed. (Downers Grove, IL: InterVarsity Press, 2003), 93.

[20]Cyril of Alexandria, *Commentary on the Gospel According to Saint John* vol. 2, Thomas Randell, trans. In *A Library of Fathers of the Holy Catholic Church*, 48:680.

In the third century the office of penitentiary presbyter was established, whose duties included receiving the repentance of those who had fallen after baptism. The need for this office arose due to a mass apostasy of Christians from the Church during the persecution of the emperor Decius (250–253) and a subsequent mass return to the Church of those who had fallen away. Socrates Scholasticus speaks of this in his *History of the Church:* "When the Novatians separated themselves from the Church because they would not communicate with those who had lapsed during the persecution under Decius, the bishops added to the ecclesiastical canon a presbyter of penitence in order that those who had sinned after baptism might confess their sins in the presence of the presbyter thus appointed."[21] Sozomenus speaks of this in still greater detail:

> Impeccability is a Divine attribute, and belongs not to human nature; therefore God has decreed that pardon should be extended to the penitent, even after many transgressions. As in supplicating for pardon, it is requisite to confess the sin, it seems probable that the priests, from the beginning, considered it irksome to make this confession in public, before the whole assembly of the people. They therefore appointed a presbyter, of the utmost sanctity, and the most undoubted prudence, to act on these occasions; the penitents went to him, and confessed their transgressions; and it was his office to indicate the kind of penance adapted to each sin, and then when satisfaction had been made, to pronounce absolution.[22]

In the late fourth century Bishop of Nectarius of Constantinople (successor to Gregory the Theologian) abolished the office of penitentiary presbyter in Constantinople. A certain woman repented before the bishop of having sinned with a deacon. The deacon was excommunicated from the Church, but this caused an uproar among the people, who were "not only offended at what had taken place, but also because the deed had brought scandal and degradation upon the Church." Then a certain priest, Eudaemon, a native of Alexandria, advised Nectarius "to abolish the office of penitentiary presbyter, and to leave every one to his own conscience with regard to the participation of the sacred mysteries: for thus only, in his judgment, could the Church be preserved from obloquy."[23] Sozomen adds:

---

[21]Socrates Scholasticus, *The Ecclesiastical History of Socrates Scholasticus* 5.19 (*NPNF*² 2:128).
[22]Sozomen, *The Ecclesiastical History of Sozomenus* 7.16 (*NPNF*² 2:386).
[23]Socrates Scholasticus, *The Ecclesiastical History of Socrates Scholasticus* 5.19 (*NPNF*² 2:128).

Nectarius . . . deposed the deacon; and, at the advice of certain persons, who urged the necessity of leaving each individual to examine himself before participating in the sacred mysteries, he abolished the office of the presbyter presiding over penance. From that period, therefore, the performance of penance fell into disuse; and it seems to me, that extreme laxity of principle was thus substituted for the severity and rigor of antiquity. Under the ancient system, I think, offences were of rarer occurrence; for people were deterred from their commission, by the dread of confessing them, and of exposing them to the scrutiny of a severe judge.[24]

It should be noted that both historians speak of confession of sins in connection with the sacrament of the Eucharist. According to them, the abolition of the office of penitentiary presbyter made confessing one's sins before communion a matter of choice, and the faithful began to be commune according "every one to his own conscience." This office was established not for ordinary confession, but for restoring to the Church those who had apostatized from it either by denying Christ or through other grave sins. It was these sins that barred the way to communion, and it was they that required remission and a penance from the confessor.

It is not entirely clear why the woman's declaration of her affair with the deacon led to the abolition of the office of penitentiary presbyter, nor how the two events were connected. Possibly the penitentiary confessor ought to have reported the matter to the bishop and failed to do so; or, on the contrary, the presbyter violated the seal of confession, thereby scandalizing the people. On the other hand, the concept of the "seal of the confessional" appears to be of later origin. At any rate, in the third century this concept had not yet taken definite form, as witnessed notably by Origen:

Observe how the divine scriptures teach us that one must not conceal sins within. . . . Only be most circumspect regarding to whom you can reveal the cause of your infirmity and who would know how to be weak with the weak, to mourn with those who mourn; who would know how to be compassionate and sympathetic. And if he tells you anything and advises you, do as he says and carry it out. If he finds and discovers that your infirmity is of a sort that must be declared and healed in the assembly of the whole Church, and that this is able to serve for the edification of others and to expedite your healing, after appropriate reflection you must do this and act on the advice of the physician.[25]

---

[24]Sozomen, *The Ecclesiastical History of Sozomenus 7.16* (*NPNF*² 2:387).
[25]Origin, *Homily on Psalm 37.6* (PG 12:1386AB). [Translated by the present translator.]

Do the above testimonies of Socrates and Sozomenus mean that, prior to the abolition of the office of penitentiary presbyter, confession of one's sins before the priest was an obligatory condition for communion? A. Almazov, who authored a study on the origin of the sacrament of confession, holds that "in the view of the ancient Church (second to third centuries) confession was required, if not before each communion, then with all possible frequency." Such confession, it his opinion, was private or secret, having as its object "only sins that were insignificant, unavoidable in a person's day to day life, due to the shortcomings of his spiritual nature."[26]

Here, it seems, the historian is involuntarily projecting a significantly later situation upon the church practice of the second and third centuries. Available sources do not give sufficient grounds for the assumption that in this period mandatory confession had to precede communion. In the early Church communion took place at every Eucharist. We have no evidence that confession was required before each Eucharist, and we do not know how often Christians communed during this period.

We know only that confession of sins varied in form in the ancient Church. First, as has been said, the Eucharist was preceded by a general confession of sins in the form of a prayer read by the priest. Here this refers specifically to a prayer, and not to confession in the sense of revealing one's sins. Second, there was confession before a bishop or a presbyter—probably public, in the presence of members of the community. This kind of confession was resorted to by Christians who had denied Christ or committed grave sins. Third, there was secret confession, where the penitent would meet privately with a priest, reveal to him his sins, and receive absolution of them. Fourth and finally, there was a custom whereby one sinner would appear before a tribunal of several presbyters (or a bishop sitting in the company of the presbyters).

It is this custom to which the author of the homily "On the Samaritan Woman," ascribed to John Chrysostom, is obviously referring: "He who now regards only the reproach of men, but when God seeth is not ashamed to do anything unseemly, and who will not repent and be converted, in that day will be made an example, not only before one or two, but in the sight of the whole world."[27] In another place, however, Chrysostom says:

---

[26]A.N. Almazov, *Tainaya ispoved'* [Secret Confession], vol. I, 43–44.

[27]John Chrysostom, *Homilies on the Gospel of Saint John* 34.3 (*NPNF*[2] 14:120–121). In Migne's *Patrologia* this composition is considered spurious.

Why are you ashamed and blush to confess your sins? Why speak of it to man, who may blame you? Why confess it to your fellow-servant, who may cause you shame? Rather show it to the Master, to Him who cares for you, who is kindly disposed; show the wound to the Physician. . . . I do not oblige you, He saith, to come into the midst of the assembly before a throng of witnesses; declare the sin in secret to Me only, that I may heal the sore and remove the pain.[28]

Thus, while acknowledging the existence of public confession, Chrysostom indicates the possibility of secret confession and recommends that penitents take advantage of this opportunity.

Which sins required repentance in public and which in secret? According to one of the rules ascribed to Blessed Jerome, public repentance is required for sins that pertain to communal rules and that set a bad example for others. Other sins require secret repentance, in the presence of the priest alone.[29] The latter include sins of thought in particular. Tertullian writes, "Sins not of *deed* only, but of *will* too, are to be shunned, and by repentance purged."[30] Cyprian of Carthage likewise calls people to confess sins of thought:

How much are they both greater in faith and better in their fear, who, although bound by no crime of sacrifice to idols or of certificate, yet, since they have even thought of such things, with grief and simplicity confess this very thing to God's priests, and make the conscientious avowal, put off from them the load of their minds, and seek out the salutary medicine even for slight and moderate wounds. . . . I entreat you, beloved brethren, that each one should confess his own sin, while he who has sinned is still in this world, while his confession may be received, while the satisfaction and remission made by the priests are pleasing to the Lord.[31]

Can we say that confession as a sacrament existed in the Ancient Church—in the period from the first to the sixth centuries—in the same sense in which we say that the sacraments of baptism and the Eucharist existed during this same period? It would appear that we cannot. First, the penitential discipline allowed for a variety of forms that can hardly be conceptualized as a single sacrament. Second, we do not know whether any rite of confession existed prior to the sixth century, in the

---

[28]John Chrysostom, *Four Discourses of Chrysostom, Chiefly on the Parable of the Rich Man and Lazarus*, F. Allen, trans. (London: Longmans, Green, Reader, and Dyer, 1869), 102.

[29]Jerome, *Regula monacharum* [The Rule for Nuns] 9 (PL 30:413).

[30]Tertullian, *On Repentance* 3 (*ANF* 3:659).

[31]Cyprian of Carthage, *On the Lapsed* 28–29 (*ANF* 5:445).

sense of an established order that included the reading of specific prayers. Third, confessing one's sins before a priest was perceived as but one means of remission of sins, and by no means the only one.[32] Fourth and finally, not a single theological work from this period devoted to the Church and the sacraments (including *The Ecclesiastical Hierarchy* of Dionysius the Areopagite and Maximus the Confessor's *Mystagogy*) mentions confession as a separate sacrament or ritual.

Nevertheless, it is certain that various forms of confession, involving the bishop, the presbyter, or a group of clerics, existed universally during the period described. The era of the early Church and the era of the Ecumenical Councils may be acknowledged as a time of gradual formation of the concept of confession as a sacrament of the Church. This concept solidified with the appearance of the order of confession, which included specific prayers and rituals.

The Service Order of Confession

The compilation of the order of the sacrament of confession is ascribed in Greek and Slavic manuscripts to John the Faster, patriarch of Constantinople (†595). The actual extent of this patriarch's involvement in compiling the order remains an open question: possibly he merely codified the prayers employed in his time, compiling them into a single service.[33] This service order continued to develop, and it is found in both complete and abbreviated versions. In general, so numerous are the various versions in the Greek and Russian traditions, and so greatly do the various versions differ from one to the next, that reviewing them all in detail is not feasible.

Certain editions notably included the reading of Psalms 6, 24, and 50, followed by Psalms 31, 69, and 101. The psalms were followed by the reading of penitential troparia. Then the priest and the penitent would make three bows, after which the priest would address the penitent with an exhortation. The penitent would then say, "I confess to Thee, Father, as the Lord and Creator of heaven and earth, all the secrets of my heart." The priest would kiss the penitent and place the latter's hand upon his neck. Then he would ask the penitent whether he had committed this sin or that. As the penitent answered each question the priest would say, "May God forgive thee." Upon completion of the confession the priest would say, "May our Lord and God and Savior Jesus Christ forgive thee all that thou hast confessed to mine unworthiness in His presence." Then the priest would read several prayers for

[32]Cf. Almazov, *Tainaya ispoved'* [Secret Confession], vol. 1, 330–335.

[33]Cf. Almazov, *Tainaya ispoved'* [Secret Confession], vol. 1, 85–91.

the forgiveness of the sins of him who had repented, say some words of instruction, and read passages from the book of the prophet Ezekiel (18.21–28) and the Gospel of Luke (5.1–10). In the conclusion of the rite of confession the trisagion prayers[34] were read, followed by penitential troparia. The priest and the penitent would then make forty bows together, and the dismissal would be given.[35]

Abbreviated versions of this same order prescribe that Psalms 50 and 69 be read, or Psalm 69 alone. Some omit the psalms altogether. The quantity and selection of prayers included in the abbreviated versions differs significantly from one manuscript to the next. The questions put to the penitent likewise vary, from the brief to the highly detailed.[36] Certain rites of confession also included a litany, intoned as a rule at the beginning of the rite.[37]

Certain editions of the service order contain prayers alternating with psalms. One tenth-century manuscript describes the following order: the initial exclamation ("Blessed is our God"),[38] the trisagion prayers, and "Lord, have mercy" forty times. Next the prayer "Lamb of God, Son of the Father, that takest away the sin of the world (have mercy on us)," thrice. Then the prayer, "Have mercy on us, O God our Savior," thrice. Then the prayerful exclamations, "Holy of holies, O God, have mercy on us," "O Lord God, receive our prayer," and "O Most Holy Lady Theotokos, pray for us sinners." Similar exclamations address by name all the archangels and heavenly hosts, John the Baptist, the prophets, the apostle Peter and the other apostles, the martyrs, and the holy hierarchs. These are followed by the great litany with petitions for the penitent. Then the troparia "Have mercy on us, O Lord, have mercy on us," and six prayers alternating with four psalms: 6, 102, 69, and 99. Of these six prayers, three—the first, second (in abbreviated form), and sixth—are included in the modern rite of confession. Next the priest "with meek face and gentle voice" asks the penitent, "What hast thou first of all, my lord brother?" The penitent replies, "I confess to thee, Lord of the heavens, all the secrets of my heart." Then the priest asks questions pertaining almost exclusively to sins against the seventh commandment (various forms of adultery and fornication). In conclusion the priest reads three prayers in which he asks forgiveness for the penitent sinner.

[34]The "trisagion prayers" consist of a series of short prayers, beginning with "Holy God, Holy Mighty, Holy Immortal, have mercy on us" (thrice) and ending with the Lord's Prayer ("Our Father").—*Trans.*

[35]Ibid., 79–80.

[36]Ibid., 87–98.

[37]Ibid., 147.

[38]In other manuscripts the exclamations "Glory to the holy" and "Blessed is the kingdom" are found. A significant number of manuscripts have no initial exclamation at all.

The greatest variety is found in two parts of the confessional rite: the prayers said by the priest and the questions that the priest asks the penitent. The prayers contained in all the known Greek and Slavic manuscripts of the rite of confession number no less than forty, yet the number of prayers in any single version of the rite did not exceed eight or nine. Of these prayers several were supplicatory in nature, others were prayers of absolution, while still others pertained solely to specific categories of penitents (for example, women or the ill).[39]

As for the questions asked by the priest at confession, these demonstrated the greatest variety. Some orders give only general instructions regarding what the spiritual father must ask the penitent—for example, "concerning faith, sacrilege, heresy, blasphemy, defiling virginity." Others concentrated almost exclusively on sins against the seventh commandment.[40] Finally, not a few orders of confession—both Greek and Russian—contain detailed lists of sins, including various sexual perversions, the mere recitation of which would shock the modern reader.[41]

Even in modern printed editions of the Book of Needs the rite of confession can differ significantly from one version to the next. In particular, certain editions include a list of sins while others omit this. The lists of sins in various editions differ significantly from one to the next.

The modern rite of confession begins with the exclamation, "Blessed is our God," followed by the trisagion prayers. The concluding exclamation is followed by "O come, let us worship" and Psalm 50. Then the troparia "Have mercy on us, O Lord, have mercy on us," "Lord have mercy" forty times, and the first penitential prayer:

> O God our Savior, who by thy prophet Nathan didst grant remission to David, repenting of his own trespasses, and didst accept the penitent prayer of Manasseh: do thou thyself, in thy wonted love for mankind, accept this, thy servant N. who repenteth of the sins he hath committed, overlooking all that he hath done, forgiving his unrighteousness, and passing by his transgressions. For thou, O Lord, hast said: "I desire not the death of the sinner, but that he turn from his way and live," and that sins shall be forgiven even unto seventy times seven. For as thy majesty is incomparable, so is thy mercy immeasurable.

[39]Almazov, *Tainaya ispoved'* [Secret Confession], vol. 1, 147–150.
[40]Ibid., 87.
[41]For example, see the order of confession according to the *Nomocanon* in the Greek manuscript from the fifteenth–sixteenth centuries and in the 1620 Slavonic edition of the *Nomocanon*, cited by Almazov in *Tainaya ispoved'* [Secret Confession], vol. 3, 29–32.

For if thou shouldest mark iniquities, O Lord, who should stand? For thou art the God of those who repent.

This is one of the most ancient prayers, and is notably included in the rite of confession from the tenth-century manuscript described above. In the opinion of A. Almazov, "this prayer undoubtedly has its origins in Christian antiquity." This is witnessed by "the simplicity of its construction, its influence on the text of other prayers compiled later, its invariable inclusion in nearly all editions of the Typicon and service orders of confession, and, finally, its inclusion in all the ancient euchologia." The researcher sets the date of this prayer's composition prior to the sixth century.[42] The prayer is woven from references to Old Testament models

Prophet Nathan and King David. The Chludov Psalter. Approx. 840–850 AD.

of repentance, biblical allusions, and individual phrases from the psalms. Mentioned among the Old Testament examples of repentance is the story of David and Nathan, as well as the prayer of King Manasseh.[43]

The second prayer of the rite is likewise of very ancient origin, as it is found in early orders of confession. Furthermore, it is encountered in the order of the liturgy of the apostle James as its final prayer.[44] This prayer also contains biblical allusions, but here episodes from the New Testament are mentioned:

> O Lord Jesus Christ, Son of the living God, Shepherd and Lamb that takest away the sin of the world, who gavest remittance unto the two debtors and remission of sins to the harlot: do thou thyself, O Master, loose, remit, and pardon the sins, transgressions, and iniquities, whether voluntary or involuntary, whether known or unknown, whether by mistake or in disobedience, which thy servant hath wrought; and if somehow, as a man bearing flesh and living in the world, having been deceived by the devil, whether in word or deed, in knowledge or ignorance he hath despised the word of a priest or hath come under the ban of a priest, or is fallen under his own anathema or bound by an oath, be pleased, O Master, since thou art good and forgetful of evil, to loose

[42]Almazov, *Tainaya ispoved'* [Secret Confession], vol. 2, 174.

[43]Concerning this prayer see vol. 4, pp. 83–84.

[44]Cf. *Sobranie drevnikh liturgiy* [Collection of Ancient Liturgies] 164.

Christ forgiving the sinful woman. Fresco. Ferapontov Monastery. Early 16th c.

this thy servant by a word, forgiving him even his own anathema and oath, according to the greatness of thy mercy. Yea, O Master and Lord, who lovest mankind, hearken unto us who are entreating thy goodness for this thy servant; and as thou art great in mercy, overlook all his transgressions and deliver him from eternal punishment. For thou hast said, O Master, "Whatsoever ye shall bind on earth shall be bound in heaven, and whatsoever ye shall loose on earth shall be loosed in heaven."

This prayer begins with a reference to the parable of the two debtors and to the forgiveness Christ granted to the sinful woman (cf. Lk 7.36–50). The prayer mentions three categories of sins: sins, iniquities, and transgressions. Special emphasis is placed on sins related to oaths and curses. The prayer is one of supplication and absolution (the prayer of absolution that is read over the coffin of one who has died is similar in content).

Then the priest addresses the penitent in language that emphasizes that it is Christ himself who receives his confession, while the priest is but a witness. This imagery is very important for understanding the role of the priest in the sacrament of confession: his is a supplementary role. He is merely present at confession as a witness, but the confession is not made to him, nor is it he that gives remission of sins. The prayer employs the traditional image of the Church as "the place of the Physician"—a hospital, where with the help of the priest as physician those who repent receive healing of their infirmities. It is likewise underscored that deliberately concealing a sin increases its gravity:

> Behold, child, Christ standeth invisibly before thee to hear thy confession. Be not ashamed, neither be afraid, and hide nothing from me. Rather, do not fear to tell me all that thou hast done, so that thou mayest receive forgiveness from our Lord Jesus Christ. Behold, his icon is before us. And I am only a witness, that I may bear witness before him of all that thou dost tell me. If thou hide anything from me, thou shalt have the greater sin. Take heed, therefore, lest having come to the place of the Physician, thou depart unhealed.

After this there a conversation begins between the penitent and the priest, which in modern practice may take various forms. Some prefer to address God in confession, or they begin confession with the formula, "I confess to Thee, O Lord my God, and to thee, reverend father, all my transgressions, voluntary and involuntary." Sometimes at confession the list of sins from the "daily confession of sins," found in the evening prayer rule, is employed. Some use guides on preparing for confession and various types of supplementary literature containing lists of sins. One fairly widespread form is to structure confession based on the ten commandments of the Mosaic Law, classifying sins in accordance with these commandments. Sometimes the Beatitudes are employed for the same purpose. Some first confess sins against God, then sins against themselves, and then sins against their neighbors.

Confession may take place in the form of questions from the priest and answers from the penitent. Despite being prescribed by the ancient orders of confession, this form can hardly be considered ideal. It may be necessary in certain cases—for example, when a person comes to confession for the first time and does not know what is sinful and what is not. Here the priest may ask certain leading questions. In other cases, however, employing the question and answer format results in the priest having to "guess" the sins the penitent may have committed, or ask him questions about sins that he has not committed.

One very widespread form of confession is an open conversation with the priest, in the course of which the penitent relates the sins he has committed in his own words, without any additional aids or leading questions. The priest listens silently to this confession, or comments briefly when necessary. Some priests say "God forgives" after each sin confessed.

How detailed must a confession be? It should not turn into a detailed account of the circumstances under which a particular sin was committed, since these are known to God, and they should not be of interest to the priest. The subject of confession must be the sin itself, which the penitent names and of which he repents. Confession should not include accounts of the sins of others, or complaints of their behavior. At confession the penitent must not justify himself for the sins he has committed; on the contrary, sins should be confessed in a spirit of self-reproach and self-condemnation.

May one ask advice of one's spiritual father during confession? This is obviously permissible at the final stage of confession, or after the confession is over. Confession should not, however, turn into a pastoral conversation. "It is important

Confession in the church

to differentiate between confession and spiritual conversation. The latter may take place outside the context of the sacrament, and it is better that it take place separately, since conversation, albeit concerning spiritual subjects, can distract and cool the ardor of the one confessing, inveigle him in theological disputes, and dull the acuteness of penitential feeling."[45] If there is a need for conversation with a parishioner regarding spiritual or everyday matters, the priest should set a separate time for this—after the service or at another time altogether.

In what degree of detail should sins against the seventh commandment be described? "Sins against the seventh commandment" is a euphemism used to denote all sins of a sexual nature (these include fornication, adultery, sexual perversions, masturbation, etc.). The priest should not ask the penitent detailed questions on these subjects, nor should the penitent relate his sins in detail. In 1998 the Holy Synod of the Russian Orthodox Church decreed "that pastors be reminded of the necessity to observe particular modesty and particular pastoral prudence when discussing issues related to various aspects of marital life with their parishioners."[46]

After the penitent has said all that he wishes, the priest may say something for his edification or impose a penance—a punishment for the misdeeds he has committed. The canons of old prescribed very strict penances for various sins, up to and including being barred from communion for several years. In our time such strict penances are not employed, since pastoral practice takes place in a different environment from the era of the ecumenical councils, and penitential discipline differs greatly from that which existed many centuries ago. Today, for example, multiple years of abstinence from communion is not perceived as a pedagogical measure that can have a positive influence on the sinner's morality. The reverse is nearer the truth: barring a person from communion may estrange or completely repulse a person from the Church. Only those persons whose way of life is incompatible with Orthodox canon law are not admitted to communion.

---

[45] Aleksandr Elchaninov, *Zapisi* [Notes] (Moscow: Russkiy Put', 1992), 121.
[46] Decree of the Holy Synod of the Russian Orthodox Church dated December 28, 1998.

When the confession is over, the priest reads a prayer that the penitent's sins may be forgiven and that he may be united to the Church. In the Christian tradition, in a sense, sin is perceived as a falling away from the Church, and so repentance is a return to the Church and reunification with it:

> O Lord God of the salvation of thy servants, merciful, compassionate, and long-suffering, who repentest concerning our evil deeds, desiring not the death of a sinner, but that he should turn from his way and live: do thou thyself now be merciful unto thy servant *N.* and grant him an image of repentance, pardon and remission of sins, forgiving him every transgression, whether voluntary or involuntary. Reconcile and unite him to thy holy Church, through Jesus Christ our Lord.

The priest then lays his epitrachelion on the head of the penitent and, signing the cross over his head, says the prayer of absolution:

> May our Lord and God Jesus Christ, by the grace and compassion of his love for mankind, forgive thee, my child *N.*, all thy transgressions, and I, an unworthy priest, through his power given unto me, do forgive and absolve thee of all thy sins, in the name of the Father, and of the Son, and of the Holy Spirit. Amen.

This formula of absolution first appeared in the middle of the twelfth century in the Kievan Book of Needs by Metropolitan Peter Mogila. From there it migrated to the 1671 Moscow Book of Needs, and since that time it has been printed in all Russian editions of the Book of Needs. Yet this formula of absolution is absent from the order of confession used in the Greek Church. The reason for this discrepancy between the Greek and Russian practices is that Metropolitan Peter Mogila borrowed the above formula from the Latin sacramentaries, in which absolution of sins was bestowed by the priest in the first person: "I absolve thee from all thy sins, in the name of the Father, and of the Son, and of the Holy Spirit. Amen." The appearance of the above-mentioned formula of absolution in Russian editions of the Book of Needs is seen by researchers as directly influenced by the Latin teaching on the sacraments, according to which a sacrament is performed by means of a certain formula. The absence of this formula in Russian editions of the Book of Needs apparently disconcerted Metropolitan Peter Mogila, whose own understanding of the sacraments, as we have seen above, was based on Latin theological assumptions, and hence he found it necessary to introduce this formula into the Book of Needs.

In the most ancient rites of confession, absolution of sins is given in the form of a prayer addressed to God: the priest asks God to forgive the transgressions of the penitent. At the same time one encounters formulae of absolution addressed to the penitent himself. One tenth-century Greek manuscript contains this formula: "May our Master and Lord Jesus Christ forgive thee all that thou hast confessed to him before me."[47] In another Greek euchologion dating back to the thirteenth century, following confession the priest says to the penitent, "Receive complete forgiveness, my spiritual child. . . . Our Lord and God himself grants thee complete forgiveness, my child, if thou hast committed anything by deed, word, and thought, through my insignificance, through the prayers of our most pure and most glorious Lady and of all the saints. Amen.[48] In both cases absolution of sins is granted by God, with the priest merely bearing witness to this.

Different prayers and formulae of absolution are also found in Slavonic editions of the Book of Needs. For example, one eleventh-century handwritten Book of Needs contains a prayer "for release of a penitent from fasting when he is vouchsafed holy communion": "O Lord God Almighty, All-powerful and Merciful God . . . mayest thou absolve this thy servant from sins, and make him also a communicant of thy most pure mysteries."[49] From its title it follows that this prayer was read at the conclusion of a penance imposed on the penitent.

In Slavonic editions of the Book of Needs the following formula is also found: "May thy transgressions be upon my neck, child, and may Christ God not require an answer of thee for them when he cometh in his glory for the dread judgment."[50] This formula owes its origin to the Greek custom of placing one's hand upon the neck of the priest during confession. In confession the priest, like the Old Testament scapegoat (cf. Lev 16), takes upon himself the sins of the penitent, thereby freeing him from punishment.

The differences between the formulae of absolution in the Orthodox East and the Latin West are thought by some researchers to be due to the discrepancy between the two traditions regarding the role of the priest in the sacrament of

---

[47]Nikolai Uspensky, *Pravoslavnaya liturgiya: istoriko-liturgicheskie issledovaniya. Prazdniki, teksty, ustav* [Orthodox Liturgy: Historical and Liturgical Studies. Feasts, Texts, Service Order], vol. 3 (Moscow: Izdatelskiy sovet Russkoi Pravoslavnoi Tserkvi, 2007), 189.

[48]A.N. Almazov, *Tainaya ispoved'* [Secret Confession], vol. 3, 13.

[49]Ibid., 100.

[50]Ibid., vol. 1, 267.

confession. The Orthodox understanding is based on the concept that it is God who forgives sins, while the Catholic formula of absolution emphasizes the power of the priest "to bind and to loose." "The issue is not of course that this formula is of Catholic origin; it runs far deeper," writes Nikolai Uspensky. "Here two views of the issue conflict: the mystic, psychological view inherent to patristic theology and the formal, juridical view common to scholastic theology."[51]

To a certain degree this is exactly the case, though in our opinion this discrepancy probably should not be overemphasized or ascribed fundamental importance. In response to the letter of Archimandrite Antonin (Kapustin) "on the differences between the Greek and Russian Churches," Metropolitan Philaret of Moscow wrote: "The priest first gives absolution in the name of Jesus Christ, and then adds, 'And I absolve thee'; but so as not to ascribe anything to his own person he says, 'Through his power given unto me,' and in a spirit of humility he also adds, 'And I, an unworthy priest.'" Based on this reasoning the hierarch concludes that the prayer contains nothing contrary to the spirit of humility.[52]

It should also be noted that certain Greek editions of the euchologion contain formulae of absolution that closely resemble the Latin. In one of these, dated to the fourteenth century, at the end of confession the priest says to the penitent, "May the all-powerful God have mercy on thee and remit all thy transgressions." He then says, "By the power I possess do I absolve thee of all thy sins that thou hast confessed to me, and of those which thou hast not remembered, that thou mightest be absolved of them in this age and in that to come."[53] As we see, here the power "to bind and to loose" is mentioned, and there is even an implicit declaration that the power of the priest has an eschatological dimension, extending to "the age to come." Of course, traces of Latin influence may be seen here as well (the fourteenth century was a time of fairly intense interaction between East and West), but there is no proof that this formula was borrowed from the Latins.

Yet another discrepancy between East and West lies in that in the Latin tradition it is customary for the priest to sit during confession, while the penitent kneels. In the Greek and Russian traditions, however, both priest and penitent typically stand facing the altar. The posture of the priest in the Latin tradition seems to

---

[51]Nikolai Uspenskiy, *Pravoslavnaya liturgiya* [The Orthodox Liturgy], vol. 3, 192.

[52]St Philaret (Drozdov), *Sobranie mnenii i otzyvov Filareta, mitropolita kolomenskago i moskovskago, po uchebnym i tserkovno-gosudarstvennyk voprosam* [Collected Opinions and Comments of Philaret, Metropolitan of Kolomna and Moscow, on Matters of Education, Church, and State], vol. 4 (Moscow: Synodal'naya tipografiya, 1886), 407.

[53]Almazov, *Tainaya ispoved'* [Secret Confession], vol. 3, 79.

emphasize his power "to bind and to loose," while in the Eastern Christian tradition the priest's posture emphasizes his solidarity with the penitent sinner. Furthermore, certain rites of confession also contain a prayer of the priest for the forgiveness of his own sins. As at the other sacraments, for the priest also participation in the sacrament of confession must be an occasion for repentance, a source of healing, forgiveness, and reconciliation with God.

Here too, however, it should be noted that this discrepancy should not be considered fundamental. One fourteenth-century Greek edition of the euchologion prescribes for the priest to sit during confession.[54] In this same period St Symeon of Thessalonica prescribes for both priest and penitent to sit during confession:

> The confessor must *sit* (καθῆσθαι/*kathesthai*) with reverence in an honorable and sacred place, alone and without clamor, and be joyous, with meekness in his soul and his gaze. . . . And the one confessing . . . must *sit* (καθίσαι/*kathisai*)[55] in the presence of him who receives (the confession), or, rather, of Christ himself, because through the one who receives the sins he confesses them to Christ, who awards forgiveness.[56]

Are all sins forgiven at confession, or only those that have been named? From the numerous surviving service orders—both Greek and Slavic, handwritten and printed—it is apparent that at confession all sins are forgiven, and not only those that are named. The prayers of intercession and absolution speak specifically of the forgiveness of all sins—"overlooking *all* that he has done, forgiving his unrighteousness, and passing by his transgressions," and, "I . . . do forgive and absolve thee of all thy sins." In certain cases it was specifically clarified that this category of "all" included forgotten sins: "I absolve thee of all thy sins that thou hast confessed to me, and of those which thou hast not remembered."

In the Orthodox Church confession is perceived as a private meeting of the penitent and his spiritual father. Certain parishes, however, practice so-called "general confession." This takes the following form: the priest goes out to the parishioners, reads the prayers before confession, and then himself names the more widespread sins, repenting of them on behalf of the faithful. After this the faithful silently come forward to have the prayer of absolution read over them. Strictly

---

[54]Cryptoferrat manuscript № 211, in *Tainaya ispoved'* [Secret Confession] by Almazov, vol. 3, 78.

[55]The Russian translation erroneously reads "stand" (*Pisaniya otsov i uchitelei Tserkvi, otnosyashchiesya k istolkovaniyu bogosluzheniya* [Writings of the Fathers and Teachers of the Church Pertaining to Explanation of the Divine Services], vol. 2, 327).

[56]Symeon of Thessalonica, *On Confession*, 257. [Translated by the present translator.]

speaking, this kind of confession is a profanation of confession, since wordless group repentance cannot be substituted for a believer's personal repentance before God with the priest acting as a witness. When possible, general confession should be eliminated from parish practice. In those parishes where the priest is physically incapable of confessing each parishioner individually, general confession may be conducted out of necessity, but it cannot completely take the place of individual confession.

A direct consequence of confession must be the person's correction, his renunciation of the sins of which he has repented. The holy hierarch Basil the Great writes:

> It is not the man who says: "I have committed a sin" and then remains in it, who acknowledges his sin, but he who according to the Psalm *hates his sin when he has found it* [Ps 35.3]. For what help for the diseased is a doctor's care when the sick man pursues what is destructive of life? In the same way there is no help in the forgiveness of wrongdoing for him who still does wrong, and in the remission of acts of licentiousness to him who remains licentious. . . . He Who wisely regulates our life wishes the man who has fallen into sins and then promises to return to a sound life, to separate off the past by a boundary and to make a beginning after his earlier sins as if entering upon a new life through repentance.[57]

In the majority of cases, however, people come to confession and confess the same sins that they confessed before. In other words, confession does not appear to be helping them to improve and to reject their sins. When this happens a person should not abandon confession; on the contrary, he must seek out the sacrament of penance again and again as a salutary medicine. There is a discourse between St Sisoes the Great (fourth century) with a certain monk, which has survived to our time:

> A brother asked Abba Sisoes: "What am I to do, abba, for I have fallen?" The elder told him: "Get up again." "I got up," said the brother, "then I fell again." "Get up again and again," the elder said, so the brother said: "Until when?"

---

[57]St Basil the Great, *Commentary on the Prophet Isaiah*. In St Basil the Great, *Commentary on the Prophet Isaiah,* Nikolai A. Lipatov, trans. *Texts and Studies in the History of Theology*, vol. 7, Wolfram Kinzig and Markus Vinzent, ed. (Mandelbachtal/Cambridge: edition cicero, 2001), 47–48.

"Until you are carried off either in the good or in the fallen state; for a person will go hence in the state in which he is found," the elder said.[58]

Furthermore, as the priest Alexander Elchaninov observes, a person cannot objectively evaluate his own spiritual progress. Frequently he himself does not notice the gradual improvement of the sins he names at confession:

> Our contrition will not be complete if, in repenting, we are not established inwardly in the resolve not to return to the sin confessed. But how is this possible, people ask? How can I promise myself and my spiritual father that I will not repeat my sin? Would not the exact opposite be nearer the truth—a certainty that the sin will be repeated? For every man knows from experience that after a while one invariably returns to the same sins again, and in observing oneself year after year one sees no improvement at all. . . . It would be frightful if this were so. But happily this is not the case. Given a pious desire to improve, regular confession and holy communion never fail to bring about beneficial changes in the soul. But the fact is that, first and foremost, we are not our own judges: a person cannot judge rightly concerning himself, whether he has worsened or improved. . . . Increased strictness with oneself, sharpened spiritual vision, and a heightened fear of sin may give the illusion that one's sins have multiplied and intensified: they are the same, or they may even have weakened, but we did not notice them so much before.[59]

---

[58]*Alphabetical Sayings of the Desert Fathers*, Sisoes, Saying 38. In *Give Me a Word: The Alphabetical Sayings of the Desert Fathers*, Popular Patristics Series 52, John Wortley, trans. (Yonkers, NY: St Vladimir's Seminary Press, 2014), 289–290.

[59]Alexander Elchaninov, *Zapisi* [Notes] (Moscow: Russkiy put', 1992), 123–124.

5

The Sacrament of Holy Orders (Ordination)

W E HAVE ALREADY SPOKEN of the Church as a hierarchal structure, of the meaning of the hierarchal priesthood, and of the three degrees of the ecclesiastical hierarchy.[1] In this section we will examine the history of the origin and development of the sacrament by which a person is elevated to a sacred rank, becoming a member of the hierarchy.

Jacob blessing the sons of Joseph. Book miniature. France. 13th c.

In the Orthodox tradition the sacrament of holy orders is understood to mean three sacred rites: the ordinations to the ranks of deacon, of priest, and of bishop. To these three rites two others are appended: the tonsure of a reader and the appointment of a subdeacon. The rites of elevation to the ranks of protodeacon, archpriest, hegumen, and archimandrite, as well as the order of the enthronement of a patriarch, are likewise contiguous with the sacrament of ordination.

ORDINATION IN THE EARLY CHURCH.
FORMULATION OF THE SERVICE ORDER

Since Old Testament times the laying on of hands[2] has been a gesture through which God's blessing is relayed from one person to another: from elder to younger, from father to son, from teacher to pupil. Jacob laid his hands upon his grandsons Ephraim and Manasseh with the words, "God, before whom my fathers Abraham and Isaac did walk . . . bless the lads . . . and let them grow into a multitude in the midst of the earth" (Gen 48.15–16). By laying his hands upon Joshua the son of Nun, Moses invested him with authority over Israel (cf. Num 27.18, Deut 34.9).

[1]Cf. vol. 4, pp. 455–458.
[2]The Russian word for "ordination," *rukopolozhenie,* literally means "the laying on of hands."—*Trans.*

The laying on of hands is likewise used to elevate a person to the ministry of the priesthood: it was through the laying on of hands that the Levites were dedicated to service to the Lord (cf. Num 8.10).

Jesus Christ used the same gesture when blessing the children (Mk 10.16) and when healing people of their diseases (cf. Mk 8.23, Lk 4.40, Lk 13.13). To his disciples Jesus commanded that they lay hands upon the sick that they might receive healing (cf. Mk 16.18). The apostles likewise employed this gesture for healing: through the laying on of Ananias' hands Paul's sight was restored (cf. Acts 9.12), and through the laying on of hands Paul restored the father of the ruler of Melita (cf. Acts 28.8). The same gesture was used to impart the gift of the Holy Spirit after baptism: by this means Peter and John imparted this gift to the Samaritans (cf. Acts 8.17), and Paul imparted it to the Ephesians (cf. Acts 19.6). The apostles received from God himself the right to impart the Holy Spirit through ordination: this right can be acquired in no other way—for example, by purchasing it for money (cf. Acts 8.18–24).

We do not know whether Christ laid hands upon the apostles when investing them with the ministry of governance and the power "to bind and to loose" (cf. Mt 18.18). What we do know is that the apostles themselves imparted this authority to their successors specifically through the laying on of hands. We first encounter a description of appointment to ministry through the laying on of hands in the account of the election of seven men to "serve tables": these men "they set before the apostles, and when they had prayed, they laid their hands on them" (Acts 6.6). Through the laying on of hands Paul and Barnabas were set apart for the apostolic ministry (cf. Acts 13.3).

Paul himself imparts the gift of the Holy Spirit to his disciple Timothy through the laying on of hands. He mentions this gift twice to Timothy: "Neglect not the gift that is in thee, which was given thee by prophecy, with the laying on of the hands of the presbytery" (1 Tim 4.14). "I put thee in remembrance that thou stir up the gift of God, which is in thee by the putting on of my hands" (2 Tim 1.6). Timothy then in turn lays hands on those whom he elects to ecclesial ministry (cf. 1 Tim 5.22).

Thus, it is through the laying on of hands, or ordination, that the apostolic succession of the hierarchy, the foundation of the Church's existence, is put into effect. Ordination becomes the channel through which the power "to bind and to loose," given by Christ to the apostles, is relayed from one bishop to the next, from generation to generation. And it is apostolic succession of ordination that becomes the primary criterion for determining the authenticity of the Church, its distinction from pseudo-church and pseudo-Christian communities.

As the Church teaches, when an ordination is performed by an apostle or a bishop, God himself is acting: "The hand of the man is laid upon (the person), but the whole work is of God, and it is His hand which toucheth the head of the one ordained, if he be duly ordained."[3] "Due" ordination means an ordination that is performed in observance of the requisite conditions—that is, performed by a canonically appointed bishop for a specific church community.

From the *Apostolic Tradition* of St Hippolytus of Rome we learn how ordination was performed in the Church in the third century. According to this historical document, the person appointed bishop must be "elected by all the people." When his candidacy has been declared and accepted by all, he must come to the church on a Sunday together with the attending bishops and presbyters. There the bishops "by consent of all lay their hands upon him, but let the presbyters stand in silence." All those present must likewise remain silent, "praying at heart, because of the descent of the Spirit." One of the bishops present, placing his hand upon the initiate, says this prayer:

> God and Father of our Lord Jesus Christ . . . grant that your servant, whom you have chosen for oversight, should shepherd your flock and should serve before you as high priest without blame, serving by night and day, ceaselessly propitiating your countenance and offering the gifts of your holy church. And let him have the power of high priesthood, to forgive sins according to your command, to assign duties according to your command, to loose every tie according to the power which you gave to the apostles, to please you in gentleness and with a pure heart, offering you the scent of sweetness. Through your child Jesus Christ, through whom be glory and might and honor to you, with the Holy Spirit in the holy church, now and to the ages of the ages. Amen.[4]

This prayer expounds on the episcopal ministry as a ministry of pastoral care, propitiation, and remission of sins. The core of this ministry is the offering of the holy gifts, that is, the performance of the Eucharist. It is for this reason that the *Apostolic Tradition* prescribes for the newly-appointed bishop to be given the kiss of peace immediately following his ordination, and then for the holy gifts to be

---

[3]John Chrysostom, *Homilies on the Acts of the Apostles* 14 (*NPNF*[1] 11:90).
[4]Hippolytus, *Apostolic Tradition* 3.1–6 (PPS 54:73–74).

offered, and for him to perform his first hierarchal Eucharist in concelebration with the presbyters.

The tradition according to which the newly ordained bishop performs the Eucharist immediately after his ordination survives today in only a few local Orthodox churches, notably the Romanian Church, where even if the patriarch presides over the ordination, immediately after the ordination all the bishops except the newly consecrated withdraw to the high place and stand there until the communion of the holy mysteries, while the newly consecrated bishop performs the Eucharist. In other Orthodox churches the newly ordained bishop takes part in serving the Eucharist together with the other bishops.

The *Apostolic Tradition* likewise contains the rites of the ordination of a presbyter and of a deacon. At an ordination to the rank of presbyter the bishop lays his hand upon the head of the candidate, and the presbyters likewise touch his head along with the bishop. At the ordination of a presbyter the bishop reads this prayer:

> God and Father of our Lord Jesus Christ, look upon this your servant and impart the Spirit of grace and counsel of presbyterate so that he may assist and guide your people with a pure heart, as you looked upon the people of your choice and directed Moses to choose presbyters whom you filled with your Spirit which you gave to your servant. And now Lord, grant that the Spirit of your grace may be preserved unceasingly in us, filling us and making us worthy to minister to you in simplicity of heart, praising you through your child Jesus Christ.[5]

The custom of the presbyters laying their hands upon the initiate along with the bishop survives today in the Roman Catholic Church. In the Orthodox Church it has fallen into disuse, and only the bishop lays his hand upon the one being elevated to the rank of presbyter.

At the ordination of a deacon, according to the *Apostolic Tradition*, only one bishop lays his hand upon the initiate, because "he is not ordained to the priesthood but to serve the bishop and to carry out the bishop's commands." The deacon "does not take part in the council of the clergy; he is to attend to his own duties and to make known to the bishop such things as are needful. He does not receive the Spirit that is possessed by the presbytery, in which the presbyters share; he receives

---

[5]Hippolytus, *Apostolic Tradition* 7.2–4 (PPS 54:96).

only what is confided in him under the bishop's authority. For this cause the bishop alone shall make him a deacon." Here the following prayer is read:

> God who created all things and ordered them by your Word, Father of our Lord Jesus Christ, whom you sent to serve your will and to show us your desire, grant the Holy Spirit of grace and sincerity and diligence on this your servant, whom you have chosen to serve your church and to present in your holy of holies that which is offered to you by your appointed high-priest to the glory of your name, that serving blamelessly and in purity he may be worthy of the rank of his exalted order and praise you through your child Jesus Christ.[6]

We find the next historical record of the rite of ordination to holy orders in the *Apostolic Constitutions*, which dates to the fourth century. Here it is written that a person who is ordained a bishop must be "blameless in all things, a select person, *chosen by the whole people.*" After he has been "named and approved" (this apparently is referring to approval by the other bishops), "let the people assemble, with the presbytery and bishops that are present, on the Lord's day, and let them give their consent." The consent of the people must be affirmed thrice:

> And let the principal of the bishops ask the presbytery and people whether this be the person whom they desire for their ruler. And if they give their consent, let him ask further whether he has a good testimony from all men as to his worthiness for so great and glorious an authority; whether all things relating to his piety towards God be right; whether justice towards men has been observed by him; whether the affairs of his family have been well ordered by him; whether he has been blameless in the course of his life. And if all the assembly together do according to truth, and not according to prejudice, witness that he is such a one, let them the third time, as before God the Judge, and Christ, the Holy Spirit being also present, as well as all the holy and ministering spirits, ask again whether he be truly worthy of this ministry, that so "in the mouth of two or three witnesses every word may be established." And if they agree the third time that he is worthy, let them all be demanded their vote; and when they all give it willingly, let them be heard.[7]

After this "one of the principal bishops, together with two others," stands near the altar, "the rest of the bishops and presbyters praying silently." Here the deacons

---

[6] Hippolytus, *Apostolic Tradition* 8.10–12 (PPS 54:103).
[7] *Apostolic Constitutions* 8.2.4 (ANF 7:481–482).

must hold an open Gospel over the head of the candidate for ordination. The senior bishop reads the prayer of consecration:

> O Thou the great Being, O Lord God Almighty, who alone art unbegotten, and ruled over by none; who always art, and wast before the world; who standest in need of nothing, and art above all cause and beginning; who only art true, who only art wise; who alone art the most high; who art by nature invisible . . . Thou who didst appoint the rules of the Church, by the coming of Thy Christ in the flesh; of which the Holy Spirit is the witness, by Thy apostles, and by us the bishops, who by Thy grace are here present; who hast fore-ordained priests from the beginning for the government of Thy people. . . . Grant by Thy name, O God, who searchest the hearts, that this Thy servant, whom Thou hast chosen to be a bishop, may feed Thy holy flock, and discharge the office of an high priest to Thee, and minister to Thee, blamelessly night and day; that he may appease Thee, and gather together the number of those that shall be saved, and may offer to Thee the gifts of Thy holy Church. Grant to him, O Lord Almighty, through Thy Christ, the fellowship of the Holy Spirit, that so he may have power to remit sins according to Thy command; to give forth lots[8] according to Thy command; to loose every bond, according to the power which Thou gavest the apostles; that he may please Thee in meekness and a pure heart, with a steadfast, blameless, and unreprovable mind; to offer to Thee a pure and unbloody sacrifice, which by Thy Christ Thou hast appointed as the mystery of the new covenant, for a sweet savour, through Thy holy child Jesus Christ, our God and Saviour.[9]

This prayer refers to the Old Testament righteous ones as the forebears of the New Testament clergy. Like the prayer from the *Apostolic Tradition,* the prayer in the *Apostolic Constitutions* expounds on the meaning of the ministry of the bishop as a pastor, a performer of the Eucharist, and one who holds the power "to bind and to loose." This grace-filled "power of the governing Spirit" Christ imparted to the apostles, and now he pours it out upon the bishops through ordinations performed by other bishops.

At the conclusion of the prayer the priests and all the people say, "Amen." The next morning the bishops install the newly ordained bishop upon his cathedra and give him the kiss of peace. Then he blesses the people, gives a sermon, and performs

[8]That is, to ordain members of the clergy (priests and deacons).
[9]*Apostolic Constitutions* 8.2.5 (*ANF* 7:482).

the Eucharist.[10] Thus, in contrast to the *Apostolic Tradition,* in the *Apostolic Constitutions* the newly ordained bishop's performance of his first Eucharist is separated by one day from his ordination.

In addition to the episcopal ordination, the *Apostolic Constitutions* contain the orders for the ordination of a presbyter, deacon, deaconess, subdeacon, and reader. The presbyter, as the manuscript states, is ordained by the bishop "in the presence of the presbyters and deacons" (there is no indication that the presbyters are to lay their hands upon the head of the candidate). Here the following prayer is said:

> O Lord Almighty, our God . . . look down upon this Thy servant, who is put into the presbytery by the vote and determination of the whole clergy; and do Thou replenish him with the Spirit of grace and counsel, to assist and govern Thy people with a pure heart, in the same manner as Thou didst look down upon Thy chosen people, and didst command Moses to choose elders, whom Thou didst fill with Thy Spirit. Do Thou also now, O Lord, grant this, and preserve in us the Spirit of Thy grace, that this person, being filled with the gifts of healing and the word of teaching, may in meekness instruct Thy people, and sincerely serve Thee with a pure mind and a willing soul, and may fully discharge the holy ministrations for Thy people, through Thy Christ, with whom glory, honour, and worship be to Thee, and to the Holy Spirit, for ever. Amen.[11]

At an ordination to the rank of deacon, which is also performed by the bishop, likewise "in the presence of the whole presbytery, and of the deacons," the following prayer is said:

> O God Almighty . . . hear our prayer . . . and "cause the light of Thy countenance to shine upon this Thy servant," who is to be ordained for Thee to the office of a deacon; and replenish him with Thy Holy Spirit, and with power, as Thou didst replenish Stephen, who was Thy martyr, and follower of the sufferings of Thy Christ. Do Thou render him worthy to discharge acceptably the ministration of a deacon, steadily, unblameably, and without reproof, that thereby he may attain an higher degree, through the mediation of Thy only begotten Son.[12]

[10]Ibid., 8.2.5–6 (*ANF* 7:483).
[11]Ibid., 8.3.16 (*ANF* 7:492).
[12]*Apostolic Constitutions* 8.3.17–18 (*ANF* 7:492).

Here the "higher degree" refers to the ministry of the presbyter. Thus, the degree of deacon is perceived as intermediate on the path to that of presbyter.

Not so the degree of deaconess, to which the bishop elevates pious women, saying this prayer: "Do Thou now also look down upon this Thy servant, who is to be ordained to the office of a deaconess, and grant her Thy Holy Spirit, and 'cleanse her from all filthiness of flesh and spirit' [2 Cor 7.1] that she may worthily discharge the work which is committed to her."[13] What exactly constitutes the "work" committed to the deaconess is not mentioned in the manuscript. The ministry of the deaconess has already been discussed above.[14] In essence it was one of the lay ministries, even if in certain eras and certain churches the deaconess was specially appointed by the bishop.[15]

The prayer at the appointment of a subdeacon expounds on the meaning of this ministry as one of assistance at the performance of the Eucharist. In particular, the subdeacon has the right to touch the eucharistic vessels:

> O Lord God, the Creator of heaven and earth, and of all things that are therein; who also in the tabernacle of the testimony didst appoint overseers and keepers of Thy holy vessels; do Thou now look down upon this Thy servant, appointed a sub-deacon; and grant him the Holy Spirit, that he may worthily handle the vessels of Thy ministry, and do Thy will always.[16]

The elevation to the rank of reader, according to the *Apostolic Constitutions,* likewise took place through the laying on of hands, during which the bishop would say this prayer:

> O Eternal God, who art plenteous in mercy and compassions, who hast made manifest the constitution of the world by Thy operations therein, and keepest the number of Thine elect, do Thou also now look down upon Thy servant, who is to be entrusted to read Thy Holy Scriptures to Thy people, and give him Thy Holy Spirit, the prophetic Spirit. Thou who didst instruct Esdras Thy

[13]Ibid., 19 (*ANF* 7.492).

[14]Cf. vol. 4, pp. 454–455.

[15]Epiphanius of Salamis writes, "<It is plain > too that there is an order of deaconesses in the church. But this is not allowed for the practice of priesthood or any liturgical function, but for the sake of female modesty, at either the time of baptism or of the examination of some condition or trouble, and when a woman's body may be bared, so that she will be seen not by the male priests but by the assisting female who is appointed by the priest for the occasion, to take temporary care of the woman who needs it at the time when her body is uncovered." *Against Heresies* 79.3. In *The Panarion of Epiphanius of Salamis, Books II and III: De Fide,* 2nd ed., trans. by Frank Williams (Leiden/Boston: Brill, 2013).

[16]*Apostolic Constitutions* 8.3.21 (*ANF* 7:492–493).

servant to read Thy laws to the people, do Thou now also at our prayers instruct Thy servant, and grant that he may without blame perfect the work committed to him, and thereby be declared worthy of an higher degree.[17]

Here the "higher degree" may be understood to mean the subdiaconate, the diaconate, and the presbytery, toward which the rank of reader is the first step. The ministry of the reader consists of reading holy scripture to the people; the *Apostolic Constitutions* likewise view it as a ministry of prophecy.

The *Apostolic Tradition* and the *Apostolic Constitutions* enable us to picture how elevation to the clerical ranks was performed in Rome in the third century and in Syria in the fourth century. From the fifth century we have the testimony of the author of the *Corpus Areopagiticum*, who describes the rites of the "sacerdotal consecrations" in his work *The Ecclesiastical Hierarchy*. Among the latter the Areopagite lists bishops, presbyters, and deacons. According to the Areopagite, the pattern for the orders for the ordination of bishops, priests, and deacons includes "conducting to the Divine Altar and kneeling—the imposition of the Hierarch's right hand—the cruciform seal—the announcement of name—the completing salutation." A unique feature of the ordination of a bishop is "the placing of the oracles[18] upon the head." The candidate for ordination to the priesthood kneels on both knees before the altar table, while the candidate for ordination to the diaconate kneels on one knee.[19]

> The Hierarch, being led to the Hierarchical consecration after he has bent both his knees before the Altar, has upon his head the God-transmitted oracles, and the Hierarch's right hand, and in this manner is consecrated by the Hierarch who consecrates him with all holy invocations. The Priest, after he has bent both his knees before the Divine Altar, has the Hierarch's right hand upon his head, and in this manner is dedicated by the Hierarch ordaining him with hallowing invocations. But the Leitourgos, after he has bent the one of two knees before the Divine Altar, has upon his head the right hand of the Hierarch who ordains him, being ordained by him with the consecrating invocations used in the ordination of the Leitourgoi. Upon each of them the cruciform seal of the ordaining Hierarch is impressed, and at each ordination the sacred proclamation of name takes place, and the concluding salutation, since every

---

[17] *Apostolic Constitutions* 8.3.22 (*ANF* 7:493).

[18] That is, the Gospel.—*Trans.*

[19] Dionysius the Areopagite, *Ecclesiastical Hierarchy* 5.3. In *The Celestial and Ecclesiastical Hierarchy of Dionysius the Areopagite*, John Parker, trans., 82.

sacerdotal person present, and the Hierarch who ordained, salute him who has been consecrated to any of the aforenamed Hierarchal orders.[20]

Ordination of St Nicholas to the diaconate. Fresco. St Therapon Monastery. Early 16th c.

Kneeling, says the Areopagite, "denotes the submissive approach of the man who draws nigh, who places under God that which is religiously presented." But inasmuch as the rank of deacon is of a supplementary nature, the candidate for ordination to the diaconate kneels on one knee only. Priests kneel on both knees, "because those who are religiously brought nigh by them are not only being purified, but have been religiously perfected by their most luminous instructions into a contemplative habit and power." A hierarch (that is, a bishop) kneels on both knees, and in addition the Gospel is placed upon his head, "as leading, through his office of Hierarch, those who have been purified by the Leitourgoi, and enlightened by the Priests, to the exact knowledge of the things contemplated by them, in proportion to their capacities; and through this knowledge perfecting those who are brought nigh, into the most complete holiness of which they are capable."[21]

According to the Areopagite, the laying on of the bishop's hand symbolizes "the protection of the primal consecrator, by whom, as holy children, they are cherished paternally, whilst it gives them the sacerdotal habit and function, and drives away their opposing powers."[22] In other words, after ordination, those who are ordained (particularly priests and deacons) remain under the patronage of the ordaining bishop. From another perspective, the laying on of hands by the bishop teaches "that all sacerdotal operations are effectual in so far as those who have been consecrated are acting under God, and have Him as Leader in every respect of their own life."[23]

The sign of the cross, which is employed at ordination, "manifests the inaction of all the impulses of the flesh, and the life of Divine imitation which looks

[20]Ibid., 5.2, 81–82.

[21]Dionysius the Areopagite, *Ecclesiastical Hierarchy* 5.3. In *The Celestial and Ecclesiastical Hierarchy of Dionysius the Areopagite*, John Parker, trans., 84–85.

[22]Ibid., 82.

[23]Dionysius the Areopagite, *Ecclesiastical Hierarchy* 5.3. In *The Celestial and Ecclesiastical Hierarchy of Dionysius the Areopagite*, John Parker, trans., 82.

unflinchingly to the life of Jesus, at once manly and most godly, Who has come even to the Cross and death, with a supremely Divine sinlessness, and stamps those who thus live as of the same likeness by the cruciform image of his own sinlessness."[24]

At the ordination of a clergyman—whether bishop, priest, or deacon—the ordaining bishop "calls aloud the name of the consecrations[25] and of the consecrated." This action, states the Areopagite, shows that the candidate "makes manifest the supremely Divine choice—not of his own accord, or by his own favour, leading those who are consecrated to the sacerdotal consecration, but as being moved by God to all the Hierarchical dedications."[26] The ministry of a clergyman must be a divine calling, and it is this calling that the bishop is indicating when he proclaims the name of the candidate and the rank to which he is being elevated.

The kiss of peace (or salutation) given to the newly ordained clergyman, according to the Areopagite, is also symbolic: it indicates "the religious communion of minds of like character, and their loving benignity towards each other, which keeps, by sacerdotal training, their most Godlike comeliness in complete perfection."[27] In other words, the kiss of peace witnesses to the fact that the one who is ordained becomes a member of the brotherhood of those who share the same rank, who must treat him with love and who are his fellow ministers.

The *Barberini Euchologion* contains an account of how ordination to the clerical ranks was performed in eighth-century Byzantium. The ordination of a deacon included the reading of this formula: "The Grace Divine, which always healeth that which is infirm, and supplieth that which is wanting, through the laying-on of hands elevateth the most devout Subdeacon *N.* to be a deacon." The candidate approaches the holy table vested in the phelonion of a reader, and kneels on one knee before the holy table. The bishop makes the sign of the cross over his head thrice, places his hand upon it, and reads the prayer, "O Lord our God, who by thy foreknowledge . . ." This is followed by the great litany, with special petitions for the one being ordained, and the bishop reads the prayer, "O God our Savior. . . ." Upon completion of the prayers the bishop removes the phelonion from the ordainee, puts the orarion on him, gives him the kiss, and entrusts him with the fan, with which he stands at the holy table.

[24]Ibid., 82–83.

[25]The rank to which the candidate is being ordained.—*Trans.*

[26]Dionysius the Areopagite, *Ecclesiastical Hierarchy* 5.3. In *The Celestial and Ecclesiastical Hierarchy of Dionysius the Areopagite*, John Parker, trans., 83.

[27]Dionysius the Areopagite, *Ecclesiastical Hierarchy* 5.3. In *The Celestial and Ecclesiastical Hierarchy of Dionysius the Areopagite*, John Parker, trans., 84.

The *cheirotonia*[28] of a presbyter, according to the Euchologion, follows the same order, with the exception that the candidate kneels on both knees, the two prayers read by the bishop are different, and the newly ordained is robed in priestly vestments.

The rite of ordination to the rank of bishop is marked by the greatest ceremony. During the liturgy, after the trisagion hymn, the senior bishop stands before the holy table. The candidate is led up to him on the right, while on the left the chartophylax (the keeper of documents) hands him a proclamation bearing the words, "By the election and mutual consent of the (senior) most holy metropolitans, the Grace Divine, which always healeth that which is infirm, and supplieth that which is wanting, through the laying-on of hands elevateth the most devout presbyter *N.* to be a bishop. Wherefore, let us pray for him, that the Grace of the All-Holy Spirit may come upon him." This proclamation is read aloud by the senior bishop for all to hear. Then he makes the threefold sign of the cross over the head of the candidate, places the Gospel upon his head, places his hand upon the Gospel, and reads the prayer, "O Master, Lord our God. . . ." At the end of the prayer one of the bishops intones the litany, "In peace let us pray to the Lord," and the other bishops reply, "Lord, have mercy." A second prayer follows, beginning, "O Lord our God. . . ."

After the prayer the senior bishop removes the Gospel from the head of the candidate and places it upon the holy table. He then places the border of his omophorion upon the head of the candidate, saying, "Axios" (Greek, meaning "worthy"), and the clergy echo his exclamation. The ordination ends with the newly appointed bishop being given the kiss of peace. After the epistle reading the newly ordained bishop says, "Peace be unto thee." He is the first of the bishops to commune.

While for the most part the rites of ordination to the diaconate and the presbytery have preserved the same elements that are described by Dionysius the Areopagite and the *Barberini Euchologion*, the order for the ordination of a bishop subsequently increased in complexity in Byzantium and, later, in Russia. The original rite was supplemented with rituals preceding the *cheirotonia* (the naming of the bishop, the hierarchical oath) and following it (the presentation of the crosier).

---

[28]Greek, literally "laying on of hands."—Trans.

APPOINTMENT OF A READER AND A SUBDEACON

In the modern practice of the Orthodox Church the responsibilities of the reader and the subdeacon are ordinarily performed by persons who have not been ordained. However, according to established tradition, the orders of elevation to the ranks of reader and subdeacon must invariably precede ordination to the higher clerical ranks. These rites are most often performed before the beginning of the liturgy at which the candidate will be ordained deacon.

In the ancient Church the reader and the subdeacon were independent minor orders of the clergy. The duties of the reader included reading all the liturgical texts and holy scripture, except for the Gospel. In addition, the reader was the keeper of the sacred books. He was likewise entrusted with lighting the lamps in the altar and the nave; in liturgical processions he would precede all with a lighted oil lamp.

The rank of reader in the ancient Church was a position of honor, and could be given as an award for particular merit or for fortitude in time of persecution. Certain Byzantine emperors were elevated to the dignity of reader (Julian the Apostate notably held this rank prior to his renunciation of Christianity). Many renowned holy hierarchs, including Basil the Great, Gregory of Nyssa, and John Chrysostom, began their ecclesiastical ministry in the position of reader.

As for the rank of subdeacon, as we have seen it is mentioned in the *Apostolic Constitutions,* as well as in other ancient Christian literary works, notably the *Letter to the Antiochenes* ascribed to Ignatius the God-bearer (second century),[29] and in the letters of Cyprian of Carthage (third century). In the ancient Church the subdeacon was assigned various supplementary functions during the divine services. Today, *subdeacon* is the term for those persons who serve during hierarchal services.[30]

The appointment of a reader takes place in the middle of the church before the beginning of the liturgy. The subdeacons lead the candidate out of the altar, and he makes three bows toward the east, then three bows toward the bishop. The bishop signs him with the sign of the cross, lays his hand upon his head, and reads the prayer at the appointment of a taper-bearer: "Array in thy fair and spotless vesture this thy servant who desireth to become a Taper-bearer . . . before thy

---

[29]Ps-Ignatius, *Letter to the Antiochenes* 12 (PPS 49:204). This letter is considered spurious.

[30]That is, in common parlance in the Russian tradition a young, unordained man is often said to serve as "subdeacon" when he assists the bishop with vesting, the dikiri and trikiri, the eagle rugs, etc. Traditionally ordained subdeacons perform these tasks, but the unordained often fulfill this role now (men cannot marry after being ordained a subdeacon, which is one reason why young unmarried men who hope to marry in the future often fulfill these tasks without being ordained).—*Ed.*

holy mysteries." This is because in the ancient Church the reader simultaneously performed the office of a taper-bearer.

Then troparia to the apostles are sung, as well as to the three theologians whom the Orthodox Church venerates as great teachers and hierarchs: Basil the Great, John Chrysostom, and Gregory the Theologian. This indicates that the office of reader is seen as linked to theology and teaching. In the ancient Church readers could preach at the divine services and perform other catechetical functions.

The bishop cuts the hair of the reader in the form of the cross with the words, "In the name of the Father, and of the Son, and of the Holy Spirit." In this instance the tonsure symbolizes his entry into the service of the Church. In the ancient Church when a person joined the clergy it was customary to shave the crown of the head. This custom existed in the West (where it survived until the twentieth century), in Byzantium, and in Russia. To cover the shaven area—in Russia this tonsure came to be called the *gumentso*—in various places different styles of hats were used. In the Russian tradition the *skufia* (in Greek, *skouphos*)[31] became widespread, and was worn at all times by the clergy. The Moscow Council of 1674 decreed, "Protopresbyters and protodeacons, priests in the world and deacons, are obligated to wear skufias, as a sign of their sacred spiritual rank and ordination by the bishop, and upon their heads to have a significant tonsure, called the gumentso, but to leave the hair around the circumference of their heads, as a representation of the crown of thorns that Christ wore."[32]

The tonsure was shaved when a person joined the clergy, specifically at his appointment to the rank of reader. The "order for the appointment of a reader" in one fifteenth-century Slavonic manuscript specifies that, after the bishop has cruciformly cut the hair of the newly appointed reader, one of the clergy shaves the tonsure upon his head.[33] A sixteenth-century reader's appointment certificate states, "That he may have the authority to sing on the kliros, and to say the prokeimena on the ambon, and to read the readings and paremiae and the Apostolos, having his crown tonsured and wearing the short phelonion."[34]

The rite of the tonsure of a reader still vests the one who is ordained in the short phelonion, though readers never subsequently wear the phelonion at the divine

---

[31]A brimless clerical hat, usually black.—*Trans.*

[32]Evgeny Golubinsky, *Istoriya Russokoi Tserkvi* [History of the Russian Church] vol. 1 (Moscow: Krutitskoe patriarshee podvorye, Obshchestvo lyubitelei tserkovnoi istorii, 1997), 579. Emphasis added.

[33]Golubinsky, *Istoriya Russokoi Tserkvi* vol. 1, 579.

[34]A. Neselovsky, *Chiny khirotesiy i khirotoniy* [The Rites of Cheirotonia and Cheirothesia] (Kamenets-Podolsk: 1906).

services. In practice, for the rite of the tonsure a special short phelonion is used, which differs from that of the priest. After vesting the candidate in the phelonion the bishop reads the prayer at the appointment of a reader: "Enable him, with all wisdom and understanding, to exercise the study and reading of thy divine words, preserving him in blamelessness of life."

After this the candidate, turning to face the east, reads a passage from the epistles. After this reading the phelonion is removed from him, and the bishop blesses him thrice. Then he is robed in the sticharion—the robe of a reader. The bishop then gives this brief instruction:

> My son, the first degree in the Priesthood is that of Reader. It behooves thee, therefore, to peruse the divine Scriptures daily, to the end that the hearers, regarding thee, may receive edification; that thou, in nowise shaming thine election, may prepare thyself for a higher degree. For by a chaste, holy and upright life thou shalt gain the favor of the God of loving-kindness, and shalt render thyself worthy of a greater ministry, through Jesus Christ our Lord.

The rite of appointing a reader concludes with the words of the bishop: "Blessed is the Lord. Lo, the servant of God, *N.*, is become a reader of the most holy church of *N.*: In the Name of the Father, and of the Son, and of the Holy Spirit." The reader is given a candle, and he stands holding it during the liturgy.

The appointment to the rank of subdeacon may be performed immediately after the appointment to that of reader. It consists of girding the candidate with an orarion worn crosswise, and the reading of a prayer in which the bishop entreats God: "And grant that he may love the beauty of thy house, stand before the doors of thy holy temple and kindle the lamps in the tabernacle of thy glory." After the prayer the subdeacons give the appointee a washbasin and place a towel upon him. The newly appointed subdeacon pours water upon the bishop's hands and offers him the towel. When the singing of the cherubic hymn begins at the liturgy the newly appointed subdeacon again offers the bishop the washbasin in which to wash his hands.

ORDINATION TO THE RANK OF DEACON

Ordination to the rank of deacon

Whereas the appointments of a reader and a subdeacon are performed in the middle of the church, ordinations to the rank of deacon, priest, and bishop are performed inside the altar, since these offices are linked to the altar and the performance of the sacrament of the Eucharist. However, in view of the fact that the deacon is not the performer of the Eucharist, but merely participates in its performance, when the ordination of a deacon takes place at the liturgy it occurs after the eucharistic canon—specifically, after the words of the bishop: "And may the mercies of our great God and Savior Jesus Christ be with you all."

The ordination to the rank of deacon may be performed not only at a full liturgy (of Basil the Great or of John Chrysostom), but also at the liturgy of the presanctified gifts. In this case it is performed after the great entrance.

To the left of the holy table a cathedra is placed, upon which the bishop sits.[35] Two subdeacons, taking the candidate by the arms with one hand and placing the other hand upon his neck, lead him from the center of the church to the altar. In the altar a deacon exclaims, "Command." Just before the candidate is led into the altar another deacon exclaims, "Command."[36] When the candidate enters the altar the senior deacon exclaims, "Command, Most Reverend Master." The first of the three deacons' exclamations is addressed to the people, the second to the clergy, and the third to the bishop. They have survived in the service order of the ordination of a deacon from the time when the consent of the people, the clergy, and the bishop to the ordination was publically asked.

In the royal doors the candidate is received by the deacons. One takes him by the left arm, the other by the right. The candidate makes a prostration before the bishop, who signs him with the sign of the cross. The deacons lead the candidate around the holy table thrice. Each time the candidate goes around he kisses the four corners of the holy table. After the first time around the holy table the candidate kisses the hand and knee of the bishop; after the second, the bishop's epigonation

[35]In practice a low stool is placed.
[36]In practice the exclamations "Command" are given by the subdeacons.

and hand; and after the third he makes three bows before the holy table (two from the waist and one prostration).

During the procession around the holy table, the clergy in the altar sing the same troparia that are sung at the sacrament of matrimony:

O holy martyrs, who fought the good fight and have received your crowns: Entreat ye the Lord that our souls may be saved.

Glory to Thee, O Christ our God, the apostles' boast, the martyrs' joy, whose preaching was the consubstantial Trinity.

Rejoice, O Isaiah! A Virgin is with child; and shall bear a Son, Emmanuel, both God and man: and Orient is his name; whom magnifying we call the Virgin blessed.

The singing of these troparia signifies that the one being ordained to this ministry is betrothed to the Church, which becomes his bride. At the same time they remind the candidate that the feat of martyrdom is the highest ideal of fidelity, dedication, and self-sacrifice. They are also a reminder of Christ as the foundation upon which the apostles built the Church.

After circling the holy table three times the candidate kneels on one knee to the right of it, laying his hands crosswise upon the corner of the holy table. The bishop rises from the cathedra and lays the hem of his omophorion upon the head of the candidate, blesses him thrice, and places his hand upon his head. The deacon exclaims, "Let us attend," and the bishop says:

The grace divine, which always healeth that which is infirm, and completeth that which is wanting, elevateth, through the laying-on of hands, *N.*, the most devout subdeacon, to be a deacon; therefore, let us pray for him, that the grace of the all-holy Spirit may come upon him.

In the eighteenth and nineteenth centuries these words were considered the "consecratory formula," it being supposed that the candidate was vouchsafed holy orders as they were pronounced. Their origin, however, is rather different: as we have seen, at the ordination of a bishop similar words were written on the document that the chartophylax would hand to the senior bishop at the ordination of a new bishop. This document was read aloud, and only after it had been read would the bishops lay their hands upon the candidate. Thus, it is not the reading of the words "The grace divine . . . ," but rather the prayers that follow it that comprised the sacrament of ordination to the rank of bishop. The same pertains to the other *cheirotonias* in which these words are used—those for a deacon and for a presbyter.

After the above words have been said the bishop reads two prayers, the text of which has existed since the eighth century (in the *Barberini Euchologion*). In the first of these prayers the bishop asks God to preserve the candidate "in all soberness of life," that he might preserve "the mystery of the faith in a pure conscience." The second prayer contains the following petition:

> O God our Savior, who by thine incorruptible voice didst appoint unto thine apostles the law of the diaconate . . . fill also this thy servant, whom thou hast graciously permitted to enter upon the ministry of a deacon, with all faith, and love, and power, and holiness, through the inspiration of thy holy and life-giving Spirit; for not through the laying-on of my hands, but through the visitation of thy rich bounties, is grace bestowed upon thy worthy ones.

While the bishop is reading these prayers the senior deacon begins to intone a litany that includes petitions for the bishop and for him "who hath now received the Laying-on of hands to be a Deacon." The clergy in the altar sing, "Lord, have mercy," while the choir traditionally sings, "*Kyrie eleison.*" The tradition of singing "Kyrie eleison" during a *cheirotonia* survives as a Russian liturgical custom from the time when the bishops in Russia were Greeks.

When the bishop completes the prayers the newly ordained arises: the bishop removes the orarion with which he had been girded crosswise, and lays it upon his left shoulder, saying, "Axios." Then, as the exclamation "Axios" is repeated, the deacon is vested in the cuffs, and at the third "Axios" a fan is placed in his hands. He kisses the bishop's shoulder, stands to the left of the holy table, "and fans the holy gifts," guarding the holy mysteries by fanning them with the fan.

ORDINATION TO THE RANK OF PRESBYTER

The order for the *cheirotonia* of a presbyter shares the structure of the order for the ordination of a deacon. However, it takes place after the great entrance, before the eucharistic canon begins, so that the newly ordained priest might take part in serving the Eucharist. This underscores the role of the priest as a performer of the sacrament. For the same reason the ordination of a presbyter is not performed at a liturgy of the presanctified gifts, at which the Eucharist does not take place.

At the great entrance the candidate goes out with the procession, bearing on his head the aer (the covering for the chalice and diskos). He is led into the altar not by subdeacons, but by deacons, and he is led around the holy table not by deacons, but by presbyters. After processing around the altar three times, he kneels on both knees to the right of the holy table, and the bishop says these words: "The grace divine . . . elevateth . . . N., the most devout deacon, to be a priest. . . ." The litany during the reading of the bishop's prayers is said not by a deacon, but by a priest. Included in the litany are petitions "for our bishop N. of N., his priesthood, succor, maintenance, peace, health and salvation; and for the works of his hands"; "for the servant of God, N., who now hath received the laying-on of hands to the priesthood, and for his salvation"; and "that the God who loves mankind will vouchsafe unto him a pure and blameless ministry."

The first prayer that the bishop reads asks that God preserve the candidate "in purity of life and in unswerving faith," that by his way of life the candidate might be worthy of the great honor of the priesthood. The second prayer contains these words:

> O God great in might and inscrutable in wisdom, marvelous in counsel above the sons of men: Do thou, the same Lord, fill with the gift of thy Holy Spirit this man whom it hath pleased thee to advance to the degree of priest; that he may be worthy to stand in innocence before thine altar; to proclaim the gospel of thy kingdom; to minister the word of thy truth; to offer unto thee spiritual gifts and sacrifices; to renew thy people through the laver of regeneration. That when he shall go to meet thee, at the Second Coming of our great God and Savior, Jesus Christ, thine Only-begotten Son, he may receive the reward of a good steward in the degree committed unto him, through the plentitude of thy goodness.

This prayer contains a list of the primary functions of the priest. First and foremost he is called to stand before the altar (the holy table), performing the eucharistic offering and prayer. He is also called to preach the gospel and to open to men the path into the Church by performing the sacrament of baptism.

When the prayers are completed the bishop removes the orarion from the newly ordained priest and vests him in the epitrachelion,[37] zōnē (belt), and phelonion. In the Russian tradition the newly ordained priest is also given a pectoral

---

[37]Since the epitrachelion is simply an orarion worn around the neck, frequently at the ordination of a priest the orarion is removed from the candidate's shoulder and placed around his neck.

cross and a service book—the book that he will use to perform the divine services. As each vestment and the cross are put on him, and also when the service book is given to him, "Axios" is intoned and sung.

After the newly ordained priest has been vested he receives a blessing from the bishop, and then "he kisses the archimandrites, and all his fellow clergy, on the shoulder," after which he goes and stands next to the senior priest throughout the entire liturgy.

After the consecration of the holy gifts the bishop breaks off the upper part of the holy lamb, bearing the inscription "XC,"[38] places it upon the diskos, and gives it to the newly ordained priest with the words, "Receive this pledge and preserve it whole and intact unto thy last breath, for thou shalt be held to account of it at the second and dread coming of our Lord God and Saviour, Jesus Christ." These words remind the priest of the responsibility entrusted to him by the Church to perform the Eucharist with reverence.

ORDINATION OF A BISHOP

The order for the ordination of a bishop resembles the orders for the *cheirotonia* of a deacon and a priest, but they are performed with considerably greater ceremony. Furthermore, an episcopal *cheirotonia* is preceded by two independent rites—the naming and the hierarchal oath.

The rite of the naming of a bishop is retained from the ancient practice in which a candidate for episcopacy was elected by the clergy and the people, after which he was ceremoniously informed of this and he would give his consent to the ordination. In the modern practice of the majority of local Orthodox churches, a bishop is elected by a general assembly of bishops or by a holy synod. The laity do not take part in the election of a bishop.

In the practice of the Russian Orthodox Church the naming of the bishop takes place in the church separately from the *cheirotonia*, using an order formulated no later than the seventeenth century.[39] The bishops vest in their mantles and seat themselves in the middle of the church in order of seniority. The bishop-elect is

[38]The abbreviation for "Christ" (the first and last letters of *Christos*, as they appear both in Greek and Cyrillic).—*Trans.*

[39]In particular see "The Rite and Order for Election of a Bishop" from the time of Patriarch Adrian, in *Iz tserkovnoi istorii vremeni Petra Velikago. Issledovaniya i materialy* [From Church History in the Time of Peter the Great: Research and Materials] by Viktor Zhivov (Moscow: Novoe literaturnoe obozrenie, 2000), 296–299.

Ordination of a bishop

led to the holy table by two archimandrites. He kisses the holy table, bows to the patriarch (or the presiding bishop, if the patriarch does not take part in the *cheirotonia*), and goes out together with them through the side doors of the altar. All three receive a blessing from the patriarch, then from each of the bishops present.

Next one of the senior presbyters (the secretary of the patriarch) reads aloud the decree of the candidate's election to the episcopal cathedra. The following declaration is made: "Honorable Archimandrite *N.*, His Holiness *N.*, patriarch of *N.*, and the Holy Synod of the *N.* Church, bless your holiness to be a bishop of the God-saved city of *N.*" Naming the city here has profound ecclesiological significance: the episcopal ministry is always linked to a specific city and region, just as the ministry of the deacon and the priest is linked to a specific church. The candidate replies, "I return thanks and accept the blessing of His Holiness *N.*, patriarch of *N.*, and of the Holy Synod of the *N.* Church, that I should be bishop of the God-saved city of *N.*, and I say nothing contrary to it."

A short moleben follows, in which traditionally neither the choir, nor the presbyters, nor the deacons take part: the patriarch intones the litanies and exclamations, while the concelebrating bishops sing. This indicates the "familial" nature of the ceremony: the bishop-elect is joining the family of archpastors—the successors and continuers of the work of the apostles.

The patriarch gives the exclamation, "Blessed is our God," and the bishops read the trisagion prayers. After the exclamation of the patriarch the troparion and kontakion of Pentecost are sung:

Blessed art thou, O Christ our God, who hast revealed the fishers most wise, sending down upon them thy Holy Spirit, and thereby catching the universe as in a net. Glory to thee, O thou who lovest mankind.

When the Most High confounded the tongues, he dispersed abroad the nations: but when he distributed the tongues of fire, he called all men into unity. Wherefore, with one accord, we glorify the all-holy Spirit.

This emphasizes that the election to the episcopal ministry takes place through the agency of the Holy Spirit.

After the bishops have sung the troparion and kontakion the patriarch intones a litany, which includes a separate petition "for the all-honourable Archimandrite N., the newly elected bishop." Then the dismissal is given, and all the bishops sit upon the cathedras prepare for them. The candidate gives a "naming address" in which he lays out his vision for his hierarchal ministry. The naming address comprises the future bishop's plan of action, as it were. At this time he also traditionally expresses his thanks to those who have been instrumental in his spiritual development.

When the candidate has finished his address the bishops rise, and the proto-deacon intones the polychronion[40] for the patriarch and all the bishops present. Then they sit, and the polychronion is intoned for the bishop-elect. Following the polychronion the patriarch sprinkles the candidate with holy water, and the candidate receives a blessing from all the bishops present.

The rite of the hierarchal oath usually takes place before the beginning of the liturgy at which the bishop-elect is to be ordained. This rite is of very ancient origin. It was mentioned in the seventh century by the holy hierarch Sophronius of Jerusalem:

An apostolic and ancient tradition has prevailed in the holy churches of God throughout the whole world, whereby those acceding to the hierarchy frankly refer in all respects to those who have administered the high-priesthood before them, as to how they should think and maintain the faith which the most wise Paul has handed on to them with the utmost safeguards, lest they run their course in vain (1 Cor 9.24).[41]

---

[40]Literally, "many years"—a prayer that God may preserve for many years the persons for whom the polychronion is intoned.—*Trans.*

[41]Sophronius of Jerusalem, *Synodical Letter* 2.6. In *Sophronius of Jerusalem and Seventh-Century Heresy,* Pauline Allen, trans. (New York: Oxford University Press, 2009), 73.

In its main features the rite of the oath used today in the Russian Church is identical to a similar rite from the seventeenth century,[42] translated from the Greek and adapted to local practice. In the beginning of the rite of the oath the bishops participating in the *cheirotonia* exit the altar in full liturgical vestments and go out to the middle of the church, where they take their seats in order of seniority. The priests stand on both sides in order of seniority. Then the protopresbyter (or senior priest) and the protodeacon (or senior deacon) take a blessing from the bishops, enter the altar, and lead out the candidate, vested in priestly liturgical garments. He is placed upon an *orlets,* or eagle rug, that lies facing west, so that he stands at the lower edge of the image. The protodeacon intones, "The God-beloved, elect and confirmed Archimandrite *N.* is led forth for consecration to the bishopric of the God-saved city of *N.*" The patriarch (or presiding bishop) asks, "Wherefore art thou come, and what dost thou ask of our humility?"[43] The candidate replies, "The laying-on hands, unto the grace of the bishop's office, Most Reverend Sirs." The patriarch asks, "And how believest thou?" The candidate reads the Symbol of Faith. When it has been read the presiding bishop blesses him with the sign of the cross, saying, "The grace of God the Father, and of our Lord Jesus Christ, and of the Holy Spirit, be with thee."

The protodeacon again intones, "The God-beloved, elect and confirmed, . . ." and the candidate is placed in the middle of the eagle rug. The patriarch says, "Reveal unto us more particularly how thou believest concerning the properties of the three Persons of the ineffable Godhead, and concerning the incarnation of the Person of the Son and Word of God." The candidate reads a synopsis of the dogma of the faith in the hypostases of the triune God. When he has finished the patriarch blesses the candidate, saying, "The grace of the Holy Spirit be with thee, enlightening, strengthening, and endowing thee with wisdom all the days of thy life."

The protodeacon intones a third time, "The God-beloved, elect and confirmed, . . ." and the candidate stands at the upper edge of the eagle rug. The patriarch says to him, "Declare unto us, also, what thou thinkest concerning the canons of the holy apostles and the holy fathers, and the traditions and regula-

[42]See for example "*Arkhiereiskoe obeshchanie Pavla, igumena Perirvinskogo monastyrya Sv. Nikolaya Chudotvortsa, pri postavlenii v arkhiepiskopy Kolomensokie i Kashirskie 30 aprelya 1676 goda*" ["The hierarchal oath of Paul, hegumen of the Prervinsk Monastery of St. Nicholas the Wonderworker, at his ordination as archbishop of Kolomna and Kashira, from April 30, 1676"], in *Iz tserkovnoi istorii*, Zhivov, 286–293.

[43]By "our humility" the patriarch (or bishop) means himself. This expression, used only in the first person, corresponds to the expressions "Your Holiness" and "His Holiness," used in the second and third person, respectively.

tions of the Church." The candidate pledges to observe the canons of the holy apostles and of the ecumenical and local councils and the rules of the holy fathers, to preserve the traditions and regulations of the Church, to maintain peace in the Church, to submit to the patriarch and the other bishops, and to guide his flock in the fear of God. In the hearing of all the candidate declares that he ascends to the archpastoral ministry not for the sake of silver or gold, but by election of the patriarch and the synod. He promises to do nothing through the coercion of the mighty of this world or of the masses, though he should be threatened with death; not to serve liturgy in another's diocese; and not to ordain clerics for another's diocese or to receive clerics from another's diocese into his own without a certificate of release. The candidate likewise promises "to visit and watch over" the flock entrusted to him, "and to inspect with diligence, and to exhort and inhibit, that there may be no schisms, superstitions and impious veneration, and that no customs contrary to Christian piety and good morals may injure Christian conduct." The candidate promises to deal gently with opponents of the Church, and to be loyal to the authorities of the country ("to be faithful to the authorities of our God-preserved land").

Upon completion of the oath the patriarch blesses the candidate and says, "The grace of the Holy Spirit, through our humility, exalts thee, most God-beloved Archimandrite, *N.*, to be the bishop-elect of the God-saved cities, *NN.*" The candidate bows thrice to the bishops and approaches each for a blessing. Then he signs the text of the oath that he has read and presents it to the patriarch. Taking the oath, the patriarch says, "The grace of the Most Holy Spirit be with thee." The candidate is led into the altar and onto a waiting eagle rug. From that moment on he is considered the "bishop-elect," though he has not yet been ordained.

The actual service for the ordination of a bishop takes place at the divine liturgy after the small entrance and the singing of the trisagion. This point in the liturgy is selected for the *cheirotonia* because after the singing of the trisagion the bishop ascends to the high place, where the newly appointed bishop takes his place among them. Furthermore, the bishop has the power not only to consecrate the gifts, but also to ordain priests and deacons, which accordingly is done after the great entrance and after the eucharistic canon.

During the singing of the trisagion the two senior presbyters lead the candidate out of the altar, stopping in front of the ambon. Then they lead the candidate up to the royal doors, where he is received by the patriarch (or presiding bishop). At the *cheirotonia* of a bishop the one who is ordained does not circle the holy table three times. Instead the candidate removes his miter[44] and phelonion and kneels on both knees directly in front of the holy table, bowing his head upon it. The patriarch blesses his head thrice, after which an open Gospel is placed upon his head, text downward. Upon the Gospel all the bishops present lay their hands. The patriarch says these words: "By the election and approbation of the most God-loving bishops and of all the consecrated council, the grace divine, which always healeth that which is infirm, and completes that which is wanting, through the laying-on of hands elevateth thee, the most God-loving Archimandrite *N.*, duly elected, to be the Bishop of the God-saved cities, *NN.*"

The patriarch then reads a prayer in which he asks God to strengthen the one elected to the episcopal ministry by the inspiration, power, and grace of the Holy Spirit, just as God strengthened the prophets and the apostles, anointed kings to kingship, and consecrated bishops. While the patriarch is reading this prayer one of the bishops reads a litany containing a petition for him who is "now ordained to be a bishop." Those present in the altar sing a threefold "Lord, have mercy." The patriarch reads a second prayer of consecration:

> O Lord our God, who, forasmuch as it is impossible for the nature of man to endure the Essence of the Godhead, in thy providence hast instituted for us teachers of like nature with ourselves, who maintain thine altar, that they may offer unto thee sacrifice and oblation for all thy people: Do thou, the same Lord, make this man also, who hath been proclaimed a steward of the episcopal grace, to be an imitator of thee, the true Shepherd, who didst lay down thy life for thy sheep; to be a leader of the blind, a light to those who are in darkness, a reprover of the unwise, a teacher of the young, a lamp to the world: that, having perfected the souls entrusted unto him in this present life, he may stand unashamed before thy throne, and receive the great reward which thou hast prepared for those who have contended valiantly for the preaching of thy Gospel.

After the prayers have been read, the sakkos, omophorion, cross, panagia, and miter are placed upon the newly consecrated bishop. For each of these items the newly consecrated bishop receives a blessing from all the bishops present, and at each "Axios" is intoned. Following the consecration all the bishops give their newly

---

[44]In the Russian tradition, a priest can receive a miter without a cross on the top as an award (here, the author describes an archimandrite removing his priestly miter before his ordination to the episcopate, after which he receives his bishop's miter). This priestly award does not exist outside the Slavic tradition.—*Ed.*

consecrated brother bishop the kiss of peace and proceed to the high place, to hear the reading of the epistle.

In the practice of the Russian Church, all the bishops present continue to perform the liturgy. The newly consecrated bishop blesses with the dikerion and trikerion[45] after the reading of the Gospel. During the communion of the clergy in the altar the patriarch imparts the body of Christ to them, while the newly consecrated bishop communes them of the holy blood.

When the liturgy is over the newly consecrated bishop receives a blessing to wear the episcopal mantle from all those who participated in his *cheirotonia*. The bishops, already in their mantles, again go out to the center of the church. The newly consecrated bishop goes out last and stands facing his brother bishops who ordained him. The patriarch (or senior bishop) traditionally gives an edifying address, in which he speaks about the meaning of the episcopal ministry. After this he presents the newly consecrated bishop with a staff as a symbol of his episcopal authority. Receiving the staff in his left hand, the bishop blesses the people.

The above rite of the *cheirotonia* of a bishop is essentially identical in all local Orthodox churches. The rites of the naming and of the hierarchal oath also vary only slightly from one church to the next. There are, however, certain liturgical elements peculiar to specific local churches.

In certain local Orthodox churches a special rite is performed following the *cheirotonia*—the enthronement of the newly consecrated hierarch, meaning his installation upon the cathedra belonging to him. If the *cheirotonia* was performed in the city where the bishop will serve, as a rule the enthronement immediately follows the *cheirotonia*. If the *cheirotonia* took place elsewhere, however, the bishop arrives at his diocese accompanied by those who participated in the *cheirotonia* and serves his first liturgy in their presence. Following this first liturgy the bishops install their brother bishop upon the cathedra belonging to him.

In the Russian Orthodox Church this custom is absent, and in the majority of cases the bishop arrives at his cathedra unaccompanied by the other bishops. The first liturgy that he performs in his own cathedral includes no special rituals.

In the Russian Church it is a rare thing for a bishop to be ordained in the city where he will serve. As a rule, bishops for Russia and for dioceses of distant countries are ordained in Moscow; bishops for Ukraine, in Kiev; for Belarus, in Minsk; for Moldova, in Chişinău. The *cheirotonia* is presided over, respectively,

---

[45]Double-branched and triple-branched candlesticks, used when a bishop serves.—*Trans.*

by the patriarch of Moscow and all Russia or by the metropolitan of Kiev and all Ukraine, of Minsk and Slutsk, or of Chişinău and all Moldova.

ELEVATION TO SPECIAL RANKS

As has been said, the rites of elevation to special ranks—protodeacon or archdeacon, archpriest or protopresbyter, hegumen, and archimandrite—are in continuity with the sacrament of holy orders.

The term *archdeacon* appeared in the fourth century to denote senior deacons attached to the church of a bishop. The term *protodeacon* is of later origin, entering into usage about the eighth century.[46] In the Russian Church today a deacon who has served a minimum of twenty years may be awarded the rank of protodeacon. The rank of archdeacon is given as an award to hierodeacons (monk deacons) after twenty years of service; the only archdeacon that is not a monastic is the senior deacon at a patriarchal cathedral. Elevation to the ranks of protodeacon and archdeacon takes place during the divine liturgy, at the small entrance. The one receiving the honorary rank is led up to the bishop, bows to him thrice from the waist, and bows his head. The bishop signs his head thrice with the sign of the cross, then lays his hands upon him and reads the prayer of elevation to the rank of protodeacon or archdeacon (the same prayer is read for both). The prayer having been read, the bishop again signs the head of the one receiving the honorary rank with the sign of the cross and intones, "Blessed is God! Lo, the servant of God, *N.*, becometh an archdeacon (*or* a protodeacon): In the Name of the Father, and of the Son, and of the Holy Spirit. Axios!" The chanters sing, "Axios," and the bishop kisses the newly elevated cleric.

The terms *protopresbyter* and *archpriest* entered into usage about the eighth century. Both signify a senior presbyter. In the Russian Church during the synodal period the rank of archpriest was awarded to distinguished priests from the white (married) clergy, while the rank of protopresbyter was awarded to the rectors of the Dormition Cathedral and the Cathedral of the Archangel in the Kremlin, the court priest (spiritual father to the tsar), and the head of the naval clergy. Today the rank of archpriest is given to priests for special merit or length of service, while the rank of protopresbyter is held by the rector of a patriarchal cathedral. The rite of elevation to the rank of archpriest or protopresbyter takes place in the same

[46]See John of Damascus, *Exposition of the Orthodox Faith* 4.15 (*NPNF*² 9:87b), and Theodore the Studite, *Penances* 1.106 (PG 99:1748B).

manner as the rite of elevation to the rank of archdeacon or protodeacon. The prayer read by the bishop particularly emphasizes that the awardee shall "stand at the head of the priests."

The term *hegumen* (or abbot) in the Greek monastic tradition has always pertained exclusively to the superiors of monasteries. In the Russian Church the rank of hegumen is given as an award to hieromonks, including those who are not the heads of monasteries, but rather are members of a monastic brotherhood or serve in parishes.[47] Nevertheless, the rite of elevation to the rank of hegumen specifically refers to the one who receives this rank as the head of a monastic brotherhood. The first prayer read by the bishop speaks first of the "reason-endowed flock," and only later of him whom God has deigned "to set over it as abbot." The second prayer refers to "the Abbot of this venerable habitation," who must become a wise "steward" of the monastic flock entrusted to him. The text of the rite of elevation to the rank of hegumen states that it is to be performed at the inauguration of a newly elected monastery superior, and not used simply as yet another award for an ordinary monastic cleric.

Conversely, the rite of elevation to the rank of archimandrite is extremely brief, containing no particular prayers. It consists solely of the deacon's exclamation, "Command"; the bishop's words, "The grace of the all-holy Spirit, through our humility, doth promote thee to be archimandrite of the venerable habitation of *N*."; and the singing of "Axios." In the Russian practice a miter is placed on the head of the archimandrite.

In the Russian Orthodox Church there are no rites of elevation to the rank of archbishop and metropolitan. The absence of special rites of elevation to the ranks of archbishop and metropolitan is due to the fact that these rites did not exist in Byzantium, since neither rank was perceived as an award. To this day in the Greek tradition the rank of archbishop or metropolitan depends not on the bishop's person, but on his episcopal see. Thus, a bishop ordained to a metropolitan see is immediately ordained with the title of metropolitan, and likewise one ordained to an archiepiscopal see is ordained with the title of archbishop.

In the Russian tradition there is a special rite of elevation to the rank of patriarch, called the *enthronement*.[48] This rite takes place at the divine liturgy after the

---

[47]In 2011 the Moscow Patriarchate discontinued this award.—*Ed.*

[48]St Moscow, the holy hierarch Job, was appointed to his ministry by an ordination similar to the episcopal cheirotonia. Subsequent patriarchs likewise were elevated to their rank through ordination and enthronement (cf. Makary Bulgakov, *Istoriya Russkoi Tserkvi* [The History of the Russian Church] vol. 6, 40, 90, 278, 316). Later, however, this procedure was abolished, and the Russian Church adopted the Greek

small entrance. Added to the appointed troparia and kontakia for the day are the troparion of Pentecost ("Blessed art Thou, O Christ our God") at the beginning, and the kontakion of Pentecost ("When the Most High descended and confounded the tongues") at the end. After the exclamation "Look down from heaven, O God," the patriarch-elect goes to the high place. Here the two senior metropolitans take his arms: one of them exclaims, "Let us attend," and the other reads aloud, "The grace divine, which always heals that which is infirm, and supplies that which is wanting, sets our father His Holiness *N.*, patriarch of the great city of Moscow and of all Russia, upon the throne of the holy first hierarchs of Russia: Peter, Alexis, Jonah, Phillip, Job, Hermogenes, and Tikhon; in the name of the Father. Amen." At these words the metropolitans seat the patriarch upon the patriarchal throne. Then they raise him, and at the words "And of the Son. Amen" they seat him again. The patriarch is then seated upon the throne a third time with the words, "And of the Holy Spirit. Amen." The senior metropolitan exclaims, "Axios," and the exclamation is taken up by the clergy in the altar and the choir on the kliros.

During the singing of "Axios" the subdeacons remove the miter and sakkos from the patriarch, and the metropolitans give him the patriarchal sakkos, in which he is vested by the subdeacons. Then the patriarch is vested in an omophorion, two panagias, and a cross. The metropolitans then bring the patriarch a miter and place it upon his head. A subdeacon goes to stand to the right of the royal doors with the processional cross; to the left stands a subdeacon with the floor candle (or *primekirion*). One of the bishops stands in the royal doors facing east, and intones a litany with a special petition "for the salvation and intercession of our father His Holiness *N.*, who is now installed as patriarch." Then one of the metropolitans reads this prayer:

> O Almighty Master and Lord of all things, Father of compassions and God of all consolation! Do thou preserve both pastor and flock, inasmuch as thou art the cause of all good things, thou art strength for the infirm, thou art a helper to the helpless, thou art the physician of souls and bodies, O Saviour who art the expectation, the life, the resurrection, and who hast joined us unto all things that are unto our eternal, salvific existence. Thou canst do all things whatsoever thou desirest: deliver therefore, preserve, protect, and compass us. Do thou also, O Lord, bestow upon him who is here present the power and the grace

---

practice of enthronement without ordination, since the rank of patriarch is not a separate holy order: the patriarch is a bishop who has primacy among his brother bishops.

Enthronement of His Holiness Patriarch Kirill

to bind that which ought to be bound, and to loose that which ought to be loosed. And do thou make wise the Church of thy Christ through thy chosen one, preserving it as a comely bride.

Following the prayer the heads or leading representatives of other local Orthodox churches, who are traditionally present for the enthronement of a patriarch, assemble around the holy table. The liturgy then continues according to the usual order. After the dismissal the patriarch divests in front of the holy table. The two senior metropolitans bring the patriarch a green mantle, in which he vests without leaving the holy table. Then, wearing the green mantle, the patriarch goes out onto the solea: one of the metropolitans gives him the white patriarchal cowl; the other, the staff. A speech of welcome is usually given at the presentation of the cowl, and another at the presentation of the staff. The patriarch blesses the people with the staff, saying, "May Christ God preserve you all by his divine grace and love for mankind, always, now and ever, and unto the ages of ages." The metropolitans lead the patriarch to the cathedra, located in the center of the church. Standing on the cathedra, the patriarch blesses in all four directions. Then the patriarch is given a cross, and with it he blesses all those present (once again in all four directions). After this one of the metropolitans brings the patriarch an icon of the Mother of God and gives a speech of welcome, followed by speeches by the heads and representatives of the local Orthodox churches. The newly appointed patriarch concludes the rite by addressing all those assembled.

6

Unction

U NCTION IS A SPECIAL CHURCH SACRAMENT, the purpose of which is to heal a person of illnesses of soul and body. In ancient times it was called by various names: oil, holy oil, anointing with oil, and oil of prayer (from the Greek ευχέλαιον/*euchelaion*). In the Russian vernacular the sacrament is called *soborovanie*, since it is performed by an assembly (*sobor*) of priests. Plant oil, usually olive oil, is use for the sacrament.[1]

OIL AS A RELIGIOUS SYMBOL. FORMATION OF THE SERVICE ORDER

In ancient times oil was one of the primary medicinal substances, and was employed particularly in the treatment of wounds (cf. Is 1.6). Olive oil was used in oil lamps (cf Ex 27.20). Along with wheat and wine, oil was one of the primary food-stuffs (cf. Deut 11.14): an abundance of oil was perceived as a blessing from God (cf. Deut 7.13, Jer 31.12), and a lack thereof as punishment (cf. Mic 6.15, Hab 3.17). As a foodstuff oil goes into a person, entering into his bones (cf. Ps 108.18). Oil was also a cosmetic: it was used to anoint the body and for fragrant rubs (cf. Am 6.6, Esth 2.12, Ps 91.11), and people would oil their hair (cf. Ps 22.5).

A table prepared for the sacrament of unction

In the Old Testament tradition oil was one of the primary religious symbols. Oil was a symbol of healing, salvation, and reunion with God (cf. Ez 16.9). Further-more, it was a symbol of joy (cf. Ps 44.8, 103.15), love (cf. Song 27.9), and brotherly fellowship (cf. Ps 132.2). Oil was a symbol of being chosen by God and of royal

[1]Burdock oil, sunflower oil, and other vegetable oils may also be used.

power, and so it was used to anoint kings and priests (this significance of oil and the symbolism of anointing is discussed above in the context of the sacrament of chrismation). Through anointing with oil (chrism) the Spirit of God was imparted to one chosen by God (cf. 3 Kg 10.1–6, 16.13).

In the Christian tradition oil has become, first and foremost, a symbol of spiritual healing. In this sense it is mentioned particularly in the parable of the Good Samaritan (cf. Lk 10.34). At the same time oil is a symbol of light, appearing in this capacity in the parable of the ten virgins (cf. Mt 25.1–13). The Greek word ἔλεος/*eleos* (mercy) sounds similar to the word ἔλαιον/*elaion* (oil), and so oil was perceived as a symbol of compassion, reconciliation, and joy.

One important aspect of the earthly ministry of Christ was the healing of illnesses, and the Gospel is filled with accounts of the numerous healings that the Savior performed. No instances of Christ using oil for healing are recorded in the Gospel; nevertheless, when he sent his disciples to preach *they went out, and preached that men should repent. And they cast out many devils, and anointed with oil many that were sick, and healed them* (Mk 6.12–13). Thus, in Christ's time oil was already used in the Christian community to heal illnesses.

In the apostolic ministry following Christ's resurrection the healing of the sick held an important place (cf. Acts 3.2–8, 5.15–16, 8.7, 9.32–34, 28.8). In the apostolic era the gift of healing was possessed not only by the apostles, but also by other members of the Christian community (cf. 1 Cor 12.9). Apparently the ministry of healing was one aspect of the work of the presbyters, as evinced by the words of the apostle James: "Is any sick among you? Let him call for the elders of the church, and let them pray over him, anointing him with oil in the name of the Lord; and the prayer of faith shall save the sick . . . and if he have committed sins, they shall be forgiven him" (Jas 5.14–15).

These words of the apostle James are the chief record of the existence of the sacrament of unction in the apostolic era (even if it was not called a sacrament and was not formulated as a separate service order). The primary elements of the sacrament are the participation of several presbyters and anointing the sick person with oil. The power of healing, however, is imputed not to the oil, but to "the prayer of faith." The sacrament must have a dual effect: it must promote physical healing and bestow forgiveness of sins.

Few accounts of this sacrament's existence are found in the works of the Eastern Christian writers of the third to fifth centuries. For example, in speaking about repentance Origen quotes the words of the apostle James about anointing the sick

with oil, but in so doing he replaces the words "pray
over him" with "place their hands on him" (which may
confirm that there was a custom of laying hands on the
sick when anointing them with oil).[2] John Chrysostom
and Cyril of Alexandria quote the words of the apostle
James, but they offer no commentary on them.[3] In
another place Chrysostom mentions those who "have
put away diseases by anointing themselves with oil in
faith and in due season,"[4] but gives no indication of
where and how this anointing took place.

The Antiochian presbyter Victor (fifth century)
wrote in more specific terms:

> James also says the same thing . . . in the Catholic
> Epistle. . . . And the oil also heals pain and is a cause
> of light and a source of cheerfulness. Therefore, the oil
> used in anointing indicates also the mercy that comes
> from God, and the healing of disease, and the illumi-
> nation of the heart, for it is manifest to anyone anywhere that prayer brings
> about everything; and the oil, so I suppose, is a symbol of these things.[5]

*Martyred unmercenaries Cosmas
and Damian. St Bessarion
Monastery. Meteora, Greece.
16th c.*

The silence of the Eastern Christian authors regarding the sacrament of unction
is understood by many researchers to mean, first, that the ancient fathers "had few
occasions to speak of the sacrament of unction, which was imparted not in the
church at a solemn service, but in private homes"; second, that the ancient fathers
of the Church viewed unction either as a supplement to penance (Origen) or as
part of the last rites; and third, "the silence of the fathers of the Church concerning
this sacrament is due to the custom of keeping sacred things secret."[6]

The latter explanation is hardly convincing: the "discipline of secrecy" (*disciplina arcani*) or "secret discipline" (*disciplina arcana*) was employed by a few second-

---

[2]Origen, *Talks on Leviticus* 2.5. Translation in *Origen: Homilies on Leviticus 1–16*, Fathers of the Church
83, Gary Wayne Barkley, trans. (Washington, DC: The Catholic University of America, 1990), 48.

[3]Chrysostom, *On the Priesthood* 3.6; Cyril of Alexandria, *On Worship in Spirit and in Truth* 6.

[4]Chrysostom, *Homilies on the Gospel of Saint Matthew* 32.9 (*NPNF*[1] 10:217).

[5]Victor of Antioch, *Commentary on the Gospel of Mark* 6.13. Translation in *The* Catena in Marcum: *A
Byzantine Anthology of Early Commentary on Mark*, Texts and Editions for New Testament Study 6, William
R. S. Lamb, trans. (Leiden: Brill, 2012), 294.

[6]Venedikt (Alentov), *K istorii pravoslavnogo bogosluzheniya* [On the History of Orthodox Worship]
(Kiev: Izdatelstvo imeni svyatitelya Lva, 2004), 17–18.

and third-century authors with regard to the sacrament of the Eucharist and several other church customs; in the fourth century, however, this sacrament was spoken of quite freely and in detail. There were no grounds therefore for shrouding the sacrament of unction in an aura of silence. A more probable explanation for the silence of Eastern Christian authors regarding unction is that this sacrament was relatively undeveloped in the period under discussion, as well as possibly the fact that it was employed but rarely—only in cases of particularly grave illness.

As for the Western writers of the fifth and sixth centuries, these explicitly mention unction as a sacrament. Pope Innocent I (402–417) mentions "the believing sick, who may be anointed with the holy oil of chrism, or of anointing." Further on, in answer to the question of whether a bishop may perform this anointing, he writes, "There is no reason to doubt the ability of a bishop to do that which a presbyter may certainly perform. The apostle speaks of presbyters because the bishops, limited by their activities, cannot visit all the sick." Finally, Pope Innocent writes of the impermissibility of imparting this sacrament to those who are under an ecclesiastical penance: "But it cannot be administered to penitents, because it is a kind of Sacrament. For how should it be supposed that one kind of Sacrament could be granted to those, who are denied the other Sacraments?"[7]

According to the instructions of the apostle James, the sacrament of unction is to be performed in the home of the sick person ("Is any sick among you? Let him call for the elders of the church"). There are, however, numerous indications that—at least from the fourth century on—the sacrament was also performed in churches. This custom was promoted by the establishment of hospitals next to churches in the sixth and seventh centuries. In the euchologia of the tenth and eleventh centuries the church is specified as the place for the sacrament of unction, and the sacrament itself is linked to the liturgy.[8] Thus, for example, an euchologion from 1027 speaks of seven priests serving the divine liturgy together, and oil being blessed before the liturgy begins. At the liturgy special troparia and readings thematically related to unction are added. The actual anointing of the sick person takes place following the prayer below the ambon.[9]

In certain liturgical manuscripts the sacrament of unction was linked to other services of the daily cycle, particularly vespers and matins. One thirteenth-century manuscript states, "On the same day when unction is appointed, seven presbyters

[7]Innocent of Rome, *Letter* 25.8.11 *To Decentius.* Translation in *The Faith of the Early Fathers, Volume 3,* William A. Jurgens, trans. (Collegeville, MN: The Liturgical Press, 1979), 181.

[8]Venedikt (Alentov), *K istorii pravoslavnogo bogosluzheniya,* 27–30.

[9]Ibid., 180–181.

shall assemble and serve vespers with a panikhida and shall sing a canon. At the conclusion of matins the seven presbyters shall serve the liturgy in different churches, then assemble in a single church, and here they shall perform the order of holy oil."[10]

As the custom of building hospitals next to churches died out in the thirteenth century, the link between unction and the divine services was also severed. The euchologia of the period that followed indicate the church and the home as two possible places for performing the sacrament.[11] Vespers was omitted, but the link with matins remained: the hymns and prayers of matins were mingled with the rite of unction, forming the first part of the service.[12]

The apostle James does not specify the number of presbyters required to serve unction. It is supposed that in the period up to the seventh century the sacrament was performed by three presbyters, and in the seventh and eight centuries seven became customary. In any case, the surviving service orders of the sacrament in the liturgical manuscripts of the ninth and tenth centuries already speak of seven presbyters.[13] Interestingly, the "Order of Holy Oil" in manuscript № 973 in the Sinai Monastery library, dated 1153, which mentions "seven presbyters," also states that "in case of necessity or want of presbyters, two or three perform the sacrament."[14]

We find similar recommendations from Symeon of Thessalonica, in the chapter devoted to the sacrament of unction:

> Others, for want of priests, summon only three; and this should not be censured, because first it is for the sake of the power of the Holy Trinity, and then also in remembrance of the witness and preaching that occurred once through Elias, when he raised the dead son of the woman of Sarepta, having prayed thrice and thrice lain outstretched upon him (cf. 1 Kg 17.21–22). . . . And there must be seven presbyters, according to the ancient custom, or out of necessity less than three, and they speak all that is commanded to say."[15]

---

[10]Alexander Petrovsky, "K istorii posledovaniya tainstva eleosvyashcheniya" [On the History of the Order of the Sacrament of Unction], *Khristianskoe chtenie* 216.1 (1903): 44–59.

[11]Venedikt (Alentov), *K istorii pravoslavnogo bogosluzheniya,* 30–33.

[12]Alexei Dmitrievsky, *Opisaniya slavyanskikh rukopisei, khranyashchikhsya v bibliotekakh pravoslavnogo Vostoka* [A Description of the Slavonic Manuscripts Kept in the Libraries of the Orthodox East] vol. 2 (Kiev–Petrograd, 1895–1917), 164–187, 197–202.

[13]Venedikt (Alentov), *K istorii pravoslavnogo bogosluzheniya,* 33–38.

[14]Dmitrievsky, *Opisaniya slavyanskikh rukopisei* vol. 2, 364.

[15]Symeon of Thessalonica, *On Unction* 283 (PG 155:517AB). [Translated by the present translator.]

It is apparent that although the service order presumes that there are seven presbyters, in reality it has not always been possible to achieve this number, and so three priests could perform the sacrament—in some cases two or even one.

In the West, beginning in the fifth century, it became the practice for the oil to be blessed by the bishop, while the presbyters anointed the sick person with the blessed oil. This practice was affirmed by a series of councils, including the Council of Trent (1545–1563), one decree of which states, "The Church has understood the matter thereof to be oil blessed by a bishop."[16] In the East the blessing of the oil was part of the actual rite of unction: it was performed by the senior of seven (or three) presbyters immediately before anointing the sick person.

In both East and West unction was served for those gravely or even mortally ill. In the East a mortally ill person was anointed in the hope that he would be healed. In the West, however, beginning in approximately the tenth century unction came to be viewed as the last rites for a dying man as he passed over into eternal life. The sacrament was given the name *extrema unction* (Latin, "the last anointing"). A decree of the Council of Trent states, "This unction is to be applied to the sick, but to those especially who lie in such danger as to seem to be about to depart this life: whence also it is called the sacrament of the departing" (*sacramentum exeuntium*).[17]

The Orthodox polemicized against this understanding of the sacrament, insisting that in accordance with the words of the apostle James, and also in accordance with the text of the rite itself, unction must be administered to the sick unto the healing of soul and body. Patriarch Nicephorus II of Constantinople (1260) refutes the opinion that unction may be administered to the dying, citing the words of the service order: "By Thy Spirit descend upon thy servant, that he may walk in Thy laws the remaining time of his life," and again, "Raise him up from the bed of sadness and the couch of suffering."[18]

Only in the twentieth century did the Catholic Church partially renounce the medieval concept of unction as last rites. Concerning unction the current Catechism of the Catholic Church says that it is imparted to those who are "seriously ill" and that it "is not a sacrament for those only who are at the point of death." In the words of the Catechism, "it is fitting to receive the Anointing of the Sick just

---

[16] *The Canons and Decrees of the Sacred and Oecumenical Council of Trent*, session 14, J. Waterworth, trans. (London: Burns and Oates, Ld., 1888), 105.

[17] *The Canons and Decrees of the Sacred and Oecumenical Council of Trent*, session 14, 106.

[18] Nicephorus II of Constantinople, *Against Those Who Say that Extreme Unction Should Be Given to the Dead* (PG 140:808C). [Translated by the present translator.]

prior to a serious operation." It also states, however, that "the fitting time . . . to receive this sacrament" is "as soon as anyone of the faithful begins to be in danger of death from sickness or old age."[19] If it is given to those gravely ill, "even more rightly is it given to those at the point of departing this life."[20] The Catechism clarifies that "in addition to the Anointing of the Sick" the Church offers the Eucharist to one who is dying as a viaticum.[21]

In the Greek Church, beginning in the twelfth century, there was a custom of performing the sacrament of unction for the dying. This custom grew out of a more ancient tradition—that of anointing one who had died with oil as one of the burial rituals. Eastern Christian authors varied in their attitudes toward this custom. In the thirteenth century Patriarch Nicephorus condemned it severely.[22] In the fourteenth century Symeon of Thessalonica exhibited a more lenient attitude toward the custom. Regarding administering unction to the deceased, he noted that "certain bishops forbid [it] as not being relayed in Scripture, while others permit it as being administered for the soul's benefit." Symeon himself held that anointing a deceased person with oil is permissible, but that "this is not the oil that was relayed by the Savior and the apostles" for the healing of the sick: "For the dead oil is offered as an offering and to the glory of God, for the sake of mercy toward the departed and forgiveness [of their sins], just as wax candles, incense, and many other things are offered for them in the churches and the sepulchers."[23]

The spread of the view of unction as a last anointing in the West, and the practice of administering this sacrament to the departed or to healthy people in the East, was facilitated by the fact that the sacrament was performed unto the remission of sins. The writers of ancient times (e.g., Origen, Chrysostom) linked this sacrament with repentance, and at a significantly later period the view of unction as a sort of supplement to confession began to spread. Some surmise that in the sacrament of unction forgotten sins are forgiven. This interpretation, however, does not follow either from the service order of the sacrament or from the theological tradition of the Eastern Church. Forgotten sins are forgiven in the sacrament of confession, as stated above.[24] As for the forgiveness of sins in the sacrament of unction, this is derived not from a need to supplement confession, but rather from

---

[19] *Catechism of the Catholic Church*, 2nd ed. (Washington, DC: USCCB, 2016), 378–379.

[20] Ibid., 381.

[21] Ibid.

[22] See quotes in Venedikt (Alentov), *K istorii pravoslavnogo Bogosluzheniya*, 520–521.

[23] Symeon of Thessalonica, *On Unction* 287 (PG 155:521C). [Translated by the present translator.]

[24] See the section on confession, p. 138.

an awareness of the fact that healing of the soul is no less important than healing of the body: without the former the latter is impossible. For this reason the prayer for healing from sickness is joined to a petition for remission of sins.

Can the sacrament of unction be administered to healthy people? To this question there is no definite answer. On the one hand, the entire service order of the sacrament shows that it is to be administered to one who is gravely ill, whose health and very life are in grave danger. On the other hand, theological and liturgical literature from the tenth century on repeatedly mentions—in one context or another—the possibility of anointing healthy people who are present at the anointing of one who is sick.[25] A Greek manuscript dated 1027 states that the household of a sick person may receive unction together with him.[26] Similar instructions are recorded in Greek and Slavic manuscripts up through the seventeenth century.[27]

In the Orthodox East the concept that unction may be administered to healthy people gave rise to the practice of so-called "general unction," where the sacrament of unction was administered en masse to all who wished. This is a fairly early practice: it existed in the Great Church of Constantinople, and from there it made its way to Russia. In the Greek Church of the seventeenth century this ritual was particularly associated with Great Thursday and Great Saturday. The Russian traveler Arseny Sukhanov, who visited Jerusalem in the mid-seventeenth century, described in detail the "general unction" that was performed in Jerusalem on Great Saturday:

> At the third hour of the day the patriarch left the church and entered his court-yard, as did all the others. And having come to his own house, and tarried in his cell, he went to the emperor Constantine[28] to bless oil for select people who contribute the most, and there he anointed them, closeted in the church. Then he blessed oil in his patriarchal cathedral porch, and all the authorities and priests, monks and other laymen here were anointed; and when he anointed anyone that person would give him an *efimok*,[29] some half of one; and the deacon stood near him with a tray, and they would place the money in the tray he held. After this all the worshippers were given a candle each, and for each candle an *efimok* was collected for the patriarch. After this, though some did so

---

[25] Archbishop Veniamin (Krasnopevkov), *Novaya skrizhal'* [New Tables], 16th ed. (Saint Petersburg: I.L. Tuzov, 1899), 383–384.

[26] Dmitrievsky, *Opisanie slavyanskikh rukopisei* vol. 2, 1018.

[27] Venedikt (Alentov), *K istorii pravoslavnogo bogosluzheniya*, 75–76.

[28] That is, to the church in Constantinople.

[29] A monetary unit.

before, they would come to the patriarch in his cell to confess their sins, monks and laymen, nuns and women. In the Great Church the church was filled with all kinds of people, and here the metropolitan blessed oil and anointed all comers, Arab Christians, men, women, and infants.[30]

Despite the fact that accounts of the practice of administering the sacrament of unction to healthy people and the practice of "general unction" are encountered fairly early, neither custom can be considered to be in keeping with the meaning of the sacrament. Furthermore, if a priest anoints himself before anointing a sick person, this does not mean that he is simultaneously administering the sacrament of unction to himself. His doing so may be explained by the widespread perception in the Orthodox Church (reflected in the words of the service orders of several sacraments) that administering a sacrament to a particular member of the Church may also benefit the one who administers it. The same should be said regarding anointing the household of the sick person: the members of his household may be anointed with blessed oil once before administering the sacrament to the sick person, or conversely at the end of the sacrament. Here the anointing signifies the blessing of the Church (similar to that given at the anointing with oil at the all-night vigil), and not the administering of the full sacrament of unction to each person present.

The Meaning and Content of the Sacrament

In Christianity illness is understood to be a consequence of sinful human nature: illness of the body is inseparably linked with the sinful state of the soul.[31]

The link between illness and sin is established in the Bible itself, according to which illnesses entered the life of man as one consequence of the fall into sin (cf. Gen 3.16–19). Frequently illness has been perceived as the punishing right hand of God (cf. Job 16.12, 19.21). On the other hand, illness may be sent to a person through the agency of Satan (cf. Job 2:7). In the Old Testament illnesses were perceived as punishment for sins; consequently, prayer for healing was accompanied by confession of sins (cf. Ps 37.2–6, 38.9–12). The Old Testament does not prohibit consulting physicians or taking medicine (cf. 2 Kg 20.7, Tob 11.10–11, Jer 8.22), but

---

[30] *Proskinitariy Arseniya Sukhanova* [The Proskinitaria of Arseny Sukhanov], 84.
[31] This is discussed in greater detail in vol. 2, p. 143.

it is sinful to consult physicians without simultaneously trusting to God's help (cf. 2 Chr 16.12).

One book of the Bible contains an entire ode to physicians and their art: "Honor a physician with the honor due unto him for the uses which ye may have of him, for the Lord hath created him. For of the Most High cometh healing, and he shall receive honor of the king. . . . The Lord hath created medicines out of the earth, and he that is wise will not abhor them. . . . Then give place to the physician, for the Lord hath created him: let him not go from thee, for thou hast need of him" (Sir 38.1–2, 4, 12). On the other hand, this same book speaks of the necessity of turning to God in prayer in times of illness and offering repentance for one's sins: "My son, in thy sickness be not negligent, but pray unto the Lord, and he will make thee whole. Leave off from sin, and order thine hands aright, and cleanse thy heart from all wickedness" (Sir 38.9–10).

The New Testament joins the Old Testament in acknowledging Satan's role as one of the causes of illness in men: of the woman who was bent over Jesus said that "Satan hath bound" her (Lk 13.16). Nevertheless, in the New Testament sin is declared to be the chief cause of illness. For this reason when healing people Jesus simultaneously remitted their sins (cf. Mt 9.2, Mk 2.5, Lk 5.20) and warned them against repeating their former sins (cf. Jn 5.14). This indicates the insufficiency of healing the body without treating the soul.

Christian tradition expounds on the question of the link between sin and illness in considerable detail. In answer to the disciples' question regarding the man who was born blind—"Who did sin, this man, or his parents, that he was born blind?"—Christ answered, "Neither hath this man sinned, nor his parents, but that the works of God should be made manifest in him" (Jn 9.2–3). In this instance the "works of God" are the miraculous healing that Christ performed. However, as Cyril of Alexandria emphasizes, it must not be thought that the man could have been born blind so that Christ might be glorified through his healing: "The man was not born blind on account of his own sins or the sins of his parents; but since it has happened that he was so affected, it is possible that in him God may be glorified."[32] In other words, the glory of God may be manifested not only in healing, but in the illness itself.

In the Christian understanding, a particular illness may result from a particular sin, but in many instances it is in no way related to a specific sin and is not caused by it. There are congenital illnesses for which a person cannot possibly be personally

[32]Cyril of Alexandria, *Commentary on the Gospel According to Saint John* vol. 2, 6:15.

responsible. Christianity does not hold a person personally responsible for his own illnesses, but it does speak of the responsibility of mankind and of each individual for mankind's common sinfulness, which is the cause of illnesses for every man.

The correlation between sin and illness can present in different ways. Barsanuphius and John of Gaza say that sometimes an illness directly results from certain sins: "Illnesses that occur through negligence or disorder are natural. . . . It is up to you to be neglectful or prodigal and to fall into those, until you reach the point of correction."[33] In other instances illness is sent from God as a punishment for sin—"for our benefit, in order that we might repent."[34] Certain illnesses are produced by "bile," that is, by physiological causes, while others are "of the demons."[35] Finally, "illness is also there to tempt us, and the temptation is there to test us."[36]

The Christian teaching on illnesses is reflected in one of the *Alphabetical Chapters* ascribed to Symeon the New Theologian.[37] Here it is said that illness is the result of corruption, which has affected the whole nature of man:

> Illness is nothing other than the loss of health. And since illness has become natural, it is natural that it does not change. Think, therefore, what tremendous power is required for what is natural, that is, the illness, to be changed into what is supernatural (that is, health). . . . Physicians who treat men's bodies . . . can by no means heal the chief natural illness of the body, that is, corruption, but they strive by numerous and varied means to restore the dysfunctional body to its former state. It however falls into yet another illness. . . . For example, the physician attempts to heal the body of dropsy . . . or of pleurisy, but not of corruption, because the body is corruptible by nature.[38]

Thus, illnesses insinuated themselves into human nature as a result of corruption, and corruption appeared due to sin. Hence the question of the author of the *Chapters*: if the treatment of secondary infirmities requires so much effort, what supernatural power must be needed to heal the primary illness of human

[33]Barsanuphius and John, Letter 521. In *Barsanuphius and John: Letters* vol. 2, *Fathers of the Church* vol. 114, John Chryssavgis, trans. (Washington, DC: The Catholic University of America Press, 2007), 117.

[34]Ibid.,

[35]Ibid., Letter 517 (Chryssavgis, p. 115).

[36]Ibid., Letter 613 (Chryssavgis, p. 198).

[37]For more on the *Alphabetical Chapters* see *Simeon Novyy Bogoslov i pravoslavnoe predanie* [Symeon the New Theologian and Orthodox Tradition] by Metropolitan Hilarion (Alfeyev), 2nd ed. (Saint Petersburg: Aleteiya, 2001), 43–44.

[38](Pseudo-)Symeon the New Theologian, *Alphabetical Chapters* 7. In Εὑρισκόμενα. Σελ./*Evriskomena. Sel.*, 53–54. [Translated by the present translator.]

nature—corruption? This power, replies the author, is the Lord Jesus Christ, the Godman. Every man who believes in him and communes of his grace receives true health.[39]

The Christian understanding of how a person must endure illnesses has a three-fold dimension. First, in ancient ascetic writings and hagiographic literature one encounters numerous indications that illnesses must be endured, being sent from above: "The bed of sickness can be a place of where one comes to know God. The sufferings of the body are frequently the cause of spiritual delights."[40]

Second, Christian writers, echoing the Bible, not only do not prohibit consulting physicians, but even extol the medical profession. Gregory the Theologian calls medicine "the result of philosophy and laboriousness."[41] He considers this art "wonderful," emphasizing that "it treats of physiology and temperament, and the causes of disease, in order to remove the roots and so destroy their offspring with them."[42]

Third, in the Christian hierarchy of values, God, being the "Physician of souls and bodies," is superior to every physician, and the healing of soul that God bestows is superior to the treatment of bodily infirmities.

It is in light of this understanding that the prayer for remission of the sufferer's sins occupies so important a place in the sacrament of unction. The sacrament may not produce healing of the illness, but it invariably produces remission of sins. This is witnessed both by the very service order of the sacrament and by many authors, particularly Symeon of Thessalonica:

> For every believer who wishes to approach the dread mysteries, especially for anyone who has fallen into sins and fulfilled the rule of repentance, and is preparing for communion and has received forgiveness from his (spiritual) father, his sins are remitted through this sacred ritual and the anointing with holy oil, as the brother of the Lord writes; and the prayers of the priests likewise facilitate this.[43]

> Having sinned, we approach the divine men and, offering repentance, make confession of transgressions; at their command we offer oil to God as a sign of

---

[39]Ibid., 7. In Εὑρισκόμενα. Σελ./Evriskomena. Sel. 54. [Translated by the present translator.]

[40]St Ignatius (Brianchaninov), Pis'ma k miryanam [Letters to Laity], 506.

[41]Gregory the Theologian, Orations 43 (NPNF[2] 7:403).

[42]Gregory the Theologian, Orations 7 (NPNF[2] 7:231).

[43]Symeon of Thessalonica, Answers to Gabriel of Pentapolis (PG 155:932CD). [Translated by the present translator.]

His mercy and compassion, in which shines the divine and gentle light of grace; for we too offer light.[44] When the prayer is made and the oil is blessed, those anointed with oil receive remission of sins, like unto the harlot who anointed the Savior's feet and from them received the anointing upon herself.[45]

Although the text of the sacrament of unction consists primarily of prayers for the healing of the sick person, this sacrament, as Protopresbyter Alexander Schmemann notes, does not guarantee healing. Nevertheless, the spiritual rebirth that this sacrament is able to produce is of no less importance—and may indeed be more important—than the healing of physical illnesses:

> A sacrament—as we already know—is always a *passage*, a *transformation*. . . . And healing is a sacrament because its purpose or end is not *health* as such, the restoration of physical health, but the *entrance* of man into the life of the Kingdom, into the "joy and peace" of the Holy Spirit. In Christ everything in this world, and this means health and disease, joy and suffering, has become an ascension to and entrance into this new life, its expectation and anticipation. . . . [I]n Christ suffering is not "removed"; it is transformed into victory. The defeat *itself* becomes victory, a way, an entrance into the Kingdom, and this is the only true *healing*. . . . Through his own suffering, not only has all suffering acquired a meaning, but it has been given the power to become itself the sign, the sacrament, the proclamation, the "coming" of that victory; the defeat of man, his very *dying*, has become a way of Life.[46]

The Service Order of Unction

The modern service order for the sacrament of unction is the fruit of many years of evolution. Its basic structure was formed by the eighteenth century: it includes the blessing of oil, the reading of a canon, seven readings from the epistles and seven from the Gospel, and the anointing of the sick person.

The rite of unction in the modern Book of Needs is titled "The Office of Holy Unction, Sung by Seven Priests Assembled in a Church, or in a House." It is prefaced by the following remark: "A small table is prepared, upon which is set

---

[44]An allusion to the lighting of lamps at the beginning of the rite.

[45]Symeon of Thessalonica, *On the Sacraments* (56) (PG 155:205BC). [Translated by the present translator.]

[46]Alexander Schmemann, *For the Life of the World: Sacraments and Orthodoxy*, St Vladimir's Seminary Press Classics 1 (Yonkers, NY: St Vladimir's Seminary Press, 2018), 123–125.

a vessel containing wheat: and on the wheat an empty shrine-lamp. And round about are set seven wands, wrapped with cotton for the anointing, and thrust into the wheat: and the book of the Holy Gospels lieth there also, and tapers are given to all the priests." Here the "empty shrine-lamp" refers to a votive lamp containing no oil. Apparently it is presumed that oil will be poured into it later, when it is to be blessed. In practice a votive lamp or other vessel filled with oil is placed upon the table at the outset.

The use of a votive lamp in the sacrament of unction is due to the custom of using the same oil with which the oil lamps are filled.[47] The significance of the wheat is not entirely clear: possibly it is linked to the blessing of the "wheat, wine, and oil" at matins, and is a holdover from the era when unction was included as part of one of the services of the daily cycle.[48] The wands for anointing are usually short wooden (or metal) rods. In ancient times the priest would anoint with his finger,[49] but later practice found this means somewhat inconvenient.

The first part of the service order is comprised of an abbreviated matins service: it includes the reading of Psalms 142 and 50, a small litany, the singing of "Alleluia," and the troparia "Have mercy on us, O Lord, have mercy on us," as well as a canon, exapostilarion, and stichera. This canon bears the superscription "A Song of Arsenius," which in all likelihood ascribes authorship to the holy hierarch Arsenius, archbishop of Kerkyra (Corfu), who lived in the ninth century.[50] The sick person is referred to here as "sorely suffering," in need of healing of soul and body, and of deliverance "from terrors and pains."[51]

After the canon an exapostilarion is read, which implies that the anointing is to take place in church: "In mercy, O Good One, cast thine eyes upon the petitions of us who today are come together in thy holy temple, to anoint thy sick servant with thine oil divine." Then special stichera are sung in which healing is asked for the sick person. Next this troparion follows: "Thou who alone art a speedy succor, O Christ, manifest thy speedy visitation from on high upon thy sick servant; deliver him from his infirmities, and cruel pain; and raise him up again to sing praises unto thee, and without ceasing to glorify thee."

Next the great litany is intoned, with additional petitions that the oil may be blessed and that the grace of the Holy Spirit may come upon the sick person. The

[47]Venedikt (Alentov), *K istorii pravoslavnogo bogosluzheniya*, 90–95.
[48]Ibid., 106–107.
[49]Ibid., 95.
[50]Ibid., 215–216.
[51]From evils and illnesses.

priest pours wine into the lamp containing the oil and reads the prayer of blessing of the oil, "that it may be effectual for those who shall be anointed therewith, unto healing, and unto relief from every passion, every malady of the flesh and of the spirit, and every ill."

Prayers for the blessing of oil have been known in the Church since the earliest centuries. The first such prayer is found in the *Apostolic Tradition,* which likewise mentions that the use of blessed oil must be "unto the healing" of those who receive it (this refers to receiving it internally, that is, consuming it as food):

> If anyone offers oil he <the bishop> shall render thanks in the same manner as for the offering of bread and wine, not saying it word for word, but to the same effect, saying: O God, sanctify this oil: grant health to all who are anointed with it and who receive it, and as you anointed kings, priests, and prophets, so may it give strength to all who consume it and health to all who are anointed with it.[52]

Concerning adding wine to the votive lamp containing the oil, mention of this custom is made in liturgical manuscripts dating back to the twelfth century. Apparently wine served as a reminder of the good Samaritan, who poured oil and wine upon the man who was wounded (cf. Lk 10.34).

Next the troparion "Thou who alone art a speedy succor" is repeated once again, followed by other troparia along the same lines, as well as troparia and kontakia to certain saints—the apostle James, St Nicholas, the great martyr Demetrius, the great martyr Panteleimon, all the holy unmercenaries, the apostle John the Theologian, and the Most Holy Theotokos. These particular saints were selected since the apostle James was the first Christian author to mention anointing the sick with oil, while St Nicholas, the great martyrs Demetrius and Panteleimon, and the unmercenaries are all venerated as wonderworkers and healers.

Following the troparia the rite itself begins, in which seven priests are to take part by turns. Consequently the rite consists of seven parts: each part includes a prokeimenon, an epistle reading, and a Gospel reading; a litany for the recovery of the sick person and for the forgiveness of his sins; and a separate prayer to which a second prayer, read at each of the seven parts, is appended. This common prayer begins with these words:

---

[52]Hippolytus, *On the Apostolic Tradition* 5.1–2.

O holy Father, Physician of souls and bodies, who didst send thine Only-begotten Son, our Lord Jesus Christ, which healeth every infirmity and delivereth from death: Heal thou, also, thy servant, N., from the ills of body and soul which do hinder him, and quicken him, by the grace of thy Christ. . . .

This prayer mentions the Most Holy Theotokos, John the Forerunner, the apostles, martyrs, and venerable fathers, and also the holy unmercenaries by name—Cosmas and Damian, Cyrus and John, Panteleimon and Hermolaus, Sampson and Diomedes, Photius and Anicetus.

The epistle and Gospel readings are not related thematically, but rather comprise two parallel selections on the theme of healing and forgiveness of sins. These two selections of readings center on the concepts of Christ as the Physician of infirmities of soul and body, the link between healing and repentance, Christian mutual aid, and compassion and love.

The first epistle reading is a passage from the epistle of James, which describes the anointing of the sick with oil (Jas 5.10–16). The second reading (Rom 15.1–7) describes Christian solidarity: the strong must bear the infirmities of the weak. The third reading (1 Cor 12.27–13.8) describes various gifts in the Church, including the "gift of healings," and speaks of love as an all-encompassing gift without which the other gifts are meaningless. The fourth reading (2 Cor 6.16–7.1) speaks of Christians as the temple of the living God and of the necessity of cleansing oneself from all impurity of flesh and spirit. The fifth epistle reading (2 Cor 1.8–11) reminds us that God has the power to deliver a person from death. The sixth reading (Gal 5.22–6.2) contains the teaching on the gifts of the Holy Spirit, and an admonition to Christians to correct one who has sinned in a spirit of meekness and to bear one another's burdens. Finally, the seventh reading (1 Thess 5.14–23) contains an exhortation to warn those who are unruly, to comfort the fainthearted, to help the weak, and to be longsuffering toward all, not rendering evil for evil and always seeking good, always rejoicing, praying continually, and giving thanks for all things.

The first Gospel reading is the parable of the Good Samaritan (Lk 10.25–37), the symbolism of which formed the basis for the sacrament of unction. The second reading (Lk 19.1–10) recounts the Lord's visit to the house of Zacchaeus the publican: this reading apparently shows unction in the home to be a visit from the Lord to one who is ailing. The third reading (Mt 10.1, 5–8) recounts how Christ gave the apostles the power "to heal all manner of sickness and all manner of disease." The fourth Gospel reading (Mt 8.14–23) relates how the Lord healed Peter's mother-in-

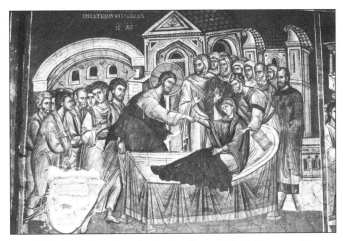

The healing of Peter's mother-in-law. Fresco. Dečani, Kosovo. 14th c.

law and others who were ill. The fifth reading (Mt 25.1–13) contains the parable of the ten virgins: characteristically, the parable employs the symbolism of oil. The sixth Gospel (Mt 15.21–28) tells of how Christ healed the possessed daughter of the Canaanite woman. The seventh Gospel passage (Mt 9.9–13) recounts how Christ called the tax collector Matthew, and contains Christ's words: "They that be whole need not a physician, but they that are sick." The true Physician is Christ, Who came "not to call the righteous, but sinners to repentance" (Lk 5.32).

The first priestly prayer, read by the senior presbyter, resembles the beginning of the anaphora at the liturgy of Basil the Great in its subject matter. Like the anaphora, it begins by addressing God the Father: "O thou who art without beginning, eternal, the Holy of Holies, who didst send down thine Only-begotten Son to heal every infirmity and every wound, both of our souls and bodies. . . ." In this prayer the priest asks God to send down the Holy Spirit and sanctify the oil, that for him who is anointed it might be "unto perfect remission of his sins, and unto inheritance in the kingdom of heaven."

The prayer read by the second priest resembles the first prayer in its content. It begins with a request for healing for the sufferer, followed by numerous reminders of God's mercy and of God's love for sinners. The prayer concludes with a petition that the sins of the person receiving the sacrament may be forgiven.

The third and fourth prayers differ little from each other in content. Both contain a request that the sufferer be healed of his bodily infirmity.

The fifth prayer stands out from the other prayers read by the priests during the sacrament of unction. In its mood and content it resembles the prayer "No one who is bound"[53] from the liturgies of Basil the Great and John Chrysostom. It speaks of the Eucharist as the central aspect of the priestly ministry. From beginning to end, his entire ministry is eucharistic, and every sacrament is linked with the Eucharist. For the priest the liturgy is a source of inspiration, and he "delights" in serving it. But the Lord has not called the priest for his own personal delight. Through the liturgy the priest becomes a mediator for the people, whom God sanctifies through the sacraments performed by the priest. The grace of the priesthood, like the gift of healing, cannot be the fruit of personal merit; for, as the same prayer goes on to say, "like unto cast-off rags is all our righteousness in thy presence" (cf. Is 64.6). Hence, in this prayer the priest reminds God of his mercy, through which the sufferer is able to be healed both in spirit and in body.

In the sixth prayer, in addition to praying for the remission of the sufferer's every sin, the priest prays for himself and all those present for the sacrament. Further on in the same prayer the priest asks God to free the sufferer from eternal torment, to fill his mouth with glorification, to direct his hands unto good works and his feet to the path of preaching the gospel, and to strengthen his mind and all his bodily members by grace.

The seventh prayer of the sacrament of unction is reminiscent of one of the prayers at the sacrament of confession. It refers to repentance and liberation from the curse that may perhaps be hanging over the person.

Upon completion of the seven prayers an open Gospel book, supported by all the priests, is laid upon the head of the sick person. The senior priest reads the following prayer:

> O holy King, compassionate and all-merciful Lord Jesus Christ, Son and Word of the living God, who desirest not the death of a sinner, but rather that he should turn from his wickedness and live: I lay not my sinful hand upon the head of him who is come unto thee in iniquities, and asketh of thee, through us, the pardon of his sins, but thy strong and mighty hand, which is in this, thy Holy Gospels, that is now held by my fellow-ministers, upon the head of thy servant, N. And with them I, also, beseech and entreat thy merciful compassion and love of mankind, which cherisheth no remembrance of evil, O God.

---

[53]The prayer of the cherubic hymn.—*Trans.*

. . . Do thou, the same Lord, receive also with thy wonted tender love towards mankind, this thy servant, *N.*, who repenteth him of his sore transgressions.

Before the beginning of this prayer the modern Book of Needs contains the following remark: "The principal priest, taking the book of the Holy Gospels, and opening it, shall lay it, with the writing down, on the head of the sick person, the book being held by all the priests. And the principal priest doth not lay on his hand." This remark apparently proceeds from a literal interpretation of the words, "I lay not my sinful hand." These words, however, may also be understood differently: "I lay not my sinful hand upon the head of him who is come unto thee in iniquities, but thy strong and mighty hand." These words would be entirely fitting for the priest to say while laying on his own hand.

That the laying on of hands was one means of healing the sick is affirmed by the Gospel, in the account of how Christ "laid his hands upon a few sick folk, and healed them" (Mk 6.5). Another passage relates how all who had sick people in their homes brought them to Jesus, "and he laid his hands on every one of them, and healed them" (Lk 4.40). Jesus likewise healed the woman who was bent over by laying his hands on her (cf. Lk 13.13). Following the Savior's example, the apostles healed people through the laying on of hands (cf. Acts 9.17–18, 28.8).

There is indisputable proof that the laying on of hands was once a part of unction.[54] Over time, however, this was replaced with placing the open Gospel upon the head of the sick person. Here the Gospel symbolizes the hand of God, which is able both to scourge and to heal. The priest asks that the mighty right hand of God be a source of healing and forgiveness of sins for the sufferer.

The service ends with a short augmented litany, the singing of the troparia to the unmercenaries and the Theotokos, and the dismissal, at which St James, the first bishop of Jerusalem, is commemorated. After the dismissal the recipient of the sacrament addresses the priests with the words, "Bless me, holy fathers, and forgive me, a sinner."

[54]Venedikt (Alentov), *K istorii pravoslavnogo bogosluzheniya*, 144–147.

7

Marriage

ACCORDING TO THE TEACHING of the Orthodox Church, matrimony is a voluntary union between a man and a woman, established for the purpose of forming a family, for the bearing and upbringing of children. The marital union is blessed by the church through a special sacrament. The service order of this sacrament is called marriage or matrimony.

The purpose of this chapter is not to examine the moral and canonical aspects of the marital union from an Orthodox perspective. Our purpose here is more narrow—to examine the Orthodox understanding of marriage as a sacrament based on the service of matrimony.

MARRIAGE AS A SACRAMENT

The teaching on marriage as a sacrament is derived from the words of the apostle Paul, that Christian marriage must resemble the union between Christ and the Church: as the Church is subject to Christ, so also wives must be subject to their husbands; as Christ loved the Church and gave himself for it, so also husbands must love their wives. Of this love Paul says, "This is a great mystery: but I speak concerning Christ and the church" (Eph 5.21–33). Here the term *mystery* (μυστήριον/*mystērion*) is used, which also means "sacrament"; many centuries later this would form the basis of the teaching on marriage as a sacrament. To be sure, the term is used not concerning the marital union, but "concerning Christ and the Church." Furthermore, as we have noted above, neither in Paul's time nor throughout the entire first millennium was this term used exclusively in the sense of a liturgical service. Nevertheless, it was the apostle Paul who formulated the ideas upon which the Christian understanding of marriage were founded, and it is he who played a fundamental role in the formation of the concept of the sacramental nature of marriage.

God bringing Eve to Adam. Mosaic.
Cathedral of Monreale. Sicily. 12th c.

This concept was a continuation and an extension of the Old Testament teaching on marriage. The Bible says that God "created man in his own image, in the image of God created he him; male and female created he them" (Gen 1.27). The creation of man was not the creation of an individual: it was the creation of two persons, united by the bonds of love. Upon creating man and woman, the Bible relates, God "blessed them, and called their name Adam, in the day when they were created" (Gen 5.2). Once again, man is not a unity, but a duality: man is "they," not "he" or "she." The fullness of mankind is realized in the marital union between a man and a woman, and the Bible emphasizes this over and over again.

The account in the book of Genesis concerning the creation of Eve from Adam's rib begins with God's words: "It is not good that the man should be alone" (Gen 2.18). The marital union is part of the Creator's original plan for man. Two must become one flesh in marriage (cf. Gen 2.24), in order that by a shared life, an inseparable union, they might carry out God's plan for themselves. The goal of the marital union is twofold. First, it is the mutual love of the husband and the wife: "Therefore shall a man leave his father and his mother, and shall cleave unto his wife" (Gen 2.24). Second, it is the bearing of children, or reproduction: "Be fruitful, and multiply, and replenish the earth" (Gen 1.28). Both commandments were given before the fall, and both must be carried out in the marital union designed by the Creator.

After the fall into sin, as with all other aspects of human existence, a sinful aspect was introduced into marital relations. The sexual attraction between a man and a woman became not only a source of blessing, but also a cause of sin. This gave rise to the need to codify the law of marriage, and to establish rules for establishing marital unions. The Old Testament legislation concerning marriage was intended not so much to secure the happiness and prosperity of the spouses as to ensure the stability of Israelite society and the propagation of God's chosen people. In other words, personal welfare was secondary to the welfare of society.[1] This gave rise to the levirate law (cf. Deut 25.5–10, Mt 22.23–33) and the prohibition against intermarriage with other nations (cf. Deut 7.1–4). This also gave rise to legalized polygamy. All these institutions obscured the original ideal of marriage as being "of one flesh," as a mystical, indissoluble union between husband and wife.

And yet this ideal permeates the whole of the Old Testament. The model for this kind of marriage was the first human couple—Adam and Eve. God created them for each other, giving them to each other without their having any choice in the matter. And they accepted each other as a gift from God, without doubts or uncertainty. Together they lived in the garden of Eden, together they found themselves exiled from paradise, together they began a life in the land of exile, together they raised their children, and together they endured the death of Abel and the other tribulations that fell to their lot. They passed away and, according to the teaching of the Orthodox Church, found themselves in hades. In the Orthodox icon of the "Descent into Hades" Christ is depicted leading up from hades both of these people, who had remained true to each other both in Eden and in Sheol, in joy and in sorrow. They lived together, died together, and were resurrected together. This is not two different life stories, but the shared story of two people who were united for all time.

In the Old Testament there are many other examples of marital unions distinguished by mutual love and blessed by God with abundant progeny. The "patriarchs" of the people of Israel—Abraham, Isaac, and Jacob—were married men, and their wives played an important role in their fate. With each of them God concluded a covenant, but putting this covenant into effect was possible only with the help of their wives, since the chief aspect of the covenant was specifically the bestowal of progeny.

The love between a man and a woman is extolled in the Song of Songs, which retains its literal meaning despite the numerous allegorical interpretations in both Jewish and Christian traditions. "Love is strong as death" (Song 8.6), proclaims this immortal book, extolling the ideal of love and marital fidelity in classic poetic language.

In the pre-Christian Greco-Roman tradition we find a completely different understanding of marriage. Here marriage is perceived not as a sacrament, but as voluntary cohabitation on a contractual basis:

---

[1] *Slovar' bibleiskogo bogosloviya* [Dictionary of Biblical Theology], Xavier Léon-Dufour, ed. (Brussels: Zhizn' s Bogom, 1990), 103.

The famous principle of Roman law, specifying that "marriage is not in the intercourse, but in the consent" (*nuptias non concupbitus, sed consensus facit*), and the definition popularized by Modestus that "cohabitation with a free woman is marriage, and not concubinage" . . . are the very basis of civil law in all modern civilized countries. The essence of marriage lies in the consent which, in turn, gives meaning and legal substance to the marriage *agreement*, or *contract*. . . . As a legal contract, whose subjects were only the parties involved, marriage did not need any third party to give it legal validity. The State, however, provided facilities for the registration of marriage agreements. Registration implied control over their conformity with the laws and provided ready material for the courts, when the latter were to rule on conflicts connected with individual marriages.[2]

The members of the early Christian Church were subject to Roman civil legislation, and so the marriage laws were fully applicable to them. In all that concerned the legal aspects of marriage, Christians followed the civil laws. Christian writers accepted Roman legislation as a given and did not dispute it. Addressing the Roman emperor Marcus Aurelius, the second-century apologist Athenagoras of Athens wrote, "Each of us [reckons] her his wife whom he has married according to the laws laid down by us."[3] John Chrysostom likewise cites "civil laws" that say marriage "arises from nothing other than habit."[4]

Nevertheless, from the very beginning the Church insisted that a marriage made according to the civil laws must be sanctified by the blessing of the Church. The hieromartyr Ignatius the God-bearer wrote in the second century, "It is proper for those men and women who are marrying to form their union with the consent of the bishop, so that their marriage may be in accordance with the Lord and not out of desire."[5] The blessing of a bishop or priest is likewise mentioned by many authors of the third and fourth centuries, notably Tertullian, Basil the Great, Gregory the Theologian, and Ambrose of Milan:

> Marriage . . . the Church cements, and the oblation confirms, and the benediction signs and seals; (which) angels carry back the news of (to heaven).[6]

[2]Meyendorff, *Marriage: An Orthodox Perspective* (Crestwood, NY: St Vladimir's Seminary Press, 2000), 16–17.

[3]Athenagoras of Athens, *A Plea for the Christians* 33 (*ANF* 2:146).

[4]John Chrysostom, *Homilies on Genesis* 56. In *Homilies on Genesis 46–67*, The Fathers of the Church 87, Robert C. Hill, trans. (Washington, DC: The Catholic University of America Press, 1992), 122.

[5]Ignatius the God-bearer, *Epistle to Polycarp* 5.2 (PPS 49:103).

[6]Tertullian, *To His Wife* 2 (*ANF* 4:48).

"Husbands love your wives" [Eph 5.25]. Although formed of two bodies you are united to live in the communion of wedlock. May this natural link, may this yoke imposed by the blessing, reunite those who are divided.[7]

Art thou not yet wedded to flesh? Fear not this consecration; thou art pure even after marriage. I will take the risk of that. I will join you in wedlock. I will dress the bride.[8]

The marriage ceremony itself ought to be sanctified by the priestly veil and benediction.[9]

Certain fourth-century fathers of both East and West speak of marriage as a sacrament. Addressing those who hold noisy, extravagant weddings, John Chrysostom asks, "Why do you publically dishonor the honorable sacrament of marriage?" And he offers a blueprint for a Christian wedding:

All this ought to be anathema . . . and priests summoned to strengthen the harmony of the union by prayers and blessings so that the love for her spouse may be increased and the maid's continence may be heightened. Thus by every means the practice of virtue will enter that home and all the devil's wiles will be kept away, and they will enjoy their life together by God's grace.[10]

The western writer Zeno of Verona (fourth century) says that "the conjugal love of two people through the venerable sacrament unites two into one flesh."[11] Blessed Augustine emphasizes that "in the marriage . . . the sanctity of the Sacrament is of more avail than the fruitfulness of the womb."[12] Augustine states that "in the Church . . . not only the bond, but also the sacrament of marriage"[13] is offered.

Of the testimony cited above, it would appear that only Zeno speaks of the sacrament as a church service. In all other cases the term *sacrament* or *mystery* apparently refers to the marital union itself. In the following passage John Chrysostom refers specifically to the marital union as "a great mystery":

[7]Basil the Great, *The Hexaemeron* 7 (*NPNF²* 8:93).

[8]Gregory the Theologian, *Orations* 40 (*NPNF²* 7:365).

[9]Ambrose of Milan, *Letters* 19, H. Walford, ed., in *A Library of Fathers of the Holy Catholic Church* (Oxford: James Parker and Co., and Rivingtons, 1881), 45:116.

[10]John Chrysostom, *Homilies on Genesis* 48 (Hill, p. 40).

[11]Zeno of Verona, *On Faith, Hope, and Love* 4. [Translated by the present translator.]

[12]Augustine of Hippo, *On the Good of Marriage* 21 (*NPNF¹* 3:408).

[13]Augustine of Hippo, *On Faith and Works* 7. Translation in *Treatises on Marriage and Other Subjects*, The Fathers of the Church 27, Marie Liguori, trans., Roy J. Deferrari, ed. (New York: Fathers of the Church, Inc., 1955), 232.

For indeed, in very deed, a mystery it is, yea, a great mystery, that a man should leave him that gave him being, him that begat him, and that brought him up, and her that travailed with him and had sorrow, those that have bestowed upon him so many and great benefits, those with whom he has been in familiar intercourse, and be joined to one who was never even seen by him and who has nothing in common with him, and should honor her before all others. A mystery it is indeed. And yet are parents not distressed when these events take place, but rather, when they do not take place; and are delighted when their wealth is spent and lavished upon it. A great mystery indeed! and one that contains some hidden wisdom.[14]

FORMATION OF THE SERVICE ORDER OF MATRIMONY

The sacrament of matrimony was shaped over the course of many centuries on the basis of three independent elements: the rite of placing wreaths on the heads of the bridal couple, the blessing of those entering into wedlock by the bishop, and the groom and the bride communing together.

In the Greco-Roman tradition a crown of flowers or leaves was a symbol of victory, a reward for military achievement, a token of merit or dignity. In the Christian tradition the crown is a symbol of victory over sin, of martyrdom, and of glory. The Bible mentions wreaths of flowers that were used at feasts (cf. Is 28.1, Ezek 23.42). A gold crown with precious stones was a symbol of royal power in Israel (cf. 2 Sam 1.10, 12.30, 2 Kgs 11.12, Song 3.11). Figuratively the wreath and the crown served as a symbol of intelligence and wisdom (cf. Prov 1.9, 4.9).

In the Christian tradition a crown of thorns became a symbol of Christ as King and Martyr (cf. Mt 27.29, Mk 15.17, Jn 19.5). The epistles speak of a crown of life (cf. Jas 1.12, Rev 2.10), a crown of glory (cf. 1 Pet 5.4), a crown of righteousness (cf. 2 Tim 4.8), and an incorruptible crown (cf. 1 Cor 9.25) as the reward that those who believe in Christ will receive from the Lord upon completing the contest of this life. The symbolism of the crown plays an important role in the Revelation of John the Theologian, where the crown is particularly interpreted as a symbol of the eschatological glory of the righteous (cf. Rev 4.4, 10) and Christ's victory over evil (cf. Rev 6.2, 14.14). The crown is depicted in this sense on ancient Christian headstones, on the walls of catacombs, and, later, on the walls of above-ground churches, over depictions of apostles and martyrs.

[14]John Chrysostom, *Homilies on Ephesians* 20 (*NPNF*[1] 13:146).

The placing of crowns upon the heads of the bridal couple was an ancient pagan tradition, mentioned in particular by Tertullian.[15] Gradually this custom became Christianized. In the sixth century a church wedding was performed at the marriage of an emperor, but this did not become the general practice. By the ninth century the church wedding was a widespread custom. During this period, however, the liturgical rite of matrimony was not set apart as an independent sacrament, but was performed along with the Eucharist. This is affirmed in particular by Theodore the Studite, according to whom the wedding was marked by a brief prayer by the bishop "before all the people" during the liturgy. Theodore cites the text (or rather, a part of the text) of this prayer:

> Do thou, O master, stretch forth thy hand from thy holy dwelling and unite thy servants and thy creation. Send down to them thy single union of minds; crown them as one flesh; make their marriage honorable; preserve their bed undefiled; vouchsafe that their mutual life might be blameless.[16]

Similar texts intended to be read during the liturgy are also found in liturgical manuscripts of the same period (for example, the *Barberini Euchologion*).[17]

From a theological standpoint, the link between marriage and the Eucharist, of which Chrysostom himself spoke, is of extraordinary importance. Symeon of Thessalonica writes that after the singing of "One is holy, one is Lord" the priest "gives Communion to the bridal pair. . . . For Holy Communion is the perfection of every sacrament and the seal of every mystery."[18] According to Nicholas Cabasilas, the Eucharist is "the celebrated marriage by which the most holy Bridegroom espouses the Church as His Bride," by which "we become 'flesh of His flesh, and bone of His bones' (Gen 2.21)."[19] As Protopresbyter John Meyendorff notes in his commentary on these words, all the sacraments of the Church "are 'completed' in the Eucharist," which "is itself a wedding feast."[20] It is the Eucharist that is the fullest manifestation of Christ's love for his bride, the Church. In this sense the Eucharist serves as an icon, a model of ideal Christian marriage, established in accordance with the teaching of the apostle Paul.

---

[15]Tertullian, *The Chaplet* 13–14 (*ANF* 3:101–102).

[16]Theodore the Studite, *Letters* 1.22 (PG 99:973CD). [Translated by the present translator.]

[17]Meyendorff, *Marriage: An Orthodox Perspective*, 21.

[18]Symeon of Thessalonica, *Against the Heresies and on the Divine Temple*, 282 (PG 155:512–513), as quoted by Meyendorff in *Marriage: An Orthodox Perspective*, 112.

[19]Cabasilas, *The Life in Christ* 4, 123–124.

[20]Meyendorff, *Marriage: An Orthodox Perspective*, 22.

The separation of matrimony from the Eucharist into an independent service, according to Meyendorff, is linked to changing civil legislation concerning marriage in the early tenth century. In his *Novella 89* the Byzantine emperor Leo VI "The Wise" (912) proclaimed that a marriage not blessed by the Church "would not be considered a marriage," and would be considered unlawful concubinage. Whereas previously marriages had been given legal status by secular law, this prerogative now passed to the Church. This meant that the Church now had the obligation to afford this status not only to marriages made in compliance with Christian morality, but also to those that contradicted it:

> The new situation, in principle, gave the Church an upper hand over the morals of all citizens; but in practice, since these citizens were not all saints, the Church was obliged not only to bless marriages which it did not approve, but even to "dissolve" them (i.e., give "divorces"). The distinction between the "secular" and the "sacred," between fallen human society and the Kingdom of God, between marriage as a contract and marriage as sacrament, was partially obliterated.[21]

The fact that the Church acquiesced to the necessity of recognizing marriages that did not comply with its teachings, according to Meyendorff, was a compromise between the Church and the secular authorities. "The only compromise which the Church could not accept, however, was to mitigate the holiness of the Eucharist." The Church could not admit to communion persons whose marriage contradicted the ecclesiastical ideal (particularly those twice or thrice married and marriages to non-believers). This created a need for a marriage ceremony that was not directly linked to the Eucharist and did not culminate in the spouses communing. In this ceremony the eucharistic chalice was replaced by a cup of ordinary wine that was merely symbolic: the spouses drank from it as a sign of their fidelity to each other.[22]

Meyendorff's view on the influence of emperor Leo the Wise's *Novella 89* on the formation of the sacrament of matrimony is one that many modern academics do not share. "An analysis of sources clearly shows that in its chief aspects the rite of holy matrimony had been formed long before Emperor Leo VI, and is found in earlier liturgical manuscripts." In particular, by the eighth century the rite of the church wedding included the crowning, communion of the holy mysteries, and

[21]Ibid., 27.
[22]Meyendorff, *Marriage: An Orthodox Perspective*, 28.

partaking of wine from a common cup.[23] Thus, communion and partaking of wine were two distinct actions.

Along with the extra-eucharistic order of matrimony, however, marriage rites that were incorporated into the liturgy continued to exist right up to the fifteenth century.[24] The link between matrimony and the liturgy remains in the modern marriage service. Many of its elements testify to its original inclusion as a part of eucharistic worship. The order of matrimony begins with the exclamation used at the liturgy, "Blessed is the kingdom." The great litany is taken from the liturgy. The structure of the order of matrimony resembles the structure of the Eucharist. Like the liturgy, matrimony includes epistle and Gospel readings. As at the liturgy before communion, at the order of matrimony the prayer "Our Father" is sung (or read) before the common cup of wine.

THE BETROTHAL

The modern service of the sacrament of holy matrimony consists of two parts: the betrothal and the crowning. In this the sacrament of matrimony resembles the sacrament of baptism, which also consists of two separate service orders (the making of the catechumen and the baptism proper), and the Eucharist, which has two parts (the liturgy of the catechumens and the liturgy of the faithful). In practice the betrothal and the crowning take place on the same day, but they may also occur at different times, since these sacred rituals differ in significance. The betrothal takes place in the narthex of the church, while the crowning takes place in the nave.

In Byzantium and in Old Russia the betrothal was a separate ritual that took place several months or even several years before the marriage service. By the fifteenth century, however, the betrothal had become a part of the sacrament of holy matrimony. The Slavonic word *obruchenie* (betrothal) is a translation of the Greek word ἀρραβών/*arrabōn* (earnest or pledge), and is related to the word *obruch* (ring). The chief action performed during the betrothal is the exchange of rings, symbolizing a pledge of the future spouses' fidelity to each other.

---

[23]Mikhail Zheltov, *"Venchanie braka"* [The Crowning of Marriage], in *Pravoslavnaya Entsiklopediya* [Orthodox Encyclopedia] vol. 7 (Moscow: Tserkovno-nauchniy tsentr "Pravoslavnaya entsiklopediya," 2004), 661–668.

[24]Alexander Katansky, *Dogmaticheskoe uchenie o semi tserkovnykh Tainstvakh v tvoreniyakh drevneishikh otsov i pisatelei do Origena vklyuchitel'no* [Dogmatic Teaching on the Seven Sacraments of the Church in the Works of the Ancient Fathers and Writers Through Origen] (Saint Petersburg: Publishing House of F.G. Eleonsky, 1877), 112, 116.

Unlike the crowning, the betrothal begins with the exclamation "Blessed is our God" (this exclamation commences the services of vespers, matins, and the hours). This is followed by the great litany, to which petitions are added for those entering into wedlock—that they may be granted children, that upon them may be sent down "perfect and peaceful love, and succor," that they might preserve oneness of mind and steadfast faith, that they might be blessed with a blameless life, and that they might be granted "an honourable marriage, and a bed undefiled." Two prayers are read:

> O eternal God, who hast brought into unity those who were sundered, and hast ordained for them an indissoluble bond of love; who didst bless Isaac and Rebecca, and didst make them heirs of thy promise: Bless also these thy servants, *N.* and *N.*, guiding them unto every good work. . . .

> O Lord our God, who hast espoused the Church as a pure Virgin from among the Gentiles: bless this Betrothal, and unite and maintain these thy servants in peace and oneness of mind. . . .

The betrothal of the groom to the bride is performed using a trinitarian formula: "The servant of God, *N.*, is betrothed to the handmaid of God, *N.*: In the Name of the Father, and of the Son, and of the Holy Spirit. Amen." The same formula is used for the betrothal of the bride to the groom ("The handmaid of God is betrothed to the servant of God"). At this point the priest puts a rings on the couples' fingers. The groom and the bride exchange rings thrice.

Then the priest reads a prayer explaining the symbolism of the wedding rings:

> O Lord our God, who didst accompany the servant of the patriarch Abraham into Mesopotamia, when he was sent to espouse a wife for his lord Isaac; and who, by means of the drawing of water, didst reveal unto him that he should betroth Rebecca: Do thou, the same Lord, bless also the betrothal of these thy servants, *N.* and *N.*, and confirm the word which they have spoken. Establish them in the holy union which is from thee. For thou, in the beginning, didst make them male and female, and by thee is the woman joined unto the man as a helpmeet, and for the procreation of the human race. Wherefore, O Lord our God, who hast sent forth thy truth upon thine inheritance, and thy covenant unto thy servants our fathers, even thine elect, from generation to generation: Look thou upon thy servant, *N.*, and upon thy handmaid, *N.*, and establish

and make stable their betrothal in faith, and in oneness
of mind, in truth and love. For thou, O Lord, hast
declared that a pledge should be given and confirmed
in all things. By a ring was power given unto Joseph
in Egypt; by a ring was Daniel glorified in the land
of Babylon; by a ring was the uprightness of Tamar
revealed; by a ring did our heavenly Father show forth
his bounty upon his son; for he saith: Put a ring on his
hand, and bring hither the fatted calf, and kill it and
eat, and make merry. . . . Wherefore, O Lord, do thou
now bless this putting-on of rings with thy heavenly
benediction: and let thine angel go before them all the
days of their life.

*Abraham's servant meeting
Rebecca by the well. Mosaic.
Cathedral of Monreale.
Sicily. 12th c.*

The prayer expresses the idea that God himself is the arranger of the marriage.
This idea is based on the patristic teaching that the marital union is a miracle and
a gift from God: "I have heard the Scripture say: Who can find a valiant woman?
[Prov 31.10] and declare that she is a divine gift, and that a good marriage is brought
about by the Lord."[25] As if to affirm this thought, the prayer cites numerous biblical
examples of God's blessing upon marital unions.

The first of these examples is taken from the book of Genesis: this is the account
of how Abraham sent his servant to find a wife for his son Isaac. This lengthy and
moving bible story (cf. Gen 24.1–61) is mentioned here as an example of a marriage contract. For the betrothal is nothing less than a marriage contract, in which
the spouses pledge fidelity to each other. And the Church asks God to ratify this
contract ("confirm the word which they have spoken") and to establish the future
spouses in faith, oneness of mind, truth, and love. It is these four virtues that must
become the foundation upon which the house of the Christian marriage will be
built.

The next series of biblical references comprises a number of diverse themes,
each of which features a ring—as a sign of power (cf. Gen 41.42, Dan 5.29), a personal effect (cf. Gen 38.18, 25),[26] or a symbol of restoration of the lost dignity of
sonship (cf. Lk 15.22). In ancient times the ring was not so much an ornament as
it was a symbol of authority. The ring was used as a signet for sealing documents,

---

[25]Gregory the Theologian, *Orations* 18 (*NPNF*[2] 7:256).

[26]The Bible mentions a signet (a small seal), bracelets, and a staff. In the Septuagint the term *signet* is
rendered as δακτύλιον/*daktylion* (ring). In ancient times the ring was used as a seal.

contracts, and wills. Like a signature, a ring belonged to a specific person. To give one's ring to someone meant to entrust that person with one's authority. To leave a ring in the hands of a person was to leave material evidence of one's presence and connection with that person (this could show either trust or extreme carelessness). The exchange of rings signifies the spouses' mutual responsibility for each other, fidelity to each other, and ownership of each other.

The prayer of betrothal is followed by the augmented litany, into which petitions for the betrothed are inserted. The rite of betrothal ends with the small dismissal, which is frequently omitted if the betrothal is immediately followed by the crowning.

The betrothal may be served apart from the crowning if the future spouses are not yet ready to actually establish a family, but are already firm in their desire to live with each other in wedlock. In this case the betrothal is a pledge of mutual fidelity, and the period between the betrothal and the crowning serves as a time of preparation for marriage.

THE CROWNING

The rite of the crowning is preceded by the singing of Psalm 127, which describes God's blessing upon a pious family. Appended to the psalm verses is the refrain, "Glory to thee, our God, glory to thee." During the singing of the psalm the groom and bride, led by the priest, process from the narthex into the nave.

The priest then asks the groom a question: "Hast thou, *N.*, a good, free, and unconstrained will and a firm intention to take unto thyself to wife this woman, *N.*, whom thou seest here before thee?" After he answers in the affirmative, the priest asks, "Thou hast not promised thyself to any other bride?" The groom replies in the negative. The bride is asked analogous questions. This questioning is necessary so that those entering into marriage might publically attest that there are no obstacles to their marriage. Only on these grounds may the crowning be performed.

The priest then intones the exclamation, "Blessed is the kingdom." The great litany is said, to which petitions are added for those being united to each other in the community of marriage and for their salvation; that their marriage might be blessed, as once in Cana of Galilee; and that they might be granted "chastity and of the fruit of the womb as is expedient for them," the joys of parenthood, a blameless life, and all things necessary for salvation.

The litany is followed by the first prayer of the rite of the crowning, in which the priest speaks of the creation of Adam and Eve, of how they were blessed to "be fruitful and multiply," and of how the two will be one flesh. Examples are cited of God's favor toward marital unions: God's blessing upon Abraham and Sarah, who begat Isaac; the blessing upon Joseph and Asenath, who begat Ephraim and Manasseh; the blessing upon Zechariah and Elisabeth, who begat John the Baptist; the birth of the Ever-Virgin "from the root of Jesse" and how she bore the Savior of the world. The prayer recalls that Christ came to the marriage in Cana of Galilee, that he might show lawful marriage and childbearing to be God's will. In the prayer the priest asks that the Lord descend upon the groom and the bride and bless their marriage, and vouchsafe them a peaceful life, length of days, chastity, love for each other in the bond of peace, "long-lived seed" (many generations of descendants), and "gratitude from their posterity" (consolation in their children). The priest asks God to bestow upon the spouses "a grown of glory which fadeth not away," to vouchsafe them to see their grandchildren, to preserve their bed "unassailed" (blameless), and to fill their house with the good things of this earth, that they might be able to share them with all those who are in need.

The conception of John the Forerunner (salutation of Zechariah and Elisabeth). Icon. Veliky Novgorod. Late 15th–early 16th c.

In the prayer that follows God is called the "Priest" of mystical and pure marriage, the Ordainer of the law of the marriage of the body, the Preserver of immortality, and the Provider of the good things of this life. Once again the prayer recalls the creation of Eve from Adam's rib, after which the priest asks God to send down grace upon the bridal couple and to grant the wife subjection to her husband, and to the husband that he may be the head of his wife. The priest repeatedly asks God to bless the bridal couple as he blessed Abraham and Sarah, Isaac and Rebecca, Jacob and all the patriarchs, Joseph and Asenath, Moses and Zipporah, Joachim and Anna, Zechariah and Elizabeth; to preserve them as God preserved Noah in the ark, Jonah in the belly of the whale, and the three youths from the fire; and to remember them as God remembered Enoch, Shem, Elijah, and the forty martyrs, upon whom he sent down incorruptible crowns. The joy of the spouses must be like the joy that was vouchsafed to the empress Helen when she found the Holy Cross.

The prayer mentions the groomsmen and the bridesmaids who are present at the crowning, as well as their parents. The priest again asks God to grant the spouses "the fruit of the womb," virtuous children, oneness of mind in spiritual and bodily affairs, abundant fruits, and that the spouses might see their grandchildren, "like a newly planted olive orchard round about their table," and that they might shine like the stars in the firmament of heaven.

The examples cited in the first and second prayers are taken from biblical history. Furthermore, the second prayer cites examples from the history of the Christian Church—the finding of the precious cross by the empress Elena in Jerusalem and the suffering of the forty martyrs of Sebaste. The finding of the cross is mentioned as a joyous occasion; at the same time the cross itself is a symbol of suffering and martyrdom. The prayer mentions the martyrs of Sebaste because, according to their hagiography, when they were in prison they heard Christ's voice: "He that believeth in me, though he were dead, yet shall he live. Be of good cheer and fear not, for you shall receive crowns incorruptible." Later, when the martyrs were in the icy water, a guard saw crowns above their heads. Thus, the prayer makes a connection between marriage and martyrdom—a connection that is reflected in the prayers and hymns that follow.

The third prayer summarizes the content of the two foregoing prayers and the entire rite of the crowning:

> O holy God, who didst create man out of the dust, and didst fashion his wife out of his rib, and didst yoke her unto him as a helpmeet; for it seemed good to thy majesty that man should not be alone upon earth: do thou, the same Lord, stretch out now also thy hand from thy holy dwelling-place, and conjoin this thy servant, N., and this thy handmaid, N.; for by thee is the husband united unto the wife. Unite them in one mind: wed them into one flesh, granting unto them of the fruit of the body and the procreation of fair children.

After this prayer and the exclamation that follows it the priest places a crown upon the head of the groom, saying, "The servant of God, N., is crowned unto the handmaid of God, N.: in the name of the Father, and of the Son, and of the Holy Spirit. Amen." The bride is crowned with analogous words. Then the priest blesses the bridal couple, pronouncing a formula based on Psalm 8.6: "O Lord our God, crown them with glory and honor." The Greek Church uses wreaths of flowers, while in the Russian Church tradition metal crowns are used. In practice, sometimes the crowns are not placed on the heads of the bridal couple, but are given to the sponsors, to be held above the heads of the groom and the bride. Nevertheless, placing the crowns on the heads of those being united in marriage is more in keeping with the significance of the sacrament.

Next follows the prokeimenon, which is based on Psalm 20.4–5: "Thou hast set upon their heads crowns of precious stones; they asked life of thee, and thou gavest it them." This is followed by the reading of a passage from the Epistle of the Apostle Paul to the Ephesians, containing the teaching on marriage as a sacrament:

> Wives, submit yourselves unto your own husbands, as unto the Lord. For the husband is the head of the wife, even as Christ is the head of the Church: and he is the Savior of the body. Therefore as the Church is subject unto Christ, so let the wives be to their own husbands in every thing. Husbands, love your wives, even as Christ also loved the Church, and gave himself for it; that he might sanctify and cleanse it with the washing of water by the word, that he might present it to himself a glorious Church, not having spot, or wrinkle, or any such thing; but that it should be holy and without blemish. So ought men to love their wives as their own bodies. He that loveth his wife loveth himself. For no man ever yet hated his own flesh, but nourisheth and cherisheth it, even as the Lord the Church: for we are members of his body, of his flesh, and of his bones. For this cause shall a man leave his father and mother, and shall be joined unto his wife, and they two shall be one flesh. This is a great mystery; but I speak concerning Christ and the Church. Nevertheless let every one of you in particular so love his wife even as himself; and the wife see that she reverence her husband.

The above text, like several other New Testament texts, emphatically expresses the need for the woman to submit to the man. This is usually explained as a Judean cultural norm in the time of the apostle Paul. We will not delve into this in detail here, as it will be discussed separately—in the chapter devoted to the moral aspects of marriage. Suffice it to say that the traditional concept of the husband as the head of the family remains in the Orthodox Church to this day (contrary to certain other Christian churches). In the Orthodox understanding, the foregoing words of the apostle Paul "are not of course about the despotism of husband or the slavery of wife, but about supremacy in responsibility, care and love. It should not be forgotten either that all Christians are called to 'submit themselves to one another in the fear of God' (Eph 5.21). Therefore, 'neither is the man without the woman, neither the woman without the man, in the Lord. For as the woman is of the man, even so is the man also by the woman; but all things of God' (1 Cor 11.11–12)."[27]

At the end of the epistle reading, "Alleluia" is sung thrice, after which the Gospel account of the wedding in Cana of Galilee is read (cf. Jn 2.1–11). The reading of this Gospel passage concerning the changing of water into wine emphasizes the sacramental nature of marriage.

The essence of every sacrament lies, as we have said, in a transformation, a change, a conversion of something into something else: bread and wine into the body and blood of Christ, a mixture of fragrant oils into holy chrism, etc. At the same time, the person participating in the sacrament is also changed: in baptism a person is changed from the old man into the new, being born again; in the Eucharist he is changed into a member of the body of Christ, being united unto Christ. What change takes place in the sacrament of holy matrimony? Obviously it is the very change that is mentioned in the Bible: "Two shall be one flesh" (1 Cor 6.16, Gen 2.24)—the changing of two individuals into "one flesh," one body, the changing of disparateness into unity, of segregation into union. As John Chrysostom says, "He is not one who is not yet [united], but the half of one. . . . For man and wife are not two men, but one man."[28] This union occurs through the power of the mutual love of the spouses: "This is friendship, that the lover and the beloved should no longer be two persons divided, but in a manner one single person; a thing which no how takes place except from love."[29]

The changing of water into wine is likewise a symbol of the transformation of day-to-day married life into a celebration: "We . . . wish you what is best," Gregory the Theologian writes to newlyweds. "Now one thing is best: that Christ be present at the wedding feast, for where Christ is, there also is order, and water is turned into wine; namely, everything becomes something better."[30] The marital union blessed by Christ, the union in which the Lord himself is invisibly present, must become a continual celebration as the spouses discover the face of God in each other, a continual "transformation into something better" of all aspects of their life together.

---

[27] *The Basis of the Social Concept of the Russian Orthodox Church* 10.5 ‹https://mospat.ru/en/documents/social-concepts/kh›.

[28] John Chrysostom, *Homilies on Ephesians* 12 (*NPNF*¹ 13:318).

[29] John Chrysostom, *Homilies on First Corinthians* 33 (*NPNF*¹ 12:197).

[30] Gregory the Theologian, *Letters* 232. In *The Fathers Speak,* Georges A. Barrois, trans. (Crestwood, NY: St Vladimir's Seminary Press, 1986), 201.

After the Gospel an augmented litany is said with petitions for the bridal couple, and the priest reads a prayer that continues the theme of the Gospel reading:

O Lord our God, who in thy saving providence didst vouchsafe by thy presence in Cana of Galilee to declare marriage honorable: do thou, the same Lord, now also maintain in peace and concord thy servants, *N.* and *N.*, whom it hath pleased thee to join together. Cause

The common cup.

their marriage to be honorable. Preserve their bed blameless. Mercifully grant that they may live together in purity; and enable them to attain to a ripe old age, walking in thy commandments with a pure heart.

After this, following the liturgical exclamation, "And vouchsafe us, O Master," the prayer "Our Father" is sung or read. A cup of wine is brought, over which the priest reads a prayer, asking God to bless it. The groom and the bride drink wine from the cup three times by turns. This action symbolizes their spiritual fellowship, their readiness to share with each other the joys and sorrows of their future family life.

As has already been said, the prayer "Our Father" is retained in the order of holy matrimony from the time when it was still included as part of the Eucharist, and the cup of wine has taken the place of the Eucharistic chalice. In the current practice of the Orthodox Church the order of holy matrimony takes place separately from the Eucharist, but quite frequently it follows immediately after the Eucharist, at which the spouses commune together of the holy mysteries. Every effort should be made to encourage this custom, since joint communion is the "daily bread" without which it is impossible to establish a strong Christian marriage. If it is not possible to commune on the day of the wedding, this may be done on one of the days immediately preceding the wedding.

The service of holy matrimony, like the sacrament of baptism, includes a procession—in this case, around the analogion with the Gospel. During this the choir sings the same three troparia that are sung at ordinations to holy orders, but in a different order: "Rejoice, O Isaiah"; "Glory to thee, O Christ God"; and "O holy martyrs."[31] The first of these troparia speaks of the birth of the child Emmanuel from the womb of the Theotokos, and reminds the spouses of their calling to childbearing. The other two troparia speak of martyric feats, of which the crowns

---

[31] The text of these troparia is found above on page 157.

worn by the bridal couple are also a reminder. The Gospel lying on the analogion reminds us that the life of a Christian family must be established on the basis of Christ's moral teaching, and that the spouses must strive to keep the Savior's commandments.

After the triple circumnavigation of the analogion the crowns are removed. In removing them the priest addresses the groom with these words: "Be thou exalted, O bridegroom, like unto Abraham; and be thou blessed, like unto Isaac; and do thou multiply like unto Jacob, walking in peace, and keeping the commandments of God in righteousness." In removing the crown from the head of the bride the priest says, "And thou, O bride: be thou exalted like unto Sarah; and exult thou, like unto Rebecca; and do thou multiply, like unto Rachel: and rejoice thou in thy husband, fulfilling the conditions of the law: for so is it well-pleasing unto God."

The crown is a symbol not only of family life in our present earthly existence, but also of the heavenly glory that awaits the spouses in the eschatological kingdom of God. Hence, in removing the crowns from the groom and the bride, the priest asks God to receive these crowns into his kingdom:

> O God, our God, who didst come to Cana of Galilee, and dist bless there the marriage feast: bless, also, these thy servants, who through thy good providence are now united together in wedlock. Bless their goings out and their comings in; replenish their life with good things; receive their crowns into thy kingdom, preserving them spotless, blameless, and without reproach, unto ages of ages.

Thus, the wedding crowns will await the spouses in the kingdom of God. This idea is based on the concept, traditional for eastern patristic thought, that not even death can destroy the marital union.

The sacrament of holy matrimony concludes with the words of the priest, invoking the blessing of the Most Holy Trinity upon the spouses:

> May the Father, and the Son, and the Holy Spirit, the all-holy, consubstantial and life-giving Trinity, one Godhead, and one Kingdom, bless you, and grant unto you length of days, fair children, prosperity of life, and faith; and fill you with all abundance of earthly good things; and make you worthy to obtain the blessings of the promise: through the prayers of the holy Theotokos, and of all the Saints. Amen.

This blessing reminds us that the spouses' oneness in marriage must be an image of the oneness manifested by the Holy Trinity—the Father, the Son, and the Holy

Spirit, who abide in indivisible and unmingled oneness, united by mutual love. As John Chrysostom says, when the husband and the wife are united in marriage they form "not a lifeless image, nor yet the image of anything upon earth, but of God Himself."[32] In this love, modeled after the Trinity, lies the pledge that the bonds of marriage will be preserved in the eschatological kingdom of God, and the crowns placed upon the spouses in this earthly life will be changed into the incorruptible crowns of life, righteousness, and glory that are prepared for those who love God and who love each other.

Great Martyr Procopius.
Chora Monastery.
Constantinople. 14th c.

The trinitarian blessing concludes the sacrament of marriage, though in modern service books it is followed by a dismissal commemorating the holy equals to the apostles Constantine and Helen and the holy great martyr Procopius. Constantine and Helen are commemorated as being the first pious rulers, who found the cross of the Lord. As for the great martyr Procopius, his life describes how before his end he exhorted twelve virgins to go to their martyric death as to a feast.[33] Once again the Church is reminding the newlyweds that wedded life is a life of martyrdom and bearing one's cross.

---

[32]Chrysostom, *Homilies on Colossians* 12 (*NPNF*[1] 13:318).

[33]Some versions of St Procopius' life record that he miraculously defeated an enemy army armed only with the cross; like the mention of St Helen, this also emphasizes the importance of the cross in the life of married people.—*Ed.*

8

Monastic Tonsure

Tʜᴇ ᴍᴏɴᴀsᴛɪᴄ ᴛᴏɴsᴜʀᴇ is customarily categorized as a rite, though the ecclesiastical writers of old (Dionysius the Areopagite, Theodore the Studite) called it a sacrament and numbered it with the sacraments. As we have said elsewhere,[1] like baptism the monastic tonsure is a death unto one's former life and a birth unto a new existence; like chrismation it is a seal of election; like marriage it is a betrothal to Christ, the heavenly bridegroom; like ordination it is a dedication to God's service; like the Eucharist it is a union with Christ. As at baptism, at the tonsure a person receives a new name and all his sins are forgiven. He renounces the life of sin and makes vows of fidelity to Christ, casting off his worldly garments and robing himself in new raiment. Being born anew, he voluntarily becomes an infant, that he might grow "unto a perfect man, unto the measure of the stature of the fulness of Christ" (Eph 4.13). In this chapter we will examine the service order of the monastic tonsure, its historical development and current form.

Fᴏʀᴍᴀᴛɪᴏɴ ᴏꜰ ᴛʜᴇ Sᴇʀᴠɪᴄᴇ Oʀᴅᴇʀ. Mᴏɴᴀsᴛɪᴄ Gᴀʀʙ

Entering monasticism takes place through a sacred rite known as the monastic tonsure. The modern service of the tonsure may be traced back to the traditions of eastern monasticism in the fourth and fifth centuries. By this time entrance into monastic life was attended by special sacred rites in which the whole community took part. The primary elements of the rite of the monastic tonsure were the vows made, the cutting of the hair, and the robing in the monastic robes. A description of "the mystery of monastic consecration" is found in the writings of Dionysius the Areopagite:

---

[1]Metropolitan Hilarion (Alfeyev), *Tainstvo Very: Vvedenie v pravoslavnoe dogmaticheskoe bogoslovie* [The Mystery of Faith: An Introduction to Orthodox Dogmatic Theology], 4th ed. (Klin: Khristianskaya Zhizn Foundation, 2004), 184–185.

The Priest stands before the Divine Altar and religiously pronounces the invocation for Monks. The Monk stands behind the Priest, neither bends both knees, nor one of them, nor has upon his head the Divinely transmitted oracles; but only stands near the Priest, whilst he pronounces upon him the mystical Benediction. When the Priest has finished this, he approaches the man being consecrated, and asks him first, if he bids farewell to all distractions—not of life only, but also of imagination. Then he sets before him the most perfect life, and warns him that it is his bounded duty to surpass the ordinary life. When the initiated has promised steadfastly all these things, and the Priest has signed him with the sign of the Cross, he crops his hair. After an invocation to the threefold subsistence of the Divine Beatitude, he strips off all his clothing, and clothes him anew, and with all the holy men present salutes him, and administers to him the supremely Divine Mysteries.[2]

Further on, speaking of the "contemplative aspect" of the service order, the Areopagite observes that the cutting of the hair "shows the pure and unpretentious life, which does not beautify the darkness within the mind by overlarding it with smeared pretence, but shows it leads by itself to the highest likeness of God, not by human attractions, but by single and monastic."[3] Regarding the change of clothing, it "seems to show a transition from a middle sort of religious life to the more perfect one; just as, in the holy Birth from God,[4] the exchange of the clothing denoted the elevation of a purified life to a contemplative and enlightened condition."[5]

From this description it follows, first, that the monastic tonsure is performed by a priest. Second, the members of the church community (that is, of the monastery) are present at the tonsure. Third, in the presence of the priest the monk vows to renounce worldly deeds and thoughts. Fourth, he listens to an exhortation from the priest on the meaning of monastic life. Fifth, the priest signs him with the sign of the cross and cuts his hair. Sixthly, the priest robes the newly tonsured monk in new garments. The rite of tonsure concludes with the newly tonsured saluting the brethren and communing of the holy mysteries of Christ.

In the current practice of the Orthodox Church monks wear their hair long, and the cutting of the hair is purely symbolic in nature, signifying that the monk

---

[2]Dionysius the Areopagite, *Ecclesiastical Hierarchy* 6.2. In *The Celestial and Ecclesiastical Hierarchy of Dionysius the Areopagite*, John Parker, trans., 86.

[3]Ibid., 87.

[4]That is, in the sacrament of baptism.

[5]Dionysius the Areopagite, *Ecclesiastical Hierarchy* 6.2. In *The Celestial and Ecclesiastical Hierarchy of Dionysius the Areopagite*, John Parker, trans., 87.

has embarked on the path of obedience. In ancient times it was another matter. Monks wore their hair short or shaved their heads, and the tonsure, instead of being merely symbolic, was an actual removal of the hair. Shaving the head was an established custom, one that most likely continued for centuries. In the eighth century Patriarch Germanus said that the head of a monk is to be shaved completely (ὁλοτελῶς/*holotelos*), in imitation of James, the brother of the Lord, of Paul, and of the other apostles.[6] In the late twelfth century Eustathius of Thessalonica described shaving the head completely as a monastic custom.[7] To what extent this custom was universal, however, remains unknown. A far more common custom, it seems, was for monks to wear their hair short. At all events, in Byzantine mosa-

Venerable Euthymius the Great.
Fresco. Church of the Savior.
Tsalenjikha, Georgia. 1384–1396.

ics and frescos monks are depicted either with short hair and no head covering, or else wearing a cowl. There is not a single known depiction of a completely shaven monk, but neither are their depictions of monks with long hair. All monks in Byzantium had beards, whether short or long.

Dionysius the Areopagite does not specify in what clothing the newly tonsured monk is robed, but we do find a list of articles of monastic clothing in the writings of the monk Evagrius (fourth century), John Cassian the Roman (early fifth century), and Abba Dorotheus (sixth century). The latter mentions a sleeveless tunic, a leather belt, an analabos, and a cowl. Evagrius likewise mentions a cloak and a staff.

The sleeveless tunic (κολόβιον/*kolóbion*) comprises a knee-length, pullover garment. The absence of sleeves, according to Evagrius, "manifests sincerity of life."[8] According to Dorotheus, a sleeveless garment symbolizes that "we have no hands for doing what the unredeemed man did." Further, "There is another sign in the tunic: it is the purple mark," symbolizing the monk's status as a war-rior of the King of Heaven.[9] Palladius likewise speaks of a scarlet-hued symbol (a cross) on the monastic clothing.[10] In the years that followed the cut of the

---

[6]Germanus of Constantinople, *On the Divine Liturgy* 19 (PPS 8:68–69).

[7]Eustathius of Thessalonica, *Inquiry into the Monastic Life* (PG 135:792BC). [Translated by the present translator.]

[8]Evagrius, *Homily on Spiritual Activity. Prologue,* 94. [Translated by the present translator.]

[9]Dorotheus, *On Renunciation.* In *Dorotheos of Gaza: Discourses and Sayings,* Eric P. Wheeler, trans. (Kalamazoo, MI: Cistercian Publications, 1977), 86.

[10]Palladius, *Lausiac History* 32.3.

Venerable Luke of Hellas.
Mosaic. Hosios Loukas
Monastery. Greece. 16th c.

monastic tunic changed, acquiring sleeves and lengthening to the ankles. This is attested by the depictions of monks in surviving Byzantine frescos, mosaics, icons, and miniatures.

The belt (ζώνη/*zonē*) that monks wear, according to Evagrius, "tears away all impurity."[11] Dorotheus sees the belt as a symbol of the fact that monks are ready for action, "for every man who wishes to do a thing first girds himself and then proceeds to act." In addition, the belt symbolizes the mortification of lust.[12] The belt is fashioned from leather.

The analabos (ανάλαβος/*analabos*) consists of a harness made of leather cords or strings. Evagrius sees the analabos as a "symbol of faith in Christ, supporting the meek, ever restraining that which hinders them, and enabling them to act without impedence."[13] In the understanding of Abba Dorotheus the analabos signifies "that we bear on our shoulders the sign of the cross, as (the Lord] says: 'Take up thy cross and follow me' [Mk 8.34]. What is the cross? It is none other than perfect mortification, which is accomplished in us through faith in Christ." The analabos, Dorotheus clarifies, "is worn cruciformly on the shoulders"—that is, it is worn crosswise on the shoulders, back, and breast.[14] John Cassian the Roman likewise speaks of the analabos, describing it as "double scarves," which, "falling down over the top of the neck and divided on either side of the throat, go round the folds (of the robe) at the armpits . . . so that they can draw up and tuck in close to the body the wide folds of the dress."[15] Whereas in the fifth and sixth centuries the analabos snugly gathered in the monastic garb, in later years the analabos became looser and longer (this change is reflected in Byzantine miniatures and frescos from the tenth century on).[16] Gradually the analabos transformed into the *paraman*—a square of material with a depiction of Golgotha and the inscription, "I bear in my body the marks of the Lord Jesus" (cf. Gal 6.17). This square is worn on the back, connected with four cords to the cross worn on the breast.

[11]Evagrius, *Homily on Spiritual Activity. Prologue,* 95.

[12]Dorotheus, *Homilies* 1.16 (SC 92:172).

[13]Evagrius, *Homily on Spiritual Activity. Prologue,* 95.

[14]Dorotheus, *Homilies* 1.17 (SC 92:172).

[15]John Cassian, *The Twelve Books on the Institutes of the Cœnobia, and the Remedies for the Eight Principal Faults* 1 (*NPNF²* 11:203).

[16]Cf. E.V. Shevchenko, "Analav" [The Analabos], in *Pravoslavnaya entsiklopediya* [The Orthodox Encyclopedia], vol. 2, 519–520 (Moscow: Tserkovno-nauchnyy tsentr "Pravoslavnaya entsiklopediya," 2001).

An indispensible part of the monastic garb is the cowl (κουκούλλιον/*kou-koulion*)—a hood resembling an infant's cap. Concerning the symbolism of the cowl Evagrius says, "The cowl is a symbol of the grace of our Savior and God, which cherishes their infancy in Christ."[17] In the writings of Abba Dorotheus we find a similar interpretation:

> We likewise put on the cowl, which is a symbol of humility. Cowls are worn by little infants (without malice), but it is not worn by the grown man. We however wear it so as to be infants in malice, as the apostle said: *Be not children in understanding: howbeit in malice be ye children* (1 Cor 14.20). What does it mean to be children in malice? A child without malice does not become angry if he is offended; and if he is honored he does not become vainglorious. If a person takes what belongs to him, he is not saddened: for he is a child in malice and does not take revenge for offences and does not seek glory. The cowl is also a likeness of the grace of God, since as a cowl covers and warms the head of an infant, so also the grace of God covers our mind.[18]

Over the tunic a cloak made of goat's hair was worn. According to Evagrius, monks wear a cloak "inasmuch as they always bear 'in the body the dying of the Lord Jesus' (2 Cor 4.10), forcing all irrational passions of the body to fall silent and cutting off the vices of the soul by a connection to good."[19] The cloak is mentioned by Palladius in the account of how Pachomius the Great beheld an angel who, among other things, said to him, "Let each of them have a worked goatskin cloak, without which they are not to eat. When they go to Communion on Saturday and Sunday, let them loosen their girdles and lay aside the skin cloak and go in with the cowl only."[20]

Evagrius likewise mentions the monastic staff,[21] but the staff is not perceived as something invariably possessed by every monk. Staffs were used by monks when traveling. In later years the staff came to be perceived as a symbol of authority, and in this capacity it came to designate the superior of a monastery or a bishop.

The monastic garments employed in the present-day Orthodox Church differ significantly from those used in the time of Evagrius and Abba Dorotheus—in

---

[17]Evagrius, *Homily on Spiritual Activity. Prologue,* 94.

[18]Dorotheus, *Homilies* 1.18 (SC 92:174).

[19]Evagrius, *Homily on Spiritual Activity. Prologue,* 95.

[20]Palladius, *The Lausiac History of Palladius* 32.3, W.K. Lowther Clarke, trans. (New York: The Macmillan Company, 1918), 113.

[21]Evagrius, *Homily on Spiritual Activity. Prologue,* 95.

style, color, and material. Today monks universally wear black clothing. Like priests, monks wear the ryassa (or exorasson) and the cassock. At the divine services, over the cassock they wear the mantle—a floor-length black cape (which in some cases has a train). On their heads monks wear the cylindrical *klobuk*, over which is worn a veil called a *namyotka* (or ἐπικαλυμμαύχιον/*epikalymmauchion*, in the Greek practice this veil is worn over the klobuk; in the Russian practice the klobuk is made with the veil attached). The cassock with its narrow sleeves and the cassock with its wide ones bear only a faint resemblance to the original sleeveless monastic tunic; the long, black mantle with its train is a distant descendant of the original monastic goatskin cloak; and the cylindrical klobuk is quite unlike the infant's cap after which the monastic cowl of old was patterned. The spherical cowl remains only as an attribute of the monastic garb of one who has been tonsured to the great schema. In certain monasteries schemamonks wear a conical hood.

THE SERVICE ORDERS OF THE TONSURES TO THE RANK OF RASSOPHORE AND TO THE SMALL AND GREAT SCHEMAS

In the current practice of the Orthodox Church there are three types of monastic tonsure: the tonsures to the rank of rassophore, to the small schema, and to the great schema. All three service orders are taken from the Byzantine practice. In many cases the tonsure to the rank of rassophore is omitted, and the layman is immediately tonsured to the mantle. On Athos and in many other Greek monasteries there is no tonsure to the little schema, and novices are immediately tonsured to the great schema. In the Russian Church, conversely, the tonsure to the great schema is a rarity: as a rule only monks who are of advanced age or are even preparing to depart this earthly life are tonsured to the great schema.

Originally the division into the ranks of rassophore, the small schema, and the great schema did not exist in monasticism. Entering monasticism was something a person did once in his life. The division between the small and great schemas appeared in the first millennium, no later than the ninth century. In any case, Theodore the Studite mentions this custom, but does not approve of it: "Do not bestow the so-called small schema, and only then the greater, as it were; for its form is one, like baptism, as was the custom of the holy fathers."[22] Nevertheless, the Typicon of Patriarch Alexis (eleventh century), which was widely circulated in Russia, already

---

[22]Theodore the Studite, *The Testament* 12 (PG 99:1820C). [Translated by the present translator.]

mentions two monastic rituals.[23] For St Theodosius of the Caves, as attested by Nestor the Chronicler, the path of entering monasticism had multiple stages:

> He admitted all gladly. However, he did not give the tonsure at once, but told the postulant to wear his ordinary attire until he had become accustomed to the life of the community. Then he would invest him with the monastic robe and test him in various services. Finally, he would give him the tonsure and the mantle. When the monk had been proved as to the purity of his life, he would be allowed to take the holy schema.[24]

Monastic tonsure of the venerable Demitrius of Priluki. Margin of hagiographical icon. 16th c.

Thus, by the time of St Theodosius monasteries were already home to novices, who wore laymen's clothing; rassophore monks; monks who had taken the small schema; and monks who had taken the great schema. The great schema was not, however, perceived as something extraordinary: all monks could take the great schema upon achieving a certain level of spiritual life. In the twelfth century, however, the great schema came to be widely viewed as a special tonsure intended for the sick and infirm. Kirik the Novgorodian asked Bishop Nifont, "I have not yet been tonsured to the schema, and I am considering: would it not be better to be tonsured in old age? Will I not be in better health then, whereas at present I am sick and infirm?" The bishop replied, "You have considered rightly in speaking of being tonsured to the schema in old age."[25]

The *tonsure to the rank of rassophore* is not an initiation into monasticism as such, since in this service no monastic vows are made. The order of the tonsure to the rank of rassophore includes the reading of two prayers by the abbot, in which he asks God to vouchsafe the one being tonsured "to live worthily in this angelic estate," to clothe him "with the robe of sanctification," and to gird his loins with chastity.[26] The novice's hair is cut in the form of the cross, after which the abbot clothes him in the cassock and klobuk, without saying any specific prayers. A third

[23]Golubinsky, *Istoriya Russokoi Tserkvi* vol. 1, 671.

[24]Nestor the Chronicler, *The Life of Theodosius*, in *The Way of a Pilgrim and Other Classics of Russian Spirituality*, Helen Iswolsky, trans., G.P. Fedotov, ed. (Mineola, NY: Dover Publications, Inc., 2012), 28.

[25]Golubinsky, *Istoriya Russokoi Tserkvi* vol. 1, 673.

[26]The text of the service order of the tonsure is taken—with minor alterations—from the translation in N.F. Robinson, *Monasticism in the Orthodox Churches* (London: Cope and Fenwick, 1916).—*Trans.*

prayer is then read, in which the abbot invokes the grace of God for "him who has received the first fruits of this holy habit," and the dismissal is given. After the dismissal the abbot traditionally delivers the newly tonsured monk to his spiritual father with the words, "Behold, I entrust to thee before God this novice, whom do thou teach to live in the fear of God and in all the virtues. Watch carefully, lest his soul perish through thy negligence, for thou shalt answer for him before God on the day of judgment." To the newly tonsured monk the abbot says, "And do thou submit to thy elder in all things as to Christ, and in all things be patient, humble, obedient, meek, and silent, and thou shalt find favor with God, and shalt be saved."

Considerably more lengthy and ceremonious is the order of the tonsure to the small schema. This takes place either at the liturgy, after the small entrance, or separately, outside the divine services. It begins with the singing of a troparion taken from the service of the Sunday of the Prodigal Son:

> Make haste to open unto me Thy fatherly embrace, for as the Prodigal I have wasted my life. In the unfailing wealth of Thy mercy, O Saviour, reject not my heart in its poverty. For with compunction I cry to Thee, O Lord: Father, I have sinned against heaven and before Thee.[27]

As this is chanted the candidate for the tonsure, clothed in a long white shirt, crawls from the narthex to the central part of the church, accompanied by two senior monks, who cover him with their mantles. The procession halts in the middle of the church, where the candidate lies face down, hands outstretched in the form of a cross. The abbot addresses him with these words: "The wise God, as a father who loveth his children, seeing thy humility and true repentance, child, receiveth thee like the prodigal son as thou repentest and earnestly fallest down before him." The abbot touches the candidate, indicating for him to rise.

The singing of the troparion, the procession, and the words of the abbot are a reminder that the monastic path is chiefly a path of mourning and repentance. The monk undertakes the labor of repentance not because he is more sinful than other men, but because he chooses repentance as a way of life. Monasticism as a path of mourning is described by St Isaac the Syrian:

> A mourner (*abila*) is he who passes all the days of his life in hunger and thirst for the sake of his hope and future good things. . . . A monk (*ihidaya*) is he who,

---

[27] *The Lenten Triodion*, Kallistos Ware and Mother Mary, trans. (South Canaan, PA: St. Tikhon's Seminary Press, 1994), 116.

making his dwelling far from the world's spectacles, has as the only entreaty of his prayer the desire for the world to come. A monk's wealth is the comfort that comes of mourning.[28]

It should be noted that in Syria a monk was referred to by the term *abila*—literally, "mourner." In the Syrian tradition, a monk is first and foremost one who mourns—for himself, for others, and for the whole world. In accordance with this view Isaac says:

What meditation can a monk have in his cell save weeping? Could he have any time free from weeping to turn his gaze to another thought? And what occupation is better than this? A monk's very cell and his solitude, which bear a likeness to life in a tomb, far from human joys, teach him that his work is to mourn. And the very calling of his name urges and spurs him on to this, because he called 'the mournful one' (*abila*), that is, bitter in heart. All the saints have left this life in mourning. If, therefore, all the saints mourned and their eyes were ever filled with tears till they departed from this life, who would have no need of weeping? A monk's consolation is born of his weeping. And if the perfect and victorious wept here, how could a man covered with wounds endure to abstain from weeping? He whose loved one lies dead before him and who sees himself dead in sins—has he need of instruction on the thought he should employ for tears? Your soul, slain by sins, lies before you; your soul which is of greater value to you than the whole world. Could there be no need for you to weep over her?[29]

After the candidate for the tonsure has risen the abbot questions him: "Why hast thou come hither, brother, falling down before the holy altar and before this holy assembly?" The candidate replies, "I am desirous of the life of asceticism, reverend father." The interrogation continues:

Question: Dost thou desire to be deserving of the angelic habit, and to be ranked in the company of those who are living as monks?

Answer: Yes, God helping me, reverend father.

---

[28]Isaac the Syrian, *Ascetical Homilies* 58. Quoted from Met. Hilarion Alfeyev, *The Spiritual World of Isaac the Syrian* (Kalamazoo, MI: Cistercian Publications, 2000), 134.

[29]Isaac the Syrian, *Ascetical Homilies* 22. Quoted from Alfeyev, *The Spiritual World of Isaac the Syrian*, 135.

Questions: Of thine own willing mind and thine own free will comest thou unto the Lord?[30]

Answer: Yes, God helping me, reverend father.

Question: Not by any necessity, or constraint?

Answer: No, reverend father.

The abbot must ascertain that the candidate is embarking on the path of monastic life voluntarily, and not under the influence of external circumstances or under pressure from anyone. In Byzantine and Russian history there have been cases where persons were forcibly tonsured in order to exclude them from political life. To this day tonsures occur that are performed not so much on a person's own initiative as at the advice of or even under direct pressure from his spiritual father. Such occurrences are a gross violation of church discipline and contradict the very idea of monasticism as a voluntary embarkment on the path of obedience to Christ, the Church, and the monastic community.

Upon ascertaining that the candidate has chosen the "angelic habit" voluntarily, the abbot receives from him the monastic vows:

Question: Wilt thou abide in the monastery and in the ascetic life until thy last breath?[31]

Answer: Yes, God helping me, reverend father.

Question: Wilt thou keep thyself in chastity, and sobriety, and piety?

Answer: Yes, God helping me, reverend father.

Question: Wilt thou until death observe obedience to the superior, and to all the brotherhood in Christ?

Answer: Yes, God helping me, reverend father.

Question: Wilt thou abide in non-possessiveness and the voluntary poverty inherent in the coenobitic life, acquiring and keeping nothing for thine own self, except for the common needs of all, and then out of obedience, and not of thine own volition?[32]

Answer: Yes, God helping me, reverend father.

[30]In some editions, "Of thine own free intent comest thou unto the Lord?"

[31]Some editions contain a more extensive version: ". . . in this monastery, or in that where thou art commanded to be out of holy obedience . . ."

[32]In some editions this question and the response thereto are omitted.

The monastic tonsure

Question: Dost thou accept all the statues of monastic coenobitic life and the rules compiled by the holy fathers and given thee by the superior?[33]

Answer: Yes, reverend father, I accept them and lovingly kiss them.

Question: Wilt thou endure all the strain and poverty belonging to the monastic life, for the kingdom of heaven's sake?

Answer: Yes, God helping me, reverend father.

The first vow is to remain in the monastery—the one where the tonsure is being performed, or another to which the monk may be sent under obedience. The monk promises to live in asceticism and to abide in chastity, virginity, reverence, obedience, and non-possessiveness. He likewise declares his readiness to observe the monastic rule and to endure the tribulations of monastic life.

The abbot gives a sermon on the meaning of monastic life, reminding the candidate of the need to be cleansed of all impurity of flesh and spirit, to acquire humble-mindedness and obedience, to renounce the ways of the world, and to endure temptations. The monk must not love anyone or anything more than God, must follow the example of the venerable fathers of old in all things, and must continually bear in mind the sufferings and death of Christ. Having called to mind these aspects of the monastic life, the abbot asks whether the monk promises to remain true to his vows, to which the monk answers in the affirmative. Addressing the monk, the abbot says, "Therefore may the all-compassionate and merciful

---

[33]In some editions this question and the response thereto are omitted.

God . . . receive, embrace, and shield thee; may he be to thee a strong tower from the face of the enemy . . . present with thee when thou liest down, and when thou risest up; comforting and cheering thine heart through the consolation of his own Holy Spirit."

The abbot then places a book on the head of the candidate and reads a prayer in which he asks God to guide the monk on the path of truth, to guard him by the grace of the Holy Spirit, and to grant him patience. Then the deacon places a pair of scissors on the Gospel, and the abbot reads another prayer for the newly tonsured monk. The abbot then says to him: "Lo, Christ is here present invisibly. See that no one is compelling thee to come to this habit. See that thou art desiring of set purpose the betrothal of the great and angelic habit." Upon being answered in the affirmative by the candidate, the abbot says to him, "Take the scissors, and give them to me." The candidate gives the scissors to the abbot three times.[34] This emphasizes once again the voluntary nature of the tonsure. Upon receiving the scissors from the candidate for the third time, the abbot says, "Lo, from the hand of Christ thou receivest them. And see to whom thou approachest, to whom thou dost promise, and whom thou dost renounce."[35] Then the abbot says the same words that are found in the sacrament of baptism: "Blessed is God, who willeth that all men should be saved, and come to the knowledge of the truth." The abbot cuts the hair of the candidate cruciformly, saying the words, "Our brother, N., is shorn in the hair of his head, in token of renunciation of the world and all that is in the world and unto the rejection of his will and all fleshly lusts, in the name of the Father and of the Son and of the Holy Spirit."

At this point the newly tonsured monk hears his new name for the first time. The custom of changing one's name upon entering monasticism is very ancient, though its precise time of origin cannot be determined. In its significance it harks back to the Old Testament custom of changing a person's name as a sign of obedience. In the Bible a name change signifies that a person has lost his independence and is now subject to the one who has changed his name (cf. 2 Kg 23.34, 24.17). At the same time a change of name may signify the beginning of a closer relationship with the one who changed it.

The name change at the tonsure is a firmly established custom, though it is not a required condition for the tonsure. The one performing the tonsure may

---

[34]Some abbots throw the scissors to the floor during the tonsure, and the candidate must pick them up from the floor three times.

[35]That is, the devil.

select the new name based on various considerations. Sometimes the candidate for monasticism is given the name of the saint commemorated that day, or of a saint that is especially venerated in that particular monastery. Frequently the monk is given a name beginning with the same letter as his former name (Nicholas becomes Nicodemus, Andrew becomes Arsenius, etc.). The candidate is not told his name beforehand, and the abbot does not consult him in the matter, since this would defeat the purpose of the name change.

Immediately following the tonsure the candidate is clothed in the monastic robes. The abbot blesses each article of clothing and gives it to the candidate, who takes it and kisses it and the hand of the abbot. Specific words are said with each article of clothing. The first to be given is the "hair shirt" (the cassock), with the words, "Our brother, *N.*, is clothed in the garment of voluntary poverty and want, and of the enduring of all misfortunes and hardships." Then the monk is given the paraman (the analavos) with the cross, and the abbot says, "Our brother, *N.*, receiveth the paraman, the betrothal of the angelic schema, as a perpetual reminder of taking upon himself of Christ's easy yoke. . . . And he takes also the sign of the Lord's cross . . . for a perpetual reminder of the . . . crucifixion and death of our Lord." The monk is then clothed in the ryassa (or exorasson)—"the garment of spiritual joy and gladness, for the putting away and trampling of all sorrows and troubles . . . and for his perpetual joy and gladness in Christ." The belt is put on him "for mortification of body and renewal of spirit." The mantia is "the robe of salvation" and "the armor of righteousness." Then the koukoulion (or klobuk) is placed on him—"the helmet of salvation and the hope that cannot be put to shame, that he will be able to stand against the snares of the devil . . . as a sign of spiritual love of wisdom." He is also clothed in sandals "in readiness for the proclamation of the Good News of peace."[36]

The words that are read as the candidate is clothed in the monastic robes describe monasticism as a path "of joy and gladness." This does not contradict the portrayal of the monk as a "mourner," as this refers not to earthly joys, but to the spiritual joy that is born of mourning and repentance. In the chapter on "joy-making mourning" John of the Ladder says:

[36]Certain editions provide a somewhat different text for the clothing in the monastic robes: "Our brother is clothed with the robe of rejoicing . . ."; "Our brother is covered with the helmet of the hope of salvation . . ."; "Our brother receives the pallion, the betrothal of the great and angelic habit . . ." (cf. the *Trebnik* [Book of Needs], 1884 edition, reverse of page 76).

Keep a firm hold of the blessed joy-grief of holy compunction, and do not stop
working at it until it raises you high above the things of this world and presents
you pure to Christ.

He who is clothed in blessed and grace-given mourning as in a wedding
garment knows the spiritual laughter of the soul.

When I consider the actual nature of compunction I am amazed at how
that which is called mourning and grief should contain joy and gladness inter-
woven within it like honey in the comb. . . . Such compunction is in a special
sense a gift of the Lord . . . for God consoles those who are contrite in heart
in a secret way.[37]

After the monk has been clothed in the robes befitting his rank, he is given a
prayer rope with the words, "Brother *N.,* receive this sword of the spirit, which is
the word of God, unto the constant prayer of Jesus, for thou must always have the
name of the Lord Jesus in thy mind, in thy heart, and in thy mouth." The prayer
rope (in Slavonic, *vervitsa*) is an integral accessory of the monk. In the Orthodox
tradition there are two types of prayer rope—leather and woven. The leather prayer
rope (called a *lestovka*) is mostly found among Old Believers. The most common
prayer ropes are woven, comprised of complex knots that transform each section of
yarn or cord into a tight, durable bead. While saying the prayer of Jesus the monk
fingers the prayer rope, counting off the number of prayers said.

Finally a cross is placed in the hand of the monk, as a reminder of the ascetic
labor of bearing his cross. He is also given a lighted candle as a reminder that a
monk is called to be a light unto the world. In concluding the ritual the abbot says,
"Our brother, *N.,* hath received the betrothal of the angelic schema and hath been
clothed in the whole armor of God, that he may be able to vanquish all the power
and warfare of principalities and powers, and rulers of the darkness of this age."

Military symbolism plays a significant role in the rite of the monastic tonsure:
the robes of the monk are perceived as the armor of a warrior, and the monastic life
as warfare with the devil. This concept is corroborated by the words of the apostle
Paul that are read immediately after the robing of the monk (the formulae of the
robing are composed chiefly of Paul's words):

Finally, my brethren, be strong in the Lord, and in the power of his might. Put
on the whole armour of God, that ye may be able to stand against the wiles of

---

[37]John Climacus, *The Ladder of Divine Ascent,* Lazarus Moore, trans. (New York: Harper & Brothers,
1959), 38–41.

Words of instruction to the newly tonsured monk on the monastic life

the devil. For we wrestle not against flesh and blood, but against principalities, against powers, against the rulers of the darkness of this world, against spiritual wickedness in high places. Wherefore take unto you the whole armour of God, that ye may be able to withstand in the evil day, and having done all, to stand. Stand therefore, having your loins girt about with truth, and having on the breastplate of righteousness; and your feet shod with the preparation of the gospel of peace; above all, taking the shield of faith, wherewith ye shall be able to quench all the fiery darts of the wicked. And take the helmet of salvation, and the sword of the Spirit, which is the word of God (Eph 6.10–17).

This is followed by a reading from the Gospel, comprised of two passages containing the entire "philosophy" of monastic life:

He that loveth father or mother more than me is not worthy of me: and he that loveth son or daughter more than me is not worthy of me. And he that taketh not his cross, and followeth after me, is not worthy of me. . . . Come unto me, all ye that labour and are heavy laden, and I will give you rest. Take my yoke upon you, and learn of me; for I am meek and lowly in heart: and ye shall find rest unto your souls. For my yoke is easy, and my burden is light (Mt 10.37–38, 11.28 30).

Thus, monasticism is presented as the most radical form of following Christ's call to perfection, self-denial, and bearing one's cross. Monasticism is the easy yoke of Christ, which the monk voluntarily takes upon himself. It is the imitation of him who was meek and lowly in heart, for the sake of whom the monk renounces parents, kinsmen, and the whole world.

The same passages from the epistles and the Gospel are read at the *tonsure to the great schema*. The rite of the tonsure to the great schema is essentially a repetition of the tonsure to the small schema, with a few changes. These include the reading of other, lengthier prayers; the exhortation of the abbot is likewise significantly longer than at the tonsure to the small schema. The chief elements, however—the vows given, the tonsure, and the clothing in the monastic robes—remain the same.

In addition to the usual monastic clothing, the schemamonk is clothed in the analavos. Here the term refers to an apron resembling an epitrachelion, but not divided into two parts, that extends only slightly below the waist. The analavos of the schemamonk, like his cowl, may be adorned with various inscriptions and symbols. Inscriptions include psalm verses ("Create in me a clean heart, O God, and renew a right spirit within me"; "Remove from me the way of unrighteousness, and with thy law have mercy on me"; etc.), while the chief image used is Golgotha—a plain cross standing on the place of the skull, with the spear and the reed on either side of the cross.

9

Burial and Commemoration of the Dead

PRAYER FOR THOSE WHO HAVE REPOSED is a tradition that dates back to the early church. Prayer for the departed is one way of heeding the apostle's exhortation to pray "for all men" (1 Tim 2.1). Since with God "all live" (Lk 20.38), the Orthodox Church makes no distinction between the living and the departed in terms of prayer: both, in its view, are in need of prayers of intercession.

The practice of praying for the departed is based on the concept that the posthumous fate of the dead may be altered through the prayers of the living for them. Among other fathers of the Church, the holy hierarch Cyril of Jerusalem gave a description of this:

> For I know many who say, "How can a soul receive profit after having left this world, either with or without sins, if it is remembered in prayer?" But surely if a king had made exiles out of certain people who had given him offense, and then their relatives wove a crown and offered it to him for those in need of help, would he not give them relief from their punishments? In the same way we also, offering our petitions to God for those who have fallen asleep, although they are sinners, we do not weave crowns, but we offer Christ slaughtered for our sins, propitiating God the lover of humanity both for them and for ourselves.[1]

Prayer for the departed is a point on which Orthodoxy differs both from Catholicism and, to an even greater degree, from Protestantism. Traditional Catholic dogma divides the kingdom of the afterlife into hell,[2] purgatory, and paradise.[3] In keeping with this division, Catholic theologians at the Council of Ferrara-Florence declared that those in paradise have no need of prayers for the departed, since they are already saved and abide with God; nor can prayer be of any help to those in hell, for deliverance from hell is impossible. Prayer for the departed can only help

---

[1]Cyril of Jerusalem, *On the Mysteries* 5.10 (PPS 57:127).

[2]In Russian there is no distinction between the words *hades* and *hell*, both of which are rendered as *ad.—Trans.*

[3]Cf. vol. 1, p. 133.

Holy Hierarch Mark of Ephesus.
Contemporary icon

those in purgatory. In the words of the Latin attendees of the Council of Ferrara-Florence, "Unless there is a purification after death, this prayer would be in vain; for this prayer is neither for those who are already in glory nor for those who are banished to hell."[4]

During its revision of Roman Catholic dogma, Protestant theology rejected various individual doctrines, while fully retaining the basis on which these doctrines were established. As a result, instead of returning to its roots, Protestantism departed considerably farther from the faith of the ancient Church than had Catholicism. In particular, while renouncing the doctrine of purgatory, Protestantism retained the Latin belief that prayer for those in paradise and in hell was futile: purgatory does not exist, ergo prayer for the departed is completely unnecessary.

Unlike Catholicism, the Orthodox Church does not recognize the doctrine of purgatory and makes no distinction between eternal torment in a hell from which deliverance is impossible, and purgatorial fire from which one may yet be saved. According to Orthodox teaching, it is possible to be delivered from the torments of hell. This deliverance occurs not out of some automatic necessity, and not because a particular sinner has "served his time" according to the sins he has committed, but by the prayers of the Church and through God's ineffable love for mankind. The idea that deliverance from the torments of hell is possible formed the basis for numerous prayers for the departed, particularly a special prayer "for those who are imprisoned in hell," read at vespers on the feast of Pentecost.

The eastern fathers of the Church expressed the opinion that prayers for the departed benefit not just one specific category of the dead, but all those who have departed this life, including those in hell. In response to the Latin theologians, Mark of Ephesus wrote:

> So also, on account of these things, we have the prayers in behalf of those fallen asleep. The Church has received these prayers from the Apostles themselves and

[4]Cardinal Julian Cesarini, *Latinorum ad Graecos capita circa purgatorium ignem* [Latin Chapters to the Greeks Concerning Purgatorial Fire] (*Patrologia Orientalis* 15:28), quoted in "The Debate Over the Patristic Texts on Purgatory at the Council of Ferrara-Florence, 1438" by James Jorgenson, *St Vladimir's Theological Quarterly* 30.4 (Winter 1986): 309–334, at 311.

the fathers, and performs them in both the Mystical Sacrifice and in certain other rites at various times. We perform them in behalf of all alike, who have fallen asleep in faith. We say that for all of these the prayers contribute and furnish something, and that power and assistance from them pass over to all. This is so even for those sinners confined in Hades, that they may obtain some small relief, even though there may not be complete release for them. . . . But the Church of God in no wise prays for such ones, but rather asks from God relief for all who have fallen asleep in faith, though they be the most sinful, praying for them both publically and privately. . . . And so if both the prayers and petitions of the Church are effective for ones such as these [great sinners], and bring much profit to them, inasmuch as they have not yet been condemned nor received the verdict of the Judge and come into Judgment, much more will prayers for those in the intermediate state bestow great benefits upon them. The prayers will either restore them to the estate of the righteous, should their sins be very small and insubstantial, or at least in the meantime will lighten the difficulties of those who remain in them and lift them up to more propitious hopes.[5]

Furthermore, in the words of the saint, prayer for the departed, especially offerings for them at the divine liturgy, "proceeds also to those who passed their lives in a righteous and holy manner, inasmuch as they are also incomplete, ever making gains in their progression toward the good and not yet enjoying the final blessedness." Thus, the saint concludes, the effects of prayer for the departed "proceeds to all, and the aid which comes from the prayers and mystical rites likewise fulfills all who have fallen asleep in faith," and for this reason "we see that there is no inherent necessity in the argument which says that this sort of aid is administered by us to those in the purgatorial fire alone."[6]

Prayer for the Departed in the Ancient Church

In the early Christian Church the primary means of praying for the departed was to commemorate them at the divine liturgy. Testimonies to this form of commemo-

[5]Mark of Ephesus, *Oratio Altera de Igne Purgatorio* [in Greek]. In *Patrologia Orientalis* 15.1 (No. 72), *Documents Relatifs au Concile de Florence I: La Question du Purgatoire à Ferrare, Documents I-VI*, 1st ed., edited and translated by Mgr. Louis Petit A. A (Paris: Firmin-Didot, 1920. Reprint, Turnhout, Belgium: Editions Brepols, 1990), 39–60, 108–51. Greek text with parallel Latin translation. English translation by Protodeacon Jeremiah Davis.

[6]Ibid.

ration abound in the writings of the fathers of the Church. In the third century Cyprian of Carthage speaks of "offerings" for one who has departed and of a "sacrifice . . . for his repose" before the altar of God.[7] Cyril of Jerusalem, commenting on the relevant place in the order of the liturgy, writes:

> Next, we make memorial and commemoration of those who have fallen asleep before us, first patriarchs, prophets, apostles, (and) martyrs, so that by their prayers and intercessions God might receive our petition. Next, for the holy fathers and bishops, who have fallen asleep before us, and, in general, for all who have fallen asleep before us, believing great profit will come to the souls for whom the petition is made as this holy and awe-filled sacrifice is being presented.[8]

We find similar accounts of commemoration of the departed at the liturgy in the writings of other fathers, particularly John Chrysostom:

> Not in vain did the Apostles order that remembrance should be made of the dead in the dreadful Mysteries. They know that great gain resulteth to them, great benefit; for when the whole people stands with uplifted hands, a priestly assembly, and that awful Sacrifice lies displayed, how shall we not prevail with God by our entreaties for them?[9]

> For it is, yes, it is possible, if we will, to mitigate his punishment, if we make continual prayers for him, if for him we give alms. However unworthy he may be, God will yield to our importunity. For if Paul showed mercy on one (who had no claims on his mercy), and for the sake of others spared one (whom he would not have spared), much more is it right for us to do this.[10]

> Not in vain are the oblations made for the departed, not in vain the prayers, not in vain the almsdeeds: all those things hath the Spirit ordered, wishing us to be benefited one by the other.[11]

Blessed Augustine likewise speaks of liturgical prayer and almsgiving on behalf of the departed:

[7]Cyprian of Carthage, *Epistles* 65 (*ANF* 5:367).

[8]Cyril of Jerusalem, *On the Mysteries* 5.9 (PPS 57:127).

[9]Chrysostom, *Homilies on Philippians* 3 (*NPNF*[1] 13:197).

[10]Chrysostom, *Homilies on Acts* 21 (*NPNF*[1] 11:139–140). [Here the Russian translation differs significantly: "For if for the apostle Paul's sake [God] saved others, and for the sake of some spared others, how can it be that he will not do the same for us?"—*Trans.*]

[11]Chrysostom, *Homilies on Acts* 21 (*NPNF*[1] 11:140).

But by the prayers of the holy Church, and by the salvific sacrifice, and by the alms which are given for their spirits, there is no doubt that the dead are aided, that the Lord might deal more mercifully with them than their sins would deserve. For the whole Church observes this practice which was handed down by the Fathers: that it prays for those who have died in the communion of the Body and Blood of Christ, when they are commemorated in their own place in the sacrifice itself; and the sacrifice is offered also in memory of them, on their behalf. If, then, works of mercy are celebrated for the sake of those who are being remembered, who would hesitate to recommend them, on whose behalf prayers to God are not offered in vain?[12]

In the tradition of the ancient Church, prayers for one who had departed were made each year on the day of his death. The third, ninth (or tenth), and fortieth days after a Christian's repose were particularly observed. On these days prayers for the departed were offered, alms are distributed in memory of the departed person, and memorial meals were held, as attested in particular by the *Apostolic Constitutions*:

Let the third day of the departed be celebrated with psalms, and readings, and prayers, on account of Him who arose within the space of three days; and let the ninth day be celebrated in remembrance of the living, and of the departed; and the fortieth day according to the ancient pattern: for so did the people lament Moses, and the anniversary day in memory of him. And let alms be given to the poor out of his goods for a memorial of him. . . . Now, when you are invited to their memorials, do you feast with good order, and the fear of God, as disposed to intercede for those that are departed.[13]

Ultimately the third, ninth, and fortieth days became the days for commemoration of the departed in the East. In the West these days came to be the seventh and thirtieth days after a person's repose. Commemoration on the seventh and thirtieth days is based on the Old Testament practice of seven days (Sir 22.11, Gen 50.10) and thirty days (cf. Num 20.29, Deut 34.8) of mourning.

We know how the departed were commemorated at the Eucharist from the surviving ancient orders of the liturgy. In particular, the liturgy of the *Apostolic Constitutions* contains the following diaconal petitions for the departed:

---

[12]Augustine, *Homilies* 272. In *The Faith of the Early Fathers* 3, William A. Jurgens, trans. (Collegeville, MN: The Liturgical Press, 1970), 29.

[13]*Apostolic Constitutions* 8.4.42–44 (*ANF* 7:498).

Let us pray for our brethren that are at rest in Christ, that God, the lover of mankind, who has received his soul, may forgive him every sin, voluntary and involuntary, and may be merciful and gracious to him, and give him his lot in the land of the pious that are sent into the bosom of Abraham, and Isaac, and Jacob, with all those that have pleased Him and done His will from the beginning of the world, whence all sorrow, grief, and lamentation are banished.[14]

The diaconal petitions are followed by a prayer that the bishop intones aloud:

O Thou who art by nature immortal, and hast no end of Thy being . . . who art the God not of the dead, but of the living: for the souls of all men live with Thee, and the spirits of the righteous are in Thy hand, which no torment can touch; for they are all sanctified under Thy hand: do Thou now also look upon this Thy servant, whom Thou hast selected and received into another state, and forgive him if voluntarily or involuntarily he has sinned, and afford him merciful angels, and place him in the bosom of the patriarchs, and prophets, and apostles, and of all those that have pleased Thee from the beginning of the world, where there is no grief, sorrow, nor lamentation.[15]

As we have seen above,[16] prayers for the departed are found in the liturgies of both John Chrysostom and Basil the Great. These prayers are offered immediately after the consecration of the holy gifts.

A highly developed rite of prayer for the departed is found in the liturgy of the apostle James.[17] He begins by commemorating the Theotokos, the prophets, apostles, evangelists, preachers, martyrs, and confessors, John the Baptist, the protomartyr Stephen, and all the saints. This commemoration is accompanied by this priestly prayer: "Lead us into this blessed assembly, unite us unto this Church, set us by thy grace amid the elect that are written in the heavens."

Further on the deacon commemorates "the divine instructors and interpreters of blameless faith, who . . . have gone to their rest, having established and passed on to us the Orthodox faith." The priest commemorates the bishops, luminaries, and teachers of the Church who have gone to their rest before us, and asks that by their prayers the teaching and confession of Orthodoxy might be established in the souls of the faithful, and that malignant heresies might swiftly be eradicated. Then

---

[14] Ibid., 8.41 (*ANF* 7:497).
[15] Ibid. (*ANF* 7:497–498).
[16] Cf. 365 and below.
[17] *The Divine Liturgy of James, the Holy Apostle and Brother of the Lord* (*ANF* 7:537).

the deacon commemorates "all the departed faithful that have reposed in the true faith, who have passed on both from this holy altar and from this habitation, and from every country," that the Lord might show them forth "worthy of remission of transgressions and absolution of sins."

The priest goes on to commemorate all the departed members of the Church: "Orthodox presbyters that have gone to their rest before us, deacons, subdeacons, psalm singers, readers, interpreters, chanters, exorcists, monks, ascetics, those who listen, perpetual virgins and laymen who have departed in the faith, and those whom each has in his soul."[18] Then the priest says a prayer for all the departed, which the people take up and conclude with these words: "Grant them rest, and pardon and remit, O God, the sins of ignorance and the transgressions of us all, known and unknown." Thus, prayer for the departed transitions smoothly into prayer for the living—those present in the church. The living do not separate the departed from themselves, but feel themselves to be members of the same ecclesial organism, the same body of Christ, to which those who have reposed in the faith belong.

The Church, which accompanies a person on his life's journey from the moment of his birth, also does not abandon him in his final hours and after death. Since ancient times the death of a Christian has been attended by special church rituals. The priest would pray with the dying person and commune him of the holy mysteries of Christ. After his repose the body of the departed would be brought to the church, where a memorial service order was performed over it. In his panegyric on his brother Caesarius, Gregory the Theologian says:

> And now our illustrious Caesarius has been restored to us, when his honored dust and celebrated corpse, after being escorted home amidst a succession of hymns and public orations, has been honored by the holy hands of his parents; while his mother, substituting the festal garments of religion for the trappings of woe, has overcome her tears by her philosophy, and lulled to sleep lamentations by psalmody, as her son enjoys honors worthy of his newly regenerate soul, which has been, through water, transformed by the Spirit.[19]

The words cited are pronounced (or at least are intended to be pronounced) during a service for the departed. The service order, as is apparent from the words of the saint, is performed in the church in the presence of the relatives, and includes

---

[18]That is, those for whom each of those present at the service is currently praying.

[19]Gregory Nazianzen, *Orations* 7.15 (*NPNF*[1] 7:234).

numerous hymns. The body of the deceased is located in the church in front of the altar (before "the altars of the martyrs"). Thus, by the fourth century it was a widespread custom for the body of the departed to be brought into the church, to have the prayers for the reposed read over it.

A detailed description of the ritual performed for the departed is found in Dionysius the Areopagite's *The Ecclesiastical Hierarchy*. Here this ritual is viewed as one of the sacraments of the Church. This sacrament, according to the Areopagite, is bright and joyous in nature, since the repose of a Christian is a joyous occasion both for the Christian himself and for his relations:

> The holy man himself, who comes to the end of his struggles, is filled with a holy consolation, and with much satisfaction draws nigh to the path of the holy regeneration. The familiar friends of him who has fallen asleep, as befits their Divine familiarity and fellowship, pronounce him blessed, whoever he is, as approaching, in answer to his prayers, the end crowned with victory. They send up odes of thanksgiving to the Author of victory, praying also that they themselves may come to the same inheritance.[20]

The relatives of the departed bring his body to the bishop, that is, to the church. The bishop "gladly receives him, and celebrates the rites fixed by reverend men, to be celebrated over those who have piously fallen asleep."[21] If the departed person was a priest, his body is placed before the altar (the holy table); if a monk or a layman, it is placed opposite the altar ("near the hallowed sanctuary, before the sacerdotal entrance").[22] The significance of this action is explained as follows:

> Not without reason does the Hierarch conduct to, and place the defunct in the place with those of the same rank. For it shows spiritually that, in the regeneration, all will be in that inheritance for which they have chosen their own life here. For example, if anyone here had a Godlike and most holy life (so far as the imitation of God is attainable by man), he will be throughout the age to come in a divine and blessed lot. But if he lead a life inferior to the divine likeness in its perfection, but, nevertheless, a holy life, even this man will receive the holy retributions of the same kind.[23]

---

[20]Dionysius the Areopagite, *Ecclesiastical Hierarchy* 7.1. In *The Celestial and Ecclesiastical Hierarchy of Dionysius the Areopagite*, John Parker, trans., 90.

[21]Ibid.,

[22]Ibid., 7.2

[23]Ibid., 7.3, 91.

In order to say the prayers over the body of the departed, the bishop "collects the revered Choir"—that is, assembles the clergy and laity—and "offers the prayer and thanksgiving to God."[24] In this prayer he "celebrates the worshipful Deity, as subjugating the unjust and tyrannical power against us all, but conducting us to our own most just judgments."[25] Next "the Leitourgoi read the faithful promises concerning our resurrection, which are contained in the Divine Lections, and chant the odes of the same teaching and power, from the Lections contained in the Psalter."[26] In other words, excerpts from holy scripture are read (apparently from the Old and New Testaments) concerning the resurrection of the dead, and hymns are sung, which, while modeled after the psalms, are actually the work of Christian hymnographers. This singing and reading is "explanatory of the most blessed inheritances into which those who have attained a Divine perfection shall be appointed. But the inheritances which await the defunct stimulate those who are still living to a similar perfection."[27]

Then "the first Deacon dismisses the catechumens."[28] After this the chief officiant "calls aloud the names of the holy people who have already fallen asleep, amongst whom he deems the man who has just terminated his life worthy of registration, as being of the same rank, and urges all to seek the blessed consummation in Christ."[29] The prayer read over the body of the departed "beseeches the supremely Divine Goodness to remit to the defunct all the failings committed through human infirmity, and to place him in the light and land of the living; in the bosom of Abraham, and Isaac, and Jacob; in a place where grief and sorrow and sighing are no more."[30] The "bosom" of Abraham, Isaac, and Jacob, according to the Areopagite, should be understood to mean "the most divine and blessed inheritance which awaits all godly men."[31]

Upon completion of the prayers "the Divine Hierarch . . . salutes the defunct, and after him all who are present."[32] "For dear and honoured, to all Godlike men, is he who has been perfected in a Divine life."[33] After this the officiant pours oil

---

[24]Dionysius the Areopagite, *Ecclesiastical Hierarchy* 7.2. In *The Celestial and Ecclesiastical Hierarchy of Dionysius the Areopagite*, John Parker, trans., 90.

[25]Ibid., 7.3, 91.

[26]Ibid., 7.2, 90.

[27]Ibid., 7.3, 91.

[28]Ibid., 7.2.

[29]Ibid.,

[30]Ibid., 7.3, 92.

[31]Ibid.,

[32]Ibid., 7.2, 91.

[33]Ibid., 7.3, 95.

upon the departed. The Areopagite sees in this ritual a reminder of the anointing with oil at baptism:

> In the course of the divine Birth from God, before the most Divine Baptism, the oil of Chrism, as a first participation of the holy symbol, is given to the neophyte, after the entire removal of the former clothing. But now, at the conclusion of all that is done, the oil is poured upon the defunct. The first anointing with the oil summons the initiated to the holy contests; but the pouring of the oil now shows the defunct to have struggled through those same contests, and to have been made perfect.[34]

When all the sacred rites are completed, and when the officiant "has offered the prayer for all, he places the body in a worthy grave, with other holy bodies of the same rank."[35] As the Areopagite notes, "If, in soul and body, the man has passed a life dear to God, there will be honoured with the devout soul also the body which contended with it throughout the devout struggles." Divine justice bestows upon the soul its due reward together with the body that belongs to it, "as companions and participators in the devout or the contrary life." For this reason also the church Typicon "bequeaths the supremely Divine participations to them both—to the soul, indeed, in a pure contemplation and in an exact knowledge of the rites celebrated; to the body, by sanctifying the whole man, as in a figure, with the most Divine Myrrh, and the most holy symbols of the Divine Communion, effecting his complete salvation, and announcing that his resurrection will be most complete by entire sanctification."[36]

The logic of this statement runs as follows: since during his earthly life the person's body participated in the church sacraments together with his soul, the Church bids farewell to the body as well as the soul as the person departs on his final journey. The sacraments of the Church, such as chrismation and communion, sanctify the whole man, including his body. Hence, posthumous honor is rendered to a Christian's body also, as being the fellow contender of the soul.

Over the centuries that followed the service orders for the departed were enriched with new hymns and sacred songs, but their essence remained unchanged. As in the ancient Church, in the Orthodox tradition prayers at the divine liturgy remain the primary means of commemorating the departed, though they are also

---

[34]Dionysius the Areopagite, *Ecclesiastical Hierarchy* 7.3. In *The Celestial and Ecclesiastical Hierarchy of Dionysius the Areopagite*, John Parker, trans., 95.

[35]Ibid., 7.2, 91.

[36]Ibid., 7.3, 95–96.

commemorated at other times during the daily cycle of services, as well as at special service orders for the departed. As in ancient times, the body of the departed is brought to the church for the funeral. As in ancient times, special commemorations are made on the third, ninth, and fortieth days, and also each year on the day of the Christian's repose.

PRAYERS AND RITUALS ATTENDING THE REPOSE OF A CHRISTIAN

The Orthodox Church ascribes considerable significance to confession and communion as sacraments that prepare a person for the passage into eternity. Healthy people confess and commune in the church, but the sick are visited by the priest in their homes for this purpose. In our time confession and communion of the sick is frequently perceived as a ritual for the dying, and so the family is afraid to invite the priest to visit the sick person, lest this give the impression that he is dying. This approach is fundamentally incorrect. Firstly, healthy people also regularly confess and commune, and there is no basis for viewing a priest making a house call as a harbinger of death. On the contrary, in many cases communing one who is gravely ill has a salutary effect not only on his soul, but on his body as well, facilitating his recovery. Secondly, it is extremely dangerous to put off confession and communion for one who is gravely ill until the last minute, since he may die before the sacraments are brought, or he may lapse into unconsciousness and prove unable to receive them. Hence, the Church recommends that the priest be summoned without delay when a person is gravely ill. Confession and communion may also be administered repeatedly over the course of the illness.

If a person is on his deathbed and it is apparent that his repose is eminent, after confessing and communing him the priest may read special prayers over him. Early printed editions of the Book of Needs, used to this day by the Old Believers, contained the "Office at the Parting of the Soul from the Body." It included two canons—one addressing Jesus Christ, the other addressing the Theotokos. In Greek editions of the euchologion and Slavonic editions of the Book of Needs, the superscription of the first canon bears name of Andrew of Crete, while the second bears that of John, metropolitan of Mauropous (ninth century). Modern editions of the Book of Needs contain a separate "Canon of Supplication at the Parting of the Soul from the Body," comprising the second of the aforementioned canons, and the "Order at the Parting of the Soul from the Body When One has Suffered for a Long Time," which includes the first canon.

The burial of St Nicholas.
Fragment of a hagiographical
icon. Circa 1607

The "Canon of Supplication at the Parting of the Soul from the Body" is penitential in nature. Its reading is preceded by the usual beginning[37] and the reading of Psalm 50. The canon is read on behalf of the one who is dying, who is no longer able to speak but can still comprehend spoken words and pray: "My mouth is silent, and my tongue speaketh not, but my heart maketh utterance: For that fire of contrition which inwardly devoureth is kindled, and in tones inexpressible invoketh thee, O Virgin." After the reading of the canon the priest says a prayer in which he asks God to absolve the one who is dying of all bonds, to pardon him his transgressions known and unknown, both those confessed and those forgotten or concealed at confession out of shame. The final lines of the prayer contain a petition that the Lord will receive the soul of the dying person in peace, and give him rest in the eternal tabernacles with the saints.

The "Order at the Parting of the Soul from the Body When One has Suffered for a Long Time," as the name suggests, is read when a person is enduring severe death agonies. The rite includes the usual beginning; Psalms 60, 142, and 50; a canon; and two prayers. As is clear from the content of the canon, it is to be read in the presence of the friends and kin of the dying person (or, if he is a monk, in the presence of the monastery brethren). The canon is filled with penitential imagery; some of its troparia are in the words of the dying person, asking the saints and the friends at his bedside for prayers. In the prayers read following the canon the priest asks God that the dying person be forgiven his sins, and asks God to release him from his unbearable sickness and give him rest with the souls of the righteous.

Some editions of the Book of Needs likewise include an "Order Following the Departure of the Soul from the Body," which includes the usual beginning, the troparia for the departed ("With the souls of the righteous"), the reading of Psalm 90, the litany for the departed, and a special canon. The same order, with the exception of Psalm 90 and the canon, is part of the rite of burial for laymen.

---

[37]The so-called "usual beginning" typically consists of the following: the priest gives the exclamation ("Blessed is our God"), and the reader continues, "Amen. Glory to thee, our God, glory to thee." He then reads the prayer "O Heavenly King" and the trisagion prayers, which the priest concludes with the exclamation, "For thine is the kingdom." The reader says, "Amen." He then reads "Lord, have mercy" twelve times, says "Glory . . . both now . . ." and concludes the usual beginning with the threefold "O come let us worship. . . ."—*Trans.*

According to the custom of the Orthodox Church, after his repose the body of a departed layman is washed and laid in a coffin. Customarily the Psalter is read over the body of a layman or a monk: it is read by laymen who were close to the departed person, and continues without interruption right up to the beginning of the office of the burial. The reading of the Psalter over the departed is a very ancient custom, being mentioned even in the *Apostolic Constitutions.*[38] At the coffin of a priest the Gospel is read—as a rule, by other priests. A departed monk is buried in full monastic robes, while a deacon, priest, or bishop is buried in full liturgical vestments.[39]

The burial of the one who has died, also called the funeral, is customarily served on the third day after his repose, though it may be served earlier or later.[40] For the funeral the body of the departed is brought to the church. The office of burial is preceded by a liturgy for the departed, during which the coffin containing the body of the departed remains in the church.

The Typicon currently in use contains four different service orders for the burial of the departed. One is served for a departed layman, another for a monk, a third for a priest, and a fourth for an infant. There is no special office for the burial of a bishop: a bishop is buried using either the monastic or the priestly rite.

THE ORDER FOR THE BURIAL OF THE DEAD (THE FUNERAL)

In the Book of Needs the order for the funeral of a layman is called "The Order for the Burial of the Dead (Laymen)." The Typicon prescribes that it be served with particular solemnity: "Whereas in other offices, even the offices of baptism and marriage, a single priest officiates, the service of burial is intended to be served with the participation of a whole assembly of clergy—if possible, with a bishop presiding."[41] This is indicated by the notes still found in the Book of Needs: "The principle Priest, or the Bishop, if one be present, shall say . . ."; "The Priests each, secretly, recite, the while, according to his rank, this prayer"; "The principal Priest . . . shall recite, aloud, the Prayer which he hath said above."

---

[38]Cf. *Apostolic Constitutions* 6.5.

[39]At the vesting of a departed bishop the same prayers are read as at the vesting of a living bishop before the divine liturgy. When the vesting is completed a lighted dikerion and trikerion are placed in the hands of the departed bishop. During the vesting the body of the departed bishop remains in a seated position.

[40]The laws in certain countries require a detailed examination to determine the cause of death, making burial on the third day impossible.

[41]St Athanasius of Kovrov, *O pominovenii usopshikh* [On Commemoration of the Departed] (Saint Petersburg: Satis, 1995), 145.

The order of burial begins in the home of the departed. The priest in his epitrachelion censes the body of the departed and all those present, and begins with the exclamation, "Blessed is our God." The usual beginning is followed by the singing of the troparia for the departed:

> With the souls of the righteous departed give rest, O Saviour, to the soul of thy servant, preserving it unto the life of blessedness which is with thee, O thou who lovest mankind.

> In the place of thy rest, O Lord, where all thy Saints repose, give rest also to the soul of thy servant; for thou only lovest mankind.

> Thou art the God who descended into Hell, and loosed the bonds of the captives. Do thou give rest also to the soul of thy servant.

> O Virgin alone Pure and Undefiled, who without seed didst bring forth God, pray thou that his soul may be saved.

A litany for the departed is intoned, and a prayer is read for the repose of the departed (this same prayer is read when the litany for the departed is intoned at the divine liturgy):

> O God of spirits, and of all flesh, who hast trampled down Death, and overthrown the Devil, and given life unto thy world: Do thou, the same Lord, give rest to the soul of thy departed servant, N., in a place of brightness, a place of verdure, a place of repose, whence all sickness, sorrow and sighing have fled away. Pardon every transgression which he hath committed, whether by word, or deed, or thought. For thou art a good God, and lovest mankind; because there is no man who liveth and sinneth not: for thou only art without sin, and thy righteousness is to all eternity, and thy word is true.

After this prayer has been read the priest gives a short dismissal, and the body of the departed is carried out of the house. The solemn burial procession progresses towards the church, "preceded by the Priest, and by the Deacon with the censer." Throughout the procession "Holy God" is sung. Concerning the place where the body of the departed is placed in the church, the Slavonic Book of Needs observes, "When we come to the Church, the remains are deposited in the porch (or in the Church, as is the custom in Russia)." As a rule, the coffin containing the body is placed in the middle of the church, opposite the royal doors, where it remains during the liturgy for the departed. The coffin may also be placed in a side chapel of the church.

The order of the burial has a twofold purpose: primarily, it is prayer for the departed; on the other hand, it is prayer intended to provide consolation and spiritual edification to the kinsmen and friends who remain on this earth. The burial of a loved one is one of those rare occasions when people who do not regularly attend services gather in the church. Unfortunately, the majority of these people do not understand the meaning of the service, which robs it of its edifying effect. The priest should see to it that the prayers are read intelligibly. The order of the burial must absolutely begin or end with a sermon by the priest.

The order of the burial is modeled after matins. It includes Psalms 90 and 118. As a rule, due to its length, the reading of Psalm 118 is generally abbreviated to a few lines. "Yet one would think it would be most desirable and comforting for believers and those who loved the departed one to sing at his coffin the same psalm that is sung at the tomb of the Savior[42]—to sing . . . this moving song of the law that makes blessed even those here on earth who walk in its way, quickening them for eternity, granting them aid at the universal Judgment."[43] When chanted in its entirety at the order of burial, Psalm 118 is divided in three parts.

The psalm is immediately followed by the troparia for the departed, preceded by the refrain, "Blessed art thou, O Lord: teach me thy statutes." The refrain is a phrase from Psalm 118, while the troparia themselves are modeled after the resurrectional troparia sung at matins of Great Saturday. They speak of the blessedness of the saints who have found "the fountain of life and the door of paradise," of the delights the Lord has prepared for those who have followed him. Then, after the small litany, other troparia are sung, beginning with the words, "Give rest with the righteous, O Savior, unto thy servant."

This is followed by Psalm 50 and a canon ascribed to the venerable Theophanes the Branded. Each ode of the canon has four troparia, of which the first is dedicated to the martyrs, the second and third contain prayers for the departed, and the fourth and final troparion addresses the Theotokos (the theme of the final troparion in all canons). After the third, sixth, and ninth odes of the canon there is a litany for the departed. After the sixth ode the kontakion and ikos are chanted:

[42]This refers to matins of Great Saturday [when the "praises" or "lamentations" are sung over Christ's burial shroud, interpolated between the verses of Psalm 118—*Ed.*].

[43]Athanasius of Kovrov, *O pominovenii usopshikh*, 147.

The funeral of His Holiness Alexy II, patriarch of Moscow and all Russia

With the saints give rest, O Christ, to the soul of thy servant, where there is neither sickness, nor sorrow, nor sighing, but life everlasting.

Thou only art immortal, who has created and fashioned man. For out of the earth were we mortals made, and unto the earth shall we return again, as thou didst command when thou madest me, saying unto me: For earth thou art, and unto the earth shalt thou return. Whither, also, all we mortals wend our way, making our funeral dirge the song: Alleluia.

Upon completion of the canon, eight stichera for the departed are sung, composed by John of Damascus, corresponding to the eight tones of the Octoechos. These stichera are "a stunning message of the vanity of all that allures us in the world, of the vanity of all that does not remain with us after death; a message that is beneficial and edifying for all those present to listen to in its entirety, from beginning to end."[44]

The stichera are followed by the Gospel Beatitudes, interspersed with troparia for the departed. Then a passage from the apostle Paul's First Epistle to the Thessalonians is read, concerning the general resurrection (1 Thess 4.13–17). A Gospel passage is also read, repeating Christ's declaration that one who hears his words and believes in him "shall not come into condemnation; but is passed from death unto life," and his words concerning the resurrection of the dead (Jn 5.24–30).

After the Gospel another litany for the departed is intoned, after which the senior priest or bishop reads aloud the prayer "O God of spirits" at the coffin

[44]Athanasius of Kovrov, *O pominovenii usopshikh,* 148.

of the departed. Then the last kiss is given to the departed, first by the clergy in order of seniority, then by the laity. During this ritual stichera are sung, the first of which begins with the words, "Come, brethren, let us give the last kiss unto the dead, rendering thanks unto God." These stichera portray in poetic form the sorrow of kindred and friends as they bid farewell to the one whom they loved. Several stichera reflect on the vanity and transience of human life. The penultimate sticheron is written on behalf of the departed, in which he addresses his kindred and friends who remain on earth, asking them to pray for him.

Next follow the trisagion prayers, the troparia "With the souls of the righteous," the litany for the departed, and the dismissal. Following the dismissal, "the bishop or the principal priest" must say thrice, "Eternal be thy memory, O our brother, who art worthy of blessedness and ever-memorable." Then he reads the "parting prayer," in which, addressing the departed, he says, "May the Lord Jesus Christ . . . pardon thee, O spiritual child, all thy deeds done amiss in this life, both voluntary and involuntary." After this the body of the departed is brought out of the church and solemnly carried to its resting place (in the cemetery), to the singing of "Holy God." At this point, before closing the lid of the coffin, the priest sprinkles earth crosswise over the body of the departed, with the words, "The earth is the Lord's, and the fulness thereof: the round world, and they that dwell therein." He then pours "oil from the shrine lamp" over the body.

In practice the order of burial is concluded somewhat differently. After the dismissal the deacon, and not the bishop, says, "Give rest eternal in blessed falling asleep, O Lord, to the soul of thy servant, *N.*, and make his memory to be eternal." The choir sings "Memory eternal" thrice, and the deacon performs the final censing. The earth, as a rule, is sprinkled into the coffin before leaving the church. Pouring oil on the body of the departed is frequently omitted in practice, despite this custom being so ancient as to have been recorded by Dionysius the Areopagite. Upon arriving at the cemetery, as a rule, a litiya (called a trisagion in the Greek tradition) for the departed is served.

Traditionally a copy of the prayer of absolution, read over the body at the end of the order of burial, is placed into the hands of the departed. This prayer, beginning with the words "Our Lord Jesus Christ, by his divine grace . . . ," may have been borrowed from the Jerusalem practice; certain of its expressions resemble the prayer of intercession from the liturgy of the apostle James.[45]

[45]Vasily Prilutsky, *Chastnoe bogosluzhenie v Russkoi Tserkvi v XVI i pervoi polovine XVII v.* [Private Worship in the Russian Church in the Sixteenth and First Half of the Seventeenth Centuries] (Kiev: Petr Barskiy, 1912), 254–255.

The above service order differs significantly from the offices for the burial of monks, priests, and infants. Each of these offices is compiled in such a way as to maximally reflect the way of life or ministry of the departed.

In particular, the *order of burial for monks* has no canon. Instead, resurrectional antiphons are sung in the eight tones. These antiphons, authorship of which is ascribed to Theodore the Studite, speak of the monk's ardent love for God, of solitude, and of dwelling in the wilderness. The antiphons alternate with stichera for the departed, also in the eight tones. The troparia at the Beatitudes, which differ in content from those chanted at the burial of a layman, focus primarily on the topic of asceticism as the path to celestial glory. Of the stichera at the last kiss, only the first four are sung; the stichera depicting in detail the sorrow of kinsmen at the loss of their loved one are omitted. As Bishop Athanasius (Sakharov) notes, "The love of monks for a departed brother is of a different nature than the love of laymen, and their sorrow at this time likewise differs in nature. It is poured out in calmer, more restrained expressions."[46]

A special *order of burial for priests* appears in Greek euchologia in the early fifteenth century, and in Russian editions of the Book of Needs towards the end of the same century, but the order did not acquire its modern form until the seventeenth century.[47] The burial of a priest is of greater complexity, solemnity, and duration than the burials of laymen and monks.[48] Five readings from the epistles and the Gospel form its basis, interspersed with psalms, antiphons, troparia, and sedalia. The majority of the readings and hymns are of a general funereal nature, but some contain reflections on the life, ministry, and death of the priest:

Thy godly minister, made a partaker of the nature divine in his translation hence, through thy life-giving mystery, O Christ,[49] is now come unto thee. Receive thou his soul in thy hand, as it were a bird, O Saviour. Establish thou him in thy courts, and in the choir of the angels.

He who lived in godliness, and was adorned as thy priest, the sacrifice and minister of thy mysteries divine, by thy divine command hath passed over from life's clamour unto thee. Save him whom, as priest, thou didst accept, O Saviour; and because of thy great mercy give unto him rest with the righteous.[50]

[46]Athanasius of Kovrov, *O pominovenii usopshikh,* 159.
[47]Prilutsky, *Chastnoe bogosluzhenie v Russkoi Tserkvi,* 271–282.
[48]Athanasius of Kovrov, *O pominovenii usopshikh,* 154.
[49]These words signify that before his death the newly reposed communed of the holy mysteries.
[50]*Order for the Burial of a Priest,* stichera at the praises.

The canon in the order of burial for a priest is modeled after the canon of Great Saturday. The sixth ode of the canon is followed not by one, but by twenty-four ikoi. As the body of the departed priest is being carried from the church to the cemetery, the irmoi of the penitential Great Canon of Andrew of Crete are sung—"He is for me unto salvation." Traditionally, before being transferred to the cemetery, the coffin containing the priest's body is carried thrice around the church.

The *order of burial for children* is fairly brief: in it all prayers for forgiveness of the sins of the departed are omitted. Emphasis is placed primarily not on mourning the departed child, who is referred to as having passed over into the heavenly habitations, but on the repentance of his living relations:

> Let us not mourn the child, but rather weep heavily for ourselves who sin always; that we may be delivered from Gehenna.[51]

> Grieve ye not for me, for I have undertaken nothing worthy of grief. But weep ye rather always for yourselves who have sinned sore, O kin and friends, the dead child crieth.[52]

During the paschal season the burial of the departed follows a specific order, in which many prayers for the departed and of repentance are replaced with paschal prayers. As the Book of Needs notes in this regard, if a person reposes during Bright Week, at his burial "very little of the customary Office for the Dead is sung, because of the majesty and honor of the joyful Feast of the Resurrection: for it is the festival of joy and gladness, not of lamentation."[53]

The Long and Short Memorial Services
(the Panikhida and Litiya, or Mnēmosyno and Trisagion)

The service called the *panikhida* in the modern usage of the Russian Orthodox Church (or the *mnēmosyno* in the Greek Church) is comprised of an abbreviated matins for the departed. In the ancient Church the term *panikhida* had an entirely different meaning, signifying an all-night vigil (the Greek word παννυχίς/*pannikhís* literally means "all-night"). The order for serving the panikhida, found in the fourteenth chapter of the Typicon, contains the rules for serving an all-night

---

[51] *Order for the Burial of a Child.* Canon, ode IV.
[52] *Order for the Burial of a Child.* Canon, ode V.
[53] *Order for the Burial of Those who Die at Holy Easter.*

vigil for the departed. In practice, however, in most cases the panikhida is served as a private service, at the request of one parishioner or several. The service order of the panikhida includes litanies for the departed, Psalm 90, Psalm 118 (omitted in practice), the troparia for the departed ("The choir of the saints"), the troparia "Give rest with the righteous," Psalm 50, the singing of the irmoi of the canon for the departed with the refrains (the troparia of the canon, as a rule, are omitted), the trisagion prayers, the troparia "With the souls of the righteous," and the dismissal. After the dismissal the deacon traditionally intones, "Give rest eternal in blessed falling asleep, O Lord, to the soul of thy servant, N., departed this life; and make his memory to be eternal." The choir sings "Memory eternal" thrice.

A *litiya* (or *trisagion*) is a short prayer service for the departed, comprised only of the ending portion of the panikhida: the trisagion prayers, the troparia "With the souls of the righteous," a single litany for the departed with a prayer, the dismissal, "Give rest eternal in blessed falling asleep," and "Memory eternal."

During the paschal season the panikhida consists of an abbreviated paschal matins, with only a handful of prayers and hymns for the departed.

Special Cases for Commemorating the Departed

All the prayers and offices for the departed found in Orthodox liturgical books pertain only to persons who have been baptized in the Orthodox Church. The church Typicon has no prayers for unbaptized persons, including unbaptized infants.[54] The prayers for unbaptized, stillborn, or aborted infants that are encountered in certain books are not part of the Orthodox order of services. This category also includes the canon to the martyr Varus, found in certain Old Russian manuscripts and containing prayers for those who have died in other faiths.[55]

The absence of prayers for non-Christians and the heterodox (both living and departed) in the church Typicon certainly does not mean that such prayers may not be offered at all by Orthodox Christians. The church Typicon pertains to the daily

---

[54]In 2018, a service for infants who died without baptism was approved by the synod of the Moscow Patriarchate (the Slavonic service text is available online: p2.patriarchia.ru/2018/07/14/1239018310/posledovanie-mlad.docx).—*Ed.*

[55]An akathist to St Varus is available in English, blessed to be read in homes by bishops in the Serbian Church in America and the Moscow Patriarchate. Isaac Lambertson, *Akathist to the Martyr Varus: Holy Intercessor for Family Members Who Reposed Outside the Orthodox Faith* (Safford, AZ: St Paisius Monastery, 2009).—*Ed.*

cycle of divine services: it says nothing regarding Christian prayer in the home, or the prayers a priest may say in special cases.

Church tradition has recorded several instances of prayers offered by Christians for departed non-Christians or heretics. In the Synaxarion of Meatfare Saturday, found in the Lenten Triodion, three such instances are mentioned. The first instance is the "account of Saint Macarius, who found the dry skull of an impious Hellenite man by the wayside and questioned it." This refers to the account from the *Alphabetical Patericon*, concerning how the venerable Macarius of Egypt, as he was walking in the desert, once saw a skull lying in the sand, and touching it with his staff he asked, " 'Who are you then?' The skull answered . . . 'I was the high priest of the idols and of the pagans who inhabited this place;

Emperor Michael and Empress Theodora. Icon. Novgorod. 16th c.

but you are the spirit-bearing Abba Macarius. Whenever you feel compassion for those in chastisement and pray for them they are a little relieved.' "[56]

The Synaxarion also relates an account mentioned in certain lives of St Gregory the Dialogist, of how the soul of the emperor Trajan was "baptized" in hell by the tears of St Gregory. Trajan was a persecutor of Christians, but he had performed one charitable act, of which St Gregory learned. Filled with pity, Gregory went to the church and prayed with tears for the soul of the persecutor until it was revealed to him that his prayer had been heard.

Finally, the same Synaxarion mentions the story of the salvation of the "unholy" emperor Theophilus (reigned 829–842) through the prayers of his widow Theodora (815–867). After the death of Theophilus, who was an iconoclast, his son Michael III (*842–867) inherited the throne, and Theodora became his regent. Theodora restored the veneration of icons, but asked Patriarch Methodius of Constantinople to absolve her deceased husband of his sins. The patriarch replied that the Church could forgive the living, but that it was unable to forgive those who had died unrepentant in a state of mortal sin. Theodora, however, said that before his death Theophilus had kissed an icon. The church council decreed that for one week prayers should be offered in all the churches of the capital for the repose of the emperor. Patriarch Methodius took a parchment and wrote upon it the names of

---

[56] *Sayings of the Desert Fathers*, Macarius the Egyptian 38 (PPS 52:191).

all the iconoclast emperors, and laid it on the altar in the Church of Hagia Sophia. In a dream he beheld an angel, who proclaimed to him that God had pardoned the emperor. In the morning the patriarch came to the church and saw that the name of Theophilus had vanished from the list of iconoclast emperors. After this incident the church council confirmed that the emperor had been absolved of his sins.

Citing the stories related in the abovementioned Synaxarion, the holy hierarch Philaret of Moscow said that an Orthodox Christian may pray for a departed Lutheran, though he felt that such prayers ought not to prayed "openly," that is, publicly. Furthermore, the hierarch permitted a deceased Lutheran to be commemorated at proskomede:

> This matter is not an easy one to resolve. As grounds for permission you wish to employ the fact that Macarius the Great prayed even for a dead pagan. It is not expedient to make a general rule of the wonderworker's boldness. Gregory the Dialogist likewise prayed for Trajan, and was informed that his prayer had not been fruitless, but that he was not to offer up such bold prayers in the future. . . . To do a thing contrary to the rules for the consolation of one, but not without scandalizing many, would not be seemly to my mind. For a living Lutheran a moleben may be served, asking upon him the grace of God, that it might draw him into the unity of the true Church, but with the deceased it is a different matter. We do not condemn him: it was not his will to remain outside the Orthodox Church to the end. Knowing several Lutherans who had respect for and faith in the Orthodox Church, but who had died outside of union with it, I permitted prayer for them—not public prayer in the Church, with which they did not unite openly during their lives, but commemoration at proskomede and panikhidas at home.[57]

As we have noted elsewhere,[58] the question of prayer for the heterodox was the subject of lively discussion on the pages of Russian ecclesiastical publications in the early nineteenth century. Archpriest E. Akvilonov wrote in a 1905 issue of *Tserkovnyy Vestnik* that prayer for a deceased Lutheran would not be accepted even by the Lutheran himself, since during his lifetime he did not believe in the power of prayer for the departed: it would be an unsolicited favor, since "at the

---

[57]Holy Hierarch Philaret (Drozdov) of Moscow, *Sobranie mneniy i otzyvov Filareta, mitropolita Moskovskago i Kolomenskago, po uchebnym i tserkovno-gosudarstvennym voprosam. Tom dopolnitel'nyy.* [Collected Opinions and Comments of Philaret, Metropolitan of Moscow and Kolomna, on Matters of Education, Church, and State. Supplemental volume] (Saint Petersburg: Synodal'naya tipografiya, 1887), 186.

[58]Cf. Hilarion (Alfeyev), *Tainstvo very,* 259.

hour of his death the reposed had no thoughts of converting to Orthodoxy." By way of example the author cites various corporations, associations, and academic and industrial communities that strictly guard their corporate boundaries, barring entrance to unauthorized persons: "Every member of the Church is obligated to cultivate in himself the true Christian, *Orthodox ecclesiastical corporate spirit,* and, not forgetting his duty to love his neighbor, to strictly uphold the banner of the Church."[59]

Archpriest Akvilonov was opposed by Vasily Sokolov, author of the book *Mozhno li i dolzhno li molit'sya v tserkvi za usopshikh inoslavnikh?* [May and Must We Pray in Church for the Heterodox Who Have Departed?] published by the Moscow Theological Academy:

> In all these discourses there is an undertone of extraordinary callousness, a squeamish, selfish concern lest one do a good turn unnecessarily and it prove to be intrusive and unwelcome. Completely forgotten in them is the fact that, despite the differences in confessions, we are all Christians, and hence, in loving our neighbors, we are obligated to render them tremendous aid. During their lives deceased Lutherans and Reformers did not believe in prayers for the departed. But what of it? We ourselves are Orthodox, after all! We believe that our prayer can be of tremendous aid to the deceased.[60]

The spirit of true Orthodoxy, the author continues, is not a "corporate" spirit, but a spirit of love, compassion, and condescension to all men, including those outside the Orthodox Church.

Recent Orthodox history has seen the advent of specially compiled orders of burial for non-Orthodox departed, approved by the ecclesiastical authorities. In 1869 one such order was instituted by Patriarch Gregory VI of Constantinople. This order consists of the trisagion prayers, the seventeenth kathisma with the customary funereal refrains, an epistle reading, a Gospel reading, and the small dismissal.[61] A similar "Service Order for Non-Orthodox Deceased" was printed shortly before the 1917 revolution at the Synodal Print Shop in Saint Petersburg. In this service order the usual beginning and Psalm 27 are followed first by Psalm 118, divided into three parts and chanted with the refrain "Alleluia," then by four

---

[59]Cited by Vasily Sokolov, *Mozhno li i dolzhno li molit'sya v tserkvi za usopshikh inoslavnikh?* [May and Must We Pray in Church for the Heterodox who have Departed?] (Sergiev Posad: Trinity-Sergius Lavra Printshop, 1906), 23.

[60]Sokolov, *Mozhno li i dolzhno li molit'sya v tserkvi za usopshikh inoslavnikh,* 23–31.

[61]Athanasius of Kovrov, *O pominovenii usopshikh,* 192.

Holy Hierarch Athanasius (Sakharov)

troparia at "The Blameless" ("The choir of the saints," "Ye who preached the Lamb of God," "Glory," and "Both now") and Psalm 38. Next come an ikos ("Thou only art immortal"), a prokeimenon, an epistle reading (Rom 14.6–9), a Gospel reading (Jn 5.17–24), the stichera at the last kiss (1, 4, 5, 8, 9, and 11), and the usual small dismissal (not for the departed).[62] Use of these service orders, however, never became widespread.

The abovementioned accounts of prayer for heterodox departed were analyzed in the mid-twentieth century by the renowned Russian liturgist and confessor, St Athanasius (Sakharov, 1887–1962), who came to the following conclusion:

Christian love, which moves us to prayer for our brethren who have gone astray, finds ways to satisfy this need without violating the canons of the Church: both in prayer in the home . . . and in public worship in the church . . . commemorating them at proskomede, on the basis of the authoritative permission of Metropolitan Philaret. If therefore the names of non-Orthodox departed may be pronounced at one of the most important commemorations—the proskomede—this means they may also be entered in commemoration books and intoned along with other names."[63]

This conclusion, however, remains to this day simply the personal opinion of a hierarch, albeit one greatly respected and numbered with the choir of the saints. In the current practice of the Orthodox Church, departed heterodox are not commemorated at proskomede and the heterodox are not named at litanies for the departed. Some priests accept commemorations slips with the names of heterodox departed, to be read silently at the liturgy. Others, on the contrary, are vigilant in their efforts to keep the names of heterodox persons off of commemoration slips. In certain parishes the ladies who run the candle desk consider it their duty to scan the commemoration slips submitted for any "non-Orthodox" names (Albert, Leopold, Janine, etc.), which if found are promptly crossed out. This vigilance, even if motivated by the worthy intention of guarding the "corporate boundaries,"

[62]Ibid., 193.
[63]Ibid.

nevertheless to our mind cannot be considered justified (the more so since, as noted above, not even all Orthodox Christians are named after Orthodox saints).

Another special case worthy of note is prayer for suicides. The ancient canons permitted liturgical commemoration of suicides only if the person who had taken his own life was "beside himself" or "out of his mind," that is, in a state of insanity. The fourteenth canon of Timothy of Alexandria states:

> *Question:* If anyone having no control of himself lays violent hands on himself or hurls himself to destruction, should an offering be made for him or not?
>
> *Answer:* The Clergyman ought to discern in his behalf whether he was actually and truly out of his mind when he did it. For oftentimes those who are interested in the victim and want to have him accorded an offering and a prayer in his behalf will deliberately lie and assert that he had no control of himself. Sometimes, however, he did it as a result of influence exercised by other men, or somehow otherwise as a result of paying too little attention to circumstances, and no offering ought to be made in his behalf. It is incumbent, therefore, upon the Clergyman in any case to investigate the matter accurately, in order to avoid incurring judgment.[64]

This canon refers to an "offering," that is, to a liturgy for the departed. No mention is made of other forms of commemoration. The longstanding practice of the Church, however, also excluded other forms of commemoration: a person who took his own life was not granted a church funeral, and panikhidas were not served for his soul. In many cases the body of a suicide was buried outside the cemetery. In refusing prayerful commemoration to the suicide, the Church leaves him solely to the mercy of God, as the holy hierarch Theophan the Recluse says concerning this:

> You ask whether one may pray for suicides. The Church does not allow it; how then can its sons and daughters pray for them? . . . This reveals an attempt to show that we are more merciful that the Church and God himself. . . . It is enough to limit ourselves to pity for them, committing their fate to the boundless mercy of God.[65]

---

[64] *The Rudder,* 898.

[65] Theophan the Recluse, *Sobranie Pisem* [Collected Letters], 4th ed. (Moscow: Pravilo Very, 2000), 58–59.

The reason for the Church's strictness toward suicides is that suicide is considered a mortal sin that a person cannot repent of during his life, since the sin and death occur simultaneously. To an equal degree, however, this strictness is pedagogically motivated: by refusing a funeral and commemoration to the suicide the Church emphasizes that a suicide essentially places himself outside the Church. In an era when religious sentiment was widespread, when Christian morality defined the standards for behavior, the prospect of being deprived of a funeral and commemoration after death was able to prevent a person from committing suicide.

The pedagogical aspect of the rule depriving suicides of all church commemoration proved considerably weakened in an era when the Church ceased to exercise a definitive influence on public morality. For this reason in the nineteenth and early twentieth centuries discussion of whether suicides might be commemorated was resumed with renewed vigor. Time and time again the increased frequency of suicide obliged pastors and spiritual fathers to revisit the issue. The venerable Leo (Leonid) of Optina wrote the following to one of his disciples, Pavel Tambovtsev, whose father had committed suicide:

> Entrust both yourself and your father's fate to the will of the Lord, which is all-wise, all powerful. Do not tempt the miracles of the All-high, but strive through humility to strengthen yourself within the bounds of tempered sorrow. Pray to the All-good Creator, thus fulfilling the duty of the love and obligation of a son ... in the spirit of the virtuous and wise, thus: "Seek out, O Lord, the perishing soul of my father: if it is possible, have mercy! Unfathomable are Thy judgments. Do not account my prayer as sin. But may Thy holy will be done!" Pray simply, without inquiring, entrusting your heart to the right hand of the All-high. Of course, so grievous a death for your father was not the will of God, but now it rests completely in the will of Him Who is able to hurl both soul and body into the fiery furnace, of Him Who both humbles and lifts up, puts to death and brings to life, takes down to Hell and leads up therefrom. . . . It remains for you to entrust the eternal lot of your father to the goodness and compassion of God, and if it is His good will to show mercy, who can oppose Him?[66]

The current practice of the Orthodox Church, based on centuries of tradition, allows for commemorating suicides if the deceased was mentally ill and not in

---

[66]Elder Leonid, first great elder of Optina. Quoted from *Orthodox Life* 26.1 (Jan.–Feb. 1976), 27–31.

control of himself at the time the sin was committed.[67] With the permission of a bishop other exceptions to the rule may also be permitted—in particular, if the suicide was a minor. Some cases that are formally classified as suicides may prove upon closer inspection to merit *oeconomia* (leniency) from the Church. Conversely, death resulting from a drug overdose or drunkenness is not formally classified as suicide, but in actuality is exactly that, even if the deceased did not intend to take his own life.

There is therefore no universal answer to the question of church prayer for suicides. In making a decision on this matter the bishop's guiding principle is that the Church punishes and exacts revenge on no one, especially posthumously. The Church grieves for every person who departs this life without repentance, and it hopes in the mercy of God. In cases where leniency may be shown in the matter of prayer for the departed, it is shown. If, however, the bishop makes the decision to deny such prayer, this is in no way motivated by a lack of compassion for the deceased, either on his part or on the part of the Orthodox Church. Rather, it is motivated by an acknowledgment that the Church is powerless to oppose the free will of a person who has voluntarily left this life and thereby placed himself outside the Church. Here too, however, hope remains in the mercy of God that knows no bounds.

---

[67] There is an opinion that every suicide is "beside himself," that is, mentally ill. This opinion was held, notably, by the renowned archpriest Boris Stark of Yaroslavl (1909–1996), who inquired, "Who in his right mind would take his own life?" This same archpriest pointed out that the time of the suicide and the time of death are not always concurrent: a person who hurls himself from ten floors up may have time to repent of it before his death. In 2011, the synod of the Moscow Patriarchate approved a "rite of prayerful consolation for the relatives of those who have taken their own lives," which may be found online in Slavonic: http://www.patriarchia.ru/db/text/1586949.html.—*Ed.*

10

The Blessing of Water

I N THE MODERN PRACTICE of the Orthodox Church there are two rites for the blessing of water: the lesser blessing and the great blessing. Furthermore, the blessing of water is a part of the order of the sacrament of baptism. At a hierarchal liturgy, before the great entrance, the prayer at the blessing of water ("O Lord our God, who didst sanctify the streams of Jordan by thy redeeming manifestation . . .") is read at the washing of the bishop's hands; this same prayer is found in the order of the consecration of a church.

Water as a religious symbol and the blessing of water at the sacrament of baptism have been discussed above in the section devoted to that sacrament.[1] In this section we will examine the service orders for the great and lesser blessings of water.

THE GREAT BLESSING OF WATER

The order of the great blessing of water takes place on the eve and on the actual day of the feast of Theophany. As early as the fourth century the water drawn on the feast of Theophany had come to be widely viewed as possessing particular sanctity. John Chrysostom says:

On this day all, having obtained the waters, do carry it home and keep it all year, since today the waters are sanctified. And an obvious phenomenon occurs: these waters in their essence do not spoil with the passage of time, but obtained today, for one whole year and often for two or three years, they remain unharmed and fresh.[2]

---

[1]Cf. pp. 34–35 and 59–64 of this volume.
[2]Chrysostom, *Discourse on the Day of the Baptism of Christ* (available online: https://oca.org/fs/sermons/discourse-on-the-day-of-the-baptism-of-christ).

In the sixth century in the Byzantine East the order of the blessing of water on the feast of Theophany was a universal custom. This practice in Jerusalem is attested by Anthony of Piacenza (570), while the practice in Constantinople was described by Paul the Silentiary. The order of the great blessing of water is set forth in ancient Greek liturgical manuscripts, including the *Barberini Euchologion* (late eighth century) and the Typicon of the Great Church (ninth and tenth centuries). Furthermore, all the primary prayers and readings presently contained in this order are already found in the earliest known manuscripts. The custom of a twofold blessing of water—on the eve of Theophany and on the day of the feast itself—is taken from the Jerusalem Typicon. In Russia the first blessing of water took place in the church, and the second at "the Jordan," that is, at a hole in the ice, in which those who wished would immerse themselves following the rite.[3] This custom of immersing oneself in the ice hole remains to this day, and has gained wide popularity in recent years.[4]

The order of the great blessing of water takes place at the liturgy after the prayer behind the ambon and two repetitions of "Blessed be the name of the Lord." The rite begins with the singing of these troparia:

The voice of the Lord upon the waters crieth out, saying: "Come, receive all of you the Spirit of wisdom, the Spirit of understanding, the Spirit of the fear of God, of Christ Who is made manifest.

Today the nature of the waters is sanctified, and the Jordan is divided, and turns back the streams of its own waters, beholding the Master baptized.

As a man thou didst come to the river, O Christ the King, hastening to receive the baptism of a servant, O Good One, at the hand of the Forerunner, because of our sins, O Lover of Mankind.

Taking the form of a servant, O Lord, Thou didst come to the voice crying in the wilderness, "Prepare the way of the Lord," asking for baptism, O Thou Who knowest not sin. The waters saw Thee and were afraid. The Forerunner began to tremble and cried out, saying: "How shall the lamp illumine the Light?

---

[3]Mikhail Zheltov, "Vodoosvyashchenie" [The Blessing of Water], in *Pravoslavnaya entsiklopediya* [The Orthodox Encyclopedia], vol. 9, 140–148 (Moscow: Tserkovno-nauchnyy tsentr "Pravoslavnaya entsiklopediya," 2005).

[4]In Greece the custom is somewhat different: on the feast of Theophany the priest throws a wooden cross into the water, and the young people dive into the water after it, competing to be the first to retrieve it.

How shall the servant lay hands upon the Master? Sanctify me and the waters, O Savior, Who takest away the sins of the world."

This is followed by three excerpts from the book of the prophet Jonah, which in the Christian tradition are viewed as a prediction of New Testament baptism. These are followed by a reading from an epistle of St Paul (1 Cor 10.1–4), which interprets the passing of the Israelites through the Red Sea as a prefiguration of baptism, and a Gospel reading (Mk 1.9–11) describing Jesus' baptism by John. Next comes the great litany with additional petitions that the water be sanctified (identical to those said at the litany during the sacrament of baptism). As the litany is intoned the priest reads the prayer, "O Lord Jesus Christ, thou Only-begotten Son . . . ," asking that the minds of the worshippers be illumined by the Holy Spirit, and that the prayers offered over the water be accepted. Then the priest intones aloud, "Great art thou, O Lord . . . ," and reads the prayer of blessing of the water, beginning with the words, "For thou, of thine own good will, hast brought into being all things which before were not."[5]

After reading the prayer the priest immerses the cross three times in a vessel of water, as the troparion of Theophany, "When thou wast baptized in the Jordan, O Lord," is sung three times.[6] The immersion of the cross in the water is what distinguishes the rite of the great and lesser blessings of water from the rite that takes place during the sacrament of baptism, where the water is sanctified through the immersion of the priest's hand and anointing the water with blessed oil.

Then the priest sprinkles holy water over the faithful in all four directions. The stichera of the feast of Theophany are sung, beginning "Let us sing, O faithful." Following the stichera the choir sings "Blessed be the name of the Lord," and the dismissal of the divine liturgy is given.

In the church Typicon, holy water that is blessed on the feast of Theophany is called "the great agiasma," or holy thing. It is customarily drunk only on an empty stomach (which, incidentally, is contrary to both the Typicon and the Menaion[7]).

[5] The text of this prayer is included above in the service order of the sacrament of baptism, on pages 61–62.

[6] The text of the troparion is found in vol. 4, pp. 291–292.

[7] See, for example, the *Typikon* [Typicon], part 2 (St. Petersburg: Redaktsionno-izdatel'skoe obedinenie "Sankt-Peterburg," 1992), 391–392: "Let all be aware concerning the Holy Water: those who abstain from drinking the Holy Water because they have eaten are not acting correctly; for the Holy Water has been provided by the grace of God for the sanctification of the world and all creation. Wherefore, it is sprinkled in all places, even dishonorable ones, and even in places where it may be trodden underfoot. Where, then, is the logic in abstaining from it? But be aware that impurity comes upon us not because of eating, but because of our abominable acts; and that we may be cleansed from them, we drink this Holy Water without doubting." [Translation taken from ‹https://stmaximus.org/files/ConfTong/140105CT.pdf›.—*Trans.*]

The Procession of the Tree of the Precious Cross. Icon. 16th c.

A vessel of holy water always stands in the church, and the faithful keep the water of Theophany in their homes throughout the year. The water blessed on Theophany is used for drinking, for anointing, and for sprinkling people, churches, homes, and various objects. In accordance with the words of the service it is perceived as "a fountain of incorruption, a gift of sanctification, a loosing of sins, a healing of sicknesses." In Old Russia there was even a special order of "communing" of holy water, and in the disciplinary canons of Byzantium (particularly the Nomocanon of John the Faster) drinking holy water was permitted to those who were barred from the sacrament of the Eucharist for canonical reasons. This, however, by no means meant that holy water was seen as a substitute for communion.

THE LESSER BLESSING OF WATER

In Constantinople the order of the lesser blessing of water was served on August 1, on the feast of the Procession of the Tree of the Precious and Life-giving Cross of the Lord. On this day in the capital of Byzantium a procession took place with the tree of the cross (described in detail in the tenth century by the emperor Constantine VII Porphyrogenitus[8]), and the life-giving tree would be immersed in water. Another tradition, which may possibly have influenced the formation of the rite of the lesser blessing, was the custom of bathing in the spring of the Church of the Most Holy Theotokos in Blachernae, Constantinople. By the twelfth century the lesser blessing of water was served in Constantinople on the first of each month. The earliest surviving manuscripts of the order of the lesser blessing date back to the eleventh and twelfth centuries.[9]

[8]Constantine Porphyrogenitus, *De Cerimoniis* 2.8 (PG 112:1005C–1008A).
[9]Zheltov, "Vodoosvyashchenie," 145.

The modern order of the lesser blessing of water begins with the exclamation, "Blessed is our God," followed by the trisagion prayers and Psalm 142. Next "God is the Lord," the troparion "Let us who are lowly and sinful, now diligently run to the Theotokos," and the troparion "Never shall we who are unworthy" are sung. Then Psalm 50 is read, after which twenty-four short troparia to the Theotokos are sung. The first troparion—"O Virgin who didst receive from the angel the salutation 'Rejoice!' and gavest birth unto thine own Creator, save them that magnify thee"—serves as the model for the other troparia, which are linked by an alphabetical acrostic.[10] Joined to this group of twenty-four troparia to the Theotokos are several short troparia to saints, followed by the exclamation, "For holy art thou, O our God." After the exclamation another four troparia to the Theotokos are sung, beginning with the words, "Now the time is drawn nigh which sanctifieth all men." One of the troparia—"O Christ, who through the waters dost rain down a fountain of healings in the all-honourable temple of the Virgin"[11]—is referring to the church in Blachernae, where this "fountain of healings" was located. Both groups of troparia, of twenty-four and of four, are found in the earliest known manuscript, which contains the rite of the lesser blessing of water and dates back to 1027 (Paris Coislin 213).

Upon completion of the troparia, which conclude with the trisagion being sung once, a prokeimenon is intoned, consisting of verses from Psalm 23, and a passage from the epistles is read (Heb 2.11–18) on the subject of sanctification and cleansing of sins through the incarnation of the Son of God. The Gospel reading describes the Sheep's Pool in Jerusalem, on which an angel would descend from time to time, and the first to enter the water after the troubling of the waters would be restored to health.

Next follows a great litany with petitions that the water be sanctified, and a prayer that differs in content from the one read at the rite of the great blessing of water:

> O Lord our God, who art mighty in counsel, and wonderful in thy deeds . . . and receivest the devout tears of all who are in distress: (For this cause thou didst come in the similitude of a servant, scorning not our image, but giving true health to the body, and saying: Lo, thou art healed, sin no more; and with clay thou didst make the man's eyes whole, and having commanded him to

---

[10]That is, each troparion begins with one of the letters of the Greek alphabet in order. In the Slavonic translation, naturally, this acrostic is lost.

[11]Most English translations mistakenly refer to Christ himself as the fountain.—*Trans.*

wash, didst make him, by thy word, to rejoice in the light, putting to confusion the enemies' floods of passion, and drying up the bitter sea of the life of the same, and subduing the waves of sensual desires heavy to be endured): Do thou, the same King who lovest mankind, who hast granted unto us to clothe ourselves in the garment of snowy whiteness by water and the Spirit, send down upon us thy blessing, and through partaking of this water, through sprinkling therewith wash away the defilement of passions.

Icon of the Theotokos the Life-bearing Font. Crete. 15th c.

The prayer goes on to mention the Theotokos and several saints. Then there are petitions for the ecclesiastical and secular authorities, for "those who hate us, and those who love us," for those in captivity and in affliction. A prominent feature of this prayer is the absence of special petitions that the water be sanctified. Thus, the water is sanctified not by invoking the Holy Spirit, but by coming into contact with the tree of the precious cross.[12]

Following this prayer and the words of the priest, "Peace be unto all," a short prayer is read from the rite of the great blessing of water ("Incline thine ear, O Lord, and hearken unto us"), after which the priest immerses a cross into the water to the singing of the troparion, "O Lord, save thy people," and then sprinkles the church and all those present with holy water. The order concludes with the singing of troparia to the Theotokos and the holy unmercenaries, a small litany, the exclamation "Hearken unto us, O God our Saviour," and the prayer "O greatly merciful Master," a prayer comprising part of the litiya at the all-night vigil and of certain other liturgical rites. Here this prayer with its commemoration of the saints takes the place of the dismissal.

In the current practice of the Russian Orthodox Church the lesser blessing of water takes place on the feast of the Procession of the Cross (August 1), on the feast in honor of the icon of the Mother of God the Life-bearing Font (on Friday

---

[12]Incidentally, the majority of editions of the Book of Needs contain "another prayer over the water." This prayer notably contains these words: "Thine unworthy servants now humbly pray and entreat thee: send the grace of the Most Holy Spirit upon this water, and by thy heavenly blessing bless, purify, and sanctify it."

of Bright Week), and at the midfeast of Pentecost. As a rule the lesser blessing of water is also served on a church's patronal feast. At the request of the faithful a lesser blessing of water is frequently served on other days as well, and may be served in the home.

Unlike the water of Theophany, water blessed using the lesser order is not drunk only on an empty stomach. In all other aspects it is used just like the water of Theophany: it is drunk unto the healing of soul and body; it is used to sprinkle churches, homes, and people; and it is used for the blessing of icons, liturgical items, vehicles, and household items.

11

The Consecration of a Church

I N THE ORTHODOX CHURCH there are several service orders related to the construction of a new church: the order used at the founding of a church, the order for placing a cross on the cupola of a church, the order for the blessing of a bell tower, and the dedication (conse-cration) of a church. In addition there is a lesser blessing of a church, served after the renovation of a previously consecrated church, if the altar was not moved in the process of renovation. The consecration of the antimension usually takes place at the same time as the consecration of the church, but it may also be served as a sepa-rate order. The orders for the blessing of various liturgical items and icons may also be served separately.

St Peter laying the foundation of Holy Dormition Cathedral. Marginal scene from a hagiographical icon. Late 16th–early 17th c.

The orders for the founding and con-secration of a church are of very ancient origin. Already in the late eighth century the *Barberini Euchologion* included a prayer at the founding of a church, an order for the blessing of a newly erected church, and an order for installing holy relics therein (later manuscripts combined these two rites into one). A detailed descrip-tion of the order for the consecration of a church is found in the writings of Symeon of Thessalonica, and its primary features remain unchanged to this day.[1]

---

[1]Symeon of Thessalonica, *On the Holy Church* (beginning at PG 155:305A).

THE FOUNDING OF A CHURCH

The Slavonic Book of Needs contains two forms of *the order of the founding of a church*—a short form and an extended form. The short order[2] is served by a bishop vested in the omophorion and epitrachelion. The order begins, as usual, with the trisagion prayers, after which the troparion is sung to the saint in whose honor the church is to be erected, "and other troparia that the rector desires." A prayer is then read in which the bishop asks God to preserve the foundations of the church "unbreakable and unshaken." A dismissal follows, after which the bishop takes a stone and, tracing a cross with it, places it at the foundation of the church with these words: "The Most High hath hallowed His tabernacle. God is in the midst of her, she shall not be shaken; God shall help her right early in the morning" (Ps 45.6). At the place where the holy altar will be located the bishop erects a cross, saying a prayer in which he asks God to bless and sanctify this site for the church. The cross is inscribed with the date of the founding of the church.

A more complete service order, found in the Supplementary Book of Needs,[3] calls for the participation of a bishop in full vestments (sakkos, omophorion, and miter). During the usual beginning the bishop censes the Gospel, located in the center, and all the excavations dug for the foundation (the censing is made in a counterclockwise circle starting at the first wall of the altar. After Psalm 142 the great litany is intoned, with special petitions added for the founding of a church. Following the exclamation, "God is the Lord" and the troparia are sung, including a special troparion for the founding of a church. Next Psalm 50 is read, during which water and oil are brought. This is followed by prayers for the blessing of the water and oil and a prayer at the erecting of a cross. The bishop and the priests erect the cross, after which they approach the excavation, where a stone lies that will be laid as part of the foundation of the church. The bishop reads a prayer over the stone, sprinkles it with holy water, and places it on the prepared site with the words, "This church is founded to the glory of our great God and Saviour Jesus Christ, in honor and memory of *N.* [the name of the feast or the name of the saint], in the name of the Father, and of the Son, and of the Holy Spirit. Amen." As the bishop pours the holy oil upon the stone he says, "Blessed and illustrious be this place for house of prayer, to the honor and glory of God, glorified in the Holy Trinity." The conclusion of the order includes a litany, with petitions for the founders of the church, and a dismissal.

[2] *Trebnik* [Book of Needs] (Saint Petersburg: 1884), reverse of 159–reverse of 160.
[3] *Trebnik* [Book of Needs], part 2 (Moscow: Moscow Patriarchate, 1956), beginning on reverse of 28.

If a wooden church is being blessed, the bishop takes an axe and strikes the middle altar log three times with the words, "This work is begun in the name of the Father, and of the Son, and of the Holy Spirit, and in the honor and memory of *N*." Then the bishop goes around all four sides of the foundation, sprinkling the logs, and on each side he strikes a log three times. At this time Psalms 86, 126, 121, and 131 are read.

Certain editions of the Book of Needs contain special service orders for erecting a cross on the cupola of the newly built church and for the blessing of a bell tower.

The Consecration of a Church and of an Antimension

The *order of the dedication (consecration) of a church*[4] takes place after the work of construction is completed. This order is served by a bishop, and only under exceptional circumstances may it be served by a priest (in which case several prayers are omitted). The order of the dedication of a church revolves around two key concepts: the first pertains to the church proper as the house of God, the receptacle of divine grace, while the second pertains to the relics of the martyr or saint that are placed at the base of the holy table. The meaning of the Christian church building, its symbolism, and its Old Testament prefigurations have already been discussed in fair detail above.[5] The significance of the martyrs for the Christian Church has also been mentioned on numerous occasions in this book.[6]

The order for the blessing of a church includes sacred rituals reminiscent of the sacraments of baptism, chrismation, and holy orders: here too water and chrism are used, the clergy vest in white vestments, and there is a circular procession. The purpose of all these sacred rituals is that the church, built of stone or wood by human hands, might acquire a spirit of life, becoming a receptacle of holy things, a house of the Living God.[7]

On the eve of the consecration of the church the all-night vigil is served with the royal doors closed and the curtain drawn. A holy table, hangings for the holy table and the table of oblation, an eileton (a square cloth), an antimension, rose water,

[4] *Chinovnik* [Hierarchal Service Book], book 2, 134–174.
[5] Cf. pp. 34–39 and 11–19 of vol. 4.
[6] Cf. pp. 157, 204.
[7] *Nastol'naya kniga svyashchennosluzhitelya* [Clergy Reference Book] (Moscow: Moscow Patriarchate, 2001), 375.

His Holiness the Patriarch signing the antimension for a church

wine, holy chrism, and a number of other items must be prepared in advance of the consecration. Before the bishop arrives, wax-mastic is prepared—a compound of melted wax, mastic, aloe, frankincense, and benzoin.

The consecration of the church takes place before the beginning of the liturgy. The bishop vests in full hierarchal vestments, over which he dons an apron and sleeve protectors. Aprons and sleeve protectors are likewise donned by the concelebrating priests. Then the bishop enters the altar with the other clergy: all laymen and altar servers leave the altar, and the royal doors are closed. Holy water is brought, and with it the bishop sprinkles the four corners of the holy table. Then boiling wax-mastic is brought: the bishop pours it on the pillars of the holy table and once again sprinkles the holy table with holy water. The prayer before the consecration of a church is read, after which the priests bring the board that will become the top of the holy table. The bishop sprinkles it with holy water on both sides, and it is placed on the four pillars of the holy table, to the reading of Psalm 144. Next Psalm 22 is read, after which the priests use stones, prepared beforehand, to drive nails into the corners of the top of the holy table. The royal doors are opened, the bishop goes out onto the ambon, and kneeling down he reads a prayer in which, recalling how King Solomon dedicated the temple in Jerusalem, he asks God to send down the Holy Spirit upon the newly erected church, and prays that this church be preserved unto the end of the age. Then the great litany is intoned, ending with the words, "For holy art thou, O our God, who restest upon the precious martyrs who have suffered for thee. . . ."

The bishop then reenters the altar, and the royal doors are closed. Warm water, wine, and rose water are brought. The bishop reads a prayer for the blessing of the water, and the water is mixed with the wine and rose water, after which the mixture is poured upon the table, and the priests wipe the table with special cloths as Psalm 83 is read. Following the words, "Glory to our God unto the ages of ages," the bishop sprinkles the antimension with the same mixture. Verses from Psalm 50 are read, and the clergy wipe the holy table with sponges. The bishop says, "Blessed is our God," and anoints the holy table crosswise with holy chrism: crosses are traced in three places on the board forming the top of the holy table, and on each of the four pillars of the holy table. The antimension is also cruciformly anointed with chrism in three places. The choir sings Psalm 132, after which the bishop exclaims, "Glory to thee, O Holy Trinity our God, unto the ages of ages." The reading of Psalm 131 begins, during which the holy table is covered with the *srachitsa,* or shroud[8] (a cubical altar covering), and tied with cord in such a way that a cross is formed on each side of the holy table. Then the holy table is covered with the inditia[9] (the outer altar covering, also cubical). Psalm 92 is read, after which the bishop exclaims, "Blessed is our God," and the table of oblation is covered. The royal doors are then opened; the bishop removes the apron and sleeve protectors and censes the altar and the entire church to the singing of Psalm 25. The bishop is accompanied by the priests, one of whom sprinkles the walls of the church with holy water, while another anoints the walls with holy chrism, using a brush attached to a long pole.

Upon returning to the altar, the bishop stands before the holy table and reads a prayer in which he recalls the sending down of the Holy Spirit upon the apostles, and asks God to fill the newly built church with his glory, that the bloodless sacrifice might be accomplished in it. After the exclamation "Peace be unto all," the following prayer is read:

> We thank Thee, O Lord God of Hosts, for as Thou hast poured out grace on Thy Holy Apostles, and on our Venerable Fathers, so Thou hast vouchsafed to extend this even unto us sinners, Thine unworthy servants, for the sake of Thy great love for mankind. Therefore, we pray Thee, O Most-merciful Master: Do Thou fill with glory, and holiness, and grace, this Altar, that the Bloodless Sacrifices which shall be offered on it may be transformed into the Most-pure Body and Precious Blood of our Great God and Savior, Jesus Christ, Thine

[8]In Greek, κατασάρκιον/*katasarkion.—Trans.*
[9]In Greek, ἐνδυτή/*endyte.—Trans.*

Only-begotten Son, unto the salvation of all Thy people and of us, who are unworthy.

After reading this prayer the bishops lights a candle and places it at the high place behind the holy table (up to this moment no lamps have been lit in the altar), takes the Gospel and a cross and gives them to the priests, and distributes lighted candles to the rest of the serving clergy. After the bishop's exclamation, "Let us depart in peace," they leave the church in solemn procession. According to the Typicon they are to go to a neighboring church, where a piece of the relics of a martyr or other saint lie prepared, which are to be brought to the newly built church. At this time troparia to the martyrs are sung:

> As with fine purple linen, Thy Church hath been adorned with the blood of Thy Martyrs throughout the world, O Christ our God. Therefore, she crieth out to Thee: Send down Thy mercies to Thy people, give peace to Thy habitation and to our souls great mercy.

> The universe offereth the God-bearing Martyrs as the first-fruits of nature, to Thee, O Lord the Gardener of Creation. Through the Theotokos and their prayers preserve Thy Church—Thy habitation—in profound peace, O Greatly-merciful One.

Upon arriving at the neighboring church, the bishop enters the altar and reads a prayer, asking God to vouchsafe the faithful to be imitators of the holy martyrs and sharers in their inheritance. The bishop censes the relics, then takes them up, lifts them over his head, and carries them thus to the newly built church. Two priests support the bishop's arms, and two or four subdeacons shade the bishop with fans, while two others carry the dikerion and trikerion. Before entering the newly built church the troparia "O holy martyrs" and "Glory to thee, O Christ God," from the order of holy matrimony and ordination, are sung.

Such are the directions for processing with the relics in the church Typicon, as reflected in the Book of Needs and the Hierarchal Service Book. In practice, however, the piece of the saint's relics are brought ahead of time not into a neighboring church, but into the church to be blessed: it is placed on the diskos, covered with the star and the aer, and placed before the icon of the Savior. After the exclamation "Let us depart in peace" the bishop leaves the church, holding the diskos with the piece of the relics above his head. In this case the procession does not go from one church to the other, then back, but around the newly built church, returning to the doors of the church as the troparia from the order of holy matrimony are sung.

When the procession reaches the doors of the church, the chanters go in and the doors are shut. The bishop and all the clergy and people remain outside the church. The diskos with the relics is placed on a small table prepared for the purpose, and the bishop exclaims, "Blessed is our God." From inside the church the chanters respond, "Amen." The bishop then intones, "Lift up your gates, O you princes, and be lifted up, O eternal gates; and the King of Glory shall enter in." The chanters respond from inside the church, "Who is this King of Glory?" The bishop censes the holy relics, the Gospel, and all those present, after which he again intones, "Lift up your gates," and the chanters again respond, "Who is this King of Glory?" Two prayers are read, in the first of which the bishop asks God to make this church steadfast unto the end of the age, while in the second he asks that the holy angels might enter the church together with the clergy. After this the bishop raises the diskos with the relics, traces the sign of the cross with it, and, as though in answer to the choir's question, exclaims, "The Lord of hosts, He is the King of Glory." The doors of the church are opened, and the bishop proceeds into the altar, all the while holding the diskos with the relics above his head.

Upon entering the altar, the bishop places the diskos with the relics on the holy table and again censes the holy relics. Wax-mastic that has "somewhat cooled" and holy chrism are brought. The bishop anoints the piece of relics with holy chrism, places it in a previously prepared reliquary, pours wax-mastic over it, and places it beneath the holy table. Another piece of relics is placed into the antimension in the same manner. A prayer is read, in which the bishop asks God for the salvation of all those present through the prayers of the martyrs. Then, kneeling together with the people, the bishop reads the final prayer of the order for the consecration, in which, calling to mind the creation of the world and God's appearance to Moses, he asks that the Holy Spirit be sent down upon all those present, and that oneness of mind and peace be preserved among them. The prayer includes a special petition for the founders of the church. The service order concludes with a litany, a dismissal, and the singing of the polychronion. The consecration is immediately followed by the divine liturgy.

If the antimension is consecrated separately from the church, a special *order for the consecration of an antimension* is used.[10] This is essentially an abbreviated order

---

[10]Cf. the *Chinovnik* [Hierarchal Service Book], part 2, 28–44. This order is called "The Order of the Consecration of Holy Antimensia by the Bishop, Upon Which the Priest Will Serve Divine Services, Where the Holy Table Does Not Contain Relics (translated from the Greek handwritten hierarchal service book)."

of the consecration of a church. Both the prayers and the rituals performed are the same as at the consecration of a church. This is because the antimension comprises a portable holy table, a kind of portable church.[11]

[11] The significance of the antimension is discussed in greater detail on pages 269–270.

12

Preparation and Consecration of Chrism

THE ORDERS OF PREPARATION and consecration of chrism are inseparably linked to the sacrament of chrismation, and they cannot be discussed in isolation from this sacrament. In and of themselves these service orders are vividly sacramental in nature. We should note that among the six sacraments Dionysius the Areopagite lists not chrismation (which in his understanding is a part of the sacrament of baptism), but specifically "the sacrament of the consecration of chrism." He describes the service order for this "sacrament" in the following words:

In the same way as in the Synaxis, the orders of the imperfect[1] are dismissed, that is, after the Bishop has made the whole circuit of the temple, attended with fragrant incense, and the chanting of the Psalms, and the reading of the most Divine Lections. Then the Hierarch takes the Myrrh[2] and places it upon the Divine Altar, veiled under twelve sacred wings, whilst all cry aloud, with a devout voice, the sacred melody of the inspiration of the God-rapt Prophets. When the Bishop has finished the prayer offered over it,[3] he uses it in the most holy perfectings of things that are hallowed, for the completion of almost every Hierarchal function.[4]

Thus, the order of consecration included a censing, the singing of psalms, the reading of holy scripture (the Gospel), the placing of a vessel of chrism on the altar (the holy table), and a prayer at the consecration of chrism to the singing of "Alleluia."[5] The Areopagite speaks of using chrism "for the perfecting of every

[1] That is, as at the Eucharist, catechumens were not present for the consecration of chrism.

[2] In modern Orthodox liturgics the terms *myrrh* and *chrism* are synonymous, *chrism* being more commonly used today.—*Trans.*

[3] The myrrh, or chrism.

[4] Dionysius the Areopagite, *Ecclesiastical Hierarchy* 4.2. In *The Celestial and Ecclesiastical Hierarchy of Dionysius the Areopagite*, John Parker, trans., 71.

[5] It is the singing of "Alleluia" that is understood to be "the sacred melody of the inspiration of the God-rapt prophets," as evinced by the explanation that follows: "As for the sacred melody of the inspiration of the God-rapt Prophets ["Alleluia"], it is called by those who know Hebrew, 'Praise of God,' or 'Praise ye the Lord'" (Ibid., 4.3, 77).

religious function";[6] in particular, he says, "the sacred consecration of the Divine Altar [is completed] by pure effusions of the most holy Myrrh."[7] We know that in the fifth century chrism was used more broadly than in the Orthodox Church today. It was used not only for the consecration of a church (anointing the four walls of the church with chrism is a part of the order of consecration of a church to this day) and the holy table (this tradition has likewise survived), but also of the blessing of icons (a tradition that has fallen into disuse).

However, the primary purpose of preparing and consecrating chrism is for the bestowal of the gift of the Holy Spirit upon one who has received baptism:

> The completing gift and grace of the Divine regeneration is completed in the Divine perfecting of the Myrrh. Hence, as I think, the Hierarch pouring the Myrrh upon the purifying font, in the form of a cross, brings to view for contemplative eyes Jesus descending to death itself through the cross, for our birth in God, and drawing up from the jaws of a destructive death, by the same Divine and resistless descent, those who, according to the mysterious saying, "are baptized into His death," from the former gulf of a destructive death, and renewing them to a godly and eternal existence. But further, the perfecting unction of the Myrrh gives to him who has been initiated in the most sacred initiation of the birth in God, the indwelling of the supremely Divine Spirit; the sacred imagery of the symbols suggesting, as I think, the gift of the Divine Spirit, by Him Who for our sakes has been sanctified as man,[8] by the Divine Spirit, in an unaltered condition of His essential Godhead.[9]

Thus, the Areopagite directly links the consecration of chrism with the sacrament of chrismation. The Areopagite sees the ritual of the cruciform pouring of chrism into the baptismal font (retained in modern practice in the crosswise form of anointing the baptismal water with blessed oil) as an allusion to Christ's descent into the waters of the Jordan.

The orders of preparing and consecrating myrrh in the usage of the Orthodox Church retain the chief aspects of the ritual described by Dionysius the Areopagite. In current practice, however, preparing chrism is the prerogative not of every bishop, but only of the heads of local Orthodox churches.[10] The ruling diocesan

[6]Ibid., 4.3, 76.

[7]Ibid.,

[8]That is, Christ.

[9]Dionysius the Areopagite, *Ecclesiastical Hierarchy* 4.3. In *The Celestial and Ecclesiastical Hierarchy of Dionysius the Areopagite*, John Parker, trans., 76.

[10]It should be noted that not all primates of local Orthodox Churches have the authority to conse-

Patriarchal moleben before beginning the preparation of chrism

bishops of a local church obtain chrism from the primate of that church, and parish priests obtain it from their diocesan bishop. Thus, through the bishops and the priests the blessing of the primate of each local church is bestowed upon every believer.

Chrism consists of a fragrant compound of a number of aromatic substances—plant oils, sweet smelling herbs, and fragrant resins. In the preparation of chrism only naturally occurring elements may be used. In the Russian Orthodox Church chrism is prepared from olive oil, white grape wine, and various fragrant substances such as frankincense; rose petals; violet, spice, and tormentil root; and nutmeg, rose, lemon, and clove oil. The list of elements and their quantities have never been strictly established. In 1671 and 1681 fifty-three elements were used in the preparation of chrism; in 1691, fifty-five; and in 1894, fifty. Currently chrism includes about forty different substances.[11]

crate chrism. For example, the archbishop of Athos obtains chrism from the patriarch of Constantinople. Obtaining chrism from Constantinople was one of the conditions on which Constantinople recognized the autocephaly of the Church of Greece in the nineteenth century: this condition is mentioned in the *tomos* (decree) of autocephaly, dated June 29, 1850. According to the *tomos* of autocephaly of the Albanian Church, dated April 12, 1937, the archbishop of Albania must likewise obtain chrism from Constantinople.

[11]Nefedov, *Tainstva i obryady Pravoslavnoi Tserkvi*, 61.

The orders of the preparation and consecration of chrism are served once a year or every few years, as needed. The elements from which the chrism is prepared are brought to the church during the third week of Great Lent (the week of the veneration of the cross). On Wednesday all the prepared elements are sprinkled with holy water, after which part of the oil is mixed with wine and cooked in a kettle. The cooked oil is poured over the fragrant substances, which have been finely ground, and they are left to steep for two weeks. On Wednesday of the sixth week of Lent the oil is poured off into vessels, and wine is poured over the substances.

The order of the preparation of chrism lasts for several days, and concludes during Holy Week. On Great Monday the patriarch or (with his blessing) another bishop, with other clergy concelebrating, performs the rite of the lesser blessing of water and reads the prayer at the beginning of the preparation of chrism. The prepared elements and the kettle are sprinkled with holy water, the patriarch pours a little holy water into the kettle, and the clergy pour in oil and wine. The patriarch blesses the kettle and lights the fire beneath it with the trikerion. For the next three days the chrism is cooked in the kettle, as the Gospel is read continually (the presbyters reading it by turns). On Great Tuesday the grape wine and fragrant substances are added to the kettle, followed on Great Wednesday by the grape wine and oil that were cooked during the fourth week of Great Lent. The preparation of chrism is concluded in the presence of the patriarch (or bishop) on Wednesday: the chrism is allowed to cool, the fragrant oils are added to the kettle, and everything is mixed thoroughly.[12]

The chrism is consecrated by the patriarch on Great Thursday at the divine liturgy. The vessels of chrism are brought ahead of time into the patriarchal cathedral from the church where the order of the preparation of chrism was performed, and to the singing of the troparion of Pentecost ("Blessed art thou, O Christ our God, who hast revealed fishermen most wise") they are placed near the table of oblation. At the same time, an alabastron—a vessel containing the chrism consecrated in previous years—is brought to the cathedral from the patriarchal stavropegial church. At the great entrance the clergy carry the alabastron and vessels out of the altar through the north door, and in the royal doors the patriarch takes the alabastron and places it on the holy table. The other vessels are placed around the holy table.

[12] *Chin mirovareniya* [The Order for the Preparation of Chrism] (Moscow: 1894); Nefedov, *Tainstva i obryady Pravoslavnoi Tserkvi*, 61–62.

Following the eucharistic canon the patriarch blesses each vessel of chrism three times, saying, "In the name of the Father, and of the Son, and of the Holy Spirit. Amen." The clergy in the altar sing, "Lord, have mercy." The patriarch reads a prayer that expounds the significance of anointing with chrism as a joining to the rank of "the royal priesthood," to a people chosen and holy. In the prayer Christians are called the "co-anointed" of Christ:

> O Lord of mercy and Father of lights, the giver of every good and perfect gift, grant to us, unworthy though we be, the grace to fulfill the ministry of this great and life-giving mystery, as thou didst give it to Moses your faithful steward, and to Samuel thy servant, and to thy holy apostles, and send thy Holy Spirit upon this chrism: Make it a royal anointing, a spiritual anointing, a safeguard of life, a hallowing of souls and bodies, an oil of gladness, which was prefigured in the Law, and which shone forth in the New Covenant: For by it were anointed priests and high priests, prophets and kings, and thy holy apostles, and all who have been reborn through the washing of new birth, by them, and by the bishops and priests who have followed them, even to this day. And so, Lord God Almighty, by the coming of thy holy and adorable Spirit, make it a garment of immortality, a perfecting seal which imprints thy divine Name, and that of thine only-begotten Son, and that of thy Holy Spirit, on those who have received thy divine washing.

After the prayer the patriarch says, "Peace be unto all." The singers reply, "And to thy spirit." The deacon intones, "Bow your heads unto the Lord," and another prayer for the consecration of chrism is read:

> To thee, O God and King of all, do we bow the neck of our heart, giving thanks because thou hast judged us worthy to become the ministers of these thy divine mysteries: we proclaim the mercy, which thou hast poured out upon us with such abundance: and we pray that we may receive thy sanctification, like the chrism which is poured upon our heads, since the chrism which is poured out is the Name of thine only-begotten Son, Christ our God, through whom the whole world, visible and invisible, is sweetly scented.

The last words contain an allusion to a verse from the Bible: "Thy name is as ointment poured forth" (Song 1.3). In the Eastern Christian tradition since the time of Origen this verse has been interpreted as pertaining to the name of Jesus Christ. Like chrism, poured out and exuding its fragrance, the name of Christ is poured out in the whole world, says Origen.[13] Echoing Origen, John Chrysostom explains that the words of the Song of Solomon concerning the "ointment poured forth" pertain to the name of Jesus Christ, and he emphasizes its universal significance and miraculous power:

> Wheresoever the Name of God is, all is auspicious. For if the names of Consuls make writings sure, much more doth the Name of Christ. . . . Marvelous is His name and great. . . . Invoke the Son, give thanks to the Father. For when the Son is invoked, the Father is invoked, and when He is thanked, the Son has been thanked. . . . Nothing is equal to this Name, marvelous is it everywhere. "Thy Name," he saith, "is ointment poured forth" [Song 1.3]. He that hath uttered it is straightway filled with fragrance. . . . By this Name hath the world been converted, the tyranny dissolved, the devil trampled on, the heavens opened. We have been regenerated by this Name. If we have this, we beam forth. This maketh both martyrs and confessors.[14]

After reading the prayer the patriarch blesses each vessel of consecrated chrism three times, adding to it a little chrism from the alabastron, and replenishing the alabastron with the newly consecrated chrism. This ritual is of great symbolic significance, attesting that, like the apostolic succession of the hierarchy, there is a direct line of succession linking the holy chrism consecrated in our own time with the chrism consecrated in the ancient Church. Thus, along with the gift of the Holy Spirit and the blessing of the primate of the Church, in the sacrament of chrismation a Christian also receives the apostolic blessing of many generations of Orthodox hierarchs—a blessing that may be traced back to the time of the apostles.

---

[13]Origen, *Homilies on the Song of Solomon* 1.4 (PG 13:41D–42A).
[14]Chrysostom, *Homilies on Colossians* 9.2 (*NPNF*[1] 13:302–303).

Orders for the Blessing of Various Objects.
Molebens and Akathists

Different editions of the Book of Needs contain numerous rites for blessing different objects, molebens (services of supplication, called in Greek a *paraklēsis* service) for various occasions,[1] and akathists. A complete review of this broad range of material would be impracticable, the more so since the content of the Book of Needs varies depending on the time and place of publication. In the seventeenth century Metropolitan Peter Mogila of Kiev appears to have collected all the rites known in his day, and also to have compiled several new ones, which he included in his own Book of Needs, published in 1646. Many of the prayers included in this collection later fell into disuse. At the same time, throughout the entire period from the mid-seventeenth century to the present, new rites, molebens, and prayers have continued to be created. In the overview below we will examine only a few service orders in the Book of Needs that remain currently in use.[2]

The Blessing of Liturgical Implements and Icons

Liturgical implements are blessed by reading special prayers and sprinkling them with holy water. For the blessing of a full set of liturgical vessels (the diskos, chalice, star, spoon, and three coverings) the *order for the blessing and sanctification of liturgical vessels* is used. This consists of the usual beginning, Psalm 23, two prayers,

---

[1] Services of supplication, either public or private, for various occasions.—*Trans.*

[2] In compiling this overview we employed the following: Trebnik [The Book of Needs] (St. Petersburg: 1995)—a reprint of the *Bolshoi Trebnik* [The Great Book of Needs] (Moscow: 1884); *Trebnik v trekh chastyakh* [The Book of Needs in Three Parts] (Kiev: 1996); *Posledovanie molebnikh peniy* [The Order of Hymns of Supplication] (Trinity-Sergius Lavra: 2003); and *Trebnik. Chinoposledovanie iz Velikago Trebnika, iz knigi molebnikh peniy i inyya* [The Book of Needs: Service Orders from the Great Book of Needs, from the Book of Supplicatory Hymns and Others] (Vladimirova [Slovenia]: 1944). All these publications differ substantially from each other in volume and in the number of service orders included.

and sprinkling the vessels with holy water. A similar rite is used for blessing each of these liturgical vessels individually, but there is a different prayer for each. There is also the *order for the blessing of new church vessels*, used for blessing items used at the divine services (the censer, water vessels, and other altar appurtenances). For blessing the eileton—the cloth in which the antimension is wrapped—the *order for the blessing of the eileton* is used. Priestly vestments are blessed using the *order for the blessing or sanctification of new priestly vestments*, and hangings for the holy table are blessed using the *order for the blessing of the endyte*. Each of these rites includes the usual beginning, a psalm, two prayers, and a sprinkling with holy water with the words, "This (*name of the item*) is blessed by the grace of the All-holy Spirit through the sprinkling of this holy water, in the name of the Father, and of the Son, and of the Holy Spirit. Amen."

The *order for the blessing of a newly fashioned cross* is of greater length. It includes the usual beginning and three psalms (131, 59, and 98); the troparion to the cross is sung; the priest reads two prayers of blessing; the cross is sprinkled with holy water; stichera to the cross are sung; and the clergy and people bow down before the cross and kiss it. In the first prayer the priest asks God to send down his blessing upon the newly fashioned cross, and to bless and sanctify it, filling it with the power and blessing of the wood to which the most pure body of the Lord Jesus Christ was nailed. The context of this prayer and those that follow shows that the service order clearly pertains to a cross of large proportions, made to be venerated by the faithful. For the blessing of a small baptismal cross the *order for the blessing of a cross to be worn on the breast* is used.[3]

As has already been noted,[4] in the ancient Church there was no special order for the blessing for icons. In Byzantium it was the custom to anoint a newly painted icon with holy chrism. Today an icon is blessed by sprinkling it with holy water and reading special prayers. The order for the blessing of any given icon includes the usual beginning, the reading of a psalm and of two prayers, and the sprinkling of the icon with holy water.

For blessing icons of the Holy Trinity there is the *order for the blessing of icons of the Most Holy Life-giving Trinity in images of the three angels, or of the Baptism, or*

---

[3]The order for the blessing of a cross raises a theological problem, to which the Book of Needs gives no direct answer. The problem is this: in the ancient Church a cross was perceived as a source of sanctification and sanctity regardless of whether or not it had been blessed. The special order for the blessing of a cross is of later origin, and was unknown in the ancient Church. In modern practice the cross is blessed by sprinkling it with holy water, but the water itself is blessed through immersion of the cross into it. It therefore remains unclear which of these is the source of sanctification: the cross or the holy water?

[4]See p. 272 of this volume.

The blessing of an icon

of the Transfiguration, or of the descent of the Holy Spirit. The very name of the rite indicates which particular icons may be considered images of the Trinity: symbolic depictions of the three persons of the Godhead in the form of the three angels (as in the icon by Andrei Rublev) and icons of the feasts of the Baptism of our Lord, Transfiguration, and Pentecost. The link between these events is discernible in this prayer from the service:

> O Lord God, Who art glorified in the Holy Trinity . . . as the Old Testament telleth us of Thine appearing in the image of the three angels to the most-glorious Patriarch Abraham, so too in the New, in a voice the Father bestowed grace upon the Son in the flesh in the Jordan, and the Holy Spirit wast revealed in the form of a dove. And again, the Son Who ascended in the flesh to Heaven, and sitteth at the right hand of God, sent down the Comforter, the Spirit, in the form of fiery tongues upon the apostles; and on Tabor, the Father in a voice, the Holy Spirit in a cloud, and the Son in truly-bright light, showed themselves to the three Disciples. Thus, as an everlasting remembrance, we confess Thee, God Who alone is glorified, not just with our mouths, but we paint an image, not to make this a god, but that when we gaze upon it with our fleshly eyes, we might see Thee, our God, in our minds.

In all four types of icons of the Holy Trinity mentioned in the order for their blessing, God the Father is not depicted. The Holy Spirit is depicted in the icon of Theophany in the form of a dove, and in the icon of Pentecost, in the form of rays and tongues of fire resting on the heads of the apostles; in the icon of the Transfiguration, as follows from the prayer, the presence of the Holy Spirit is symbolized by the cloud. This rite may not be used for blessing any icons of the Holy Trinity in which God the Father or the Holy Spirit is depicted in the form of a dove outside the context of the Theophany of our Lord (such as the "New Testament Trinity," the "Paternity," etc.). These icons are not eligible to be blessed or to be in church at all, since they violate the strict prohibition against all depictions of God the Father.[5]

For blessing icons of the Savior or a feast of the Lord a corresponding rite is used, which includes a prayer briefly outlining the theological basis of iconography and mentions the account of the Mandylion (the "Icon Not Made By Hands"), sent by Christ to Abgar of Edessa. Separate rites exist for blessing icons of the Mother of God, a saint or group of saints, and for "various icons." A special rite is used for blessing a reliquary in which holy relics are kept. Certain editions of the Book of Needs also include an *order for the blessing and sanctification of an iconostasis.*

MOLEBENS FOR VARIOUS OCCASIONS

In the Orthodox Church there are a large number of molebens, hymns, and prayers for various occasions.

The *moleben for the New Year* is served on the eve of the New Year according to the civil calendar.[6] This is at once a service of thanksgiving and of supplication. It begins with the exclamation from the liturgy, "Blessed is the kingdom," and includes the reading of Psalm 64, the great litany with special petitions "that He will bless the beginning and continuance of this year," the singing of troparia of thanksgiving, readings from the epistles (1 Tim 2.1–6) and the Gospel (Lk 4.16–22), the augmented litany with additional petitions of thanksgiving, a prayer of thanksgiving read by the priest, the singing of the great doxology, and the dismissal. Sometimes in place of the great doxology the early Christian hymn "We praise Thee, O God," attributed to St Ambrose of Milan, is sung.

---

[5]See Steven Bigham, *The Image of God the Father in Orthodox Theology and Iconography* (Crestwood, NY: St Vladimir's Seminary Press, 1995).—*Ed.*

[6]In the Russian Church some priests serve this moleben on the eve of September 1 Old Style (September 14 New Style), when the "Beginning of the Indiction" or church New Year is celebrated. Others serve it on the eve of the "Old New Year" (January 1 O.S., January 14 N.S.). The most widespread practice in recent decades, however, has been to serve this moleben on the eve of the civil New Year (New Style)—that is, on the eve of December 31.

The *moleben for the beginning of the instruction of children* is served as a rule at or before the beginning of the school academic year (in Russia, on September 1 N.S.) The service order contains special petitions that God "will send down upon these children the spirit of wisdom and understanding, and will enlighten their minds and lips, and enlighten their hearts, unto the receiving of precepts of good instruction."

The *moleben for the sick, whether one or many,* is served for those who are gravely ill. The rite contains prayers for the healing of illnesses and that the souls and bodies of the sick may be cured, and that their transgressions may be forgiven, both voluntary and involuntary. Certain prayers are taken from the service order of the sacrament of unction (in particular the prayer "O Physician of souls and bodies").

The *moleben of thanksgiving for the receiving of a petition and for every good gift from God* is usually called the thanksgiving moleben. It is served at the request of a believer who wishes to give special thanks to God for a benefaction he has been granted or for deliverance from danger, illness, or affliction. The moleben includes the singing of the troparia of thanksgiving ("We, Thine unworthy servants, O Lord, grateful for Thy great benefits given unto us"), readings from the epistles (Eph 5.8–21) and the Gospel (Lk 17.12–19), a litany with special petitions, a final prayer of thanksgiving, and the hymn "We praise Thee, O God."

Special molebens are served in times of natural disasters—*want of rain (drought), inclement weather* (prolonged heavy rain), *earthquake, flood,*[7] and *devastating epidemic and ruinous pestilence.*

Several services in the Book of Needs have to do with war and military action. The Orthodox Church has never taken a position of absolute pacifism, and it has always blessed soldiers to do battle with foreign foes, offering up prayers for victory over enemies in times of war. In Russia in wartime it was customary to serve the *moleben sung in time of war against adversaries.* There is also an *order for the blessing of a military standard, or banner, and for the blessing of soldiers for battle,* which includes sprinkling the standards, soldiers, and officers with holy water and blessing the warriors to do battle. Certain modern editions of the Book of Needs also include the *order for the blessing military weapons,* which includes the prayer, "O Lord our God . . . send down Thy heavenly blessing upon these weapons, and

---

[7]The order of the moleben in time of flood was first served on November 14, 1824, in the Kazan Cathedral in Saint Petersburg, on the seventh day of the most catastrophic flood in the history of the northern capital, when nearly the entire city was inundated, houses were destroyed, and many people perished.

grant strength and might to this Thy servant *N.* to bear them unto the fortification and defense of Thy Holy Church, of orphans and widows, and of those on earth who desire Thy holy inheritance." According to the directions in the Book of Needs, during the reading of this prayer the weapons are placed on a special table before the ambon. Following the prayer they are sprinkled with holy water. For the blessing of a battleship there is the *order for the blessing of a battleship being launched against the foe.*

The Church accompanies those departing on a long journey with special prayers: for this the Book of Needs contains the *order of blessing for a journey* and the *order of blessing for them that are about to travel by water.* A ship is blessed using a separate rite, for which there is the *order for the blessing of a new ship or boat.* In the twentieth century these service orders were supplemented by the *order for the blessing of a chariot* (that is, a motor vehicle), the *order for the blessing of an airship* (an airplane), and the *order for the blessing of a journey by air.*

For blessing houses, private apartments, and office spaces the *order for the blessing of a new home,* included in certain editions of the Book of Needs, is used. It includes the usual beginning and Psalm 90, after reading which the priest prays that the Lord may bless the home and its inhabitants and preserve it unharmed by adversaries. Then the priest blesses oil, sprinkles all the walls of the home with holy water, and anoints the four walls of the house or apartment with the oil. After this the Gospel account of Zacchaeus the Publican (Lk 19.1–10) and Psalm 100 may be read. The rite ends with the augmented litany, the dismissal, and the polychronion.

For the blessing of a cemetery there is an *order for the blessing and sanctification of the place where the bodies of Christians who have reposed will be buried.* Certain editions of the Book of Needs likewise include the *order of the blessing and sanctification of the cross over a grave.*

The digging of a well is accompanied by two service orders: at the beginning the *order of prayer at the digging of a well and the finding of water* is served; at the end, the *order of the blessing of a new well.*

The Great Book of Needs includes a rite called the *order of supplication for the infirm who are beset by unclean spirits.* This rite contains several psalms, the "canon of supplication to our Lord Jesus Christ, to the Most Holy Theotokos, to the bodiless hosts, to the apostles, and to all the saints," a litany, the prayer for one who is ailing from the sacrament of unction, and five prayers of exorcism ascribed to Basil the Great. These prayers, translated from the Greek, originate from the early

Christian practice of exorcism—driving demons out of those possessed by them. Today Basil the Great's prayers of exorcism are used by a few solitary spiritual fathers, about whom congregate those who are possessed or believe themselves to be so: the reading of the prayers is made into a ritual (in the vernacular called *otchitivanie* or *otchitka*—a "reading out" of the evil spirit), during which those possessed throw themselves on the floor, scream in inhuman voices, froth at the mouth, etc. Extreme caution must be exercised in assessing these phenomena, since at times psychological disorders or abnormal behavior can be mistaken for demonic possession. And if a person is psychologically unstable, being present at this kind of ritual is by no means conducive to his recovery.

MOLEBENS AND AKATHISTS.
WORSHIP ACCORDING TO AND OUTSIDE THE TYPICON

The molebens and other prayers included in the various editions of the Book of Needs comprise service orders for special occasions in addition to the daily cycle of services, or else for particular needs related to various circumstances in the life of a Christian. For many centuries the prayer life of a Christian in the Church revolved around the Eucharist and participation in the services of the daily cycle, which are regulated by the Typicon. There were no "private" services for individual needs, served at the particular request of a believer. Only in extraordinary cases were prayer services conducted outside those prescribed by the church Typicon.

Over the last two centuries, however, the practice of performing various service orders for individual needs—"customized" divine services—has become widespread in the Russian Orthodox Church. Not content, so to speak, with public worship, the modern parishioner can request a special service for himself, which the priest serves following the liturgy or the all-night vigil. Private services have become a regular custom in most churches—a sort of separate liturgical cycle, existing alongside what is prescribed by the Typicon, but unregulated by any rules or regulations.

Molebens in particular are served in most churches on a regular, often daily basis. In many churches a moleben is served after every liturgy. In these cases the so-called *general moleben* is used as a basis. Paradoxically, the order of the general moleben is not found in most editions of the Book of Needs. The reason for this is that the moleben is not a standalone service, but rather a greatly abbreviated and significantly altered matins service.[8] In compiling molebens, parish rectors usually follow an oral tradition. The moleben may be dedicated to the Savior, the Mother of God, one of the icons of the Mother of God, or saints (one or several). Composite molebens—for example, to the Savior, the Mother of God, and several (if not several dozen) saints—are also widespread.

The moleben begins with the exclamation "Blessed is our God," the singing of "O Heavenly King," the reading of the trisagion prayers, and Psalm 142. Then the great litany is intoned, followed by the singing of "God is the Lord" and troparia to those to whom the moleben is dedicated (in the case of a "composite moleben" there may be several—or several dozen—such troparia). The troparia are followed by Psalm 50. At the moleben a canon to the saint or saints may be chanted; in practice, however, the canon is replaced by brief refrains: "O Sweetest Jesus, save us"; "O Most Holy Theotokos, save us", "Holy Hierarch Father Nicholas, pray unto God for us"; etc. Each refrain is sung by the clergy, then repeated by the choir (they are repeated to correspond to each of the odes in the canon, though the text of the canon is omitted). The refrains are interspersed with troparia, kontakia, and litanies. A prokeimenon and a Gospel reading are also inserted (the Gospel reading depends on the whom the moleben calls upon). After the completion of the refrains, "It is truly meet" is sung, followed by an augmented litany commemorating the names, with various additional petitions. At the end of the moleben a special prayer is read, after which the dismissal is given. There are various abbreviated forms of the moleben: the usual beginning is omitted, the psalms are omitted, the refrains are sung only three times, the refrains are not sung at all, the Gospel is omitted, etc.

In many parishes and monasteries a *moleben with an akathist* may also be served. Here the akathist—to the Savior, the Mother of God, in honor of one of the icons of the Mother of God, or to a saint—is inserted after the first six repetitions of the refrains, before the reading of the Gospel. Some parishes and monasteries have a practice of combining molebens with akathists made up of several different akathists: the first ikos and kontakion may be taken, for example, from the akathist to Sweetest Jesus; the second ikos and kontakion, from the akathist to the Theoto-

---

[8]The description that follows below corresponds to the Russian practice. The Greek *paraklēsis* service is related, but quite different. It is an abbreviated matins service, but still contains a full canon, which is sung according to traditional melodies (in contrast, Russian canons are never composed in poetic meter to match a melody, see Vol. 4, p. 93). In Greek practice, the Great and Small Paraklēsis to the Theotokos are chanted on alternating evenings in the Dormition Fast, and general in times of peril, hardship, temptation, or suffering.—*Ed.*

kos; the third, from the akathist to John the Forerunner; the fourth, to St Nicholas; etc. This kind of creative liturgics has no basis in the church Typicon, and is not found in a single liturgical book or a single edition of the Book of Needs.

With regard to the widespread usage of molebens and akathists the following should be noted. The practice of serving molebens and akathists everywhere and every day has become widespread in the Russian Church over the last hundred and fifty to two hundred years. Unlike hard-to-grasp Byzantine hymns, the texts used at molebens and akathists require neither any particular intellectual effort nor any special theological training to understand: they are simple in content and easy to digest. These factors are largely responsible for their popularity among the laity.

A moleben is essentially a matins service that has been stripped of all the texts that are hardest to understand. For whereas the matins elements richest in theology are the stichera and the canons, at the moleben stichera generally are not sung at all, and of the canon only the refrains remain. The almost universal proliferation of molebens in the Russian Church is a sign that the development of liturgical piety has been following a trajectory of semantic simplification, replacing the more ancient, lengthy, and complex texts with those that are simpler, shorter, and easier to understand.

Similar processes have occurred in various eras in Protestantism and Catholicism, in which the ancient, theologically rich liturgical texts were replaced with chorales and canticles. In the Catholic Church the final stage of combining and simplifying liturgical ritual was the liturgical reforms of the Second Vatican Council. In Protestantism an analogous reform took place at the moment of its inception. In both cases richness of theological content was sacrificed in the name of making the divine services understandable and accessible. To a significant degree, however, their divine services ceased to be a school of theology and religious thought, and are now at best no more than a school of piety.

The widespread proliferation of akathists is also linked to a waning interest in the liturgy and the other appointed services. Only one akathist is known to the Orthodox Typicon—the one sung on Saturday of the fifth week of Great Lent. Other excellent akathists were later patterned after this akathist for home use, such as those to Sweetest Jesus and to St Nicholas. In the eighteenth and nineteenth centuries, however, numerous akathists were composed to various saints or individual icons of the Mother of God. Some of these are composed on a subpar theological and literary level, replacing theology with piety, and religious thought with mere religious talk.

Among the faithful of the Russian Orthodox Church certain voices are heard calling for reform in Orthodox worship, to make the divine services easier to understand. But if understandability in the services is achieved at the cost of subsequently eliminating the prescribed liturgical texts from use and replacing them with "folk hymnography," such a reform is unlikely to bear good fruit.

This discussion must, in all likelihood, take place in the context not so much of "reforming" the divine services as of returning them to the sphere of the church Typicon, so that the believer might regain access to the treasury of Orthodox theology and religious thought contained in these prescribed liturgical texts. First and foremost, efforts must be made to ensure that the divine liturgy once again assumes the sole and central place that rightfully belongs to it—and to it alone—in the consciousness of Orthodox Christians.

Abbreviations

ANF   *The Ante-Nicene Fathers*. Edited by Alexander Roberts and James Donaldson. 10 vols. Buffalo, 1885–1896. Reprint, Peabody, MA:Hendrickson, 1994.

CUA   The Fathers of the Church: A New Translation (Patristic series). Washington, DC: Catholic University of America Press. 1947–

NPNF¹ *The Nicene and Post-Nicene Fathers*, Series 1. Edited by Philip Schaff. New York, 1886–1889. 14 vols. Reprint, Peabody, MA: Hendrickson, 1994.

NPNF² *Nicene and Post-Nicene Fathers*, Series 2. Edited by Philip Schaff and Henry Wace. New York, 1890. 14 vols. Reprint, Peabody, MA: Hendrickson, 1994.

PG   Patrologia Graeca [= Patrologiae cursus completes: Series graeca]. Edited by J.-P. Migne. 162 vols. Paris, 1857–1866.

PPS   Popular Patristics Series. Crestwood, NY [Yonkers, NY]: St Vladimir's Seminary Press, 1996–

SC   Sources Chrétiennes. Paris: Les Éditions du Cerf, 1942–

Select Bibliography

A Small Book of Needs. South Canaan, PA: St. Tikhon's Monastery Press, 2012.

Almazov, A. N. *Tainaya ispoved' v Pravoslavnoy Vostochnoi Tserkvi* [Secret confession in the Orthodox Eastern Church]. 3 vols. Odessa, 1894. Reprint, Moscow: Palomnik, 1995.

Ambrose of Milan. *Exposition of the Holy Gospel according to Saint Luke.* Translated by Theodosia Tomkinson. Etna, CA: Center for Traditionalist Orthodox Studies, 2003.

Ambrose of Milan. *On the Holy Spirit. NPNF²* 10:93–158.

Ambrose of Milan. *The Letters of Ambrose.* Translated by S. F. Wood and B. H. Walford. Vol. 45 of *A Library of Fathers of the Holy Catholic Church.* Oxford, 1881.

Apostolic Constitutions. ANF 7:385–508.

Asmus, Valentin. "Gimny prepodobnogo Simeona Novogo Bogoslova v bogosluzhebnikh knigakh Russkoi Tserkvi" [The Hymns of the Venerable Symeon the New Theologian in the Liturgical Books of the Russian Church]. Lecture at the international conference in honor of the 1000-year anniversary of the Baptism of Russia, 2004.

———. "Gimny Simeona Novogo Bogoslova v bogosluzhebnikh knigakh Russkoi Tserkvi" [The hymns of Symeon the New Theologian in the liturgical books of the Russian Church]. *Bogoslovskiy Vestnik* 4 (2004): 209–219.

Athanasius of Alexandria. *Defense against the Arians. NPNF²* 4:97–148.

(Pseudo-)Athanasius of Alexandria. *Pseudo-Athanasius on Virginity.* Edited by David Brakke. 2 vols. CSCO 592–593. Louvain: Peeters, 2002.

Athanasius of Kovrov. *O pominovenii usopshikh* [On the commemoration of the departed]. Saint Petersburg: Satis, 1995.

Athanasius (Yevtich), [Bishop]. *Christ: The Alpha and Omega.* Alhambra, CA: Sebastian Press, 2007.

Athenagoras of Athens. *A Plea for the Christians. ANF* 2:129–148.

Augustine of Hippo, *Explanation of John.*

Augustine of Hippo, *On the Good of Marriage. NPNF¹* 3:397–416.

Augustine of Hippo. *On Faith and Works.* Translated by Marie Liguori, in *Treatises on Marriage and Other Subjects,* ed. Roy J. Deferrari, Fathers of the Church 27, 215–282 (Washington, DC: Catholic University of America Press, 1955).

Augustine of Hippo. *On Visiting the Infirm* 2.4. PL 40:1147–1158.

Barrois, Georges A., trans. *The Fathers Speak*. Crestwood, NY: St Vladimir's Seminary Press, 1986.

Barsanuphius and John. *Letters*. Translated by John Chryssavgis. 2 vols. Fathers of the Church 113–114. Washington, DC: The Catholic University of America Press, 2006–2007.

Basil (Krivocheine), [Archbishop]. *In the Light of Christ: St Symeon the New Theologian; Life, Spirituality, Doctrine*. Translated by Anthony P. Gythiel. Crestwood, NY: St Vladimir's Seminary Press, 1987.

Basil the Great. *Commentary on the Prophet Isaiah*. Translated by Nikolai A. Lipatov. Texts and Studies in the History of Theology 7. Mandelbachtal/Cambridge: Edition Cicero, 2001.

_____. *Exhortation to Baptism*.

_____. *The Hexaemeron*. NPNF² 8:51–107.

_____. *Letter 93: To Caesaria, Concerning Communion*. NPNF² 8:179.

_____. *The Rule of St Basil the Great*. Translated by Anna M. Silvas. Collegeville, MN: Liturgical Press, 2013.

_____. *Sermon 13*.

_____. *The Short Rules*.

Bigham, Steven. *The Image of God the Father in Orthodox Theology and Iconography*. Crestwood, NY: St Vladimir's Seminary Press, 1995.

Blackmore, Richard W. *The Doctrine of the Russian Church*. Aberdeen: A. Brown and Co., 1845.

Bouillé, Louis. *O Biblii i Evangelii* [On the Bible and the Gospel]. Brussels: Zhizn' s Bogom, 1998.

The Canons of the Holy and Altogether August Apostles. NPNF² 14:594–600.

Cæcilius, on the Sacrament of the Cup of the Lord. ANF 5:359–362.

Cesarini, Julian, [Cardinal]. *Latinorum ad Graecos capita circa purgatorium ignem* [Latin chapters to the Greeks concerning purgatorial fire]. Patrologia Orientalis 15:25–38.

Catechism of the Catholic Church. 2nd ed. Washington, DC: USCCB, 2016.

Chin mirovareniya [The Order for the Preparation of Chrism]. Moscow, 1894.

Chinovnik [Hierarchal Service Book].

Clement of Alexandria. *The Stromata*. ANF 2:299–588.

Constantine Porphyrogenitus. *De Cerimoniis*. PG 112.

Cyprian of Carthage. *Epistles*. ANF 5:275–420.

_____. *On the Lapsed*. ANF 5:437–447.

_____. *On the Lord's Prayer*. ANF 5:447–457.

Cyril of Alexandria. *Commentary on the Gospel According to Saint John.* Vol. 2, *S. John IX–XXI*, trans. Thomas Randell. Vol. 48 of *A Library of Fathers of the Holy Catholic Church.* London, 1885.

_____. *Explanation of the Gospel of Luke.* PG 72:475–950.

_____. *Explanation of the Gospel of Matthew (Fragments).* PG 72:365–474.

_____. *Five Tomes against Nestorius.* Vol. 47 of *A Library of Fathers of the Holy Catholic Church.* Oxford, 1881.

_____. *On Worship in Spirit and in Truth.* PG 68.

Cyril of Jerusalem. *Catechetical Lectures. NPNF²* 7:1–157.

_____. *Lectures on the Christian Sacraments: The Procatechesis and the Five Mystagogical Catecheses Ascribed to St Cyril of Jerusalem.* Translated by Maxwell E. Johnson. Popular Patristics Series 57. Yonkers, NY: St Vladimir's Seminary Press, 2017.

Dionysius the Areopagite. *The Celestial and Ecclesiastical Hierarchy of Dionysius the Areopagite.* Translated by John Parker. London: Skeffington, 1894.

The Divine Liturgy of James, the Holy Apostle and Brother of the Lord. ANF 7:537–550.

Dorotheus of Gaza. *Dorotheos of Gaza: Discourses and Sayings.* Translated by Eric P. Wheeler. Kalamazoo, MI: Cistercian Publications, 1977.

Elchaninov, Alexander. *Zapisi* [Notes]. Moscow: Russkiy put', 1992.

Epiphanius of Salamis. *The Panarion* [=*Against Heresies*] *of Epiphanius of Salamis, Books II and III:* De Fide. Translated by Frank Williams. 2nd ed. Leiden: Brill, 2013.

Etheria. *The Pilgrimage of Etheria.* Translated by M. L. McLure and C. L. Feltoe. London: Society for Promoting Christian Knowledge, 1919.

Eustathius of Thessalonica. *Inquiry into the Monastic Life.* PG 135:729–908.

Evagrius Ponticus, *Homily on Spiritual Activity.* SC 170; 171.

Firmilian of Caesarea. *Epistles of Cyprian* 74. ANF 5:390–397.

Gavrilyuk, Pavel. *Istoriya katakhizatsii v Drevnei Tserkvi* [History of catechesis in the ancient church]. Moscow: Svyato-Filaretovskiy pravoslavno-khristianskiy institut, 2001.

Germanus of Constantinople. *On the Divine Liturgy.* Translated by Paul Meyendorff. Popular Patristics Series 8. Crestwood, NY: St. Vladimir's Seminary Press, 1984. Germanus of Constantinople.

Golubinsky, Evgeny. *Istoriya Russkoi Tserkvi* [History of the Russian Church]. Moscow: Krutitskoe patriarshee podvorye, Obshchestvo lyubitelei tserkovnoi istorii, 1997.

The Great Book of Needs. 5 vols. South Canaan, PA: St. Tikhon's Monastery Press, 1998–99.

Gregory of Nazianzus. *Festal Orations.* Translated by Nonna Verna Harrison. Popular Patristics Series 36. Crestwood, NY: St Vladimir's Seminary Press, 2008.

_____. *Orations. NPNF²* 7:185–434.

_____. *Letters.* Select letters available in *NPNF²* 7.

Gregory of Nyssa. *Against Eunomius.* *NPNF²* 5:33–248.

_____. *Catechetical Discourse: An Ancient Catechist's Handbook.* Translated by Ignatius Green. Popular Patristics Series 59. Yonkers, NY: St Vladimir's Seminary Press, 2019.

_____. *On Infants' Early Deaths.* *NPNF²* 5:372–381.

Hilarion (Alfeyev), [Metropolitan]. *Simeon Novyy Bogoslov i pravoslavnoe predanie* [Symeon the New Theologian and Orthodox tradition]. 2nd ed. Saint Petersburg: Aleteiya, 2001.

_____. *The Spiritual World of Isaac the Syrian.* Kalamazoo, MI: Cistercian Publications, 2000.

_____. *Tainstvo very: Vvedenie v pravoslavnoe dogmaticheskoe bogoslovie* [The mystery of faith: An introduction to Orthodox dogmatic theology]. 4th ed. Klin: Khristianskaya Zhizn Foundation, 2004.

Hilarion (Troitsky), [Archbishop]. "Bogoslovie i svoboda Tserkvi: o zadachakh osvoboditel'noi voiny v oblasti russkogo bogosloviya" [The theology and freedom of the Church: On the goals of the war of liberation in the sphere of Russian theology]. In *Collected Works,* vol. 2.

Hippolytus. *On the Apostolic Tradition.* Translated by Alistair C. Stewart. 2nd ed. Popular Patristics Series 54. Yonkers, NY: Saint Vladimir's Seminary Press, 2015.

Ignatius (Brianchaninov), [Bishop]. *Pis'ma k miryanam* [Letters to laity].

_____. *Sochineniya svyatitelya Ignatiya Bryanchaninova. Tom IV: asketicheskaya propoved'* [The writings of the Holy Hierarch Ignatius Brianchaninov. Vol. 4: Ascetic preaching]. Moscow: Pravilo Very, 1993.

Ignatius of Antioch. *The Letters.* Translated by Alistair Stewart. Popular Patristics 49. Yonkers, NY: St Vladimir's Seminary Press, 2013.

Innocent of Rome. *Letter to Decentius.*

Irenaeus of Lyons. *Against Heresies.* *ANF* 1:315–567.

Isaac the Syrian. *Ascetical Homilies.* Brookline, MA: Holy Transfiguration Monastery, 2011.

Iswolsky, Helen, trans. *The Way of a Pilgrim and Other Classics of Russian Spirituality.* Edited by G. P. Fedotov. Mineola, NY: Dover Publications, Inc., 2012.

Jerome. *Regula monacharum* [The rule for nuns]. PL 30:403–439.

John Cassian. *Conferences.* *NPNF²* 11:291–545.

_____. *The Twelve Books on the Institutes of the C{**XC 167,1 }nobia, and the Remedies for the Eight Principal Faults.* *NPNF²* 11:201–290.

John Chrysostom. *Discourses Against Judaizing Christians.* Translated by Paul W. Harkins. Fathers of the Church 68. Washington, DC: Catholic University of America Press, 1979.

_____. *Discourse on the Day of the Baptism of Christ.* Translation available online from the Orthodox Church in America website: https://oca.org/fs/sermons/discourse-on-the-day-of-the-baptism-of-christ.

_____. *Explanation of Psalm 110.*

_____. *Four Discourses of Chrysostom, Chiefly on the Parable of the Rich Man and Lazarus.* Translated by F. Allen. London: Longmans, Green, Reader, and Dyer, 1869.

_____. *Homilies on Acts. NPNF¹* 11:1–328.

_____. *Homilies on Colossians. NPNF¹* 13:257–321.

_____. *Homilies on Ephesians. NPNF¹* 13:49–172.

_____. *Homilies on First Corinthians. NPNF¹* 12:1–269.

_____. *Homilies on Genesis 46–67.* Translated by Robert C. Hill. Fathers of the Church 87. Washington, DC: The Catholic University of America Press, 1992.

_____. *Homilies on the Gospel of Saint John. NPNF²* 14:1–332.

_____. *Homilies on the Gospel of Saint Matthew. NPNF¹* 10.

_____. *Homilies on Hebrews. NPNF¹* 14:333–522.

_____. *Homilies on Philippians. NPNF¹* 13:181–255.

_____. *Homilies on Romans. NPNF¹* 11:329–564.

_____. *Homilies on Second Corinthians. NPNF¹* 12:271–420.

_____. *Instructions to Catechumens. NPNF¹* 9:157–171.

_____. *On the Priesthood.* Translated by Graham Neville. Popular Patristics Series 1. Crestwood, NY: Saint Vladimir's Seminary Press, 1977.

_____. *On Repentance and Almsgiving.* Translated by Gus George Christo. Fathers of the Church 96. Washington, DC: The Catholic University of America Press, 1998.

John Climacus. *The Ladder of Divine Ascent.* Translated by Lazarus Moore. New York: Harper & Brothers, 1959.

John of Damascus. *An Exact Exposition of the Orthodox Faith. NPNF²* 9:1b–101b.

John of Kronstadt. *Mysli o pokayanii i prichashchenii* [Thoughts on Penance and Communion]. Moscow: Palomnik, 1997.

Jorgenson, James. "The Debate Over the Patristic Texts on Purgatory at the Council of Ferrara-Florence, 1438." *St Vladimir's Theological Quarterly* 30.4 (Winter 1986): 309–334.

Jurgens, William A. *The Faith of the Early Fathers.* 3 vols. Collegeville, MN: The Liturgical Press, 1970–1979.

Just, Arthur A. Jr., ed. *Luke.* Ancient Christian Commentary on Scripture, New Testament 3. Downers Grove, IL: InterVarsity, 2003.

Justin Martyr. *First Apology. ANF* 1:163–187.

Kappes, Christiaan. "A New Narrative for the Reception of Seven Sacraments into Orthodoxy." *Nova et Vetera* 15.2 (2017): 465–501.

Katansky, Alexander. *Dogmaticheskoe uchenie o semi tserkovnykh Tainstvakh v tvoreni-yakh drevneishikh otsov i pisatelei do Origena vklyuchitel'no* [Dogmatic teaching on the seven sacraments of the Church in the works of the ancient Fathers and writers through Origen]. Saint Petersburg: Publishing House of F.G. Eleonsky, 1877.

Kenrick, Francis Patrick. *A Treatise on Baptism*. Philadelphia, PA: King and Baird, 1843.

Lambertson, Isaac. *Akathist to the Martyr Varus: Holy Intercessor for Family Members Who Reposed Outside the Orthodox Faith*. Safford, AZ: St Paisius Monastery, 2009.

Lampe, G. W. H. *A Patristic Greek Lexicon*. Oxford: Oxford University Press, 1991.

The Lenten Triodion. Translated by Kallistos (Ware) and Mother Mary. South Canaan, PA: St. Tikhon's Seminary Press, 1994.

Léon-Dufour, Xavier, ed. *Slovar' bibleiskogo bogosloviya* [Dictionary of Biblical Theology]. Brussels: Zhizn' s Bogom, 1990.

Makary [Archimandrite]. *Dogmaticheskoe bogoslovie* [Dogmatic Theology]. 2 vols. Moscow: 1786.

Makary (Bulgakov), [Metropolitan of Moscow]. *Pravoslavno-dogmaticheskoe bogoslovie* [Orthodox dogmatic theology]. 5th ed. 2 vols. St Petersburg: Tipo-litografiya R. Golike, 1895.

Mark of Ephesus. *Oratio Altera de Igne Purgatorio* [in Greek]. In *Patrologia Orientalis* 15.1 (No. 72), *Documents Relatifs au Concile de Florence I: La Question du Purgatoire à Ferrare, Documents I-VI*, 1st ed., edited and translated by Mgr. Louis Petit A. A., 39–60, 108–51. Paris: Firmin-Didot, 1920. Reprint, Turnhout, Belgium: Editions Brepols, 1990.

McGuckin, John Anthony. *The Orthodox Church*. West Sussex: Wiley-Blackwell, 2011.

Meyendorff, John. *Byzantine Theology*. 2nd ed., rev. New York: Fordham University Press, 1983.

_____. *Marriage: An Orthodox Perspective*. 3rd ed. Crestwood, NY: St. Vladimir's Seminary Press, 2000.

Nastol'naya kniga svyashchennosluzhitelya [Clergy reference book]. Moscow: Moscow Patriarchate, 2001.

Nefedov, Gennady. *Tainstva i obryady Pravoslavnoi Tserkvi* [The sacraments and rites of the Orthodox Church]. Moscow: Palomnik, 2002.

Neklyudov, Constantine, and Alexander Tkachenko. "Vino" [Wine]. In *Pravoslavnaya entsiklopediya* [The Orthodox encyclopedia], 8:519–520. Moscow: Tserkovno-nauchnyy tsentr "Pravoslavnaya entsiklopediya," 2004.

Neofit (Osipov), [Archimandrite]. "*Mysli ob Imeni*" [Thoughts on the Name]. *Nachala* 1–4 (1998): 51–58.

Neselovsky, A. *Chiny khirotesiy i khirotoniy* [The rites of *cheirotonia* and *cheirothesia*]. Kamenets-Podolsk: 1906.

Nestor the Chronicler. *The Life of Theodosius.*

Nicephorus II of Constantinople. *Against Those Who Say that Extreme Unction Should Be Given to the Dead.* PG 140:805–808.

Nicholas Cabasilas. *The Life in Christ.* Translated by Carmino J. deCatanzaro. Crestwood, NY: St Vladimir's Seminary Press, 1998.

Nicodemus the Hagiorite. *The Rudder.* Translated by Denver Cummings. Chicago, IL: Orthodox Christian Educational Society, 1957.

Origen. *Homilies on Leviticus 1–16.* Translated by Gary Wayne Barkley. Fathers of the Church 83. Washington, DC: The Catholic University of America, 1990.

_____. *Homilies on Luke.* Translated by Joseph T. Lienhard. Fathers of the Church 94. Washington, DC: The Catholic University of America Press, 1996.

_____. *Homilies on the Psalms.* PG 12:1053–1684.

_____. *Homilies on the Song of Solomon.* PG 13:37–197.

Orthodox Daily Prayers. 2nd ed. South Canaan, PA: St. Tikhon's Seminary Press, 2008.

Orthodox Life 26.1 (Jan-Feb, 1976).

Palladius. *The Lausiac History of Palladius.* Translated by W. K. Lowther Clarke. New York: The Macmillan Company, 1918.

Petrovsky, Alexander. "K istorii posledovaniya tainstva eleosvyashcheniya" [On the history of the order of the Sacrament of Unction. *Khristianskoe chtenie* 216.1 (1903): 44–59.

Philaret (Drozdov), [Metropolitan of Moscow]. *The Longer Catechism of the Holy, Catholic, Eastern Church.* Pp. 445–542 in *The Creeds of Christendom: With a History and Critical Notes.* Vol. 2: *The Greek and Latin Creeds, with Translations.* Edited by Philip Schaff. New York, NY: Harper & Brothers, 1877.

_____. *Sobranie mnenii i otzyvov Filareta, mitropolita kolomenskago i moskovskago, po uchebnym i tserkovno-gosudarstvennyk voprosam* [Collected opinions and comments of Philaret, Metropolitan of Kolomna and Moscow, on matters of education, church, and state]. Vol. 4. Moscow: Synodal'naya tipografiya, 1886.

_____. *Sobranie mneniy i otzyvov Filareta, mitropolita Moskovskago i Kolomenskago, po uchebnym i tserkovno-gosudarstvennym voprosam. Tom dopolnitel'nyy* [Collected opinions and comments of Philaret, Metropolitan of Moscow and Kolomna, on matters of education, church, and state. Supplemental volume]. Saint Petersburg: Synodal'naya tipografiya, 1887.

Pisaniya otsov i uchitelei Tserkvi, otnosyashchiesya k istolkovaniyu bogosluzheniya [Writings of the fathers and teachers of the Church pertaining to explanation of the divine services]. 2 vols. St Petersburg, 1856.

Posledovanie molebnikh peniy [The order of Hymns of Supplication]. Trinity-Sergius Lavra, 2003.

Prilutsky, Vasily. *Chastnoe bogosluzhenie v Russkoi Tserkvi v XVI i pervoi polovine XVII v.* [Private worship in the Russian Church in the sixteenth and first half of the seventeenth centuries]. Kiev: Petr Barskiy, 1912.

Prolygina, Irina. "Katekhizatsiya i chin kreshcheniya v Antiokhii" [Catechesis and the rite of baptism in Antioch]. In *Svyatitel' Ioann Zlatoust. Oglasitel'nye gomilii* [Saint John Chrysostom. Catechetical homilies], ed. and trans. Irina Prolygina, Tver: Germenevtika, 2006.

Proskinitariy Arseniya Sukhanova [The Proskinitaria of Arseny Sukhanov]. *Psaltir' Sledovannaya* [The Liturgical Psalter]. Leningrad:

Pseudo-Ignatius. *Letter to the Antiochenes.* Pp. 199–205 in *The Letters*, by Ignatius of Antioch, translated by Alistair Stewart, Popular Patristics Series 49. Yonkers, NY: St Vladimir's Seminary Press, 2013.

Pseudo-Symeon the New Theologian, *Alphabetical Chapters 7.* In Εὑρισκόμενα. Σελ./ *Evriskomena. Sel.,* 53–54. [Translated from Russian. —*Trans.*]

Richardson, Cyril C., trans. *The Library of Christian Classics.* Vol. 1, *Early Christian Fathers.* Philadelphia, PA: The Westminster Press, 1953.

Rufinus. *History of the Monks of Egypt.*

The Russian Orthodox Church Department for External Church Relations. *The Basis of the Social Concept of the Russian Orthodox Church* 10.5. Accessed January 16, 2019. https://mospat.ru/en/documents/social-concepts/kh.

Schmemann, Alexander. *The Eucharist: Sacrament of the Kingdom.* Crestwood, NY: Saint Vladimir's Seminary Press, 2003.

———. *For the Life of the World: Sacraments and Orthodoxy.* St Vladimir's Seminary Press Classics 1. Yonkers, NY: St Vladimir's Seminary Press, 2018.

———. *Of Water and the Spirit.* Crestwood, NY: Saint Vladimir's Seminary Press, 1974.

The Seven Ecumenical Councils: Antioch in Encaeniis. NPNF[2] 14:103–121.Dmitrievsky, Alexei. *Opisaniya slavyanskikh rukopisei, khranyashchikhsya v bibliotekakh pravoslavnogo Vostoka* [A description of the Slavonic manuscripts kept in the libraries of the Orthodox East]. 3 vols. Kiev–Petrograd, 1895–1917.

Shevchenko, E. V. "Analav" [The *Analabos*]. In *Pravoslavnaya entsiklopediya* [The Orthodox encyclopedia], 2:519–520. Moscow: Tserkovno-nauchnyy tsentr "Pravoslavnaya entsiklopediya," 2001.

Skaballanovich, Mikhail. *Tolkovyi Tipikon: Ob"iasnitel'noe izlozhenie Tipikona s istoricheskim vvedeniem* [The Typikon Interpreted: An explanatory presentation of the Typikon with a historical introduction]. 1st ed. Kiev, 1910. Reprint, Moscow: Palomnik, 1995.

Sobranie drevnikh liturgiy [Collection of ancient liturgies].

Socrates Scholasticus. *The Ecclesiastical History of Socrates Scholasticus.* NPNF² 2:1–178.

Sokolov, Vasily. *Mozhno li i dolzhno li molit'sya v tserkvi za usopshikh inoslavnikh?* [May and must we pray in church for the heterodox who have departed?]. Sergiev Posad: Trinity-Sergius Lavra Printshop, 1906.

Sophronius of Jerusalem. *Synodical Letter.* In *Sophronius of Jerusalem and Seventh-Century Heresy: The Synodical Letter and Other Documents*, edited and translated by Pauline Allen, 67–160. Oxford Early Christian Texts. Oxford: Oxford University Press, 2009.

Sozomen. *The Ecclesiastical History of Sozomenus.* NPNF² 2:179–427.

Stewart-Sykes, Alistair. *On the Lord's Prayer: Tertullian, Cyprian, & Origen.* Popular Patristics Series 29. Crestwood, NY: St Vladimir's Seminary Press, 2004.

Stewart-Sykes, Alistair, ed. *On the Two Ways.* Popular Patristics Series 41. Yonkers, NY: St Vladimir's Seminary Press, 2011.

Suslova, A.V., and A.V. Superanskaya. *O russkikh imenakh* [On Russian names]. Leningrad: Lenizdat, 1985.

Symeon Metaphrastes. *Prayers.*

Symeon of Thessalonica. *Answers to Gabriel of Pentapolis.* PG 155:829–953.

_____. *On the Holy Church.* PG 155:305–361.

_____. *On Repentance.* PG 155:469–504.

_____. *On the Sacraments.* PG 155:175–237.

_____. *On Unction.* PG 155:515–535.

Symeon the New Theologian. *Catéchèses* [Catechetical Discourses]. SC 96; 104; 113.

_____. *The Discourses.* Translated by C. J. deCatanzaro. Mahwah, NJ: Paulist Press, 1980.

_____. *Divine Eros: Hymns of St Symeon the New Theologian.* Translated by Daniel K. Griggs. Popular Patristics Series 40. Crestwood, NY: St Vladimir's Seminary Press, 2010.

_____. *The Epistles of St Symeon the New Theologian.* Translated by H. J. M. Turner. Edited by Henry Chadwick. New York: Oxford University Press, 2009.

_____. *On the Mystical Life: The Ethical Discourses.* Vol. 1, *The Church and the Last Things*, translated by Alexander Golitzin. Popular Patristics Series 14. Crestwood, NY: St. Vladimir's Seminary Press, 1995.

_____. *Traités théologiques et éthiques* [Theological Discourses]. SC 122, 129.

Tertullian. *On Baptism.* ANF 3:669–679.

_____. *The Chaplet.* ANF 3:93–104.

_____. *To His Wife.* ANF 4:39–49.

_____. *On Repentance.* ANF 3:657–668.

Testa, Benedetto. *Tainstva v Katolicheskoi Tserkvi* [Sacraments in the Catholic Church]. Moscow: Khristianskaya Rossiya, 2000.

Theodore the Studite. *Lesser Catechism.*

———. *Letters.* PG 99:903–1682.

———. *Penances.* PG 99:1733–1757.

———. *Prohibitions.* PG 99:1733–1757.

———. *The Testament.* PG 99:1813–1824. [Translated from Russian. —*Trans.*]

Theophan the Recluse. *Pervoe poslanie k Korinfyanam* [First Epistle to the Corinthians].

———. *Pis'ma o raznykh predmetakh* [Letters on various subjects]. Moscow: Pravilo Very, 2008.

———. *Put' ko spaseniyu* [The path to salvation].

———. *Sobranie pisem* [Collected letters]. 4th ed. Moscow: Pravilo Very, 2000.

Theophilus of Antioch. *Theophilus to Autolycus. ANF* 2:89–122.

Thomson, H. O. "Yahweh." In *Anchor Bible Dictionary*, 6:1012. New York: Doubleday, 1992.

Trebnik [Book of Needs]. Moscow: Moscow Patriarchate, 1956.

Trebnik [Book of Needs]. Saint Petersburg, 1884.

Trebnik [The Book of Needs]. Moscow, 1884. Reprint, St. Petersburg, 1995.

Trebnik v trekh chastyakh [The Book of Needs in three parts]. Kiev, 1996.

Trebnik. Chinoposledovanie iz Velikago Trebnika, iz knigi molebnikh peniy i inyya [The Book of Needs: Service orders from the Great Book of Needs, from the Book of Supplicatory Hymns and others]. Vladimirova [Slovenia], 1944.

Typikon. Part 2. St. Petersburg: Redaktsionno-izdatel'skoe obedinenie "Sankt-Peterburg," 1992.

Typikon. Leningrad, 1992.

Uspensky, Nikolai. *Pravoslavnaya liturgiya: istoriko-liturgicheskie issledovaniya. Prazdniki, teksty, ustav* [Orthodox liturgy: Historical and liturgical studies. Feasts, texts, service order]. Vol. 3. Moscow: Izdatelskiy sovet Russkoi Pravoslavnoi Tserkvi, 2007.

Venedikt (Alentov). *K istorii pravoslavnogo bogosluzheniya* [On the history of Orthodox worship]. Kiev: Izdatelstvo imeni svyatitelya L'va, 2004.

Veniamin (Krasnopevkov-Rumovsky), [Archbishop]. *Novaya skrizhal'* [New tables]. 16th ed. Saint Petersburg: I. L. Tuzov, 1899.

Victor of Antioch. *Commentary on the Gospel of Mark.* Translation in *The* Catena in Marcum: *A Byzantine Anthology of Early Commentary on Mark*, trans. and ed. William R. S. Lamb, Texts and Editions for New Testament Study 6, 213–460. Leiden: Brill, 2012.

Vorobyev, Vladimir. "Podgotovka ko svyatomu prichashcheniyu" [Preparation for Holy Communion]. Report given at the round table "Preparation for Holy Communion: Historic Practice and Modern Approaches to the Issue," held on December 27, 2006, at Saint Daniel Monastery in Moscow.

Waterworth, J., trans. *The Canons and Decrees of the Sacred and Oecumenical Council of Trent.* London: Burns and Oates, Ld., 1888.

Whitaker, Edward Charles. *Documents of the Baptismal Liturgy.* Revised and expanded by Maxwell E. Johnson. 3rd ed. Collegeville, MN: Liturgical Press, 2003.

Wortley, John, trans. *Give Me a Word: The Alphabetical Sayings of the Desert Fathers.* Popular Patristics Series 52. Yonkers, NY: St Vladimir's Seminary Press, 2014.

Zeno of Verona. *On Faith, Hope, and Love.*

Zheltov, Mikhail. "Venchanie braka" [The crowning of marriage]. In *Pravoslavnaya Entsiklopediya* [Orthodox encyclopedia], vol. 7, 661–668. Moscow: Tserkovno-nauchniy tsentr "Pravoslavnaya entsiklopediya," 2004.

———. "Vodoosvyashchenie" [The Blessing of Water]. In *Pravoslavnaya entsiklopediya* [The Orthodox encyclopedia], vol. 9, 140–148. Moscow: Tserkovno-nauchnyy tsentr "Pravoslavnaya entsiklopediya," 2005.

Zhivov, Viktor. *Iz tserkovnoi istorii vremeni Petra Velikago. Issledovaniya i materialy* [From church history in the time of Peter the Great: Research and materials]. Moscow: Novoe literaturnoe obozrenie, 2000.